Importing Faith

Importing Faith

The Effect of American "Word of Faith" Culture on Contemporary English Evangelical Revivalism

Glyn J. Ackerley

FOREWORD BY
Martyn Percy

☙PICKWICK *Publications* • Eugene, Oregon

IMPORTING FAITH
The Effect of American "Word of Faith" Culture on Contemporary English Evangelical Revivalism

Copyright © 2015 Glyn J. Ackerley. All rights reserved. Except for brief quotations in critical publications or reviews, no part of this book may be reproduced in any manner without prior written permission from the publisher. Write: Permissions. Wipf and Stock Publishers, 199 W. 8th Ave., Suite 3, Eugene, OR 97401.

Pickwick Publications
An Imprint of Wipf and Stock Publishers
199 W. 8th Ave., Suite 3
Eugene, OR 97401

www.wipfandstock.com

ISBN 13: 978-1-4982-1947-1

Cataloguing-in-Publication Data

Ackerley, Glyn J.

Importing faith : the effect of American "word of faith" culture on contemporary English evangelical revivalism / Glyn J. Ackerley, with a foreword by Martyn Percy

xiv + 312 p. ; 23 cm. Includes bibliographical references.

ISBN 13: 978-1-4982-1947-1

1. Faith movement (Hagin). 2. Prosperity theology. 3. United States—Church history—20th century. 4. Evangelicalism—Great Britain—20th century. 5. Pentecostalism. I. Percy, Martyn. II. Title.

BR1643.5 A242 2015

Manufactured in the U.S.A.   10/22/2015

Contents

Foreword by Martyn Percy | vii
Acknowledgements | ix

Introduction | 1

Part One: Introducing the Word of Faith Culture
CHAPTER 1 Current Literature on Word of Faith | 13
CHAPTER 2 Performative Rhetorical Approach and American Historical Background | 31
CHAPTER 3 Word of Faith and American Religion | 76

Part Two: Three Case Studies in England
Introduction | 125
CHAPTER 4 The Rhetoric and Faith Theology of Colin Urquhart | 129
CHAPTER 5 The Rhetoric and Faith Theology of Michael Reid | 150
CHAPTER 6 The Rhetoric and Faith Theology of Jerry Savelle | 179

Part Three: The Effect of Word of Faith on Some English Revivalist Churches

Introduction | 209

CHAPTER 7 Using Insights from Congregational Studies, Organizational Theory, and Anthropology | 211

CHAPTER 8 The Charisma of Leaders | 236

Summary | 261

Appendix | 269

Bibliography | 281

Index | 299

Foreword

"Abusive religion" is never far from the public imagination and the media gaze. Yet all denominations are prone to the charge at some level. Any glance at the media coverage of paedophile priests in Roman Catholic churches, for example, reveals a scale of abuse unimagined a quarter of a century ago. And of course, the problem is not confined to Roman Catholicism by any means.

Yet despite all churches aspiring to be arks of salvation, some Christian movements are prone to abusive behavior than others. And in this highly readable, yet also deep and scholarly book, Glyn Ackerley introduces us to the "Health, Wealth and Prosperity Movement" (HWPM)—sometimes known as the "Name It and Claim It" churches. Dr. Ackerley's carefully researched monograph arises out of his doctoral study, which in turn was prompted by his own pastoral concern for parishioners who turned up at his Vicarage door, with lengthy, exasperating, and occasionally tragic tales of religious abuse. His ministry—and now this book—are the mature fruits of his own investigations and reflections. Ackerley pursues his thesis with a measured and sober assessment.

Ackerley's work is much more measured than many studies of religious abuse—Roland Howard's more alarmist *Charismania: When Christian Fundamentalism Goes Wrong* (1997) come to mind. Like Ackerley, Roland Howard rubbed shoulders with prophets, healers, mega ministries, and charismatic preachers, but has not been impressed. Howard is an investigative journalist, and in his pacey and sharp expose, based on his experiences of the varieties and vagaries of contemporary Charismatic Renewal, he offers a sharp critique of abusive religion. It is a quite deliberate focus on some of the more colorful and absurd elements of a movement that has enjoyed widespread popularity. Both Howard and Ackerley's work serve as critical counterweights to the more fabulous and favorable claims made by those who see this brand of Christianity as the "cure-all" for an over-rational and secular Western Europe. Howard, and now Ackerley, see it as a nadir, and pursue their theses with vigor.

Howard's method, for its time, was a simple, but effective. He offered a series of case-studies, most of which have at one time or another featured in national newspapers. The "Toronto Blessing" (RIP: 1994–97), sexual abuse at the London healing Mission, Morris Cerullo's ministry and uncorroborated accounts of healing, and dangerous dalliances with dubious doctrines of demonology were but a few. In each case, Howard offered a mixture of journalistic observation and analysis, eye-witness accounts, and some academic reflection. The totality of this made for some very disturbing reading, and alarmed critics and supporters alike. At times the critique was devastating and damming.

Ackerley's concerns are similar, but his method far more nuanced and scholarly than that of Howard. Ackerley knows there are plenty of sane and balanced people who operate quite happily within Charismatic Renewal, who neither perpetuate nor experience abuse. Yet the force of Ackerley's argument is to press a generic problem for all churches, namely that of accountability and trust.

What is so disturbing about the instances Howard cited was the corruption of power and authority. When, as in one case, some bizarre form of sexual abuse was being peddled as "ministry," the relevant authorities failed to act for fear of a scandal. No one, it appears, was willing to intervene in or stop an apparently successful ministry. Ackerley writes about abusive charismatic ministries too. What Ackerley really presents us with is a plea—a sort of mandate for accountability. Keeping the scandal at bay is the easy part. It is the ability to own our mistakes, face the truth and one another, which in turn requires maturity and trust, that is in the end, the making of the real church.

The focus of Ackerley's book is the "Health, Wealth and Prosperity Movement" (HWPM), which has gained a surprising degree of prominence in the United Kingdom during the twenty-first century, and can claim some limited influence within Christian fundamentalism, Evangelicalism, Pentecostalism, and Charismatic Renewal. Strictly speaking, there is no "Health and Wealth" movement *per se*. It is, rather, an ideology that can be traced to several seminal preachers and teachers, who in turn advocate and emphasize slightly different doctrines and practices that are connected with the health and wealth concerns of Christians. The range and variants of belief and practice are considerable. Some health and wealth exponents will argue that the Bible demands *tithing* (i.e., individuals giving 10% of income). Correspondingly, those who fail to do this, it is argued, could not expect

God to reward them with financial success, prosperity, and good health. Put another way, "godly giving" is the only real way of ensuring that God will bless the individual.

Other HWPM exponents have more complex and novel ideologies. Some argue that God will not only match the gifts of believers with assurance and blessing, but will actually *multiply* those gifts, and return them to the individual. Exponents of this teaching—such as Morris Cerullo—have suggested that believers can expect a "sevenfold" increase on their gift or investment. For every one dollar that believers donate, they could expect to receive the equivalent of seven back, either through promotion at work, good fortune, or other means. Ironically, Cerullo has appealed for such generous giving from supporters in order to help him evade the deepening debt that had threatened to curtail his ministry. A variant on this teaching would be the "seed faith" practice of Oral Roberts. Believers are encouraged to make their offering, even if (or especially if) they are in financial difficulty. Only by giving will believers be able to receive—"your return, poured into your lap, will be great, pressed down and running over" (Roberts, quoted in Hadden and Shupe, 1988, p. 31).

Others exponents have suggested that the gospel *guarantees* health and wealth to believers who have realized their sanctified and empowered status. Thus, all the believer needs to do is have the necessary amount of faith to claim their God-given heritage—a mixture of heavenly and earthly rewards. Correspondingly, poverty is seen as the outcome of a lack of faith. The ultimate premise of the health and wealth ideology—sometimes called "name it and claim it"—is that there is no blessing or gift that God would wish to deny [his] people, because God is a God of life, generosity, and abundance. "God does not want you to be poor" is the frequently cited mantra of the movement. Again, examples of this in practice might include Oral Roberts' advocacy of a "Blessing Pact"; in return for donations from believers, their financial, spiritual, relational, and health concerns will be addressed.

The roots of the "Health and Wealth" movement are complex. Culturally, they can be traced to the very origins of American entrepreneurial frontier religion—the independent preacher that went from town to town, "selling" the gospel, and establishing networks of followers who supported the ministry by purchasing tracts and subscribing to newsletters that tended to develop distinctive and novel teachings that were not found within mainstream denominations. Fused together with "New Thought," pragmatism and materialism, the movement is, in a sense, distinctively American. Indeed, the HWPM gospel can be said to be rooted in a distinctive "American dream" (success, prosperity, etc.), even though the movement is now encountered all over the world.

Key influences upon the movement have included Norman Vincent Peale ("the power of positive thinking"), whose legacy was most obviously manifest in Robert Schuller's ministry and the once startling Crystal Cathedral in California. Another obvious influence upon the movement, sociologically, is a belief in an ever-growing economy. Although exponents of health and wealth would not explicitly articulate such a view, their actual assumption about investment and return assumes a pattern of economic growth. Correspondingly, a serious recession tends to lead to a downturn in the fortunes of health and wealth exponents, although we should note that some individuals will try and give more during times of hardship, as they believe that this will be their best means of returning to prosperity.

HWPM teaching has become and enduring feature of the Protestant Evangelical and Pentecostal landscape of North America. Pat Robertson, Kenneth Copeland, William Branham, and Oral Roberts are names that have commanded respect. Whilst Jim Bakker, Morris Cerullo, and Jimmy Swaggart have suffered from financial and personal crises that have cast some doubt on the movement as a whole. Further afield, Paul Yonghi Cho, pastor of the world's largest church in Seoul, South Korea, offered a distinctive brand of health and wealth teaching fused to Korean culture and its newly modernized economic expectations. In Brazil, Edir Macedo's Universal Church of God's Kingdom claimed more than six million followers spread over eighty-five countries. Macedo, a former sales assistant in a lottery shop, headed a church that owned a bank, a soccer team, and various media outlets (radio, TV, newspapers, etc.), with the organization once having an estimated annual turnover of over $1 billion (USD). HWPM churches are successful, in financial terms; and they like to talk about their success, and encourage followers to share in that success "that God wills for his own."

Steve Bruce (1990) identified three distinctive emphases that characterize the movement. First, health and wealth teaching is linked to a revival of the Pentecostal emphasis on physical healing and well-being. Second, the teaching is linked to the "discovery" that the Bible proclaims not only spiritual salvation for the believer, but also material and physical prosperity. Third, the teaching emphasizes "positive confession"—a crude cocktail of confidence and assertion, under the guise of faith, that claims that in order to receive healing or wealth, the individual must *first* believe and act as though the miracle has already been reified, even if all the evidence still points to the contrary. As Kate Bowler's masterly thesis points out (2013) the favored biblical text that underpins this dogma is found in Mark 11:24: "... whatever you desire, when you pray, believe that you shall receive them, and you shall have them . . . ." It is on the basis of this last point that the health and wealth movement is dubbed "name it and claim it'

"Unsurprisingly, the health and wealth exponents have had many critics within Christianity. Liberation theologians have attacked the movement for its absorption with material prosperity, and its capacity to exploit the poor and vulnerable in developing nations and poor communities. Others have attacked the movement for its deficient hermeneutics, and for the psychological and pastoral damage that can be done to those who fail to receive either health or wealth, and are forced to conclude that this is their own fault, due to a lack of faith. Others regard the movement as a deviant form of Christian orthopraxy that is disreputable and highly manipulative. Others, that its teaching is heterodox. In their defence, health and wealth exponents defend their stance as a "daring" theology that testifies to the generosity and goodness of God. They speak of the "universal law of divine reciprocity." Or, as the old Pentecostal mantra puts it, "as you sow, so shall you reap."

These points aside, the teaching of the movement continues to have a beguiling and almost mesmerizing effect upon its followers. It offers a worldview—a kind of "theological construction of reality"—that is remarkably resistant to a reckoning with any antithesis, which is in turn centered upon a world that offers promises and guarantees about health and wealth, despite evidence to the contrary. To reify their blessings, all the believer need do is "plant the seed of faith," and give.

Thus, committed believers who follow the health and wealth teachings may find that they believe they will be cured of cancer, even though the disease is in their liver, and they have only days to live. Others will believe that by giving away their money, they will receive more. On a personal note, I can recall a conversation with a young man in 1987, who was a follower of Reinhardt Bonnke. The follower explained to me that after the prayer rally at which Bonnke was speaking, he was going outside to collect his new car—a large Volvo estate—which God had promised him, to help him with his new, emerging ministry. In prayer, God had apparently told him that all he needed to do was believe, and he would receive. As an act of faith, God had asked him to choose a color scheme for the car, so he would recognize it as his. When he stepped out of the meeting, there was indeed a brand new Volvo parked outside the main exit. But as the follower explained to me afterwards, he knew it wasn't his—"because it was the wrong color."

Ackerley's perceptive book helps us to understand the role of HWPM churches and their leaders. It is a distinctive and brave thesis that probes and presses the issue of abusive religion (i.e., bad faith), and thereby constantly invites another question: what might good faith actually look like?

The Very Revd Professor Martyn Percy,
Dean of Christ Church, University of Oxford

Further Reading:

Bowler, K. *Blessed: A History of the American Prosperity Gospel.* New York: Oxford University Press, 2013.

Bruce, S. *Pray TV: Televangelism in America.* London: Routledge, 1990.

Hadden, J., and A. Shupe. *Televangelism: Power and Politics on God's Frontier.* New York: Holt, 1988.

Howard, R. *Charismania: When Christian Fundamentalism Goes Wrong.* London: Mowbray, 1997.

McConnell, D. *A Different Gospel: A Historical and Biblical Analysis of the Modern Faith Movement.* Peabody, MA: Hendrickson, 1988.

Acknowledgements

I would like to extend my sincere thanks to all those who have helped me and encouraged me throughout this exacting task. I am grateful to the people of St. Philip and St. James Church, Chatham and St. Peter and St. Paul, Shorne, who have coped with the extra burden of this work upon their vicar and allowed me space in which to complete this thesis.

Special thanks are due to the Following. First of all I would like to thank Robin Gill for opening my eyes to the wonders of theology and social structure. I want to thank Lesley Harrison for her help with transcription of my early interviews. I would also like to thank Eric Clouston and David Green for valuable discussions while they served as my curates at St. Philip and St. James. Without doubt I would not have been able to complete this thesis without interviews and conversations with adherents and various leaders associated with my case study ministries. I am most grateful for the insights you were able to give me. I am also grateful for the many helpful conversations with fellow students at King's College London's Centre for theology, Religion and Culture.

I would like to thank Andrew Walker, who was my principal supervisor for one year and who started me off on this thesis but also acted as my second supervisor while being unwell. Without doubt I am most indebted to two people. My supervisor Martyn Percy, for his inspirational guidance, profound insights, and gentle encouragement. Finally, my wife Philippa, who did a Master's degree in theology stimulated by my research and has been my constant companion and sounding board over the years of this work. She has been my continuous support in periods of frustration and self-doubt.

I am further sincerely grateful for the financial support received from the Diocese of Rochester, Ministry and Training department and the Bishop and Archdeacon of Rochester.

A study of this nature inevitably involves sacrifice of time and leisure as well as a measure of isolation from friends and family. Thank you all for being so understanding.

Glyn Ackerley
Shorne, Kent
January 2015

Introduction

THIS BOOK IS ABOUT persuasion. I am concerned with the use of rhetorical devices, both verbal and performative, to convince religious adherents in contemporary charismatic churches of the leader's ability to reify the power of God in the form of miracles and divine provision.

It is also about the globalization of culture. Globalization is a worldwide phenomenon; distinctive cultures around the globe are increasingly interacting with the vast increase of communication in recent decades. However, the most significant manifestation of this has been Americanization, the globalization of American cultural ideas around the world. This has been greatly aided by the vast influence of the Internet, Microsoft, Apple, and satellite and cable television. American influence on worldwide Christianity is an example of this and has affected cultures significantly more resistant than English culture.[1] However, this book specifically notes the importing of American cultural ideas into the UK.

Most significantly, this book is about North American pragmatism. Many people think of pragmatism as being a British attitude, and indeed pragmatism and the closely allied commonsense philosophy have European origins.[2] However, pragmatism is, as I will argue throughout this book, a distinctively American philosophy and, although pragmatists have always been identifiable in British culture, British theology, on the whole, has been more influenced by the European skepticism and liberalism of Kant and Schleiermacher.[3] However, over the last century and particularly

---

1. See the study of the Swedish charismatic church "Livets Ord" in Coleman, *The Globalisation of Charismatic Christianity*.
2. See Hamner, *American Pragmatism*.
3. See Murphy, *Beyond Liberalism and Fundamentalism*, 5.

since the 1960s, American pragmatism has had an increasing influence on English evangelicals, especially over those naturally disposed to this way of thinking.[4]

Contemporary English evangelical revivalist Christians are looking for a religion that works with results that confirm their faith. The embracing of a pragmatic approach to religion by leaders and adherents alike is the interconnecting thread that runs throughout this book. American culture is being beamed into our living rooms and uncritically absorbed by those watching television and surfing the net, but my primary interest is the way Christian praxis is being molded by those who are persuaded by, and enthusiastic about, ideas they have picked up from their contacts with American Christians.

Only a few years ago, at a meeting of Anglican revivalist leaders, I noted with interest that one vicar was happy to admit that his preaching and praxis were influenced significantly by his uncritical viewing of God TV and other American revival channels available on Sky.

This is reminiscent of an earlier study, Stephen Pattison's book *The Faith of the Managers*,[5] that first awakened my interest in the importing of American cultural ideas. This book, together with his earlier essay "Mystical management" (1991),[6] are a fascinating attempt to make a theological analysis of modern management. "Mystical Management" sets out Pattison's view that "the new managers are deeply involved in religious activity . . . indeed a religious activity which has close analogies with charismatic evangelical Christianity,"[7] of which, to a large extent, they are unaware. To him, this is most obvious in the religious language used by managers, e.g., "vision," "mission statements," "doom scenarios," and so on.[8] He is concerned that managers ought to become aware of the religious nature of management language and ideas and apply to their "faith" some of the critical spirit that theologians have applied to religious belief.[9]

Pattison significantly develops this thesis in his book *The Faith of the Managers*, in which he fleshes out his arguments and, towards the end of the book, applies his thinking to the introduction of managerial theories and practices into the life of the church.

---

4. See Warner, *Reinventing English Evangelicalism*.
5. Pattison, *The Faith of the Managers*.
6. Pattison, "Mystical Management."
7. Ibid., 17.
8. Ibid., 23.
9. Ibid., 18, 25.

In the coda at the end of the book entitled *An Essay on Management to Its Religious Admirers*,[10] Pattison refers to a Church of England report,[11] which is critical of the "pick and mix" approach of postmodern faith that replaces traditional Christianity with beliefs and practices from all sorts of religious systems. He then comments,

> It may seem ironic, therefore, that the churches themselves are apparently unconcerned about importing ideas and practices from management, which can itself be seen as a kind of religion.[12]

The application of management to the church might well concern those who are alerted to what Pattison says appears to be the origin of many of its concepts in fundamentalist North American sectarianism.[13] In a similar way, and importantly for this book, is the importation of ideas and practices into the English church, through contemporary evangelical revivalism. These ideas and practices, I argue, originate in the nineteenth-century American mind-science cults,[14] and indeed the distinctive cultural environment in which they developed. For the sake of clarity, I understand the term cult in this context in a similar way to Braden who writes:

> By the term "cult" I mean nothing derogatory to any group so classified. A cult, as I define it, is any religious group which differs significantly in some one or more respects as to belief or practice, from those religious groups which are regarded as normative expressions of religion in our total culture.[15]

Interestingly, the material that is increasingly influencing some leaders in the church in England today is saturated with late capitalist positive American thinking. For example, Peter Brierley's book *God's Questions*[16] makes uncritical reference throughout to American self-help and management books and articles.

10. Pattison, *The Faith of the Managers*, 157–66.

11. The Church of England Board of Mission, *The Search for Faith and the Witness of the Church*.

12. Pattison, *The Faith of the Managers*, 159.

13. Ibid., 35.

14. In using the term mind-science cults I mean particularly "New Thought" originating in the teaching of Phineas P. Quimby, Warren Felt Evans, and others and also Mary Baker Eddy's "Christian Science." The use of the term "cult" to refer to these movements has been defended by a number of scholars working in this area, e.g., McConnell, *A Different Gospel*, 15–20.

15. Braden, *These Also Believe*, xii.

16. Brierley, *God's Questions*.

Stimulus for This Study

For fifteen years, I was Vicar of St. Philip & St. James, Chatham, in the Diocese of Rochester in the Church of England.[17] Pip & Jim's, as the church has been affectionately known for many years, has been consciously evangelical since the 1960s; and during the twenty-three-year incumbency of my predecessor, Ken Gardiner, it became one of the leading renewal/revivalist churches in the diocese.[18] For at least the first ten years of my ministry at St. Philip & St. James, I sought to maintain and develop this revivalist emphasis.[19] However, during the 1990s and into the next decade, the long-standing evangelical and renewal ethos of the church attracted a significant number of "refugees" from other local revivalist churches, where there had been disenchantment and even allegations of abuse. I myself became more and more critical of the rhetoric and practices that were widespread in the movement.[20] I felt uneasy about allegations of psychological, financial, and even physical abuse towards the refugees from their former leaders.

English revivalist evangelicalism in the early years of the twenty-first century has many disillusioned adherents. This study was stimulated by my pastoral relationship with some of the local "refugees" I encountered. Many of these individuals were attracted by the way their former churches presented themselves, and some were initially very happy and excited by

---

17 From May 1994 to November 2009.

18 My predecessor, Canon Ken Gardiner, led the church into the charismatic movement from the beginning of his ministry at St. Philip & St. James, Chatham, starting in 1970. Ken's experience of "charismatic renewal" as it is known began during his first curacy at Holy Trinity Sydenham (1963–67). Ken's active leadership in the diocesan renewal group and, to an extent, his role as a diocesan advisor on the paranormal made him well known among charismatic evangelical Christians of all denominations, both in the Chatham area and further afield. Ken managed to lead the church in renewal while keeping the church firmly in the Anglican fold. His faithful service in these roles and as the Rural Dean of Rochester was formally recognized by the Bishop of Rochester when he was made an honorary Canon of the Cathedral in 1988.

19 My own background had been in charismatic renewal, both in my curacy at St. Peter & St. Paul, Tonbridge, and before ordination training at St. Mary's Rushden, Northamptonshire. During my time at St. Philip & St. James, Chatham, I visited the Toronto Airport Christian Fellowship (January 1996) and regularly attended New Wine, and for two years attended New Frontiers International's Stoneleigh Bible Week.

20 I became increasingly critical of fresh "moves of God" and words from the Lord to keep charismatic Christians "happy." After the Toronto blessing, people were encouraged to go to the Pensacola Revival. Medway churches had a visit from Ed Silvoso, a charismatic Argentinean evangelist, and recently people were even attracted by the strange and distinctly neo-Gnostic miracle ministry of Todd Bentley and the Lakeland Revival. I later became aware that this sort of activity might well be stimulated by fear of the rise of secularization. See Warner, *Reinventing English Evangelicalism*.

the vision of church presented. However, in time, for most there has been a realization that the rhetoric of their former church leaders and churches did not produce what it had promised.

In churches from what is known as the Health, Wealth, and Prosperity Movement (HWPM),[21] it is common for people to be taught that, if they have enough faith and follow simple steps, or consistently apply specific principles to their lives, they will never be sick or poor but will be healed of all their diseases and will never be in financial want. Of course, many find that certainly, as far as they can see, this does not work. Although they have devoutly and obediently followed their churches' teaching, they have still remained sick or poor.

As well as welcoming people as refugees from these churches, we also had members leave St. Philip & St. James to join Colin Urquhart's Kingdom Faith. It became clear, in conversation with one of these people, that she was seeking a form of charismatic religion that "works" and brings definitive answers to her life questions. She left looking for deeper understanding and knowledge of the principles that, if applied to her life, would bring her a more immediate experience of God's presence and power.

Case Studies

In this book, I intend to consider three representative examples of "faith ministries" that were active in the South East of England during my time at St. Philip and St. James, and which had a significant impact upon members of our church. They are:

Michael Reid

Until 2008, Reid was the leader of Peniel Church, an independent Pentecostal church in Brentwood, Essex, which had a University College (linked to Oral Roberts University), a school, and even a financial advice company offering financial products to its members.[22]

My awareness of this church grew out of my pastoral relationship with a man who has been a member at St. Philip & St. James for many years. In 1989,[23] his wife started to go to midweek meetings at Peniel and then Sun-

---

21 I will use this acronym throughout the book.

22. In 2008, Reid resigned as Pastor of Peniel Church after allegations of an eight-year affair with the choir leader.

23. This incident occurred during my predecessor's incumbency and the information comes from interviews with the couple's son and Canon Ken Gardiner.

day services, attracted by the life of the church and the teaching of Michael Reid. In 1992, she went on holiday with the church. The following year she went on a similar holiday with the church from which she did not return. She and her husband have been separated ever since, and they have recently divorced. Their three sons all moved to Brentwood with her and became involved in the church. All of the sons eventually became disenchanted with the church, and one of them returned (in 2002) to live with his father and attend St. Philip & St. James. It was at his wedding in 2006 that I met a number of disenchanted past and present members of the church. I have attended Peniel since Reid's departure, but most of my information comes from videos of Reid's ministry,[24] teaching found in his books and publications, and interviews with key individuals.

Colin Urquhart

Urquhart is the leader of Kingdom Faith, a denomination or group of churches situated across the UK. Kingdom Faith has its own Bible teaching training college, known as Roffey Place,[25] and runs its annual Faith Camp, similar in style to New Wine or Spring Harvest.

Most of my information comes from Urquhart's numerous books and his biographies, but also publications, tapes, videos,[26] and sermons from the church and Roffey Place.

Some of my information about the ministry comes from informal discussions with two former members of St. Philip & St. James, who have attended the college and ended up working for Kingdom Faith. I have also visited the college and the organization's main church known as The National Revival Centre.

Jerry Savelle

Savelle is an American, closely associated with Kenneth Copeland. Copeland might be considered to be the leading figure of the HWPM worldwide, and Savelle preaches and communicates the ideas he has learned from him. Savelle has an international ministry with UK offices in Monmouthshire, Wales, but has had a significant influence on churches in the South-East of

---

24. Many of Reid's miracles and key sermons are, at time of writing, available on websites such as YouTube.

25. Roffey Place is the Kingdom Faith training college situated on the Old Crawley Road, Horsham, West Sussex.

26 Videos of Urquhart's ministry are, at time or writing, available from the internet.

England. The main focus of my encounter with Savelle is his influence on the ministry of the pastor of an independent Pentecostal church in Medway. Towards the end of the ministry of this particular pastor, I encountered a number of refugees from the church, some of whom now attend St. Philip & St. James. Others have moved to more mainstream denominational churches in the Medway area. I also visited the Hillsongs church in London, when Savelle was preaching there. My information about the Chatham church, its ministry, and Savelle come from interviews, taped sermons, videos,[27] and publications by Savelle.

The main research questions of this book are:

> What social and theological construction of reality, and what factors or reasons, make these ministries appealing to people, and what is the true nature of what these ministries offer?

My rhetorical analysis of the case studies raised further questions namely:

> Are there certain types of people who are attracted to the claims of Faith teachers such as my case studies?

> Can I discover reasons that people are persuaded by these teachers other than they believe them to be biblically correct?

> What gives teachers of this sort so much charisma?

> Why are some people enchanted but then disenchanted by these ministries, and what sort of ecclesial environment facilitates this?

> What can we learn from the nature of the churches involved, and how are they different to mainstream churches?

> What accounts for the belief that giving money will result in receiving even more in return?

> Why do people continue to believe these ministries when clearly there are people who remain unhealed and still poor?

> Are there socio-economic reasons that people are drawn to these churches?

Providing possible answers to the above questions should help the wider church understand why there might be refugees from these ministries, and how and why these ministries continue and grow. I give my answers in the summary at the end of the book.

---

27. Many videos and other material regarding Savelle's ministry have been downloaded from the internet.

Structure of the Book

This book is in three parts: Part One includes a literature review of other material about the Word of Faith or Health Wealth and Prosperity Movement in chapter 1, and then my initial methodology early in chapter 2. This is followed, in the same chapter, by a historical interpretive theory, which is a general background of American historical cultural theory that examines the concept of American exceptionalism and the distinctiveness of American evangelicalism compared to English evangelicalism. This historical theory continues by examining the national religious heritage, originating from the early Puritan settlers and their Calvinism, and associated "extreme biblicism"[28] and electionism. It suggests that this environment, compared to English skepticism, led to a lack of challenge to revivalism and notes the arrival of Scottish commonsense philosophy and the embracing of pragmatism by the early Puritan leaders. It notes, following Weber, that Puritan ascetic culture was ideal for the rise of capitalist attitudes to all life, including religion. Finally, it notes suggestions of neo-Gnostic tendencies among North American Protestants. A religious interpretive theory follows in chapter 3 that examines the roots of Word of Faith in American culture. It plots the rise of positive thinking, American Transcendentalism, New Thought, and the mind-cure, noting the influence of Subjective Idealism, Swedenborgianism, Unitarianism, and Mesmerism. It examines the theology of the likely founder of the mind-cure, Phineas P. Quimby, and other key metaphysical[29] teachers leading to the possible link to E. W. Kenyon and to Word of Faith theology.

Part Two is a rhetorical analysis of my three case studies, and as such is a subordinate, supportive, but vital piece of work that not only illustrates the nature of my case studies' performative rhetoric but reveals the significant pragmatism at work in these ministries.

The rhetorical analysis of part two raises questions about the sort of people who are drawn to these ministries and the charismatic leaders involved. What sort of churches result from the teachings of these leaders? Why do people think that giving money away, especially to leaders, will result in them receiving more back for themselves? Why do people continue to be drawn to ministries of this sort when there are many who are not healed and remain poor? Are there socio-economic reasons that people are drawn to these churches?

---

28. I understand this term to mean total dependence on a literalist approach to bible texts with no place for theological reason or consideration of the context of biblical statements.

29. See definition of "metaphysics" early in chapter 1.

Part Three is an attempt to answer these questions. This demands further methodology drawing insights from congregational studies, psychology, organizational theory, and Maussian analysis in chapter 7, and then, in chapter 8, looking at the nature of the charisma of my case studies and the concepts of enchantment, disenchantment, and *habitus*. I also briefly consider the theory of cognitive dissonance, the nature of neo-Gnosticism evident in these ministries, and the relationship between attraction to these ministries and social class. I then summarize the thesis before making my final conclusions.

Part One:
Introducing the Word of Faith Culture

CHAPTER 1

Current Literature on Word of Faith

BEFORE THE ASSUMPTIONS AND initial methodology of this researcher are set out, this chapter will review material relevant to this book, which others have written, about the Word of Faith or Health Wealth and Prosperity Movement. The material is divided into three categories:

1. critical confessionally based approaches
2. apologetic confessionally based material
3. scholarly critiques

It should be noted that most, if not all, of the confessional critiques consider their approaches to be scholarly. All of the confessional critiques are written by evangelical authors, some writing from a Pentecostal/Charismatic perspective, others from a cessationist perspective.[1]

The critiques labeled scholarly are mainly sociological/anthropological in nature.

Before I consider the critical and apologetic literature, it is necessary to introduce Essek W. Kenyon, the person who many critics allege effectively syncretized ideas from New Thought metaphysics with evangelical revivalism. Before I do, I need to explain the use of the terms "metaphysics" and "metaphysical" used throughout this book. In this context, "metaphysics" is not the strict definition of classical philosophy, which understands metaphysics as the branch of philosophy that deals with the basic nature of all that is. The term originates with Andronicus of Rhodes (first century BC),

---

1. Cessationists take the view that spiritual gifts, e.g., the gift of tongues or the gift of healing, ended with the apostles, and that alleged spiritual gifts today are counterfeit.

who arranged the writings of Aristotle (382–322 BC). Andronicus put the writings that Aristotle called *First Philosophy* After the writings on *Physics*, hence meta-physics (after physics) and is a term used in recent philosophy, for example in the writings of A. J. Ayer,[2] to cover any aspect of the subject that is neither analytic or scientifically verifiable.

What I understand by "metaphysics" or "metaphysical" in this book, particularly in discussing New Thought metaphysics and its antecedents, is the same as that of Charles Braden, who understood metaphysics to be a religious orientation that is common to a variety of religions and beliefs such as American New Thought, Theosophy, Christian Idealism, Spiritualism, and Christian Science. "This broad complex of religions," he wrote, "is sometimes described by the general term "metaphysical" because its major reliance is not on the physical, but on that which is beyond the physical."[3] I am also indebted to J. Stillson Judah for his description of "metaphysics" as a "practical type of philosophy," that is, "both scientific and religious." He quotes an American metaphysical source as saying, it "stands for the deeper realities of the universe, the things which stand above and beyond the outer phenomenal realm . . . it especially concerns itself with the practical application of that absolute Truth of Being in all the affairs of our daily and hourly living."[4]

1.1 E. W. Kenyon

Dan McConnell records that Kenyon was converted between the ages of fifteen and nineteen and preached his first sermon in a Methodist church when he was nineteen. In 1886, he was ordained a deacon in that church.[5] What McConnell does not say, or appear to know at that time, was that, despite an early enthusiastic evangelistic ministry, Kenyon became disillusioned and became an agnostic.[6] Joe McIntyre records the testimony of Kenyon's first wife, who said that her husband was disillusioned by,

> "disgust arising from the many inconsistencies in the motives and lives of Christian leaders," and some failings in his own life, namely, "the pride of life, desire for fame and money in his own nature."[7]

2. See Ayer *Language, Truth and Logic*.

3. Braden, *Spirits in Rebellion*, 4.

4. Judah, *The History and Philosophy of the Metaphysical Movements in America*, 21, 11.

5. McConnell, *A Different Gospel*, 30.

6. McIntyre, *E. W. Kenyon*, 3–8.

7. Ibid., 7.

In 1892, Kenyon moved to Boston where he attended the Emerson College, or Emerson School of Oratory, as it was known.[8] McIntyre records that from an early age Kenyon wanted to be an actor and attended the college to get ready for the stage.[9] According to McConnell, both the school's founder Charles Wesley Emerson and many of the students and tutors had a strong affinity for New Thought.[10] Bearing in mind that Kenyon was going through an agnostic stage, it seems likely to me that his state of mind and his own natural failings would have left him open to influence by New Thought, even if he subsequently rejected the movement's major teachings. New Thought was very popular in New England in the time that Kenyon was at Emerson College, and McConnell argues that, while disagreeing with the theology of the movement, he unwittingly took on board some of its key practical principles and syncretized them into his gospel, resulting in a blend of evangelical revivalism and New Thought metaphysics.[11] So McConnell concludes that some of the principles that Kenyon taught originated in the mind-science cults of the nineteenth century, specifically New Thought metaphysics.

1.2 Critical Confessional Material on the Faith Movement

1.2.1 Gordon Fee

Many of the earlier critics of the movement attempted hermeneutical critiques, arguing that the teaching of the movement is theologically unorthodox. Perhaps one of the best of these is Gordon Fee's *The Disease of the Health and Wealth Gospels*.[12]

Fee does not refer to Kenyon at all in this book, but does refer to those who were influenced by his teaching, including Kenneth Hagin and Kenneth Copeland. Fee was a widely respected biblical scholar, especially among charismatics and Pentecostals, and is an ordained minister in the Assemblies of God; his approach is to point to the hermeneutical misunderstandings of the movement. For example, Fee points to a key biblical

---

8. McConnell, *A Different Gospel*, 29, 34.

9. McIntyre, *E. W. Kenyon*, 15.

10. McConnell, *A Different Gospel*, 38–41. New Thought, otherwise known as New Thought Metaphysics, is a way of thinking that originated in early nineteenth-century America in particular through the teaching of Phineas P. Quimby.

11. Ibid., 48.

12. Fee, *The Disease of the Health and Wealth Gospels*.

text used by Faith teachers, 3 John 2 (KJV): "Beloved, I wish above all things that thou mayest prosper and be in health, even as thy soul prospereth." Fee notes[13] that Faith teacher Kenneth Copeland interprets this to mean, "John writes that we should prosper and be in health."[14] Fee then comments on this text,

> In the first place, the Greek word translated "prosper" in the KJV means "to go well with someone," just as a friend in a letter two days ago said, "I pray that this letter finds you all well" (cf. 3 John 2 in the KJV, GNB, NEB, RSV, etc.). This combination of wishing "things to go well" and for the recipient's "good health" was the standard form of greeting in a personal letter in antiquity.[15]

Fee points to a large collection of similar personal letters from the same era.[16] He also comments,

> To extend John's wish for Gaius to refer to financial and material prosperity for all Christians of all times is *totally foreign* to the text. John neither intended that, nor could Gaius have so understood it. Thus it cannot be the "plain meaning" of the text. We might rightly learn from this text to pray for our brothers and sisters that "all will go well with them," but to argue from the text that God wills our financial prosperity is to abuse the text, not use it.[17]

1.2.2 John MacArthur

From a fundamentalist perspective, there are those who do not distinguish between the Health, Wealth, and Prosperity Movement (otherwise known as Word of Faith) and the charismatic movement in general, and who critique the Faith Movement as yet another charismatic error. An example of this is *Charismatic Chaos* by John MacArthur (1992). MacArthur dismisses the entire charismatic movement in what his book calls "biblical evaluation" and analysis of "the doctrinal differences between charismatics and

---

13. Ibid., 10.
14. See Copeland, *The Laws of Prosperity*, 14.
15. Fee, *The Disease of the Health and Wealth Gospels*, 10.
16. See, for example, the collection of ancient personal letters in the Loeb series: Hunt and Edgar (eds.), *Select Papyri*, 269–395.
17. Fee, *The Disease of the Health and Wealth Gospels*, 10.

non-charismatics in the light of scripture."[18] However, in his critique of the Word of Faith Movement, MacArthur significantly points to the critique of D. R. McConnell, who describes himself as a charismatic.

1.2.3 Dan McConnell

Three key critiques of the Word of Faith Movement's theology are written by people who are themselves charismatic evangelicals: McConnell, Simmons, and Bowman. However, as the argument of each of the three is slightly different, I will review their contribution to the debate somewhat comparatively.

Perhaps the most well known analysis of the movement is *A Different Gospel* by D. R. McConnell.[19] Published in the UK as *The Promise of Health and Wealth*,[20] the book is a reworking of his Master's thesis submitted to the Oral Roberts University in 1982: "The Kenyon Connection: A Theological and Historical Analysis of the Cultic Origins of the Faith Movement." McConnell describes himself as "a confirmed, unapologetic advocate of and participant in the charismatic renewal."[21]

Dan McConnell considers the idea of revelation knowledge distinct from sensory knowledge to be key because, as he says, it is the epistemology of the Faith Movement.[22] This, he argues, is an epistemology that is both dualistic, in the sense that it reduces reality to two opposite principles, and fideistic, in the sense that religious truth can only be based on faith, not on sensory evidence. He concludes, "both the dualistic and fideistic aspects of Revelation Knowledge come from the metaphysical cults."[23] British scholars Walker, Wright, and Smail acknowledge their indebtedness to D. R. McConnell and his book *A Different Gospel*[24] for their understanding of Hagin and his revelation knowledge.[25]

McConnell's thesis is that while Kenneth Hagin, leader of the movement for many years, claimed that his teaching was based on direct revelation from God, he did, in fact, extensively plagiarize the writings of an earlier preacher, E. W. Kenyon.[26] McConnell demonstrates this with exam-

---

18. MacArthur, *Charismatic Chaos*, back cover and 18–19.
19. McConnell, *A Different Gospel* (originally published 1988).
20. McConnell, *The Promise of Health and Wealth*.
21. Ibid., xx.
22. McConnell, *A Different Gospel*, 102.
23. Ibid., 102–3.
24. Ibid.
25. Smail, et al. *The Love of Power or the Power of Love*, 79.
26. McConnell, *A Different Gospel*, 6–13.

ples of significant parallel passages from both writers to argue that Hagin plagiarized Kenyon's books. McConnell introduces this section of his book by saying: "Hagin has, indeed, copied word-for-word without documentation from Kenyon's writings. The following excerpts of plagiarisms from no less than eight books by E. W. Kenyon are presented as evidence of this charge. This is only a sampling of such plagiarisms. Many more could be cited."[27] McConnell argues that Kenyon's thinking on healing and prosperity has its origin in New Thought, otherwise known as New Thought Metaphysics, a way of thinking that originated in early nineteenth-century America in particular through the teaching of Phineas P. Quimby.[28] Quimby was interested in alternative medicine, mesmerism, and healing, and believed that people's problems and sicknesses are caused by problems of the mind. McConnell states that Mary Baker Eddy was healed through Quimby,[29] and she adopted much of his thinking in her writing of *Science and Health*,[30] and in the formation of the Christian Science Church.[31]

Walker, Wright, and Smail comment with regard to Kenyon's dependency on New Thought, "This might be unproblematic if such writings were secondary to Faith teaching, but they would appear to provide their very *raison d"etre*."[32]

McConnell's book was first published in 1988, so the substance of his argument is twenty-five years old and has not remained unchallenged.[33] He points to a key approach to receiving healing from God, in Kenyon's writings, which he describes as the "Denial of Sensory Reality."[34] (See my reflections on Denial of Sensory Reality at section 3.8.4.) According to McConnell, Kenyon's idea of revelation, imported into the Faith Movement, has at its root the epistemological error of Gnosticism. (See my reflections on neo-Gnosticism at section 2.3.3.5.)

---

27. Ibid., 8.

28. Ibid., 37–38. Many of those who adhere to New Thought acknowledge Quimby as the founding father of the movement; see, for example, Anderson and Whitehouse, *New Thought*.

29. McConnell, *A Different Gospel*, 38. For more detail on the thinking and practice of Quimby, see Simmons, *E. W. Kenyon and the Postbellum Pursuit of Peace, Power and Plenty*, 209.

30. Baker Eddy, *Science and Health*.

31. McConnell, *A Different Gospel*, 42.

32. Smail, et al. *The Love of Power or the Power of Love*, 76.

33. See the challenges of Bowman and McIntyre noted in sections 1.2.5 and 1.3.1 of this thesis.

34. McConnell, *A Different Gospel*, 104.

1.2.4 Dale H. Simmons

A scholarly approach to the life and theology of Kenyon (from more or less the same time as Joe McIntyre's book, *E. W. Kenyon: The True Story*)[35] is to be found in *E. W. Kenyon and the Postbellum Pursuit of Peace, Power and Plenty* by Dale H. Simmons 1996.[36] This is a reworking of Simmons's PhD thesis on Kenyon. "Postbellum" means "after war," and the title refers specifically to the desire of Americans, after their terrible civil war, to seek power over wealth and health, both mental/spiritual and physical. Both Simmons and McIntyre fill in many of the gaps in McConnell's knowledge of Kenyon's life and theology. At the time McConnell's book was written, a biography of Kenyon had never been attempted.[37]

According to Simmons, the main purpose of his book was to focus on Kenyon and the historical development of Kenyon's thought. However, he also had a secondary goal, a comparison of New Thought and Evangelical sources.[38] In Simmons's opinion,

> although the two groups differed in their definitions of the nature of the individual's power source, the methods employed in tapping into this power and the promised results of its proper exercise were strikingly similar . . . on a practical level, New Thought and the Higher Christian Life movement were birds of a feather emerging from the same gilded cage. This is not to say that the two groups were of the same species, but it is to recognize that they were certainly of the same genus.[39]

He also argues that,

> a thorough investigation of Kenyon's writings makes it clear that both the teachings of the Higher Christian Life movement and New Thought played a central role in the development of his own thought.[40]

---

35. McIntyre, *E. W. Kenyon*.
36. Simmons, *E. W. Kenyon*.
37. McConnell, *A Different Gospel*, 29.
38. Simmons, *E. W. Kenyon*, xiii.
39. Simmons, *E. W. Kenyon*, xiii.
40. Ibid., xi.

1.2.5 Robert M. Bowman Jr.

Another important book that examines the Faith Movement is *The Word-Faith Controversy* by Robert M. Bowman Jr. (2001).[41] Bowman disagrees with McConnell, and argues that Word-Faith theology does not have its roots in New Thought Metaphysics, but in the evangelical faith cure movement of the late nineteenth century.[42]

Bowman goes to great lengths in demonstrating that Kenyon's thought is similar, if not identical, particularly in teachings about healings, spiritual laws and positive confession (or avoiding negative attitudes), to the teaching of evangelical leaders of the previous generation, A. B. Simpson and John G. Lake, thus placing Kenyon in this more orthodox stream of teachers.[43] Interestingly he admits that,

> the possibility exists that the evangelical faith cure movement and early Pentecostalism were also influenced in some respects by metaphysical thought.... Many of the ideas and expressions one finds in all of these movements, Christian and non-Christian, seem to have been "in the air" in late nineteenth-century American culture.[44]

At this point, one might ask, what difference does it make whether Kenyon was influenced by New Thought, or the faith cure movement, if the faith cure movement was itself influenced by metaphysical thought? If Bowman is right his view does not change the origin of these ideas; their origin is the metaphysical cults.[45]

Bowman considers Kenyon to be the grandfather of the Word-Faith Movement with its gospel of health and wealth and principles of positive confession.[46] He further thinks of Kenneth Hagin as one of the "fathers" of the movement, who used Kenyon's material and doctrines, and added his own developments to the teaching. Other "fathers" who he says have influenced the movement are William Branham and Oral Roberts.[47] Bowman argues that the Word-Faith Movement is an extreme form of Pentecostalism, or as he says, "Pentecostalism at its (near) worst."[48] He considers

---

41. Bowman, *The Word-Faith Controversy*.
42. Ibid., 11.
43. Ibid., 72–76.
44. Ibid., 82.
45. See definitions of "cult" and "metaphysical" in the introduction of this thesis.
46. Ibid., 36.
47. Ibid., 86–89.
48. Ibid., 12.

the Word-Faith views on healing and prosperity to be the least problematic aspects of their theology.[49]

In the view of both Bowman and Simmons, McConnell and those who have utilized his thesis (for example, Hank Hanegraff in his book *Christianity in Crisis*)[50] have failed to acknowledge the significant influence of the "Higher Life," often called the "Keswick," faith cure teachings of the nineteenth century on Kenyon.

Bowman takes a different view to Simmons on the similarity between Higher Life and New Thought and is keen to distinguish between the movements. In his view,

> New Thought is thoroughly heretical; the Higher Christian Life movement, while deservedly subject in my opinion to some theological criticisms, is an orthodox Christian tradition.[51]

Bowman fails to recognize that Simmons is not talking so much about doctrines but about common practices. Kenyon's practical teaching has much in common with the practices of New Thought and Christian Science. As Bowman himself acknowledges in a table in his book,[52] all three believed that the main causes of sickness are mental/spiritual, that healing is primarily through the mind or spirit, and that humans are basically spiritual beings. Higher Christian Life and Word-Faith writers utilize in practice, in the same way, the same biblical verses as New Thought teachers. All do so without consideration of their context or original meaning.

1.3 Apologetic Confessional Material

As I said earlier, McConnell's thesis has not remained unchallenged. In response, adherents and supporters of the Faith Movement have attempted to make a defense of the teaching by pointing to weaknesses of detail in his argument.[53] They have particularly pointed to the orthodox and evangelical nature of Kenyon's teaching in contrast to the thinking of New Thought Metaphysics and Christian Science.

---

49. Ibid., 11.
50. Hanegraff, *Christianity in Crisis*.
51. Bowman, *The Word-Faith Controversy*, 58.
52. Ibid., 47.
53. For example, DeArteaga, *Quenching the Spirit*.

1.3.1 Joe McIntyre

A more recent detailed book in defense of Kenyon from this viewpoint is *E. W. Kenyon: The True Story* by Joe McIntyre (1997).[54] McIntyre has examined the books, diaries, and sermon notes of Kenyon in an attempt to demonstrate that Kenyon's influences were purely orthodox. Although McIntyre points to what appears to be the clearly evangelical influences on Kenyon, he fails to explain some of the stranger, more metaphysical sayings that appear in Kenyon's books.[55]

In the section that follows, I seek to set out the background of these ideas in the writings of leading Word of Faith teachers, and their original expression in Kenyon's books.

In order to identify their presence in the case study material we might ask what are the principles, insights, and practices of positive confession as taught by the Faith Movement? What are Faith teachers, following Kenyon's lead, saying about God and faith?

Recognizing that Kenyon is the teacher, through whom many of these ideas have come into the Faith Movement, as the principal commentators do (McConnell, McIntyre, Simmons, Bowman, etc.), it is interesting to look at his thinking on these principles and how others have built on them.

1.3.2 Don Gossett

First of all is the idea of creative speech or "what you say is what you get," which incidentally is the title of a book by Don Gossett, a well known Faith teacher.[56] Gossett, like many of the Faith teachers, simply passes on ideas that originated in Kenyon. In fact, Gossett has written two books in which he puts his own thoughts alongside the teaching of Kenyon and cites him as his co-author.[57]

Kenyon argues that God himself had faith when he created the universe. He wrote, "Faith-filled words brought the universe into being, and faith-filled words are ruling the universe today."[58] He argues that God's words "let there be" caused the creation to come into existence. He points to

---

54. McIntyre, *E. W. Kenyon*.

55. In reading Kenyon's books the narrative is very much what a reader might expect from a revivalist author of this period until one reads a phrase which seems to be "metaphysical" and strangely out of place in revivalist writing.

56. Gossett, *What You Say is What You Get*.

57. Gossett and Kenyon, *The Power of Your Words* & *The Power of Spoken Faith*.

58. Kenyon, *The Two Kinds of Faith*, 20.

Hebrews 11:3 that says, "By faith we understand that the worlds have been framed by the word of God," and that from Hebrews 1:3 Christ is "upholding all things by the word of his power."[59]

Now the suggestion by Kenyon and those who have followed is that instead of the creation being created directly by the will of God, he himself spoke in faith, thus operating within some sort of spiritual laws that govern the universe along with the laws of physics. Kenyon describes these laws as "the great spiritual laws that govern the unseen forces of life. . . . They are to the spirit realm what iron, copper, gold and other metals are to the mechanical realm."[60]

1.3.3 Kenneth Hagin

Kenneth Hagin has built on the teaching of Kenyon to suggest that words spoken in faith by anyone according to these unseen laws or principles will result in that person getting what they say. Hagin claimed that in December 1953, Jesus appeared to him when he was "in the Spirit" and gave him a sermon with four points.[61] Jesus apparently said, "If anybody, anywhere, will take these four steps or put these four principles into operation, he will always receive whatever he wants from Me or from God the Father."[62] The four steps were (1) Say it, (2) Do it, (3) Receive it, and (4) Tell it.

The first and key point was "Step 1: Say it." During this first point Jesus gives, as an example of this "speech faith," the actions of the woman with the issue of blood in Mark 5:28: "For she said, If I may touch but his clothes, I shall be whole." According to Hagin, Jesus said, "That is the first thing she did: She said."[63] In Hagin's vision, Jesus continued, "Positive or negative, it is up to the individual. According to what the individual says, that shall he receive."[64]

Hagin suggests that Jesus told him that the woman could have been negative, and she would not have been healed. He goes on to apply this positive/negative thinking idea to the struggles of life as well as just sickness. He writes, "If you talk about your trials, your difficulties, your lack of faith, your lack of money—your faith will shrivel and dry up. . . . If you confess sickness, it will develop sickness in your system. If you talk about your doubts

---

59. Ibid.
60. Kenyon, *The Hidden Man*, 35.
61. Hagin, *How To Write Your Own Ticket With God*, 3–5.
62. Ibid., 5.
63. Ibid., 8.
64. Ibid.

and fears, they will grow and become stronger. If you confess your lack of finances, it will stop the money from coming in."[65]

Building on Kenyon's thoughts, Hagin teaches that if believers discover these "spiritual laws" they can be used for their own ends. Hagin writes,

> In the Spiritual realm God has set into motion certain laws, just as He set laws in the natural realm. Those laws in the natural realm work don't they? Just as you get into contact with those natural laws or put them into practice they work for you. Over the spiritual realm the same thing is true. I have come to the conclusion that the law of faith is spiritual law, that God has put this law into motion, and that as surely as you come into contact with it, it will work for you.[66]

1.3.4 Kenneth Copeland

Kenneth Copeland repeats this idea in his teaching particularly in the area of prosperity. It is clear that Copeland believes that if people follow certain "spiritual laws," they can become prosperous. One of these spiritual laws is to do with giving. He encourages the depositing of money "in your heavenly account"[67] by tithing to the church, giving to the poor, investing in the gospel and giving as a praise to God. According to Copeland, these deposits attract returns of 100 to 1 based on what Jesus says in Mark 10:29–30.[68] This money can be withdrawn later.[69] Of course, another of the spiritual laws that Copeland teaches is positive confession.[70]

This is also taught by Jerry Savelle as we shall see in chapter 6 of this book.

1.4 Scholarly Treatments of "Word of Faith"

1.4.1 Andrew Perriman

In 1994 ACUTE (The Evangelical Alliance Commission on Unity and Truth among Evangelicals) identified the "prosperity gospel" as a theme for study.

---

65. Ibid., 10.
66. Hagin, "The Law of Faith," 2.
67. Copeland, *The Laws of Prosperity*, 76.
68. Ibid., 76–92.
69. Ibid., 92.
70. Ibid., 98–99.

A working group was appointed,[71] chaired first by Dave Cave and then David Hilborn, to undertake an analysis of the prosperity movement. This study was initially stimulated by the ministry in the UK of Morris Cerullo and "the direct link he [Cerullo] appeared to make between the level of donors' contributions to his own particular ministry and the extent of God's blessing upon those donors' lives."[72] The book *Faith, Health and Prosperity*[73] is the result. Although this is a report from the Evangelical Alliance on Word of Faith and Positive Confession theologies and, therefore, undoubtedly a confessional critique, it is also a thorough and critical academic work. On its back cover, Andrew Walker describes it as "a critical but by no means dismissive report on the Faith Movement by leading evangelical scholars." And Paul Gifford describes it as

> a comprehensive, perceptive and nuanced examination of the biblical sources and theological tradition regarding the power and generosity of God. The report can be critical of the Faith Movement, but its eirenic and respectful tone, its determination to understand rather than condemn, will make it a tool for fruitful dialogue. It is a model of its kind.[74]

This book offers a detailed history of the Faith Movement. It starts with a chapter introducing the main beliefs and leading representatives of the movement—Kenneth Hagin, and Kenneth and Gloria Copeland—and describes the globalization of the movement. The book continues with an analysis of the basic premises of the movement and looks at their beliefs about creation, the fall of Adam and the nature of the atonement.

The report points, on one hand, to the Word of Faith Movement's assertions that "we may transcend the limitations of human understanding by receiving 'revelation knowledge' directly from God; and on the other, that by activating certain spiritual 'laws' that have been built into the universe, the most important being the law of faith, we may gain access to a supernatural power than can dramatically change our material circumstances."[75]

---

71. The Working Group consisted of Rev. Roger Abbott (British Evangelical Council), Rev. Hugh Osgood (Pastor, Cornerstone Christian Church, Bromley, Kent), Dr. Keith Warrington (Lecturer in New Testament, Regent College, Nantwich), Dr. David Allen (Lecturer in Church History, Mattersey Hall, Doncaster), and Mrs Pauline Summerton (Associate Chaplain, Whittington Hospital, London).

72. Perriman, *Faith, Health and Prosperity*, x.

73. Ibid.

74. Ibid., back cover.

75. Ibid., 30.

Chapter 5 of the book looks at the philosophical and theological background of the movement. The analysis then proceeds by examining the hermeneutics of Word of Faith and highlighting the movement's "highly utilitarian use of the biblical texts. Scripture," the report points out, "is treated as a contractual or covenantal document whose practical value lies almost entirely in the fact that it comprises a set of promises, rules, laws, conditions, etc., which must be appropriated and activated by the believer in order to achieve spiritual and material success."[76] The report further comments that Word of Faith teaching "operates with a naive hermeneutic which largely disregards historical and literary distinctions within the text and refuses to engage in dialogue with the scholarly community."[77]

Following chapters make a critical analysis of the movement's theology of double atonement (that Christ died both physically and spiritually), Christ as the second Adam, his alleged descent into hell and subsequent rebirth, and the relationship between salvation and material prosperity. The questions of healing in the atonement and the relationship of God's will to physical health are also addressed.

In the final chapter, the authors make the following observation,

> In order to ensure the efficacy of faith in the life of the ordinary believer, the Word of Faith Movement has developed a highly functional and formulaic spirituality. Success in the spiritual life is not a haphazard affair: we can be certain of achieving our spiritual objectives if we act in accordance with the various laws that were embedded by God in the universe at creation—rather as the Jews were guaranteed prosperity if they observed the rules prescribed in the Torah.[78]

They further add,

> Word of Faith spirituality is dominated by the determination to get results, to prosper, and this is where the legalism comes into play: the practical outworking of the spiritual life, whether as personal sanctification or as ministry, is governed by the operation of spiritual laws.[79]

This book is a very thorough work and, while making a strong confessional assessment, it gives a great deal of information on the roots and development of the movement. However, it is not without its critics, for

---

76. Ibid., 82.
77. Ibid.
78. Ibid., 196.
79. Ibid.

example, Sally Jo Shelton critiques the work as having British disdain for the "faith message" because it is an American export exhibiting American exuberance and optimism. She also says the book's attempt to summarize the key teachings of the movement is problematic because of the wide diversity of teachings of faith teachers, so the report's attempt to generalize them is speculative. She also finds problems with the personal tone of the discussion. The greatest criticism from Shelton is the failure of the report to address certain topics fully because of the lack of consensus among evangelicals themselves.[80]

1.4.2 Milmon Harrison

Harrison's book *Righteous Riches*[81] is an ethnography that explores the Word of Faith Movement and particularly, towards the end, its African-American forms. He is himself a former Word of Faith adherent and utilizes participant observation by drawing on the testimony of several informants active in the movement, some of whom he has apparently known for years. In conducting formal interviews, with twenty primarily lay people, he seeks to show how these people seek to apply the message they hear in church to everyday life.

Harrison's assessment of the movement is fair and free from too many negative criticisms about the movement as he attempts an objective and simple sociological analysis. He starts with a summary of the key figures in the movement and their teachings and the way the movement has developed. While he refers to McConnell's book, he stops short of describing Hagin's indebtedness to Kenyon in his writing as plagiarism.[82]

Harrison then offers a concise summary of the Word of Faith message that he considers under three basic points. First, the Gnostic principle of knowing who you are in Christ;[83] second, the practice of positive confession;[84] and third, the argument that every Christian has the God-given right to prosperity and health.[85] He then goes on to list common critiques of these ideas, that these teachings are the result of poor exegesis of scripture, that they are an oversimplified formulaic approach to faith that

---

80. Shelton, Review of Andrew Perriman, *Faith, Health and Prosperity*.
81. Harrison, *Righteous Riches*.
82. Ibid., 5–8.
83. Ibid., 8–10.
84. Ibid., 10–11.
85. Ibid., 11–12.

is viewed by some critics as in the realm of witchcraft and the "New Age."[86] However, the distinctive analysis of this book is of the African American manifestation of "Word of Faith." Harrison describes a typical experience of being a new member of a black Word of Faith church by observing the fictitiously named Faith Christian Centre in Sacramento.[87] Here, he demonstrates how religious meaning is constructed in this sort of context. The author provides an "illuminating" discussion on the distinct influences of black Word of Faith theology including precursors like Johnnie Coleman and Rev. Ike (Significant leaders who have gone virtually unexplored until now).[88] He also investigates aspects of contemporary black culture and economics that cause black churches to be strategically situated for prosperity theology.[89] Overall this book gives a good explanation of the key differences between Classic Pentecostalism and the Word of Faith Movement and the author makes a good attempt to demonstrate the connection between New Thought and the Word of Faith Movement and how New Thought influences the movement more than Pentecostalism.[90]

1.4.3 Simon Coleman

The Globalisation of Charismatic Christianity[91] sounds like it should be an all-embracing work describing the spread of charismatic Christianity across the world. However, Simon Coleman undertakes an ethnographic, anthropological study of Livets Ord (Word of Life), a charismatic church/movement in Sweden. In doing this, he aims to show that the church is not only part of the global prosperity or Word of Faith Movement, but that its members' beliefs and behavior reflect the sort of global processes indicated by theories of globalization put forward by Roland Robertson, Arjun Appadurai and others.[92] Coleman also draws on insights from Berger and Luckmann, and their concept of the social construction of reality,[93] in his analysis of how the church's members' lives and faith are a local manifestation of globalization. Coleman's aim is to show how exactly this works in this particular example.

86. Ibid., 12–14.
87. Ibid., 81–2.
88. Ibid., 134–36.
89. Ibid., 131–40.
90. Ibid.
91. Coleman, *The Globalisation of Charismatic Christianity*.
92. Ibid., 4.
93. Ibid., 6.

The analysis centers on three interrelated dimensions of this local form of globalization: media, forms of organization, and orientation.[94] Under each heading, Coleman goes to great depths with insights from various scholars to unearth the local/global aspect of this movement and the way that individuals relate to it and view it.

So in thinking about media, Coleman does not just look at techniques, such as television, video, and the internet, to communicate a local message, he examines how these things make the movement global. Videos, for example, become like "quasi-relics" that transmit sacred power to non-locals. When it comes to organization, he emphasizes how the local church sees itself as a focus that transmits its products, not just locally but nationally and globally. In his understanding of orientation, Coleman describes something like Bourdieu's *habitus*,[95] learned attitudes, habits, style, taste, body language, etc., through which particular groups structure their lives.[96] So members of Livet's Ord have a definite attitude, they see themselves as not just local and global but of this world and the spiritual world. They have taken on board Word of Faith principles, and in practicing them, they understand physical health and prosperity to be manifestations of the Spirit's activity in the movement. They are like capitalist consumers of religion, part of a worldwide movement of which Sweden is the northern center.

They understand Christian mission as being focused on nations, and they see themselves as agents of their movement, seeking to change first Sweden and its identity and also, as a part of the global movement, to change the world. Coleman observes that they offend many fellow Swedes, who see Livet's Ord not merely as unswedish, but as an invasion of American culture.[97]

Conclusion

Most of the books in this literature review are confessional materials that concentrate on the historical development of the movement and its biblical exegesis. While McConnell and others critique the movement's erroneous theology, Coleman (and to an extent Harrison) attempt to explain with sociological and anthropological methodologies how the Faith Movement works and operates. While all of the literature in the review gives valuable information, my aim in this book is to examine the rhetoric, self-presentation,

---

94. Ibid., 55–65.
95. Ibid., 62–64.
96. Ibid., 141.
97. Ibid., 208–9.

and persuasive, performative actions, sayings of my case studies, and their use of media and suggestion. I want to investigate how people are persuaded to follow the lead of the charismatic leaders that I use as my case studies. Thus, I will set out my initial methodology in the next chapter.

CHAPTER 2

Performative Rhetorical Approach and American Historical Background

This book primarily focuses on a branch of Christian faith—the health, wealth, and prosperity movement—that is often understood to be shaped by techniques of persuasion, aspects of American culture and various forms of popular and widely disseminated mechanistic-pragmatism. The book is broadly set within a practical theological framework, and is effectively a study that pays particular attention to critical correlative approaches that in turn draw on insights from rhetorical theory, sociology, anthropology, psychology, and congregational studies.

Cameron, Richter, Davies, and Ward describe the critical correlational approach thus:

> Depending on the particular experience facing a local church, the researcher selects a traditional theological doctrine or biblical text . . . insights of tradition are brought into dialogue with the contemporary situation. As the text or doctrine and the contemporary situation correlate with each other, a dialogue, or conversation, develops as traditional understandings interplay with contemporary explorations.[1]

Guest, Tusting, and Woodhead observe that this approach, "brings insights of doctrine and tradition into dialogue with the contemporary situation."[2]

---

1. Cameron, Richter, Davies, and Ward, *Studying Local Churches*, 24–25.
2. Guest et al. *Congregational Studies in the UK*, 13.

The idea of critical correlation in theology originates in the writings of Paul Tillich. His view was that theology is a correlation of existential questions that emerge from cultural experience and answers from the Christian message.[3] This understanding was built on by David Tracy. In his view theology "correlates the confessional beginning point of theology with questions shaped both by faith and by other aspects of our cultural experience."[4] This is refined even further by Don Browning.[5] My task in this book is to understand, to make sense of three ministries and associated religious communities. In order to do this I engage in a form of qualitative research, examining key texts and other media. Browning's book is a highly significant account of how church practice is the underlying foundation of theological enquiry as a whole. He argues that as well as being communities of memory and tradition, religious communities are communities of practical wisdom and practical reason.[6] I understand this to mean that all Christian leaders and their discourse communities are constantly doing practical theology through dialogue or conversation.

Browning asserts that "The sub-specialities of descriptive theology, historical theology, systematic theology, and strategic practical theology become movements within a fundamental practical theology."[7] Based on Gadamer's hermeneutical theories, Browning proposes a radically new theory of the structure of theological studies. He proposes, "that we conceive theology primarily as fundamental practical theology,"[8] he continues, "Under this general rubric, I envision theology . . . as having the four sub-movements of descriptive theology, historical theology, systematic theology, and strategic or fully practical theology."[9]

In this book my approach is a correlation of these sub-movements, particularly descriptive and historical theology, describing and analyzing what I see in the performative rhetoric of my three case studies. Browning justifies the use of theology in the full task of describing situations, for example congregations, it is not just secular disciplines such as psychology, sociology, economics and anthropology that can be used. However, these disciplines can be used together with theology in a critical correlational approach to understanding congregations. This sort of approach is exemplified

3. Tillich, *Systematic Theology. Volume 1*. 36.
4. Ibid.
5. Browning, *A Fundamental Practical Theology*.
6. Ibid., 2.
7. Ibid., 36.
8. Ibid., 42.
9. Ibid.

in James Hopewell's book *Congregation*.[10] I make use of Hopewell's approach later in this book. It is important to note that I'm not primarily seeking to be dogmatic but listening and reflective. This attitude to practical theology is carefully summarized by Poling and Miller.

> Practical Theology is a critical and constructive reflection within a living community about human experience and interaction, involving a correlation of the Christian story and other perspectives, leading to an interpretation of meaning and value.[11]

In the rest of this chapter I intend, first of all, to set out my initial methodology by discussing what I mean by persuasion; to do this I glean insights from rhetorical studies and social constructionism. Secondly, I will develop the first of two cultural "tools" or "resources," both of which are used later in the book to give insights into my case study material.

The first of these tools is a general, background, American historical cultural theory. The second, developed in the next chapter, is a religious interpretive theory. This second tool is more about the development, from the 1830s onwards, of American transcendentalist and revivalist traditions (more transcendentalist than revivalist), their pertinent characteristics, and their significant interaction in the later nineteenth and early twentieth centuries.

2.1 Methodology

This book is a sociological and practical theological study that is set against the background of rhetorical analysis. It employs a process of critical correlation between the theological rhetoric of my case studies and observations from rhetorical theory, sociology and anthropology of religion, psychology, congregational studies, and organizational theory.

My main focus is on wider performative rhetoric rather than just speech. While this is not a classic participant-observer study,[12] I draw on the perspective of an observer as participant. Denzin defines participant observation as a "strategy that simultaneously combines document analysis, interviewing of respondents and informants, direct participation and observation, and introspection."[13]

---

10. Hopewell, *Congregation*.
11. Poling & Miller, *Foundations for a Practical Theology*, 62.
12. See Whyte, *Street Corner Society*; Coleman, *The Globalisation of Charismatic Christianity*; Bender, *Heaven's Kitchen*.
13. Denzin, *The Research Act*.

While attending the churches is helpful, it is not necessary to undertake exhaustive classical fieldwork involving spending months physically encountering each ministry.

In a very real sense, my own church and ministry,[14] and our relationship with these ministries, are the "field." The rhetoric of Reid, Urquhart, Savelle, and their churches and movements is delivered to me in the post and via the internet on video streams. I can read them, hear them, and see their performance. If I cannot spend a lot of time visiting the churches, I can have the next best thing. What I have been doing is what Geertz, citing James Clifford, describes as "deep hanging out."[15]

In my research, I analyze books, web-streaming video, DVDs, CDs, and tapes, both video and audio. I also conduct interviews and record notes from conversations with key figures. The majority of interviews have been recorded on a high quality digital recorder and have subsequently been transcribed. In the interviews of refugees, I have simply asked them to tell me their story: why they started going to the church concerned, and why they became disenchanted and left. Some interviewees, while willing to be interviewed, did not want to be recorded, so I made basic notes in my journal, which I annotated after the interviews.

In the analysis of this data, I have been interested in the performative nature of these ministries. All of the ministries concerned are keen to market their teaching in the form of books, DVDs, web-streaming videos, VHS videos, CDs, MP3 tracks, and tapes. In doing so, their performative rhetoric is distributed widely.

In all three cases, books associated with these ministries are based on sermons and other teaching. While they might well have been refined and edited, they clearly reflect the ideas and approaches to faith and life in the churches concerned.

Web-streaming videos found at each of the ministries' websites (either free or to be purchased) often simply depict each of the preachers preaching and in a sense performing to the camera; this is also true of DVDs and videos.

In the cases of CDs and taped sermons, the visual performance is missing, but the taped sermons have a level of detail and "roughness" that are not so apparent in books. At least two people interviewed have suggested that editing of material that appears on tapes, CDs and MP3 tracks might well have taken place.

---

14. During the main period of research.
15. Geertz, *Available Light*. 107–10.

Interviews have provided more personal detail of how individuals have encountered the ministries, and they have filled in details that are not available in media.

Visits to the churches, or places in the UK where the teachers have ministered, have given me a personal insight into the nature of each ministry. My interaction with those attending has helped in my understanding of what motivates adherents to these ministries. I have also observed the nature and indeed the significant placing of publicity from each church.

It ought to be said at this point (for the sake of clarity) that although all three case studies show clear signs of being influenced by Word of Faith teaching, they have subtle but significant differences. Reid and Urquhart's ministries are significantly focused on healing, while Savelle's ministry is almost totally focused on prosperity. Reid and Urquhart are both British; Savelle is American, but has, at times, been a significant missionary on behalf of the HWPM in the UK and across the world. While both Reid and Urquhart teach, Reid is more of a "hands-on" healer. They all have produced media of various types that some UK Faith teachers openly describe as "product."[16] This, I think, reveals an attitude to church that is more uncritically capitalistic, entrepreneurial, and pragmatic, and I will discuss this in the first of my cultural tools developed later in this chapter.

I would also like to make it clear at this point that while Jerry Savelle knows he is a Word of Faith teacher and stands firmly in that tradition, Colin Urquhart would almost certainly reject the label. Indeed, many of his followers might be shocked to see his faith principles compared to the spiritual laws of the HWPM. Michael Reid, however, has been clearly influenced by Word of Faith teachers such as T. L. Osborn and Benson Idahosa, and publicly acclaims their ministries. Strangely, he also might reject the label Word of Faith teacher, but I think this is more about his concerns of how the British public might perceive him than the principles and methods that he has learned from Osborn and Idahosa.

Performative rhetoric seeks to create trust; it attempts to persuade. It is not just about the preacher's words; it is their image, their character, their perceived expertise, the trust and respect they are accorded by their followers. When preachers and ministries gain the trust of followers, those followers can often be unaware that some of what they are being taught has origins that are cultural and psychological rather than theological. In an attempt to tease out these cultural elements, I intend to develop, in this and the next chapter, the two cultural, interpretative tools.

16. For example, Paul Scanlon, based in Bradford, UK, describes his materials as product on a taped sermon I have of his. This reveals an entrepreneurial, capitalistic attitude similar to that observed in my case studies.

In understanding how performative rhetoric creates trust, I have used insights from the canons of rhetoric.[17] While the canons of rhetoric originate in antiquity and were formulated to teach oratory, we shall see that they can be used "in reverse" to show why an orator might be more effective in convincing those watching and listening.

I have not sought to apply these rhetorical canons in a formulaic way; instead, I have followed the advice of rhetorical theorists Black and Klyn. Black argues that "critical method is too personally expressive to be systematized."[18] Likewise, Klyn states, "rhetorical criticism, I think, only means intelligent writing about works of rhetoric . . . in whatever way the critic can manage it." He believes that rhetorical criticism "does not imply a prescriptive mode of writing, any categorical structure of *judgment* or even any judgmental necessity."[19] Therefore, the rhetorical critic should be "uninhibited methodologically and free to use his mind as well—perhaps as unconventionally—as he can."[20] Campbell and Jamieson suggest that "a concern with form and genre does not prescribe a critical methodology."[21] In light of these remarks, I merely allow the rhetorical examples to speak to me, noting the obvious features of each Faith teacher.

After providing some background and character (memory/ethos) of each of my Faith teachers, I consider the nature, or likely nature, of their readers or hearers. Then I focus on their lines of argument, that is, on the development and organization of their material, after which I will discuss their style and delivery.

Analysis of the discourse of Faith teachers is a helpful starting point in trying to understand how they induce co-operation in their hearers and why this form of religious teaching continues to persuade people. One can listen to, or watch, an individual preacher and know within a short time whether that person is influenced by Faith teaching. Many Faith teachers employ the same language. Many of them have similar preaching styles, and most of them apply the same arguments and evidence. However, it is not just the words, it is the whole performance—the way they dress, their gestures, the way they hold their Bible, the way they walk around and in a sense hold the stage.

---

17. The five canons of rhetoric (probably catalogued by Cicero) in the anonymous *Rhetorica Ad Herennium* are *memoria* (memory), *pronunciatio* (delivery), *dispositio* (organization or arrangement), *inventio* (development) and *elecutio* (style).

18. Black, *Rhetorical Criticism*. x.

19. Klyn, "Toward a Pluralistic Rhetorical Criticism," 147.

20. Ibid., 156.

21. Campbell and Jamieson (eds.), *Form and Genre*, 21.

In the analysis of the teachings of the three persons considered (and their mentors), I am interested in their pragmatic instrumentality, exemplified by their use of mechanistic language and concepts such as principles, steps and keys, to describe how their teachings can work for people's benefit.

2.2 Works on Rhetoric

At the heart of this book is an analysis of the rhetoric of my chosen Faith teachers and their associated movements and mentors. In understanding how rhetorical analysis can help in understanding the popularity and relative success of Faith ministries, I have found the work of two scholars particularly helpful. First, I have gleaned insights from the approach of Stephen J. Pullum and his book *Foul Demons, Come Out: The Rhetoric of Twentieth Century American Faith Healing*.[22] Second, I have attempted to follow the lead of linguistic and rhetorical scholar Annabelle Mooney and the methodology set out in her book *The Rhetoric of Religious Cults*.[23] She, in turn, is dependent on the thinking of Roy Wallis and his book *The Elementary Forms of the New Religious Life*,[24] and John M. Swales and his concept of the discourse community.[25]

2.2.1 Pullum

Pullum introduces his methodology of rhetorical analysis and then applies this to American Revivalist faith healers of the twentieth century, namely, Aimee Semple McPherson, William Branham, Oral Roberts, A. A. Allen, Ernest Angley, Kathryn Kuhlman, and Benny Hinn. In this section, I add my own reflections based on Pullum's work and cite other helpful sources.

At the outset, Pullum chooses the ancient definition that rhetoric is "the faculty of observing in any given case the available means of persuasion."[26]

This definition was a part of theories of rhetoric that provided guidelines for the construction of speeches, and for aiding rhetors to conduct themselves in a manner that would convince audiences. Rhetorical analysis

---

22. Pullum, *Foul Demons, Come Out*.
23. Mooney, *The Rhetoric of Religious Cults*.
24. Wallis, *The Elementary Forms of the New Religious Life*.
25. Swales, *Genre Analysis*.
26. Aristotle, *Rhetoric*, 5.

is often used today to understand and explain why certain orators are successful persuaders.²⁷

Pullum points to a more contemporary definition of rhetoric from Brock, Scott, and Chesebro who define it as "the human effort to induce co-operation through the use of symbols."²⁸ While they are aware that this definition, like most others, "gives rise to troublesome questions of inclusion and exclusion,"²⁹ they are simply pointing out that the aim of rhetoric is to persuade using symbols, whether they be spoken or written, verbal, or non-verbal. Rhetorical analysts or critics examine, dissect, and categorize the persuasive discourse of politicians and, indeed, of any speaker who seeks to persuade, including preachers. This discourse, as Brock, Scott, and Chesebro point out, is not limited to verbal communication. A rhetor's whole life, their life story, their family, their knowledge and their trustworthiness can all be wittingly or unwittingly used as instruments of persuasion. Christian preachers' whole lives and associated ministries can be understood as rhetorical constructs.

In my own understanding of this, I have found it helpful to think of this rhetoric as contributing to "the grammar of assent that forms the theological construction of reality for participants."³⁰ Percy explains how "the divine and human pulses, activity and performances are conflated in such a way to make 'religion.'" He adapts Berger and Luckmann's phrase "the social construction of reality"³¹ and speaks of "the theological construction of reality."³²

As Jonathan Potter writes, "Recent work on rhetoric by Michael Billig³³ has maintained that rhetoric should not be confined to obviously argumentative or explicitly persuasive communication. Rather rhetoric should be seen as a pervasive feature of the way people interact and arrive at understanding."³⁴ Potter points out that Herbert Simons has argued that

---

27. For example, Ramzy, "Communicating Cosmopolitanism"; Cloer, "Profiles in Evangelistic Persuasion"; Martin, "A Rhetorical Analysis of the Illustrative Technique of Clovis G. Chappell, Batsell Barrett Baxter, and Lynn Anderson"; Lewis, "Charismatic Communication and Faith Healer."

28. Brock, Scott, and Chesebro, *Methods of Rhetorical Criticism*, 14.

29. Ibid.

30. Percy, *Power and the Church*.

31. Berger and Luckmann, *The Social Construction of Reality*.

32. Percy, *Power and the Church*, 10.

33. Billig, *Arguing and Thinking*.

34. Potter, *Representing Reality*. 106.

"part of the job of the rhetorical analyst is to determine how constructions of "the real" are made persuasive."[35]

Pullum notes that Andrews includes this approach when he succinctly defines rhetorical criticism as "the systematic process of illuminating and evaluating the products of human activity."[36] Here, Andrews is clear that the rhetoric is not just "talk" but "human activity." In his opinion, rhetorical criticism questions, "What potential did the message have to influence what audience or audiences in what ways?"[37]

I understand this human activity, included in rhetoric, to be implicit in community.

Anthropologist Clifford Geertz believes, with Max Weber, "that man is an animal suspended in webs of significance he himself has spun."[38]

So the rhetoric of an individual and associated movement can be something that is not wholly deliberately created by the individual but often unintentionally and mutually created. The discourse community contributes to the rhetoric associated with its leader by the building of a reputation that is appreciated within the movement and is presented to those outside the movement.

Pullum points to Walter who reminds us not to ignore the existence of implicit rhetorical theories. While he observes that few societies—for example, Greco-Roman and Western civilizations—have produced explicit rhetorics, he notes that all societies have an implied or implicit theory of rhetoric. These implicit theories are "a theory of how communication ought to proceed, and what is appropriate, dangerous, unusual, or saintly."[39] He writes,

> Unexpressed and implicit theories of rhetoric exist in all cultures and subcultures: in aboriginal tribes, in slum culture in our large cities, and "in groups" and "out groups." These implicit theories of communication are the distinctive marks that stamps one as a . . . child of the slums, as a product of a university education, as an introvert or an extrovert.[40]

---

35. Simons, "Introduction: The Rhetoric of Inquiry as an Intellectual Movement," 11.

36. Pullum, *Foul Demons come out*, xi–xii. Citing Andrews, *The Practice of Rhetorical Criticism*, 4.

37. Ibid. 6.

38. Geertz, *The Interpretation of Cultures*, 5.

39. Walter "On the Varieties of Rhetorical Criticism," 169.

40. Ibid., 169–70.

In other words, what assumed code governs the discourse of, for example, a university graduate, a blue-collar worker, a homeless person, an introvert or an extrovert; and what are their distinctive phrases, terminologies, mechanisms, tricks and argument structures?

We might well ask at this stage, what implicit rhetorical theory might apply to Faith teachers and their associated discourse communities? Faith teachers associated with the HWPM have had an increasing impact in the United States throughout the twentieth century and increasingly all around the world, including the South-East of England. Most people outside and even inside the movement have not given any consideration to the distinctive nature of its rhetoric, although those within the movement may use it or be those who are looking and listening, albeit mainly uncritically. We might ask, what theological construction of reality accounts for the popularity and apparent success of these Faith ministries? Pullum cites Walter who notes the value of "unexpressed" rhetorical theories because they "reveal the ways in which such groups both communicate and evaluate the communication they hear."[41] If similar implicit rhetorical practices can be seen to be common to different Faith teachers, it might help us to understand how this form of religion functions, and why their discourse continues to influence people in the UK, where one might expect a healthy skepticism rather than a pragmatic positivist approach to religion common in the United States.

It is beyond the scope of this book to undertake a complete rhetorical analysis of each of my three faith teachers. My aim is to identify and evaluate striking rhetorical devices and techniques in each case, to comment on possible origins of these devices and techniques, and to note the influence of my case studies' mentors and other figures in the Word of Faith Movement.

I will examine each of the orators separately, starting with Colin Urquhart. Then in subsequent chapters, I will examine the rhetoric of Michael Reid and Jerry Savelle. I will then compare their rhetorical practices and the possible cultural influences behind them.

2.2.2 Mooney

I have found Annabelle Mooney's approach to be particularly helpful as she works on the rhetoric of each of the three "cults" she examines: Scientology, the Jehovah's Witnesses, and the Family, with just one particular significant text from each. I want to take a similar approach with significant, persuasive stories or illustrations that act as rhetorical devices for each of my three Faith teachers, thus revealing significant information about the nature of

---

41. Ibid., 170.

their rhetoric. I should say very clearly at this point that I am not classifying my Faith ministries as cults in a pejorative sense. In fact, Mooney argues that the three religious groups she considers are not properly called "cults," and that the recruiting practices of these groups are no different from any other recruiting, including that of corporations or indeed the genre of advertising in general.[42] Instead, she suggests "marginal movements" as a less offensive and loaded term.[43]

Mooney's work develops a new rhetorical framework for undertaking text analysis. Her primary aim was to try to find out if there is anything distinctive about "the textual strategies that are used to recruit people into these movements." She discovers that "the techniques of persuasion that cults use are also used by those who argue against them."[44] Mooney is clear that she is not a theologian and is not able to deal with religious questions that are raised.[45] Of course, in my analysis, consideration of theological questions that are raised is eventually exactly what I want to do.

Mooney uses Wallis's[46] three-way distinction between religious movements along with Aristotle's classification of three kinds of proof that can be used in a rhetorical argument: *logos, ethos,* and *pathos.* Wallis suggests that New Religious Movements can be categorized into three groups: the world-affirming, the world-rejecting, and the world-accommodating.[47]

World-affirming groups are characterized by

> coping with the demands made upon us to succeed in modern capitalist societies . . . with the dilemmas of *individual achievement* . . . personal success in securing the valued goals of this world: improved income and personal relationships, greater confidence and self-esteem, enhanced ability to cope with life's vicissitudes.[48]

Mooney observes that Scientology falls into this world-affirming category.[49] So do Faith ministries. Wallis adds,

> The logic of the market is wholly compatible with the *ethos* of such movements. Thus the salvational product will be tailored

---

42. Mooney, *The Rhetoric of Religious Cults*, 2.
43. Ibid., 3.
44. Ibid., 3.
45. Ibid., 4.
46. Wallis, *The Elementary Forms of the New Religious Life*, 4–39.
47. Ibid.
48. Ibid., 28–9.
49. Mooney, *The Rhetoric of Religious Cults*, 12.

for mass production, standardising content, instructional method, and price, distributing it through a bureaucratic apparatus which establishes or leases agencies, just as in the distribution of Kentucky Fried Chicken or Ford motor cars.[50]

Mooney places the Jehovah's Witnesses in the category of world-accommodating, in that they make at least some "distinction between the spiritual and the worldly."[51] This category could also hold for my case studies and many other charismatic/evangelical churches.

In the third category of world-rejecting movements, Mooney places the Family, previously known as the Children of God. They tend to separate themselves from the world, which they consider to have rejected the divine plan. There might be a sense in which Michael Reid's church could be seen to be world-rejecting, with its own college and school, and also Colin Urquhart's Kingdom Faith, with its own college in a quite geographically isolated position.

So we could consider churches to be on a spectrum:

World Accommodating　　　　　World Affirming　　　　　World Rejecting

◄───►

I discuss this spectrum in chapter 7.

Mooney refers to three well-known ways of persuasion or proof through speech: *ethos* (argument that depends on the character of the speaker), *logos* (structure and argument that puts the audience into a certain frame of mind), and *pathos* (persuasion that depends on the proof, or apparent proof, provided by the words of the speech itself). So *ethos* is associated with the perceived character of the speaker, *pathos* is about influencing the audience through emotions, and *logos* is providing an apparent or real argument.

All three of my Faith teachers depend to a great extent on their own credibility; Colin Urquhart, as a former Anglican vicar, refers to his many years of experience and the fact that he is the author of many books to establish the reliability of his character. Michael Reid relies heavily on his past in the police to establish his credibility. Jerry Savelle proudly presents many stories about his family and the successes associated with his ministry.

50. Wallis, *The Elementary Forms of the New Religious Life*, 33.
51. Ibid., 35.

Mooney cites Aristotle, who says

> Persuasion is achieved by the speaker's personal character when the speech is so spoken as to make us think him credible. We believe good men more fully and more readily than others: this is true generally whatever the question is, and absolutely true where exact certainty is impossible and opinions are divided. This kind of persuasion, like the others, should be achieved by what the speaker says, not by what people think of his character before he begins to speak.[52]

All three of my Faith teachers rely heavily on telling their own stories; the credibility of their ministries are strongly linked to their own characters. This understanding fits well with Mooney's argument. She cites Aristotle who says of a speaker, "his character may almost be called the most effective means of persuasion he possesses."[53]

All three of my Faith teachers use the manipulation of emotion or *pathos*. Mooney quotes Aristotle's definition: "persuasion may come through the hearers, when the speech stirs their emotions. Our judgements when we are pleased and friendly are not the same as when we are pained and hostile."[54]

Argument that exploits emotion in relation to television advertising has been examined by Schmidt and Kess.[55] They suggest a link between *pathos* and other persuasive techniques: "People with a high level of personal involvement in a topic tend to pay closer attention and base their decision primarily on such factors as the number and quality of arguments presented in the message."[56]

It will be interesting to see which, if any, of these ways of persuasion dominate in the rhetoric of the three subjects.

Memory. This was originally about how an orator was to remember his speech, but in the analysis of texts, it becomes the effect it has on an audience or reader in terms of how they remember and act on the discourse. Ancient rhetorical theory understood memory to be aided by using architectural or other visual forms as a mnemonic. In the medieval period, memory became associated with the character of the speaker. As Mooney writes, "It is possible to interpret memory as an inventive choice, one that relates to reflection on one's own life experiences and the inclusion of these in the

---

52. Aristotle, *Rhetoric*, 6.
53. Ibid., 6.
54. Ibid., 6.
55. Schmidt and Kess, *Television Advertising and Televangelism*.
56. Ibid., 18–19.

persuasive text. In this way, memory would come close to persuasion by *ethos*."[57] So memorable life-incident stories might be attractive illustrations around which a speech is constructed, but they also have the psychological effect of making the audience think that the orator is someone like them, who has family, friends, and so on; someone who can be trusted. There is overlap here with the work of Fisher and his narrative paradigm, as we shall see early in chapter 4 (see section 4.4).

Delivery. This has been associated with effective use and tone of the voice along with gesture and speed of presentation. However, in my analysis, it could also be seen to be how the orator's message is presented or delivered to those inside and outside the movement. Some of the techniques associated with delivery might also fall under the canon of style, but under this heading, I want to focus on layout, presentation and the coding used to communicate with people. At this point there needs to be a distinction made between those who are acquainted with the codes commonly used in the movement and those who are not. As Mooney does,[58] I want to use John Swales's[59] concept of the discourse community. There are at least two audiences for the texts and other media I am analyzing; as Mooney writes, "the way discourse practices are represented to the outside world may well differ significantly from the way discourse is actually conducted within the community."[60] She adds, "outsiders do not necessarily view or understand the community in the same way as members."[61] Words can be used in such a way that they have a simple meaning for those unfamiliar with other hidden meanings understood by the community. Associated with delivery, the placing and location of publicity *may* reveal the sort of people the ministry is seeking to recruit into membership. For me, this has been particularly important and noticeable in the case of Reid's ministry, as we shall see later.

Organization. Otherwise known as "arrangement," this involves the construction of a coherent argument. In simple terms, this might be seen as like structuring an essay. A well-proven approach is to establish the credibility of the orator's own position and then, while taking an ethical, respectful, gentle and concerned approach to undermine the arguments of others.

Such an argument might start with a startling illustration, possibly about the orator, which draws attention to the orator's expert knowledge and trustworthiness. The argument might then continue with the neutral

---

57. Mooney, *The Rhetoric of Religious Cults*, 19.
58. Ibid., 23.
59. Swales, *Genre Analysis*.
60. Mooney, *The Rhetoric of Religious Cults*, 24.
61. Ibid.

presentation of facts that those listening might accept as independently accepted and not just the opinion of the orator. Then the case for the orator's opinion can be presented, involving a persuasive argument for what the listener should do or believe as a result. This might be followed by a respectful but effective refutation of opposing arguments; while the orator might respect those he disagrees with, he can seek to show they are sadly mistaken. A conclusion will remind those listening of key points and encourage them not just to agree but to act on what they have heard.

Development. Otherwise known as "invention," this is about what is included or indeed omitted from an argument, and how the thought pattern is constructed; it involves paradigmatic choice. There is of course an overlap with the canon of organization, in which premises come first, in which order should the arguments be made. There is also overlap with style.

Style. This final canon goes beyond just stating the facts or making a reasoned argument. It uses word constructions in such a way that the hearer can be impressed purely by the orator's skill with words. It uses techniques such as reversal, for example, "Ask not what your country can do for you; ask what you can do for your country,"[62] and triples, for example, "God, Queen and Country." Style involves the use of slick, memorable phrases that are certainly not absent from the orations of Faith teachers and are obvious in the orations of Savelle and Reid.

2.2.3 Another Significant Rhetorical Tool: Mental Suggestion

As I will observe in chapter 3, Phineas Quimby initially studied and practiced mesmerism/hypnosis to heal people. At first, he used a clairvoyant to diagnose his patients and to prescribe a medicinal remedy. After a while, Quimby substituted a cheap alternative to the medicine that the clairvoyant prescribed which worked just as well. He concluded that it was not the medicine that made them better, but their belief. So he gave up mesmerism/hypnosis in favor of mental suggestion.

Modern psychologists who study hypnosis are divided over the exact nature of the practice. Some, often described as "state" theorists, understand hypnosis as a definite and distinct "state" in which it is suggested subjects are able to achieve things that someone who has not been hypnotized cannot. Other psychologists who work in this area are described as "non-state" theorists. This latter group understands what is called hypnosis in terms of a

---

62. John F. Kennedy's speech at his swearing in as president of the United States, 20th January 1961.

set of relaxation or suggestive persuasion techniques in which a person does not need to be put into an apparent trance state.[63] This appears to be the sort of technique that Quimby was using, albeit in a rudimentary form.

Psychologists such as Robert Baker[64] and Graham Wagstaff[65] claim that what we call hypnosis is actually a form of learned social behavior, a complex hybrid of relaxation, social compliance, and suggestibility that can be used to bring relief to many. Other modern medical psychologists prefer the more modern methods of healing through psychology, such as Freudian psychoanalysis, Jungian analytical psychology or a variety of composite methods in modern psychotherapy.[66] Interestingly Both Freud and Jung studied hypnosis in their early careers. As time progressed Freud gave his full attention to psychoanalysis. However, he continued to see the value of suggestion and later reintroduced its use to hasten the results of psychoanalysis.[67] Some of those who have built on the work of Jung have also returned to the use of hypnosis and see it as a helpful tool alongside Jung's analytic psychology.[68]

Benjamin Beit-Hallahmi and Michael Argyle, like Baker and Wagstaff still understand religious healings in terms of earlier psychological methods of healing initially developed by Franz Mesmer, James Braid, and Émile Coué. These same psychologists understand that what happens at revival meetings can be interpreted as suggestion.[69] Beit-Hallahmi and Argyle cite a number of studies that show a much greater suggestibility among religious conservatives who had experienced dramatic conversions compared to more radical Christians. It is certainly recognized that some people are more suggestible and susceptible than others and religious conservatives and revivalists are among the more suggestible.[70]

I think this is a key issue, particularly in examining what is happening in the healings of Michael Reid that we will consider in chapter 5. As I have said, many modern psychologists argue that deep trance is not strictly necessary, and much depends on the effect a strong leader figure can have

---

63. See Pintar and Lynn, *Hypnosis*, 126–30.
64. Baker, *They Call It Hypnosis*.
65. See Wagstaff, "Compliance, Belief, and Semantics in Hypnosis."
66. See Weatherhead, *Psychology Religion and Healing*, 251–98.
67. Freud, "Lines of Advance in Psychoanalytic Therapy."
68. See Hall, *Hypnosis*.
69. Beit-Hallahmi and Argyle, *The Psychology of Religious Behaviour, Belief and Experience*, 171.
70. Ibid.

on a suggestible person, merely tapping into their potential for role playing and compliance. As Thouless writes,

> If we say that the religious orator may be using suggestion as one of his means of influencing people, we clearly do not mean that his audience are hypnotized. They may, however, be in the condition of heightened suggestibility which we may call the *hypnoidal state*.[71]

Much of this depends on the rhetoric and charisma of the leader or person that is doing the persuading. As Weatherhead writes,

> The condition depends partly on the person offering the suggestion. Any lack of confidence he has in himself, or doubt as to whether or not his suggestions will be carried out, conveys itself to the patient and decreases the suggestibility of the later. The fame, prestige and impressive character of the operator are also important factors, as every child knows.[72]

Robert H. Thouless comments that suggestibility evident in the subjects of religious orators, "may also be increased by factors emphasising the prestige of the minister such as the wearing of special clothes and the occupation of an elevated position."[73]

Special clothing and the performance of my case studies seem to be highly significant, as I've noted elsewhere in this book.[74]

I am not suggesting that Reid was, in any way, consciously using hypnosis techniques. I am suggesting that his methods of healing in front of a congregation as an audience may well have added to the likelihood of compliance from those with psychosomatic illnesses, resulting in their "healing."

The social constructionism and role-taking *theory* of hypnosis suggests that individuals are enacting (as opposed to merely *playing*) a role and that, actually, there is no such thing as a hypnotic trance. A socially-constructed relationship is built, depending on how much rapport has been established between the hypnotist and the subject.

In a highly significant article for this book, Wagstaff[75] describes the case of a seventy-three-year-old woman who was described as ataxic. She was unable to walk properly and, typical of this problem, had a wide gait staggering from left to right. Many medical and neurological tests had

---

71. Thouless, *An Introduction to the Psychology of Religion*, 24.
72. Weatherhead, *Psychology Religion and Healing*, 124.
73. Thouless, *An Introduction to the Psychology of Religion*, 24.
74. See section 8.3 of this thesis.
75. Wagstaff, "The Semantics and Physiology of Hypnosis as an Altered State."

proved negative, including a CT scan. Hypnosis was suggested, but she refused, saying she was frightened. Instead, Wagstaff used a technique that utilized imagery and suggestion with no hypnotic induction procedure or mention of hypnosis. They used an imagination technique in which she was told that she could be "cured" by generating images that would correct her posture. She was asked to imagine that her feet were stuck in cement and she had an iron rod in her back keeping her back in place. She was told she could release each foot from the cement and walk a few steps, and she was to imagine she was walking through a narrow corridor that would prevent her from swaying from side to side. After just a week, she walked to a shop half a mile away and then walked unaided for an hour. In his report, Wagstaff gave two possible explanations. One was compliance, that the woman had originally feigned the symptoms to gain attention after the death of her husband but now needed an excuse or permission to be cured. The other was that, for various reasons, she had convinced herself that she could not walk, but now the techniques gave her the belief that she could walk.

This sort of behavior could account for a number of the healings attributed to Reid. Almost all of the videos of healings deal with arthritis, rheumatism, and so on, where the person is unable to bend or walk properly, or they involve debilitating illnesses like ME.

I understand that in using suggestion, psychologists are using a sort of rhetorical device. An explanation of many of Reid's "miracles" may well also be due to response by the sick person to Reid's persuasive rhetoric, his suggestions. Of course, it is likely that Reid is not consciously doing this; it may well be a technique or process he has absorbed from observing others and that he uses intuitively.

2.3 Cultural Analysis: Historical Interpretive Theory

I now turn to the cultural tools mentioned earlier. I intend to use an interpretative methodology employing two cultural frameworks to deconstruct the Movement's rhetoric and apply this to the writings, webcasts and other teaching materials marketed by these ministries.

Before I proceed further, I ought to make some statement about what I mean by the terms "culture" and "cultural," particularly as I speak of American "Word of Faith" culture effecting contemporary English revivalism in the title of this book. Culture is a very difficult concept to define. As Raymond Williams comments,

> Culture is one of the two or three most complicated words in the English language.... This is so partly because of its intricate historical development, in several European languages, but mainly because it has now come to be used for important concepts in several distinct and incompatible systems of thought.[76]

The term culture has an agricultural origin. The Latin *cultivare* meaning—to till the soil, led to the original meaning of culture which was "the care and tending of crops and animals,"[77] with the aim of improving them. According to Stanley Grenz, "The idea of a specifically *human* culture, indicating our use of the term, was likely a metaphorical extension of this 'tending' process to the human person."[78]

In Enlightenment Europe "culture" became associated with education and refining artistic and intellectual gifts resulting in what could be termed "high culture." While this idea still exists a significant change in the meaning of the term came about in the 1920s among anthropologists. As Grenz comments, "Rather than denoting an ideal—the goal of an education process—*culture* came to refer to an already given dimension in human life. Culture now consisted of the customs and rituals of a particular social group."[79] In one sense culture was understood to be about humanity in general by anthropologists such as Claude Levi-Strauss and Marcel Mauss. However the study of culture became the study and comparison of "cultures," the practices of human beings in particular groups. As Melvin Herskovitz commented in 1948, "culture is essentially a construct that describes the total body of belief, behaviours, knowledge, sanctions, values and goals that mark the way of life of a people."[80] Writing more recently in 1996 William Romanowski understands the term culture to refer to,

> The network or system of shared meaning in a society, a conceptual collection of ideals, beliefs and values, ideas and knowledge, attitudes and assumptions about life that is woven together over time and widely shared among a people. It is a kind of invisible blueprint—a map of reality that people use to interpret their experience and guide their behaviour. The term *culture* refers directly to this fabric of meaning that is a people's way of life, and

---

76. Williams, *Keywords*, 87. See also Williams, *Culture and Society 1780–1950*.
77. See Warren, *Seeing Through the Media*, 41.
78. Grenz, "What does Hollywood Have to do with Wheaton?" 304.
79. Ibid.
80. Herskovitz, *Man and His Works*, 625.

its general usage also describes the "texts" of everyday life and material works that are a manifestation of a cultural system.[81]

This description of culture speaking of blueprints and fabric of meaning reflects the highly influential thinking of anthropologists who in recent decades have thought of culture in terms of systems of meaning in need of interpretation. Perhaps the most well-known example of the interpretive approach is from Clifford Geertz who, describes cultures as the "webs of significance" that humans spin.[82] It is clear to me that there is a distinctive American culture that is intertwined with the nations religious heritage and the theology of the Puritan Calvinist settlers, indeed the first of the cultural frameworks or tools I mention above is a historical interpretative theory which acknowledges the distinctive influence of Calvinist Puritanism and its electionism, pragmatism, Scottish commonsense realism, the Protestant work ethic linked to capitalism and even neo-Gnosticism that are an explanation of the roots and the continuing development of this way of thinking in American culture (and the globalization of its religion). In this, I will seek to establish that many of these influences flow out of beliefs about America being a nation founded and established by God, which in turn flow out of America's Puritan past and its ongoing Puritan legacy.

The second framework in the next chapter is a more religious interpretation that explains the nature of the Word of Faith Movement's ethos and worldview, its philosophy and epistemology. In this I explore the development of the positive thinking new thought sub-culture within American culture and plot the likely paths of its fusion with revivalist culture to form what I term "American 'Word of Faith' Culture." Later in the book these frameworks are used to interpret my case study ministries and their associated congregational cultures.

2.3.1 American Exceptionalism

My thesis depends, to a large extent, on the identification of a general cultural difference between English and American evangelicalism. Looking at American culture in general there is something that could be called American ethnicity, "a set of traits or cultural turns characterizing those born, or born again, in the United States."[83] With the rise of the American Studies discipline over recent decades, there has been much discussion over

---

81. Romanowski, *Pop Culture Wars*, 306.
82. Geertz, *The Interpretation of Cultures*, 5.
83. Albanese, *A Republic of Mind and Spirit*.

the concept of "American exceptionalism." That is the idea that the United States is culturally unique, a concept that originated from Alexis de Tocqueville in the 1840s, who observed that the developing American culture was exceptional.[84]

This wider cultural debate has had an impact on comparative studies of American and English evangelicalisms. In a significant recent article, key British scholar David Bebbington asserted that the characteristics of American and British evangelicalisms "are very similar, and their essence is identical."[85] This view is challenged by the views of a number of other scholars, both before and after Bebbington's assertion. Key to this discussion is the notional dating of the phenomenon of evangelicalism in Britain and the United States. While acknowledging that historians link the term "evangelical" to the churches of the Reformation,[86] Bebbington asserts from the outset of his highly influential 1980s book, *Evangelicalism in Modern Britain*,[87] that "Evangelical religion is a popular Protestant movement that has existed in Britain since the 1730s."[88]

Bebbington's working definition in the above work of four characteristics of evangelicalism—conversionism, activism, biblicism, and crucicentrism (known as the quadrilateral)[89] along with his thesis that evangelicalism had been shaped since the 1730s first by the Enlightenment, second by Romanticism, and thirdly by modernism,[90] was happily received by the vast majority of his peers. Bebbington's argument is framed in such a way that it appears that evangelicalism is essentially an eighteenth-century phenomenon, linked with revivalism and stimulated by Enlightenment philosophy. Bebbington's thesis has, in the period since its publication, gained very wide acceptance.

However, the specific placing of evangelical origins in eighteenth-century Britain has been questioned by recent scholarship. For example, W. R. Ward in his 2006 book, *Early Evangelicalism*,[91] challenges earlier scholarship of the evangelical movement which, in his view, did not date the origins of evangelicalism early enough and failed to give a coherent

---

84. See de Tocqueville, *Democracy in America*, 517–18.
85. Bebbington "Not So Exceptional After All," 4.
86. Bebbington, *Evangelicalism in Modern Britain*, 1.
87. Bebbington, *Evangelicalism in Modern Britain*.
88. Ibid., 1.
89. Larsen, "The Reception Given *Evangelicalism in Modern Britain* Since Its Publication in 1989," 25.
90. Ibid., 30.
91. Ward, *Early Evangelicalism*.

picture of evangelical identity.⁹² Instead, Ward points to the 1670s and argues that evangelicalism as an intellectual movement influenced Protestants throughout Europe and the American colonies. He argues that, in response to the dry Protestant orthodoxy of seventeenth-century Lutheran and Reformed thinkers, many longed for a more personal pietistic faith that was the forerunner of modern evangelicalism. Despite being separated by geography and language, there was a definite "evangelical movement" that spanned continents and religious traditions. He cites the example of leading American Puritan, Cotton Mather, who was an admiring correspondent of Francke, a Lutheran Pietist.⁹³

Bebbington's claim that evangelicalism began in the 1730s was only a concern for a handful of reviewers when *Evangelicalism in Modern Britain* first came out. Indeed, as Larsen points out, Bebbington's definition has become the standard definition of evangelicalism and has been warmly received and cited by many scholars. Without doubt, his quadrilateral should be central to any definition of modern evangelicalism, and is extremely helpful in understanding the development of evangelicalism since the early eighteenth century. However, it is perhaps surprising that it took nearly twenty years for the appearance of a volume rethinking his dating of the movement.⁹⁴

As Larsen points out, a number of reviewers have raised concerns from confessional angles.⁹⁵ However, he cites others who point out the controversy and weakness of Bebbington's lack of acceptance of continuity between evangelicalism and its precursors.⁹⁶ Paul Helm points out that Calvin believed in religious conversion, he was foremost in stressing the principle of *sola scriptura*, that Christ was central to Calvin's understanding of theology, and evangelism was a key priority.⁹⁷ In the same volume, Gary J. Williams indicates that in many ways, the quadrilateral characteristics and Bebbington's other factor, activism, were evident in the lives of the Reformers.⁹⁸

Alister McGrath argues that the term "evangelical" emerged from Italian Benedictine monasteries in the late fifteenth century, and that it was

---

92. Ibid., 1.
93. Ibid., 6.
94. Larsen, "The Reception Given *Evangelicalism in Modern Britain*."
95. Ibid., 23–24.
96. Ibid., 24.
97. Helm, "Calvin, A. M. Toplady and the Bebbington Thesis."
98. Williams, "Enlightenment Epistemology and Eighteenth-Century Evangelical Doctrines of Assurance."

used prominently in the writings of the early reformers in the early sixteenth century.[99]

It seems clear to me that the early Puritan settlers in America were, in a very real sense, part of the developing evangelical movement. From those very early days, American culture has been influenced by evangelicalism. So Kyle is right to assert that "evangelicalism and American popular culture have interacted extensively since the colonial era."[100]

However, this interaction has not just been evangelicalism's influence over American culture; evangelicalism as a phenomenon has been significantly influenced by American culture. As Kyle writes, "While its roots can be found in Europe, if evangelicalism were a garment its label would read: 'Made in America.'" He continues,

> the relationship has been complex and paradoxical. It has run in both directions. In its attempt to create a Christian American, evangelicals have shaped the nation's public values. The influence, however, has run more in the other direction. The popular culture has had a tremendous impact on evangelicalism—so much so that many conservative protestants regard evangelical and American values as one and the same.[101]

A number of other writers make the same or similar points.[102]

Bebbington summarizes Kyle's critique of American evangelicalism in the following way.

> Evangelicalism has capitulated, he argues, to the forces of Americanism—individualism, pragmatism, populism, democracy, free enterprise, and so on. In trying to convey the gospel to the United States, the movement has assimilated the values of the nation . . . Evangelicals have tried to be countercultural, but, paradoxically, they have been thoroughly pressed into the mould of their setting.[103]

Bebbington, however, sees Kyle's verdict as "pessimistic" and instead prefers to note the large numbers of similarities between American and British evangelicalism. This is consistent with his earlier stance in the essay

---

99. McGrath, *Evangelicalism and the Future of Christianity*, 11–13.

100. Kyle, *Evangelicalism*, ix.

101. Ibid.

102. Sweeney, *The American Evangelical Story*; Reimer, *Evangelicals and the Continental Divide*; Sheler, *Believers*; El-Faizy, *God and Country*.

103. Bebbington, "Not So Exceptional After All," 2.

"Evangelicalism in Modern Britain and America,"[104] where he counters the view that the American form of evangelicalism is entirely distinctive. As an example, he refers to Nathan Hatch who, he says, argues that "the evangelicalism of the United States possesses unique American characteristics."[105] Bebbington further states that Hatch is arguing that American evangelicalism "expresses the views of commoners, who have unbounded confidence in their ability to grasp total truth," and at its core is "democratic."

He quotes Hatch's argument as follows: "Where but in America could a converted seaman . . . make bold to undertake the same rational study of biblical prophecy that had taxed the mind of . . . Isaac Newton?"[106] Bebbington responds,

> The expected answer is nowhere, but the accurate answer is that similar studies were published aplenty by converted butcher's assistants, grocer's assistants and other humble folk in nineteenth- and twentieth-century Britain. It is assumed that evangelicalism was in this respect distinctive to the United States, when in reality it was not.

Hatch chooses an unfortunate example, and Bebbington makes a valid point here. However, he does not give sufficient attention to the ongoing confidence American evangelicals have in their perceived status as a nation "founded" by God,[107] and their confidence that the ordinary person is as capable of interpreting the Scriptures as accurately as anyone else,[108] as we shall see later in this chapter.

Bebbington argues that the movement originated simultaneously in both countries, with Jonathan Edwards in 1734, and Howell Harris and Daniel Rowland in Wales, and George Whitefield and John Wesley in England in 1735. He comments that the American and British branches of the movement have remained connected over the years and he notes the "transatlantic influence," with preachers going back and forth across the Atlantic Ocean, especially from America to Britain. Visitors from America to Britain he names as Lorenzo Dow, James Caughey, Dwight L. Moody,

---

104. Bebbington, "Evangelicalism in Modern Britain and America—A Comparison."

105. Ibid., 184.

106. Hatch, "Evangelicalism as a Democratic Movement." Hatch refers to Hal Lindsey and his book *The Late Great Planet Earth*.

107. Marsden, *Religion and American Culture*, 22.

108. This approach to the scriptures is revealed in the teaching of R. A. Torrey who argued, "In ninety nine out of one hundred cases the meaning that the plain man gets out of the Bible is the correct one"; see McLoughlin *Modern Revivalism*, 372. The original source is not clear, but dates from 1906 and is cited in Marsden, *Understanding Fundamentalism and Evangelicalism*, 165.

from the nineteenth century, and Billy Graham and John Wimber in the later half of the twentieth century. A significant traveller in the opposite direction he names as John Witherspoon, who went from Scotland to be President of Princeton, and was the only minister of religion to sign the American Declaration of Independence. He also mentions F. B. Meyer, but only as a visitor.[109] In a recent article, Bebbington mentions recent British influences on American evangelicalism such as F. F. Bruce, J. I. Packer, John Stott, and strangely C. S. Lewis (who would not have described himself as an evangelical). A recent British influence he names as Nicky Gumbel and his Alpha Course.[110]

While Bebbington names these transatlantic emigrants and visitors, he does acknowledge that the flow has been especially from North America to Britain.[111] In his more recent article he says,

> Although the 20th-century influence of America over the British movement has been far stronger, especially through Billy Graham, there has been a longstanding and in some measure enduring influence of Britain over American evangelicalism.[112]

This, Bebbington argues, counters the idea of American exceptionalism, that American religion is entirely different from European religion, and that evangelicalism can be presented as distinctively American (as, for example, presented in Kyle's book). While I would not subscribe entirely to the idea of American exceptionalism, and agree with Bebbington that evangelicalism is, in its entirety, not something distinctively American, I would not agree with his assertion that the characteristics of American and British evangelicalism "are very similar, and their essence is identical."[113]

2.3.2 Accounting for Differences between American and British Evangelicalism

Of course, I agree with Bebbington that British and American evangelicalisms have interacted extensively and agree with Marsden that

> from the time of the Puritans down through the awakenings to the end of the nineteenth century British and American

---

109. Bebbington, "Evangelism in Modern Britain and America," 186.
110. Bebbington "Not so Exceptional After All," 4.
111. Bebbington, "Evangelism in Modern Britain and America," 186.
112. Bebbington "Not so Exceptional After All," 4.
113. Ibid.

evangelicalism had been in many respects parts of a single transatlantic movement.[114]

However, I note the precision of Marsden's statement that they are in "many respects" parts of a single transatlantic movement; there are some notable differences and divergences. Indeed, as Marsden argues in this article, American and British evangelicals in general responded in quite different ways to the arrival of Darwinism and higher critical views of Scripture. In America, controversy over these issues intensified from the 1860s to the 1920s, while in Britain, most of the controversy over evolution had passed by 1869 and controversy over the nature of Scripture by 1890.[115] To explain the relative lack of militancy among English evangelicals compared to their American counterparts, Marsden suggests a number of significant factors—social, religious, and intellectual—that might have led to militancy among the Americans. Instead of these just being factors that led to differences over enthusiasm for fundamentalism, I would like to suggest that these factors indicate considerable differences in the nature of American and British evangelicalism going back at least to the time of the first Great Awakening.

I now intend to consider the significant nature and characteristics of each of these factors, following Marsden, but building significantly on his work.

Before introducing pertinent cultural differences, I want to reflect briefly on social factors, mentioned by Marsden,[116] which particularly molded American evangelicalism. Most significant is that America, still a developing nation in the nineteenth century, was affected by its geographical vastness. Poor communications led to poor communication of ideas and a lack of challenge of religious assumptions. Another factor was the lack of interaction between denominations which meant that innovations in evangelical thought were experienced in different parts of America as much as generations apart.[117] To this, I would like to add that the culture of revival camp fireside meetings and the "frontier spirit" led to the rise of American transcendentalism and particularly New Thought Metaphysics (sometimes simply called American religion), developed by Quimby and others (see chapter 3). The thinking of this movement about the use of the mind and

---

114. Marsden, "Fundamentalism as an American Phenomenon: A Comparison with English Evangelicalism," 216.

115. Ibid., 217–18.

116. Ibid., 224.

117. This was a point made at the time by Newman, "Recent Changes in the Theology of Baptists."

that thoughts can change situations was, I believe, absorbed into the popular teaching of nineteenth century American revivalist evangelicals.

2.3.3 The Differences

2.3.3.1 Puritanism

The first of my "differences" is Puritanism and its associated Calvinism and electionism. One of the major cultural influences on the United States has to be its Puritan heritage. Perry Miller commented, "Without some understanding of Puritanism, it may safely be said, there is no understanding of America."[118]

Miller understood Puritanism to be a "philosophy of life" or "code of values" brought by seventeenth-century settlers to New England. He writes,

> It has become one of the continuous factors in American life and American thought. Any inventory of the elements that have gone into making the "American mind" would have to commence with Puritanism.[119]

He adds,

> Its role in American thought has been almost the dominant one, for the descendants of Puritans have carried at least some habits of the Puritan mind into a variety of pursuits, have spread across the country, and in many fields of activity have played a leading part . . . it has inspired certain traits which have persisted long after the vanishing of the original creed.[120]

Calvinism. Puritanism has its roots in European Calvinism and was a movement that wanted to purify the church from what it viewed as Roman Catholic excesses.

In the 1530s, before the Puritan movement was evident, Anabaptists fleeing persecution in mainland Europe came to Britain. They faced less possibility of opposition in England because of support from those who had been supporters and sympathizers towards John Wyclif and Lollardy in the fourteenth century. As Puritanism developed throughout the sixteenth century, and particularly during the reign of the Protestant Elizabeth I, Anabaptists were among the most extreme in the movement. The majority

---

118. Miller, "The Puritan Way of Life," 36.
119. Ibid., 35.
120. Ibid., 36.

of Puritans were committed to the Church of England and its practice of infant baptism which was in line with the approach of reformers throughout Europe, whether they be Calvinist, Lutheran, or Zwinglian.[121]

Extreme biblicism. The Anabaptists totally refused to accept the validity of infant baptism in what they viewed as their rigorous adherence to the New Testament.[122]

So the more extreme end of the Puritan movement tended to an "extreme biblicism"[123] that had no place for theological reason on such issues. The Puritans who settled in New England, were among the more radical.[124] While the majority in the Puritan movement would have been opposed to this biblicism, there is no doubt that Anabaptist thought crossed over to America. Its biblicism was there among the early settlers, and it had a lasting impact on the progress of American evangelicalism in the centuries to follow.

The Puritan movement in England suffered a severe setback in the period 1553–58 when the Roman Catholic Mary Tudor was on the throne. This was a dangerous time for Protestants, culminating in the burning of Thomas Cranmer, Hugh Latimer, and Nicholas Ridley as heretics in 1555–56. Many high profile Puritans fled from London; Adam Winthrop (grandfather of John Winthrop, the first governor of the Massachusetts Bay Colony), for example, retreated to his family's lands in Suffolk to avoid close scrutiny of his religious views.[125]

Sola Scriptura. Others fled to the continent, to Holland and to Calvin's Geneva. When these exiles returned to England, they were not pleased to find the Elizabethan Compromise (or Settlement) in place where Episcopal government and much Catholic ritual were retained alongside Protestant doctrine; they wanted to press for the Bible alone as the guide for the church.[126]

When Elizabeth I of England died in 1603, she was succeeded by James Stuart, King of Scotland. In Scotland, the Stuarts barely tolerated the Calvinist Presbyterian Church. They ruled England for most of the seventeenth century and had a strong dislike for English Puritans.[127] It was in this environment that a small group of extreme Puritans left the Church of England

---

121. Ibid., 40. See also Dyton, "Anabaptists."
122. Dyton "Anabaptists."
123. See section 2.3.3.1 of this thesis.
124. Miller, "The Puritan Way of Life," 41.
125. Bremer, "William Winthrop," 285.
126. Marsden, *Religion and American Culture*, 20.
127. Ibid., 21.

and at the same time felt they should leave England itself. They founded the Plymouth Colony in 1620. Tension worsened when Charles Stuart came to the throne in 1625. Charles rejected Calvinism in favor of a theological position closer to traditional Catholicism. Even more Puritans felt they had to leave for America to form a society based on Puritan principles.

A model Christian state and a nation founded by God. This society, the Massachusetts Bay Colony, was described by its first governor, John Winthrop, as "a city upon a hill." It was hoped to be a model Christian state.[128]

Convinced they were commissioned by God to play a major role in world history, the early Puritan settlers in America were Calvinists and believed that their new home was a nation founded by God. They even viewed themselves as the New Israel, God's new chosen people.[129] This is a view that has persisted to the present day; Hamner writes,

> From the first Puritan's step onto New England soil, Puritanism has been a concept fissuring from within. Nevertheless, the concept of Puritanism consistently has sustained mythic portraits of America as a uniquely religious country with a God-given mission and constituted by God-intoxicated persons.[130]

Marsden notes that, according to Bercovitch's exposition of the American Puritans' understanding of their own identity, based on typologies in the history of God's people in his *Puritan Origins of the American Self*,[131] they had a vision that New England's corporate mission was of the same type as the mission of the Old Testament nation of Israel.[132]

Electionism. As I have said, at the heart of Calvinism was the theology of electionism. In practice, New England churches restricted membership, as well as political authority, to the "elect" who could prove they were recipients of God's grace.[133] This, of course, limited the numbers of those who were seen to be the visible church, something that later revivalists reacted to by modifying electionism, as I will point to as I consider early pragmatism in American evangelicalism.

Puritanism led to revivalism being almost unchallenged. The predominantly Calvinist religion of the Puritan settlers demanded intellectual assent to "precisely formulated statements of religious truth in opposition to

---

128. Ibid., 22.
129. Ibid.
130. Hamner, *American Pragmatism*, 7.
131. Bercovitch, *The Puritan Origins of the American Self*, 36.
132. Marsden, "America's 'Christian' Origins," 242.
133. Cotton, "Letter to Lord Say and Seal."

all error,"[134] whereas the Anglican majority in England fostered a spirit of moderation and restraint.

Revivalism was almost unchallenged in America, while in England it was restrained by the influence of the established church and the universities, and the evangelicalism in nineteenth-century England was somewhat curtailed by the draw of the High Church movement on people of traditional temperament.[135] In America, the effectiveness of methods associated with revivalism would have been in tune with the thinking of those who were among the early pragmatists.

Unopposed revivalism often led to anti-intellectualism, and the tendency to think in terms of simple dichotomies and dualism.[136] As Marsden observes of nineteenth-century American revivalists, "The universe was divided between the realm of God and the realm of Satan; the supernatural was sharply separated from the natural; righteousness could have nothing to do with sin. The central impulse of revivalism was to rescue the saved from among the lost, and its whole way of conceiving reality was built around this central antithesis. In such a dichotomized view of things, ambiguities were rare."[137] Anti-intellectualism and its development in American life has been described famously by Richard Hofstadter,[138] but more recent treatments examining the relationship between pietism, revivalism, pragmatism, and anti-intellectualism have been made by Os Guinness[139] and Mark Noll.[140]

2.3.3.2 Scottish Commonsense

Closely linked with pragmatism is Thomas Reid's Scottish commonsense realism, brought to America when his student John Witherspoon became the President of Princeton. From that point onwards, this philosophy had a deep and lasting influence on the thinking of ordinary Americans.

The Princeton School was strongly influenced by a synthesis of Scottish commonsense realism and Baconian inductive philosophy.[141] Scottish commonsense philosophy began to have an influence on Princeton when John Witherspoon (1723–94), a former student of the respected Scot-

---

134. Marsden, "Fundamentalism as an American Phenomenon," 227.
135. Ibid., 226.
136. Ibid.
137. Ibid.
138. Hofstadter, *Anti-Intellectualism in American Life*.
139. Guinness, *Fit Bodies, Fat Minds*.
140. Noll, *The Scandal of the Evangelical Mind*.
141. Marsden, "Fundamentalism as an American Phenomenon," 228.

tish philosopher, Thomas Reid, came from Scotland to become the sixth President of Princeton. The great theologians of Princeton—Charles Hodge, A. A. Hodge and B. B. Warfield—followed the thinking of Reid in preference to Locke and Hume.[142] This had a profound influence on American thinking during the nineteenth century, the effect of which was a straightforward practical approach to everything including the Bible, which many held could be understood to be the Word of God, independent from its historical and literary context. The Bible was not just a book for scholars to interpret for the masses but was a book that could be directly understood by ordinary Americans.[143] In contrast, the skepticism associated with Hume, and the rationalism and liberalism associated with Kant and Schleiermacher, was much more influential in Britain and the rest of Europe.

2.3.3.3 Pragmatism

American pragmatism is an extremely important cultural factor for this book. In the section that follows, I examine the highly significant interrelationship between revivalism and pragmatism. Perhaps revivalism could have been considered in the religious interpretive theory of chapter 3, but for the sake of clarity (not fracturing the argument), I consider revivalism in this chapter and section.

William James (1842–1910) in his essay *Pragmatism* (1907)[144] points to Charles S. Peirce (1839–1914) as the founder of the modern pragmatic movement and originator of the term "pragmatism."[145] He also points to others in the past for the origins of this sort of thinking, such as Socrates, Aristotle, Locke, Berkeley, Hume, and James Mill.[146] While he does this, he does not explore any American roots and therefore does not explain why pragmatism flourished in America to the extent that it became "justly regarded as a distinctly American philosophy."[147]

Benjamin Franklin. In his book *Recovering Benjamin Franklin*,[148] James Campbell, building on his earlier essay "The Pragmatism of Benjamin

---

142. Marsden, *Fundamentalism and American Culture*, 14–15.

143. See Reuben Torrey's comment, "the meaning the plain man gets out of the Bible is the correct one," in McLoughlin, *Modern Revivalism*, 372.

144. James, "Pragmatism: A New Name for Some Old Ways of Thinking."

145. Ibid., 8, and 341–42 n. 9.

146. Campbell, *Recovering Benjamin Franklin*, viii.

147. Bruce Aune, quoted in Hamner, *American Pragmatism*, 3.

148. Campbell, *Recovering Benjamin Franklin*.

Franklin,"[149] points to a pragmatic tradition in America, including Frederick Douglas (1818–95), Walt Whitman (1819–92), Elizabeth Cady Stanton (1815–1902), and Henry David Thoreau (1817–62),[150] at whose head is Benjamin Franklin (1706–90).[151] Campbell's book and essay is an excellent attempt to explore "what H. S. Thayer calls the "nascent" pragmatism of Benjamin Franklin."[152] Campbell quotes Clinton Rossiter,

> Pragmatism as a rule of conscious political action has never had a more eminent exponent than Benjamin Franklin . . . in Franklin's life and political arguments this method became an acknowledged if yet nameless American fundamental. . . . He was not a political philosopher; he was not a philosopher at all. He was prepared to investigate every principle and institution known to the human race, but only through practical and un-speculative methods. He limited his own thought-process to the one devastating question: *Does it work?*, or more exactly, *Does it work well?*[153]

This question "what makes things work well?" is a key priority in American thinking through to the present.

Of course, other key figures of the time—for example, Jefferson and Adams—were also pragmatists, and Jonathan Edwards, the most influential of Puritans, was affected by pragmatism, which was "in the air" in early eighteenth-century America.[154]

Puritan thought was insistent that God is holy and transcendent and all human organizations including the church were fickle and inconsistent. In New England, it was assumed God's covenant with his people could only include those who were convinced of their salvation through God's unfathomable grace. The church's mission was not understood in terms of saving souls; that was the prerogative of God as creator and judge. Their role instead was to gather and shepherd the elect and build the New Jerusalem.[155]

---

149. Campbell, "The Pragmatism of Benjamin Franklin."
150. Campbell, *Recovering Benjamin Franklin*, ix.
151. Ibid.
152. Ibid.
153. Campbell, *Recovering Benjamin Franklin*, 199.
154. Conkin, *Puritans and Pragmatists*.
155. Williams, "Visions of the Good Society and the Religious Roots of American Political Culture," 10.

By 1740, a "half-way covenant" had been created, opening membership of the church and therefore full citizenship to the baptized, who had not experienced what they perceived to be mystical regeneration.[156]

Solomon Stoddard and his grandson, Jonathan Edwards, of the then frontier town of Northampton, Massachusetts, included this new inclusive approach into Puritan theology. Stoddard believed that the more exclusive form of Puritanism would not work on the frontier, where the very nature of life encouraged equality and individualism. So Stoddard's Calvinism was modified to reach the masses. Experience leading to conversion was preferred over an intellectual approach.[157] In essence, this meant that the church was assumed to be everyone baptized, which usually meant the whole community; the elect would be revealed in experience. Stoddard expressed the approach as: "Let the Church include the whole town [and then] let God do the selecting."[158]

Revivalism in the form of the first Great Awakening, associated with Jonathan Edwards and John Whitfield, was characterized by this more inclusive Calvinist theology. This revival, while it remained theocentric, with the view that God alone could change people's hearts and lives, gave priority to experience over intellect. Experience became the validation of God's activity. The second Great Awakening associated with Charles G. Finney (influenced by the Wesleys) softened Calvinism, preferring Arminian theology. In order to win more souls, Finney introduced "new measures" to bring in revivals, making conversion to be about personal response, for example, coming forward in a church meeting to sit on the mercy seat in response to the preached gospel. Finney's addresses on revival read like a recipe with steps and principles on a how to bring about a revival.[159]

He and his contemporaries adopted methods that worked. In doing this, they were behaving in a pragmatic way. As Thomas writes,

> an important controversy with respect to revivals was over their rationalised methods, which struck some as manipulation and therefore unworthy of the gospel. It was also argued that these measures "worked-up" faith and conversions, faith created by humans and not the truly regenerating faith that is a gift from God. The revivalists defended their activity by arguing that anything that effected conversion was appropriate and required;

---

156. Marsden, *Jonathan Edwards*, 30. See Also Heimert and Delbanco, *The Puritans in America*, 194.

157. Stoddard allowed a much wider basis for admission to the sacrament of the Lord's Supper, see Ziff, *Puritanism in America*, 197.

158. Reichley, *Religion in American Public Life*, 69.

159. Finney, *Finney on Revival*.

> they thereby were the early developers of American pragmatism. . . . Opponents flatly rejected the autonomous mechanics of means coupled with free will, in the tradition of Edwards ([1742] 1974, 407) who had explicitly condemned such pragmatism as an "erroneous principle."[160]

Of course, it might well be said, and I would like to argue, that Edwards and Stoddard had already taken a more pragmatic line themselves by including the theology of the half-way covenant.

Pragmatism is often referred to as American pragmatism because it is the only distinctively American philosophy. We might well ask, what is American about American pragmatism and what is its nature? This is a question discussed by Gail Hamner in her book *American Pragmatism*.[161] Hamner argues that,

> American pragmatism marks a repositioning of British and European science, especially psychology, within theories of human knowing and being that emphasise the purposive and disciplined production of the self through habits (Peirce) or will (James).[162]

She identifies the driving force behind this repositioning as "America's slippery but persistent 'Puritan imaginary,'" and she attributes "the American quality of pragmatism to an insistent, non doctrinal Puritan legacy that operated during the mid- to late nineteenth century."[163] In her conclusions, Hamner links her understanding of Puritanism and its evolution in American history to national identity and the nature of religion in America today.[164]

To the pragmatist, religious ideas have to prove their worth in concrete ways in order to be true; as James writes, "If theological ideas prove to have a value for concrete life, they will be true, for pragmatism, in the sense of being good for so much."[165]

Much American religious thought has adopted pragmatism in its approach to truth. If it "works," it must be good is a common way of thinking in American Christianity. In effect, subjective religious experience causes individuals to follow whatever spiritual path, method or theory "works" for them.

---

160. Thomas, *Revivalism and Cultural Change*, 73.
161. Hamner, *American Pragmatism*.
162. Ibid., 4.
163. Ibid.
164. Ibid. and ibid., 152–73.
165. James, *Pragmatism and Other* Writings, 36.

In their desire to grow their churches and ministries, many American evangelicals have adopted a pragmatic approach to everything, from answering life's problems to bringing about church growth and even revival.

As Os Guinness writes,

> The overall results of such different trends as prosperity piety, positive thinking, engineered revivalism, and the church growth movement has been to stamp pragmatism indelibly on the evangelical soul. The concern "Will it work?" has long overshadowed "Is it true?" Theology has given way to technique. Know-whom has faded before know-how. Serving God has subtly been deformed into servicing the self.[166]

Another aspect to the pragmatic approach to life and theology is pragmatism's instrumentalism. This interpretation of pragmatism was added by John Dewey, who defined instrumentalism as

> an attempt to constitute a precise logical theory of concepts, of judgements and inferences through their various forms, by considering primarily how thought functions in the experimental determinations of future consequences.[167]

In effect, this means that the workings of religion are seen to be in steps or by using keys to make things work. It is precisely this pragmatism and instrumentality that I intend to illustrate in the writings and teachings of my case study ministries throughout this book.

As pragmatism developed, it became clear that it was about simple methods that worked. (*Pragma* is Greek for "action," from which our words "practice" and "practical" come.)[168] This simple approach to life had much in common with the Scottish commonsense philosophy of the Princeton school and the early fundamentalists. As a form of religion, it was about people doing things to bring themselves into the kingdom rather than waiting for God to call them.

In response to pragmatism, many left more evangelical opinion in favor of the more social gospel of the Unitarians or, alternatively, followed the thinking of men like Quimby and his New Thought Metaphysics, which was equally pragmatic, but also, as I shall argue, neo-Gnostic.

---

166. Guinness, *Fit Bodies, Fat Minds*, 59.
167. John Dewey, quoted in Thayer, *Meaning and Action*, 169.
168. James, *Pragmatism and Other Writings*, 25.

2.3.3.4 Spirit of Capitalism

I would like to suggest that due to America's particularly Puritan/Calvinist heritage, American evangelicalism and American culture in general has a particularly capitalist mindset. Marsden argues that "the connection between the 'spirit of capitalism' and the Protestant ethic can readily be illustrated in a New England line of descent from Cotton Mather to Benjamin Franklin."[169] This, according to Ahlstrom, led to "a 'gospel' of work that was undergirded by the so-called puritan Ethic."[170]

The Calvinist doctrine of double predestination led, as Weber famously described,[171] to the view that only the elect would succeed in business, which in turn led to the desire to succeed even through Protestant ascetic lifestyle. This is turn led to "the spirit of capitalism" and the capitalist mindset.[172]

Weber's life work as a sociologist was no less than the comparative analysis of world civilizations. He was fascinated by the differences between western civilization and the civilizations of the east. Why did Western civilization in particular give rise to modern western capitalism and the industrial revolution? Weber's answers to this question were given is his famous essay, *The Protestant Ethic and the Spirit of Capitalism*.[173] Indeed, the title names the two factors which, in his view, provide the answers to the question. In his book, *The Spirit of Capitalism and the Protestant Ethic*,[174] Michael Lessnoff depicts the Weber thesis schematically as a causal chain involving four terms. The "Protestant ethic" (PE), the "spirit of capitalism" (SC), "modern Western capitalism" (MWC) and the "Industrial Revolution (IR). If the arrows below represent causal relationships then

$$PE \rightarrow SC \rightarrow MWC \rightarrow IR$$

He makes the observation that it is somewhat difficult to distinguish between the "spirit of capitalism" and "modern Western capitalism" because the latter is a pattern of economic behavior and the former is a set of ideas that lead to that behavior.

169. Marsden, "America's 'Christian' Origins," 243.
170. Ahlstrom, *A Religious History of the American People*, 1972, 1090.
171. Weber, *The Protestant Ethic and the Spirit of Capitalism*.
172. Roy M. Anker, *Self-Help and Popular Religion in Early American Culture*, 45–46.
173. Weber, *The Protestant Ethic and the Spirit of Capitalism*.
174. Lessnoff, *The Spirit of Capitalism and the Protestant Ethic*, 2.

In seeking to define the spirit of capitalism, Weber bases his ideas on the thinking of culturally Puritan writers of the eighteenth century, particularly Benjamin Franklin. Weber quoted Franklin early in his work; for example:

> For six pounds a year you may have the use of one hundred pounds, provided you are a man of known prudence and honesty. He that spends a groat a day, spends idly above six pounds a year, which is the price for the use of one hundred pounds. He that wastes idly a groat's worth of his time per day, one day with another, wastes the privilege of using one hundred pounds each day. He that idly uses five shillings worth of time, loses five shillings, and might as prudently throw five shillings into the sea. He that loses five shillings, not only loses that sum, but all the advantages that might be made by turning it in dealing, which by the time that a young man becomes old, will amount of a considerable amount of money.[175]

Weber then concludes,

> Truly what is here preached is not simply a means of making one's way in the world, but a particular ethic. . . . It is not mere business astuteness, that sort of thing is common enough, it is an ethos.[176]

He then makes the following comment about Franklin,

> Now, all Franklin's moral attitudes are coloured with utilitarianism. Honesty is useful, because it assures credit; so are punctuality, industry, frugality, and that is the reason they are virtues.[177]

He continues,

> The earning of money within the modern economic order is, so long as it is done legally, the result and the expression of virtue and proficiency in a calling; and this virtue and proficiency are, as it is now not difficult to see, the real Alpha and Omega of Franklin's ethic.[178]

---

175. Weber, *The Protestant Ethic and the Spirit of Capitalism*, 50, quoting Franklin's *Necessary Hints to Those that Would be Rich* (1736) and *Advice to Young Tradesmen* (1748).

176. Ibid., 51.

177. Ibid., 52.

178. Ibid., 53–54.

In Franklin's writings, Weber saw early signs of the spirit of capitalism before there was any established capitalistic order in the American colonies.

Weber's focus is on behavioral elements of modern Western capitalism that he finds peculiar. In particular the continuous pursuit of maximum profit, which might be mistaken for a simple expression of selfishness but is in fact nothing of the kind. Instead of gain being seen as a means to ease and enjoyment, these things are rejected because they get in the way of the maximization of profit which became an end in itself. In fact, it became a duty. This is the "spirit of capitalism." Weber calls it an "ethic";[179] the ethic specifies both an end, and a number of means to that end. Among these means are such virtues as industry, frugality, punctuality, and honesty.

The spirit of capitalism is a peculiar set of motivating ideas that require an explanation; his explanation is another set of ideas: the Protestant ethic.

One obvious difference between these two sets of ideas is that those who exhibit the spirit of capitalism are businessmen, whereas the ideas and values of the Protestant ethic are put forward by men of religion.

Nevertheless, Weber calls the Protestant ethic a secular ethic, that is, an ethic for this world, even though it is derived from more fundamental religious principles. The relationship between the two sets of ideas amount to a religious influence on economic conduct.

It might be expected that the Protestant ethic and the spirit of capitalism are fundamentally the same, but an examination of Weber's argument reveals this is not so. To explain this, it is necessary to understand Weber's thinking about the development of Protestant doctrine in the sixteenth and seventeenth centuries. The key doctrine of Protestantism is *sola fide*—salvation by faith alone in which there is no idea of justification by works, although Protestantism does have a doctrine of works where works are important in living a life that is pleasing to God. It is the interaction of these two doctrines over time that led to what Weber calls the "Protestant ethic." This, he said, became fully elaborated in the "ascetic Protestantism" of the Calvinist reform churches, though not by Calvin himself.

However, both Luther and Calvin played an essential background role. Not only did Luther expound the doctrine of salvation by faith alone, but he also changed Christian thinking about good works through his doctrine of the calling.[180] Weber's analysis of Luther's thinking starts with the observation that Luther rejected the Roman Catholic idea that the religious orders were called to be on a higher moral plane, interceding between the sinful masses and the deity on their behalf. From the point of view of Weber's

179. Ibid., 51.
180. Ibid., 79–81.

thesis, the central achievement of the Reformation was the acceptance of secular life as equal, if not higher, in moral value to life in the religious orders, where withdrawal from the world was seen as valueless from a religious point of view. The "godly life" was now for all believers, regardless of their station. The earthly calling is, in effect, every legitimate and social role, conceived as part of the divine order for men. To perform the duties of such a calling is to serve and love one's neighbor as commanded by God and is, therefore, "the only way to live acceptably to God."[181] According to Weber, the significant change in this doctrine from past thinking is that it views "fulfilment of duties in worldly affairs as the highest form which the moral activity of an individual could assume."[182]

In his writings, Weber makes frequent use of the term "asceticism." Traditionally, those who practiced asceticism were the monks and nuns of religious orders, often by complete withdrawal from the world. However, after the Reformation, a form of Protestant asceticism developed in which self-denial was practiced without withdrawal from the world. Indeed, with the notion of the "calling," this self-denial was applied to work, with the result that these ascetic Protestants worked hard, but reinvested the profits of their labor rather than spending money on themselves in displays of conspicuous consumption.

In Weber's argument, Calvin contributed the salvation doctrine of absolute double predestination.[183] Expressed simply, this is the idea that, from the beginning of time, God has chosen a small minority of human beings for salvation through his grace (the elect) and to damn the rest (the reprobate) by withholding his grace from them. This doctrine became more important to Calvin's followers than it was to Calvin. Among Calvinists, the predestination doctrine produced extreme anxieties about salvation which were experienced in profound "inner isolation."[184] This led Calvinists to seek assurance of their salvation in some way. They were taught that "intense worldly activity" may be taken as a sign of salvation.[185] To gain that assurance, Calvinists engaged in remarkably disciplined economic activity; consequently, many accumulated considerable amounts of capital which, following religious strictures, was reinvested.[186] According to Weber's thesis, the "ethic" and the later "spirit" caused substantial economic

181. Ibid., 81.
182. Ibid., 80.
183. Ibid., 98–127.
184. Ibid., 108.
185. Ibid., 112.
186. Ibid., 68.

growth in Protestant nations, specifically in those influenced by Calvinism and its derivatives. However, it is surely the case that the reverse is true, that modern evangelicalism descended from Calvinism has been affected by its relationship with capitalism. This has been especially true in America, with its strong Calvinist influence. This is a possible explanation as to why American evangelicalism has tended to be more capitalist, having an interest in the success of churches and their leaders through the sales of books and media, and through the promotion of their programs and teachings. There is a tendency in many American evangelical churches to see God's blessing in terms of personal wealth, whereas in England—more influenced by Anglicanism and the Catholic past with its "evangelical counsels" of poverty, chastity and obedience—apparent, if not actual, poverty are often thought to accompany deeper spiritual commitment and holiness.

In line with America's mainly Puritan/Calvinist origins and ancestry, one might expect the idea of the financial blessing of the elect, or chosen, to be firmly embedded in the national values. Since these national origins and ancestry are spiritual, rather than merely political, I would also expect this idea to be more clearly evident in American churches and ministries than British ones.

2.3.3.5 Neo-Gnosticism

As I observe in chapter 3, according to McConnell, E. W. Kenyon's idea of revelation imported into the Faith Movement has at its root the epistemological error of Gnosticism. While being clear that there is no historical link implied between ancient Gnosticism and Faith theology there are, in McConnell's opinion, distinct parallels between the thought of the metaphysical cults and Gnostic thinking about knowledge. Following an article by Rudolf Bultmann,[187] McConnell argues that three key aspects of the Gnostic understanding of knowledge are present in both the metaphysical cults and the Faith Movement.

The first of these, he argues, is dualism. The Gnostics separated knowledge of God from all other knowledge; this involved suspension of sensory knowledge. The second is anti-rationalism; to the Gnostics, knowledge of God is "radically distinguished from rational thought." The third is classification, dividing believers into classes, the highest of which is divine.[188]

---

187. Bultmann, "*ginōskō*," 692–96.
188. McConnell, *A Different Gospel*, 107.

Philip J. Lee, in his 1987 book *Against the Protestant Gnostics*,[189] argues that something similar to ancient Gnosticism is evident in our time, particularly in North American Protestantism. The *gnosis*, he argues, has become so intermingled with authentic Christianity that it is very difficult to separate them. Furthermore, Lee suggests that this modern Gnosticism is doing great harm to both the church and the world.[190]

Lee notes that it would be practically impossible to trace the history of Gnosticism down through the ages. So instead he suggests that a connection between ancient and modern Gnosticism can be made by the construction of a Weberian "ideal type" in a similar way to Troeltsch's study of the "Church" and "Sect" types.[191]

In stating the nature of his ideal type, Lee observes that Gnosticism is usually born out of a mood of despair. He quotes Troeltsch, saying that this mood was often birthed in the decline of an over-ripe and static civilization, whose delight in life and vitality had been drained out of it, and which in dull dissatisfaction with itself was seeking for something new, . . . it was satiety, exhaustion, and fatigue.[192]

He says that in the first century, this might have been a failure of apocalyptic hope. My observation is that, in our time, it might be the creeping ascendancy of secularization.

Lee then observes that the Gnostic will have some sort of saving religious knowledge that will be the answer to the state of despair.[193] He states that,

> It is generally accepted that gnosticism is a world-denying faith and that it inevitably leads to escapism. What is not always recognised is that before there can be a deliberate escape from the real world into an alternatively designed world, there first must be a deliberate escape from the real God to an alternatively designed God. This, in fact, is the Gnostic trick.

So there is usually a redefinition of "God" and his "laws." Lee suggests that the escape is from anything but the self and always leads in an egocentric direction. This leads to religion being about satisfying the demands of self in the end and ultimately the worship of self. Lee adds that feelings of importance (or rather lack of it) before things like the creation, matter,

---

189. Lee, *Against the Protestant Gnostics*.
190. Ibid., xiv.
191. Ibid., 6.
192. Ibid., 7.
193. Ibid., 8.

time, suffering, and death can be overcome by denying God's power over the "spiritual self." This is achieved by asserting total power within the "spiritual" realm and perhaps by finding methods or laws that empower the individual.[194] He further notes Nock's observation that this leads to an importance linked to self-sufficiency that then results in self-intoxication, narcissism,[195] and elitism.[196] Finally Gnosticism is syncretistic, as whatever is available is used to answer the needs of Gnostic faith, that is, the needs of the self.

Lee then compares the above characteristics of Gnosticism with what he calls "ordinary" or "historic" Christianity and notes six major contrasts.

An alienated humanity versus the good creation.[197] Lee argues that in 1987, there was much despair among Protestants about the state of humanity and even creation itself. He suggests that this despair was caused by a number of factors: the assassination of a president and also a leading black cleric, failure in Vietnam, and the shame of the Watergate scandal.[198] There is good reason to think that the despair that Lee writes of is even more advanced today, following 9/11 in New York and the 7/7 London bombings on the public transport system. These bombings carried out by Islamist extremists, motivated by the Iraq war, may well cause some people to look for spiritual answers in the face of uncertainty in life and even the threat of death.

Knowledge that saves versus knowledge of mighty acts.[199] Lee is not criticizing legitimate knowledge. As such, he points to knowledge that is essential to the faith as Yahweh's mighty acts in his relationship with Israel and in the new covenant with the church.[200] He points instead to a fascination that many American Protestants have with a special saving knowledge[201] or formula that he describes as Gnostic. He is not "writing off" theocentric salvation and regeneration, but the feeling of being "born again" generated by what the believer has achieved psychologically through stirring up their own feelings or by psychological manipulation applied by charismatic leaders.

Salvation through escape versus salvation through pilgrimage.[202] Lee describes various ways in which American Protestants have been attracted by the escapism of an otherworldly approach to religion rather than the

---

194. Ibid., 9–10.
195. Ibid., 10.
196. Ibid., 11.
197. Ibid., 16–19.
198. Ibid., 99.
199. Ibid., 19–23.
200. Ibid., 22.
201. Ibid., 113.
202. Ibid., 23–26.

ordinary and perhaps somewhat mundane experience of Christian pilgrimage. In a more recent article, he writes,

> The pilgrimage, which is the "ordinary" Christian's journey toward salvation, involving "many dangers, toils and snares," requires a continuing confession that "we have left undone those things which we ought to have done and done those things which we ought not to have done." The pilgrimage depends on constant nourishment through Word, sacrament, and prayer and recognizes the likelihood that we will end our earthly sojourn not like Elijah, carried off by a band of angels, but like our Lord, crucified (with him), dead and buried. Rather than longing for an escape from this world, ordinary Christians adhere to the words of the Nicene Creed: we "look for the resurrection of the dead: and the life of the world to come." Ordinary Protestants recall Jesus' prayer for his people: "I am not asking you to take them out of the world, but I ask you to protect them from the evil one" (John 17:15).[203]

Lee gives examples of various examples of the escalation of escapist Christianity, including Tim LaHaye and Jerry B. Jenkins's *Left Behind* series of novels built around the concept of "the Rapture," Benny Hinn's prosperity message, and Creflo Dollar's methods for creating successful lives. Lee comments, "These escape routes are ways to avoid the pilgrimage—the hard tasks demanded by the disciples of the cross."[204] This trying to make religion easy or comfortable is no new thing. Indeed, Seldes, writing in 1928, observes a very similar phenomenon among nineteenth and early twentieth century revivalists when he writes, "they tried to reproduce in the masses and in a single moment of time the psychological experience which the great saints have gone through in solitude and after long travail."[205]

The knowing self versus the believing community.[206] Lee notes a shift from Protestantism's historical focus on the gospel itself to an emphasis on individual response to the gospel.[207] This individualism, he argues, leads to the presence (in 1987) of the growing phenomenon of self-centered faith with very little social and environmental concern.[208]

---

203. Lee, "Protestant Gnosticism Reconsidered," 37–40.
204. Ibid., 38.
205. Seldes, *The Stammering Century*, 142.
206. Lee, *Against The Protestant Gnostics*, 26–33.
207. Ibid., 157.
208. Ibid., 199.

A spiritual elite versus ordinary people.[209] Lee observes a similarity between the elitism of the ancient Gnostics and certain modern Protestants.[210] He observes those who see themselves as being "born again" in a special way and somehow different and superior to those becoming Christians by ordinary baptism. Those who have been through a conversion "experience" are often seen as the real Christians as opposed to ordinary churchgoers. They are sometimes singled out as "believers" as if no one else believes.[211]

Selective syncretism versus particularity.[212] In 1987, Lee observed that when religion becomes centered on the self, almost anything goes. What would not be tolerated is Christian faith based on the particularity[213] of Jesus Christ the Lord, his life, death, resurrection and ascension. In today's climate, Lee observes his prediction has come true, with the present orthodoxy being "there is no such thing as heresy."[214] Although most of those in the Faith Movement have not rejected "ordinary" Christianity, they do not prefer to promote it. Instead, they prefer the experiential elitism that seems to lack discernment when embracing new teachings, especially if a new "move of God" is seen to be occurring.

Conclusions

So while it is true that both American and British evangelicalism share the characteristics of conversionism, activism, biblicism, and crucicentrism, as Bebbington argues,[215] American evangelicalism has been distinctively influenced by Puritanism and Calvinism, leading, as Weber has argued, to a spirit of capitalism that still seems to pervade much of modern American evangelicalism.[216] American evangelicalism has also been influenced by the distinctively American philosophy of pragmatism, as well as New thought Metaphysics, as I will argue in the next chapter. Also, American evangelical-

---

209. Ibid., 33–40.
210. Ibid., 161–75.
211. Lee, "Protestant Gnosticism Reconsidered," 39.
212. Lee, *Against The Protestant Gnostics*, 40–44.
213. Ibid., 275–76.
214. Lee, "Protestant Gnosticism Reconsidered," 39.
215. Bebbington, *Evangelicalism in Modern Britain*, 3. See also Bebbington, "Evangelism in Modern Britain and America," 185 and Bebbington, "Not so Exceptional After all," 1.
216. Of course Weber's thesis might well also indicate reasons for the lifestyle and attitudes of British people with puritan roots, e.g. Wesley and the early Methodists, Salvationists etc.

ism has been influenced by Scottish commonsense realism, as opposed to the rationalist skepticism more prevalent in Britain.

In summary, American evangelism is different to English evangelicalism, but they have a significant relationship, which means often that English evangelicals are charmed by the direct and simple way that Americans present their faith. Simply put, American evangelicals have been influenced by or can be characterized by:

1. seeing themselves as God's chosen people, the right and the blessed—an attitude received from their Puritan heritage;

2. believing theology can be easily comprehended by the "common man" without reference to academia—a view resulting from the influence of commonsense philosophy, which can also be seen to be associated with anti-intellectualism and a suspicion of theology and questioning;

3. accepting a mechanistic, programmatic approach to religion, where "success" is achieved by following "steps" and "keys" (received from America's pragmatism);

4. running churches as businesses that especially results from America's early Calvinist influences and associated spirit of capitalism; and

5. practicing a Gnosticism demonstrated in a readiness to share with the world insights into authentic Christianity that they have discovered.

CHAPTER 3

Word of Faith and American Religion

3.1 The Roots of "Word of Faith" in Popular American Culture

3.1.1 Introduction

As we have seen in the cultural theory section of the previous chapter, there are a number of movements, beliefs, and attitudes that have been of particular significance in the development of American thought: Puritanism and its Calvinist emphases on predestination, electionism, and the associated spirit of capitalism; the Puritans' "extreme biblicism"[1] and principle of *sola scriptura*; the "frontier spirit"; and anti-intellectualism, pragmatism, and Scottish commonsense philosophy. To the Puritan mind, America was a nation founded by God; they were God's new chosen people.

These things are closely related to a number of religious factors and developments that are also of interest in this book. Historical and religious ideas flow and develop out of each other as observed over eighty years ago by H. Richard Niebuhr in his *Social Sources of Denominationalism*,[2] where he writes,

> The victory of the Bourgeosie over Calvinism, however, was to be made even more complete than appeared in later English Puritanism. It remained for America to carry the accommodation of the faith to bourgeois psychology to its extremes. A single line of development leads from Jonathan Edwards and his great

---

1. See section 2.3.3.1 of this thesis.
2. Niebuhr, *The Social Sources of Denominationalism*.

system of God-centered faith through the Arminianism of the Evangelical revival, the Unitarianism of Channing and Parker and the humanism of transcendental philosophy, to the man-centered, this worldly, lift-yourself-by-your-own-boot-straps doctrine of New Thought and Christian Science.[3]

This was written in 1929, and I suggest we would now want to trace the influence of this popular religious psychology on American evangelical religion even further to take in the positive thinking of Norman Vincent Peale and then Robert Schuler,[4] but also Kenyon, Kenneth Hagin, and, in the present day, such figures as Kenneth Copeland, Joel Osteen, and, of course, my case studies: the American Jerry Savelle, and the English Michael Reid and Colin Urquhart.

When it comes to understanding the development of American religious culture throughout the eighteenth and nineteenth centuries, I would like to point to two streams of thought that, while in many ways distinct, inevitably interacted. The first of these I would simply label revivalism and its embracing of pragmatism (already considered in chapter 2). The second I would label as positive thinking, transcendentalism, and the mind cure; *this theme is the major focus of this chapter*. In order to aid navigation through its complexities I insert the following flowchart figure 3.

---

3. Ibid., 104.

4. It perhaps needs to be said that Peale, Schuler, and so on, are only of background interest in the development of the movement I am examining in this book.

78 PART ONE: INTRODUCING THE WORD OF FAITH CULTURE

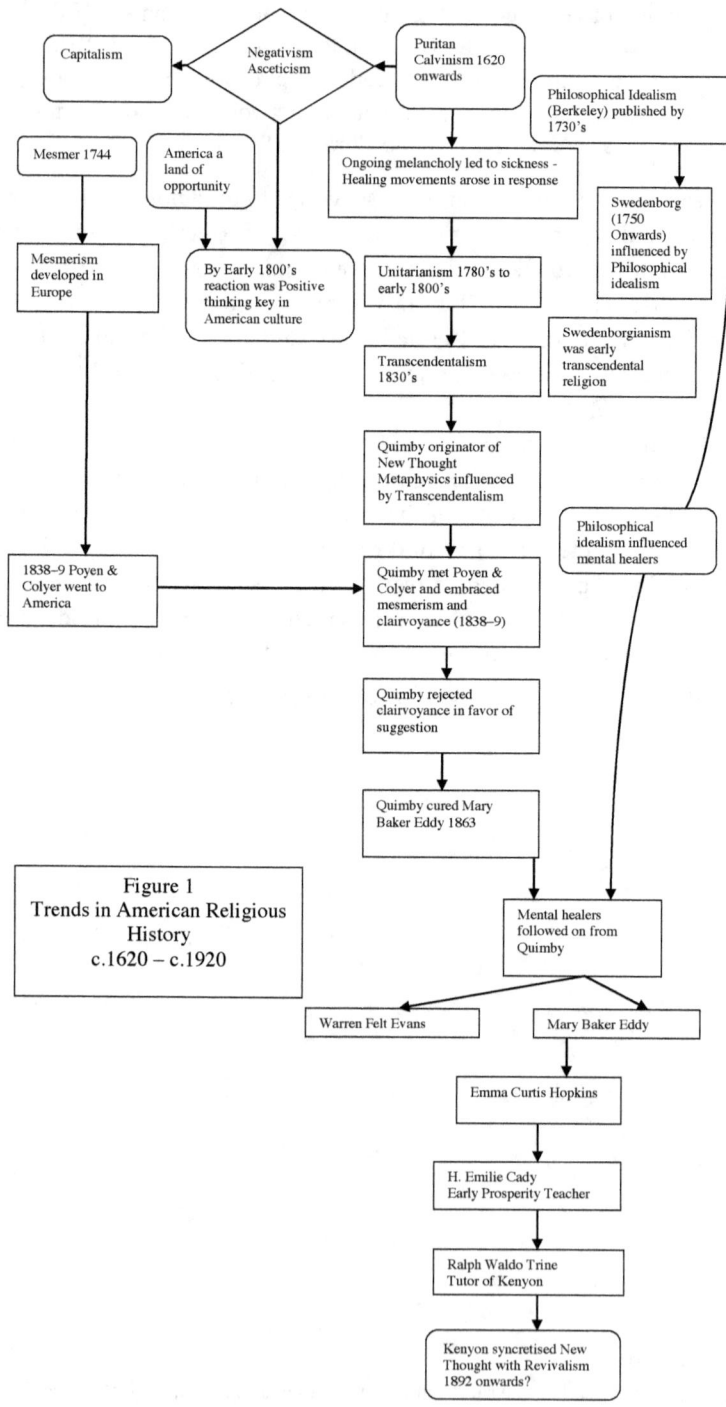

Figure 1
Trends in American Religious History
c.1620 – c.1920

In Simmons's opinion, writing of transcendentalism and revivalism,

> although the two groups differed in their definitions of the nature of the individual's power source, the methods employed in tapping into this power and the promised results of its proper exercise were strikingly similar . . . on a practical level, New Thought and the Higher Christian Life movement were birds of a feather emerging from the same gilded cage. This is not to say that the two groups were of the same species, but it is to recognize that they were certainly of the same genus.[5]

(This observation about the methods used in tapping into power is particularly important in my chapters that consider the methods and teaching of Urquhart and Reid.) Simmons also adds that the two streams,

> if indeed they had an enemy, it was not primarily each other (at least not early on), but the rigid orthodoxy of old school Calvinism. . . . As a result, their shared rebellion against this overly strict and emotionally constipated Calvinist father only served to solidify their familial bonds.[6]

3.1.2 Background to These Themes

In the early seventeenth-century (1620s) American colonies in New England and, to a lesser extent, in Virginia, the Protestant ascetic ideology, associated with Calvinism, helped the Puritan settlers to survive. However, many of the settlers struggled to survive Calvinism itself. Their religion made them sick with "depression" and self-loathing; it led to religious melancholy. Children, from infancy, were taught that if their sins were not pardoned, they would go to hell.[7] Of course, America was not the only place where Calvinism had this effect; indeed, in seventeenth-century England, a wave of religious melancholy afflicted the nation.[8] But for the early American settlers, this religious melancholy was intensified by the extreme conditions of the new world, and it persisted so that, two hundred years later, it was still very much

---

5. Simmons, *E. W. Kenyon*, xiii.
6. Ibid., 283.
7. See, for example, the distress of Betty Sewell cited in Miller, *The American Puritans*, 241. This sort of religious melancholy seems to be evident in some of the religious refugees I have encountered in the course of this project, including some from Peniel.
8. See, for example, Robert Burton, *The Anatomy of Melancholy*, 580.

present in New England. For example, revivalist preacher George Beecher was so tortured by his religious fear that he committed suicide in 1843.[9]

People were sick; and so healing, associated with the revivalist and Higher Life movement, and the mind cure, associated with the positivist transcendentalist movement, arose in response.

In this chapter, my major concentration will be on the development of the mind cure/New Thought, as it is one of the contentions of this book that revivalism has been subtly affected by the "values" and "principles" of New Thought.

3.2 Positive Thinking, Transcendentalism, and the Mind Cure

3.2.1 Why Positive Thinking is a Key Element of American Culture

Many observers have attributed the positive attitude that exudes from many Americans to the fact that America was, and still sees itself, as a land of opportunity.[10] When the original settlers arrived in America, they came to a new world where there was almost endless opportunity to claim land and to build a new life.

However, there might well be other explanations of this positive thinking. I tend to agree with Barbara Ehrenreich[11] that positive thinking might well be better understood as a reaction to the extreme negativity of the Calvinism that the founding fathers brought with them to New England. In basic terms, the Calvinists believed that the elect would be seen to be blessed by God and, therefore, materially successful. In order for material success to be observed, Puritans lived austere and frugal lifestyles, pouring their profits back into their businesses. So the harsh Protestant asceticism associated with Calvinism led to the Protestant ethic and associated spirit of capitalism (as discussed in chapter 2) that persisted into the twenty-first century. In America, busyness was admired in the 1980s and 1990s, and this in turn had an influence on British culture (see Reagan, his positive thinking, and its impact on Thatcher's Britain).[12] This late capitalist influence on

---

9. Rubin, *Religious Melancholy and Protestant Experience in America*, 161.

10. Turner *The Frontier in American* History, 201. See also Berkin et al., *Making America, Volume 2*.

11. Ehrenreich, *Smile or Die*. See particularly chapter 3, "The Dark Roots of American Optimism."

12. Meyer, *The Positive Thinkers*, 375–93. See also Milton Friedman and his positive

Britain is an interesting and perhaps a reinforcing cultural backdrop to what I observe to be the religious capitalism of my case studies.[13]

In the early American centuries, Calvinist negativity held sway; however, for many Americans, by the early nineteenth century this Calvinist gloom was beginning to break. The building of roads and rail ushered in an age of possibility.[14]

This change of attitude affected the religious mood of many, as Ralph Waldo Emerson wrote,

> Why should we grope among the dry bones of the past. . . . The sun shines today also. There is more wool and flax in the fields. There are new lands, new men, new thoughts. Let us demand our own works laws and worship.[15]

An increasing number of workmen, small farmers, and wives "insisted on the primacy of individual judgment."[16] One such person was Maine clockmaker Phineas Parkhurst Quimby (1802–66), the originator of New Thought Metaphysics, who is a key figure in this book. Before we examine Quimby further, I would like to survey New Thought's religious antecedents.

3.2.2 Transcendentalism and New Thought

Towards the end of America's second Great Awakening (1830s), transcendentalism, a new and alternative religious movement, started to develop in New England in reaction to Calvinism (see section 3.2.7). New Thought was a philosophical religious movement which was a manifestation of this transcendentalism. In order to understand significant ideas that were held by those involved in the mind cure movement and, I will argue, have been passed into the Faith Movement, I would like to survey and identify the origins of these ideas in the sections that follow before considering transcendentalism and New Thought in more detail.

---

economics, Friedman was the key architect of Reagan and Thatcher's monetarist policies during the 1980s. See Thomas, *Research Concepts for Management Studies*, 62.

13. See my comments on Weber's thesis in chapter 2.
14. Turner, *The Frontier in American History*, 1–24.
15. Emerson, *Nature*, 1, quoted in Albanese, *A Republic of Mind and Spirit*, 165.
16. Ehrenreich, *Smile or Die*, 79.

3.2.3 Subjective Idealism

The philosophical background underpinning the claims of New Thought is a subjective idealistic approach to mind and matter. According to the subjective idealism of the influential Irish Bishop and philosopher, George Berkeley (whose ideas were widely published by the 1730s), things do not exist unless they are perceived by the human mind.[17] Berkeley denied the existence of material substance and contended that familiar objects like tables and chairs are only ideas in the minds of perceivers, and as a result cannot exist without being perceived.[18] As Berkeley put it, for physical objects, *esse est percipi* ("to be is to be perceived"). So Berkeley, in effect, removed the distinction between thoughts and matter. He further suggested that as ideas exist just in the human mind, then everything exists just in the mind. According to Berkeley, mind is primary, matter is secondary.

Mental healers such as Warren Felt Evans took a further step; mind's relation to matter is causative; hence the term, "mind over matter." Evans, perhaps the earliest of mind cure writers, understood the miracles of Christ to be mind over matter. He writes,

> In Christ's miracles, or marvels of healing, there is no infraction of the laws of nature; we only witness the predominance of a higher over a lower law,—of spirit over matter, of the mind over the body.[19]

The argument of mental healers was: if the mind can be changed, then changes in matter will follow. Working on this basis, they believed all they had to do was to discover the inner laws of the mind and their applications. (These inner laws or hitherto undiscovered laws seem very similar to the principles taught by my case studies Colin Urquhart and Michael Reid.)

Berkeley's work, along with Hegel's and Emerson's versions of idealism, had a profound influence, their writings being quoted widely in early mind science literature. Idealism became the "dominant type of philosophy" by the early 1900s.[20] Evans, who was healed by and profoundly influenced by P. P. Quimby, and was the earliest advocate of mind cure to be extensively published, often made reference to Berkeley, Hegel, and other well known idealists in his linking of subjective idealism and metaphysical healing.[21]

---

17. Phelan, *Philosophy Themes and Thinkers*, 18–19.

18. Berkeley was a key influence on Warren Felt Evans, perhaps the earliest published New Thought writer. See Albanese, *A Republic of Mind and Spirit*, 307.

19. Evans, *The Divine Law of Cure*, 239.

20. Macquarrie, *Twentieth-Century Religious Thought*, 23, 25.

21. Braden, *Spirits in Rebellion*, 87–88.

3.2.4 Swedenborgianism

Swedenborgianism (otherwise known as the Church of the New Jerusalem) had a significant influence on mind cure teachers. Two of the most prominent figures in the New Thought movement were profoundly influenced by Swedenborg. When Evans first visited Phineas Quimby, he was already well versed in Swedenborg. Later he published the earliest books on mental science, applying the ideas of Swedenborg to healing.[22] Horatio W. Dresser, whose parents were keen disciples of Quimby, and who became the leading historian and significant teacher of New Thought, was also a Swedenborgian. He was appointed as a lecturer at the Swedenborgian Seminary, and in 1919 was ordained as a Swedenborgian minister. So Swedenborg's thought was an obvious influence on mind cure.[23]

Emmanuel Swedenborg (1688–1772) claimed to have been visited by angels who imparted to him special knowledge regarding the real meaning of scripture.[24] His subsequent writing in his series of volumes, *Arcana Coelestia* (or "Heavenly Arcana," published between 1749 and 1756 and written in Latin) unfolded what he claimed to be the "internal sense" of Scripture. This "internal" or "spiritual" meaning of Scripture became a common feature of mind cure/New Thought. These "revealed" interpretations of Scripture were the basis for new teachings that were radically different from orthodox interpretations. In the *Arcana Coelestia*, Swedenborg argued that "the mere letter of the Word" does not reveal the "deep secrets of heaven ... there are internal things which never appear at all in the external things."[25]

Some of the mental healers' Scripture interpretations "are patterned after Swedenborg, whose writings have been somewhat extensively read by New Thought teachers."[26]

Another idea characteristic of metaphysical religion that came from Swedenborg was the doctrine of correspondence, in which it is argued that the material world corresponds directly to the spiritual world; physical phenomena are reflections of a spiritual reality. He saw the two worlds in a cause and effect relationship. In Swedenborg's view,

> The whole natural world corresponds to the spiritual world ... and as a consequence every thing in the natural world that springs from the spiritual world is called a correspondent. It

---

22. Ibid., 81.
23. Ibid., 141.
24. Swedenborg seems to be a prime example of late Gnosticism.
25. Swedenborg, *Arcana Coelestia*, Vol. 1, 1.
26. Dresser, "The New Thought and the New Church," 8.

must be understood that the natural world springs from and has permanent existence from the spiritual world, precisely like an effect from its effecting cause.[27]

According to Swedenborg, humans have both an outer and an inner mind. The outer mind perceives the natural or external world; the inner mind is affected by the spiritual realm; receiving divine truth he calls "divine influx." He considered this spiritual knowledge more important than normal sensory perceptions which he believed often obscured spiritual truth. Writing of man, he says, "his mind is interiorly spiritual but exteriorly natural; therefore by means of his interiors he communicates with spirits, while by means of his exteriors he communicates with men."[28] Also, he argues, man's light "is obscured by the fallacies that arise from the appearances pertaining to the external bodily senses and that are believed in."[29] Metaphysical religion in general emphasized that physical senses are unreliable and that spiritual or intuitive senses are much more reliable. This is also true of Kenyon's thought as we shall see.

In Swedenborg's view, the physical body is the projection of the inner or spiritual man; changes in the internal mind cause changes in the external man. He believed that "all things that take place and come forth in the external or natural man take place and come forth from the internal or spiritual man."[30] Also, "everything of man's life is from the spiritual world; and therefore if his spiritual life sickens, evil is derived there from into the natural life also, and becomes a disease there."[31] He did not extensively apply this to health; this step was made by the early mind cure teachers.

Swedenborg's preference of spiritual knowledge over sensory perception is a form of anti-rationalism that leads to what McConnell calls the "denial of sensory reality" evident in Kenyon and the Word of Faith teachings. The doctrine of correspondence manifests itself in Word of Faith and in my case studies as a belief that full healing (and, in some cases, material provision) has been achieved in the atonement; all a person needs to do is to believe what is spiritually true, and material circumstances will change accordingly.

---

27. Swedenborg, *Heaven and Hell*, 37.
28. Swedenborg, *The True Christian Religion*, 394.
29. Ibid., 393.
30. Swedenborg, *Heaven and Hell*, 38.
31. Swedenborg, *Arcana Coelestia, Vol. 6.*, 539.

3.2.5 Mesmerism

Franz Anton Mesmer (1734–1815) was a German physician who, in 1744, pioneered the use of magnets in healing. Other magnetic practitioners of the time explained their practice by suggesting that magnets could be used to realign disturbed body electricity. Healing, according to Mesmer, was linked to his method of using animal magnetism on a patient;[32] animal magnetism was transferred to the patient through the medium of a universal permeating fluid by magnetic direction. Of this "universal fluid," Mesmer said, "It is more than likely that all of the bodies and elements of nature are penetrated by this elemental matter."[33] Psychologist Ernest R. Hilgard observed that Mesmer explained animal magnetism in terms of physical science: "Mesmer's basis involved nothing outside of naturalistic science." And

> If Mesmer found evidence of a familiar organic disease or ailment, he sent the patient to a physician practicing the accepted methods of contemporary medicine. Only if the difficulty appeared to be a "nervous" condition would he accept the patient for treatment.[34]

This universal fluid was similar in concept to the phlogiston of early chemical theory.[35]

Mesmer's theories were discredited by a French royal commission but, after his death, were developed into two different schools of thought, fluidistic and animalistic, by his former colleagues. The fluidists held that magnetism resulted from "a universal fluid of electrical nature,"[36] while the animalists explained magnetic influence as "a purely mental effect of the magnetizer's will upon the subject's consciousness."[37] In the fluidistic school, Count Maxime de Puysegur replaced magnets with just touch and verbal commands. Puysegur discovered the two central elements of hypnosis: artificially induced somnambulism and posthypnotic amnesia. Zwieg

---

32. See extract from Mesmer's "Précis Historique des Faits Relatifs au Magnetisme Animal Jusqu"en Avril 1781," Appendix I, in G. Bloch, *Mesmerism*, 135–37.

33. Bloch, 34–35.

34. Bloch (introduction by Hilgard), xix.

35. Plogiston was a hypothetical substance formerly thought to be a volatile constituent of all combustible substances, released as flame in combustion. This was a popular theory until the role of oxygen in combustion was discovered.

36. Bloch, xx.

37. Zweig, *Mental Healers*, 97–98.

goes so far as to say that "the modern science of psychology was born" with Puyseguer's discoveries.[38]

The animalistic school, led by Chevalier Barbarin took the view that magnetism was a mental rather than a physical force. He claimed that the will of the magnetisers influenced the patient's mental state; this in turn affected the nervous condition. Thirty years later, this thinking was developed by James Braid in *Neurypnology* (1843).[39] Barbarin claimed

> that the so-called magnetic influence was exercised by a purely mental effect of the magnetizer's will, upon the subject's consciousness . . . an outlook which is obviously transitional to Christian Science, mind cure, and Coueism.[40]

In the early nineteenth century, European mesmerists, such as Charles Poyen, travelled to America, thus exporting their ideas and their practices. Quimby's encounter with Poyen, as we shall see in section 3.2.8, was life changing.

Mesmer was perhaps the first scientific practitioner of mental healing, although he was not the founder of mind cure; Quimby and others would achieve that by the combination of suggestion therapeutics with metaphysical idealism. However, the mind cure movement owed much to the thinking of Mesmer. Zweig, writing in 1931, claims "it is undeniable that all the psychotherapeutic methods of today derive by one route or another from the discoveries of Franz Anton Mesmer." Also,

> Mesmerism was equally creative in its influence upon the religious and mystical movement of mind cure, and upon the development of autosuggestion . . . besides Eddyism, Coueism, and Freudism . . . the "occult" sciences, all the telepathic and telekinetic experiments . . . owe much to Mesmer.[41]

Mesmer uncovered principles of mental suggestion and mental laws for physical healing; much of his work was foundational for modern psychology. I have already discussed in chapter 2 Quimby's initial dependence on mesmerism in his healing work, but also his later shift to mental suggestion.

---

38. Ibid., 72.

39. Braid, *Neurypnology*.

40. Zweig, *Mental Healers*, 97–98. Émile Coué (1857–1926) was a French psychologist and pharmacist who advocated psychotherapy by autosuggestion.

41. Zweig, *Mental Healers*, 96, 98–99.

3.2.6 Unitarianism

By the early nineteenth century, many Americans had rejected Puritan Calvinism in favor of Unitarianism.[42] A number of New England churches had already changed to a universalist view of salvation; and while still remaining Congregationalist, many ministers had adopted anti-Trinitarian and Arminian views. James Freeman of Kings Chapel in Boston had done so by 1785.[43] Unitarianism developed as a schism of these "liberal Christians" (as they liked to be called) from Congregationalism. This can be seen from the titles of some of the earliest Unitarian periodicals, such as *The Liberal Preacher* and *The Liberal Christian*.[44] This more liberal form of Christianity quickly spread west to the frontier. As Hankins, quoting Boles, observes, "Methodist preacher James Smith, itinerating near Lexington, recorded in 1795 that 'the Universalists, joining with the Deists, had given Christianity a deadly stab hereabouts.' About that same time, David Barrow reported that 'deists, nothingarians, and anythingarians' were predominant in Kentucky and were strengthened by the recent publication of Thomas Paine."[45]

Unitarians made radical changes to Protestant theology; they rejected such doctrines as the Trinity, the divinity of Christ, electionism, revivalism's insistence on spiritual transformation, and the need to be saved by God's grace from one's sins. At the beginning of the nineteenth century, they still believed that miracles verified the truth of Christianity and that Christ was uniquely the Son of God, but in practice their religion was mainly about living a moral life and keeping rules. The Unitarians' strongly anti-orthodox attitude was foundational for mental healers. These theological revisions were driven by Enlightenment thinking which included an epistemology combining skepticism, empiricism, and rationalism. Utilitarian ethics and a deistic outlook in general were also influential. All of these things would have a significant impact on the nineteenth-century mind cure movement.[46]

Deism, however, was only in part acceptable to mental healers. They rejected the Deist view of God being removed from creation in favor of an immanent view, but they shared the Deists' skepticism regarding

---

42. Marsden, *Religion and American Culture*, 89. See also Hankins, *The Second Great Awakening and the Transcendentalists*, 25.

43. Wright, *A Stream of Light*, 4–5.

44. See Cooke, *Unitarianism in America*, 260.

45. Boles, *The Great Revival*, 17–18. Hankins quotes Boles in *The Second Great Awakening and the Transcendentalists*, 3. Paine's book *The Age of Reason*, 1794, advocated Deism, promoted reason and freethinking, and argued against institutionalized religion in general and Christian doctrine in particular.

46 Atkins, *Modern Religious Cults and Movements*, 220–22.

supernatural theology. The traditional church was mistaken that miracles were the suspension of natural law; they were, to Unitarians and mental healers, events achieved through the application of previously unknown laws. For examples of the deistic belief that miracles are explainable by natural laws, see Peter Gay (ed.), *Deism*,[47] and for the view of a Unitarian minister of this, see Minot J. Savage, *Belief in God* (1881).[48] Mental science believed that its task was to discover and make use of these laws to explain and reproduce the effects previously known as miracles.

Utilitarianism and its associated pragmatism were also influential. Important questions for acceptable practice in the application of metaphysical theory, in line with pragmatism, were simply "Does it work?" or "Is it beneficial?"

Unitarianism was the religious seedbed for metaphysical religion in a number of ways. It fostered anti-orthodox attitudes, it revered natural law, and it stressed the importance of reason for the inner life. So it is not surprising many of the leaders of the mind cure were Unitarians or people with similar views. In New Thought, "the tendency on the whole is to adopt a Unitarian view," theologically.[49] They reacted to what they felt was dry religion, longing for a deeper spiritual experience.[50] They were not looking for revivalist conversion but rather a mystical, ethereal, individualistic oneness with nature.[51]

3.2.7 Transcendentalism

So, to an extent, transcendentalism arose out of dissatisfaction with Unitarianism. Its leader was Ralph Waldo Emerson and the movement was strongly influenced by his book *Nature* (1836),[52] which became known as the manifesto of transcendentalism.[53]

Transcendentalism combined a number of views and approaches which were key to metaphysical religion and the mind cure. These were subjective idealism, monism (drawn from Hinduism), and a deified view of human potential. Along with these went an epistemology that was both intuitive and

---

47. Gay, *Deism*, 78–79.
48. Savage, *Belief in God*, 78–79, 122–23.
49. Dresser, "The New Thought and the New Church," 7. See also Atkins, *Modern Religious Cults and Movements*, 226.
50. Timko, "Ralph Waldo Emerson and American Identity."
51. Hankins, *The Second Great Awakening and the Transcendentalists*, 25.
52. Emerson, *Nature*.
53. Hankins, *The Second Great Awakening and the Transcendentalists*, 23.

subjective, and, of course, the Swedenborgian doctrine of correspondence (that changes in the physical world are caused by changes in the spiritual world). In *A Participant's Definition* (1852), William Henry Channing gave one of the best summaries of the movement by one of its own:

> Transcendentalism was an assertion of the inalienable integrity of man, of the immanence of Divinity in instinct. . . . On the somewhat stunted stock of Unitarianism—whose characteristic dogma was trust in individual reason as correlative to Supreme Wisdom—had been grafted German Idealism . . . and the result was a vague yet exalting conception of the godlike nature of the human spirit.[54]

Emerson and others owed much to their exploration of Eastern thinking, often citing Hindu sacred literature. Not only did they read "the Hindu and Buddhist holy books,"[55] but they viewed them as highly as the Christian scriptures. Thoreau wrote, "That age shall be rich indeed . . . when the Vaticans shall be filled with Vedas and Zendavestas," and that the exclusive Christian should, "commune with Zoroaster then, and through all the liberalizing influence of all the worthies, with Jesus Christ himself, and let 'our church' go by the board."[56]

At this point, it might be useful to explain the distinction between the concepts of monism, pantheism, and panentheism. Huw Owen explains that, "Pantheists are 'monists' . . . they believe that there is only one Being and that all other forms of reality are either modes (or appearances) of it or identical with it."[57] While pantheism means all things are identical to God, panentheism means *God is in all things*, neither identical to, nor totally separate from all things.[58] Such a concept, some may argue, is more compatible with God as personal while not barring a bridge between God and creation. Unlike Hindus, most mind curists were not fully pantheist; the majority held to a panentheism that held to the immanent nature of the divine. Modern New Thought scholars Anderson and Whitehouse describe the difference between pantheism and panentheism in their helpful book

---

54. Miller, *The American Transcendentalists*, 36–37.
55. Reid, *Dictionary of Christianity in America*, 1184
56. Thoreau, *Walden, or, Life in the Woods*, 68, 70–71.
57. Owen, *Concepts of Deity*, 65.
58. The German philosopher Karl Christian Friedrich Krause first used the term panentheism meaning "all in God" when seeking to reconcile monotheism and pantheism in 1828 in his writing *Vorlesungen über das System der Philosophie* ("Lectures on the System of Philosophy").

about New Thought spirituality.[59] This characteristic of their thinking they inherited from the transcendentalists, although some mental scientists were influenced by their own reading of Eastern philosophy. Emerson's worldview might be "classified as a qualified monism, which has been also characteristic of the metaphysical sects," one of the chief qualifications being the retention of individual selfhood.[60] The division within the movement concerning pantheism (monism) can be represented by two of its outstanding leaders: Warren Felt Evans, who generally guarded both individual and divine personality, and Emma Curtis Hopkins, who through her study of eastern religion maintained a straightforward pantheism.

For example, Emerson taught that Christianity had made the error of making Christ divine and calling human beings to subordinate themselves to Christ. Instead, he argued that people need to realize that they also are capable of divine inspiration.[61]

He understood that, in nature, all people are eternally connected to all living things and are part of the "Oversoul," which is an over abiding presence of absolute goodness, a higher power of supreme intelligence, that is, "God" or "the creator." He expresses this when he writes, "This is the ultimate fact which we so quickly reach on this, as on every topic, the resolution of all into the ever-blessed ONE."[62] Also,

> God reappears with all his parts in every moss and cobweb. . . . Thus is the universe alive. Essence, or God, is not a relation or a part, but the whole . . . swallowing up all relations, parts and times within itself.[63]

Emerson also writes,

> That great nature in which we rest as the earth lies in the soft arms of the atmosphere that Unity, that Over-Soul, within which every man's particular being is contained and made one with all other.[64]

His view results in, to an extent, the deification of humanity. Each soul blended into the Divine, in this optimistic transcendental philosophy, has

---

59. Anderson and Whitehouse, *New Thought*, 8; see also 142–47.

60. Judah, *The History and Philosophy of the Metaphysical Movements in America*, 32.

61. Hankins, *The Second Great Awakening and the Transcendentalists*, 29.

62. Emerson, *The Complete Works of Ralph Waldo Emerson*, 70. See also Emerson "Humanity and the Over-Soul," 72.

63. Emerson, "Compensation," 150, 156.

64. Emerson, "Humanity and the Over-Soul," 72.

unlimited potential. He writes, "The soul refuses limits, and always affirms an Optimism, never a Pessimism."[65] There is "no bar or wall in the soul, where man, the effect, ceases, and God, the cause, begins.... One mode of the divine teaching is the incarnation of the spirit in a form—forms, like my own."[66] Emerson writes to consciously "become divine," you must "place yourself in the middle of the stream of power and wisdom which animates all whom it floats.... Then you are the world, the measure of right, of truth, of beauty."[67] This is clearly similar to view of human potential held by New Thought. Both transcendentalism and New Thought distrusted the physical senses to be reliable when it comes to revealing reality; truth could be more reliably known by the human spirit's inner perception. According to the transcendentalists, "revelation knowledge" can be received by "direct influx" of divine wisdom to the soul of the individual from the Over-soul. "Swedenborg, Emerson and the metaphysical leaders believed that intuition rather than the senses revealed a spiritual reality . . . transcending the natural science of the physical world."[68] Emerson's concession of "utter impotence to test the authenticity of my senses, to know whether the impressions they make on me correspond with outlying objects" was basic to his idealism and epistemology.[69]

He writes, "The soul is the perceiver and revealer of truth. We know truth when we see it, let skeptic and scoffer say what they choose. . . . We distinguish the announcements of the soul . . . by the term *Revelation*. . . . For this communication is an influx of the Divine mind into our mind."[70]

"Revelation knowledge" is a significant concept in mind-science and in the writings of E. W. Kenyon and Faith theology, as we have already seen in this book. The concept of "divine influx" has its origin in the thinking of Swedenborg; Emerson openly cited him and drew heavily from his mysticism. Emerson, plainly a champion of the inner life, confessed that "Swedenborg's mythus is so coherent and vital and true to those who dwell within, so arrogant and sanitary to those without."[71] "The influence of Emmanuel Swedenborg cannot be underestimated as one source for the seeds of idealism that blossomed forth in transcendentalism and in the

---

65. Emerson, "Compensation," 157.

66. Emerson, "The Over-Soul," 201–2.

67. Emerson, "Spiritual Laws," 161.

68. Judah, *The History and Philosophy of the Metaphysical Movements in America*, 26.

69. Emerson, "Nature," 20.

70. Emerson, "The Over-soul," 203.

71. Bosco and Myerson, *The Later Lectures of Ralph Waldo Emerson 1843–71*, Volume 1, 69.

metaphysical movements."[72] For Emerson, human potential was related to receiving this divine influx to human potential; he also used Swedenborg's spiritual hermeneutic and his doctrine of correspondence. Divine influx was a means of deification: "The simplest person who worships God, becomes God; yet for ever and ever the influx of this better and universal self is new and unsearchable."[73] In his explanation of correspondence, Emerson says, "Swedenborg saw gravity as an external of the irresistible attractions of affection and faith."[74] Emerson also lauds "the opening of the internal sense of the Word, in the language of the New Jerusalem Church."[75]

John K. Simmons summarizes Emerson's thought:

> Swedenborg ... taught ... that the Divine and the natural are consubstantial in God and man. Everything that exists visibly, in day to day experience, reflects patterns laid out in the spiritual world and is the end product of spiritual force.[76]

Many of the mental scientists referred to Emerson and his ideas in their writings.[77] He did not apply his thinking to healing, but it is clear that Emerson was a direct influence on the New Thought movement. Emerson did imply, at least, that the real self (spirit) could not be sick—which became a premise for metaphysical healers. "The soul will not know either deformity or pain.... For it is only the finite that has wrought and suffered; the infinite lies stretched in smiling repose."[78]

This thought is significant in that, according to Dan McConnell, it continued via Emerson to Quimby and New Thought to the key figure of early twentieth century, evangelist E. W. Kenyon.[79] Swedenborg's ideas were popularized by Emerson and by Jonathan Chapman (otherwise known as Johnny Appleseed), who peddled fruit trees among frontier settlers while fulfilling the role of a missionary of the Swedenborgian society.[80] The key

---

72. Judah, *The History and Philosophy of the Metaphysical Movements in America*, 26.

73. Emerson, "The Over-soul," 207.

74. Emerson "Poetry and Imagination," 204.

75. Emerson, "The Over-soul," 204. The New Jerusalem Church is another name for Swedenborgianism.

76. Simmons, "Christian Science and American Culture," 63.

77. Ahlstrom, *A Religious History of the American People*, 1030. See also Tyner, "The Metaphysical Movement," 315.

78. Emerson, "Spiritual Laws," 159.

79. McConnell, *A Different Gospel*.

80. Williams, *America's Religions*, 332.

person who seemed to draw on this thinking in the development of New Thought was Phineas P. Quimby.

3.2.8 New Thought

The acknowledged originator of the movement of positive thinking called New Thought Metaphysics is Phineas Parkhurst Quimby (1802–66). Quimby was a successful clockmaker in Belfast, Maine.[81] He became interested in mesmerism as a possible cure for the sick.[82] While he was just a young man, he had an illness for which conventional medicine had no solution. Quimby came to believe that "the priest and the medical faculty have assumed sway, and one pretends to look after the body and the other the soul. So between both they have nearly destroyed soul and body."[83]

Since the time of the ancient Greek philosophers, there has been much speculation on the connection between magnetism and life. Franz Anton Mesmer (1734–1815) provided an explanation of the connection between human experience and the spiritual realm.[84] As John K. Simmons writes,

> Mesmer provided the very principle interconnecting the human and the spiritual realms: "animal magnetism," a subtle, universal substance that when properly manipulated could give vitality to the dying and the sick.... In a world that preceded the great war between science and religion and amongst people who had been raised to view earthly phenomena from a practical common-sense aperture, Swedenborg and Mesmer gave scientific validity to their quest for self-understanding and religious assurance.[85]

In 1838, Quimby attended a lecture in Belfast, Maine, by French mesmerist Charles Poyen. The demonstration of the powers of animal magnetism made a deep impression on Quimby. He followed Poyen from town to town until he himself became proficient in the theory and practice of mesmerism.[86] It seems he also encountered another mesmerist, an Englishman, Robert Collyer, from whom he also learned.[87]

---

81. Ahlstrom, *A Religious History of the American People*, 2nd edition, 1020–21. See also Braden, *Spirits in Rebellion*; Dresser, *Health and the Inner Life*; Peel, *Mary Baker Eddy*.
82. Anker, *Self-Help and Popular Religion in Early American Culture*, Vol. 1, 181–86.
83. Quimby, *The Quimby Manuscripts*, 217.
84. Simmons, "Christian Science and American Culture," 63.
85. Ibid.
86. Anker, *Self-Help and Popular Religion in Early American Culture*, Vol. 1, 183.
87. Ibid. See also Braden, *Spirits in Rebellion*, 44.

In 1859, Quimby gave up his clockmaking to become a successful mesmerist and healer.[88] He worked with a young man, Lucius Burkmar, who was easily put into a trance, and in that state seemed to have gifts of clairvoyance and telepathy. Quimby used Burkmar's clairvoyant gifts to diagnose patients' illnesses and then prescribe medicine.[89] The accuracy of his diagnoses caused patients to believe Quimby's power to cure. After some time, Quimby became suspicious of Burkmar and started to think that he was reading patients' minds to find out what they already believed were the causes of their sicknesses. Eventually, Quimby concluded that it was not the medicine that made them better but their belief. He gave up mesmerism and hypnosis in favor of mental suggestion. I have already offered some thoughts on susceptibility, suggestion, compliance, and belief in chapter 2, section 2.2.3. The efficacy of mental suggestion from a powerful "charismatic" figure can be immense.[90] It can be something of which the person doing the suggesting is not really aware, but is part of their intuitive practice.

Quimby stopped his collaboration with Burkmar[91] and concluded that the real cause of people's illnesses were their wrong beliefs.[92] He wrote, "Man is made up of truth and belief; and, if he is deceived into a belief that he has, or is liable to have, a disease, the belief is catching and the effect follows it."[93]

Quimby realized that he had wrongly believed that it was animal magnetism or displaced magnetic fluids that caused the sicknesses of many. Instead, he theorized that their problems were caused by their wrong thoughts about themselves. He wrote, "all disease is in the mind or belief . . . to cure the disease is to correct the error, and as disease is what follows the error, destroy the cause, and the effect will cease."[94] He also wrote, "Disease is what follows an opinion, it is made up of mind directed by error, and Truth is the destruction of this opinion."[95]

Quimby developed what became known as his "talking cure." In his view, he had to "come in contact with your enemy, and restore you to health and happiness. This I do partly mentally and partly by talking until I correct the wrong impression and establish the Truth, and the Truth is the cure."[96]

---

88. Simmons, "Christian Science and American Culture," 63.
89. Fuller, *Mesmerism and the American Cure of Souls*, 119–20.
90. See my discussion of charismatic authority at section 8.2.1.
91. Simmons, *E. W. Kenyon*, 209.
92. Fuller, *Mesmerism*, 121.
93. Quimby, *The Quimby Manuscripts*, 29.
94. Ibid., 175.
95. Ibid., 171.
96. Ibid., 183.

He talked his patients into changing their thoughts, using "his clairvoyant faculty to get knowledge in regard to the phenomena which does not come through his natural senses, and by explaining it to the patient gives [another] direction to the mind, and this explanation is the science or the cure."[97]

In his talking cure, Quimby sought to convince people that the universe is benevolent and that, by becoming one with the universal mind, they could use their minds to cure or correct their ills. His healing ministry was based on a fusion of mind techniques and Christian teaching.

3.3 Quimby and His Teaching

People often describe Quimby as the founder of the New Thought movement, although this is frequently disputed. Warren Felt Evans, one of Quimby's patients and pioneer New Thought writer, is seen by some to be the first real leader of New Thought, building on the thinking of Quimby.[98] Pointing to Quimby as the pivotal figure in the movement was perhaps aided by Horatio W. Dresser (son of Julius and Annetta Dresser, who were keen followers of Quimby). Horatio Dresser was himself a Quimby disciple and the first major historian of New Thought.

Quimby's thinking on healing and theology should be of interest to us as a significant origin for the ideas that have been carried forward in the New Thought movement and into the environment in which nineteenth-century revivalism developed. There are a number of different versions and editions of Quimby's writings that are available to us today. His papers that are the basis for the manuscripts were deposited in the Library of Congress by Horatio W. Dresser, who received them from Quimby's son who acted as his secretary for many years.[99] The references that follow are from the 1921 version (republished 2008) produced by Horatio W. Dresser, entitled *The Quimby Manuscripts*, note page numbers in other versions vary.[100] It should be stated, perhaps at this point, that anyone trying to read or make sense of the Quimby manuscripts has an extremely difficult task ahead of them. Quimby's style of writing often seems very confused, with apparently contradictory statements even in the same sentence or paragraph. As shall be seen he uses words like science, God, Christ, death, and disease in his own specific way.

---

97. Ibid., 180.
98. Ahlstrom, *A Religious History of the American People*, 2nd edition, 487.
99. Braden, *Spirits in Rebellion*, 433.
100. Quimby, *The Quimby Manuscripts*.

3.3.1 Sickness

Quimby held that sickness or Disease is caused by wrong belief. In response to a question often put to him—"Is Disease a Belief?"—Quimby replies,

> I answer that it is, for an individual is to himself just what he thinks he is, and he is in his belief sick. If I believe I am sick, I am sick, for my feelings are my sickness, and my sickness is my belief and my belief is my mind. Therefore all sickness is in the mind or belief. . . . To cure the disease is to correct the error . . . destroy the cause, and the effect will cease.[101]

Disease is the result of disturbance of the mind (that he calls spiritual matter). The mind is diverted by error (or wrong thinking). The patient is, in fact, perfectly well, they just think they are unwell; they have the wrong attitude. This wrong attitude is put right by speaking the truth to a patient. Quimby writes, "Disease is what follows the disturbance of the mind or spiritual matter. . . . Disease is what follows an opinion, it is made up of mind diverted by error, and Truth is the destruction of this opinion."[102] He repeatedly states the mental basis of disease; his response to this in patients is to approach the problem mentally (that is, through clairvoyance), and then by talking to a patient until they change their mind. In an article dated December 1859, he put it this way:

> The trouble is in the mind, for the body is only the house for the mind to dwell in. . . . Therefore, if your mind has been deceived by some invisible enemy into a belief, you have put into it the form of a disease, with or without your knowledge. By my theory or truth, I come in contact with your enemy, and restore you to health and happiness. This I do partly mentally, and partly by talking till I correct the wrong impression and establish the Truth, and the Truth is the cure.[103]

Also, writing of himself in the third person, as he did rather frequently, in an article dated January 1860, and entitled "How Dr. Quimby Cures," he gave this explanation:

> Dr. Quimby, with his clairvoyant faculty, gets knowledge in regard to the phenomena, which does not come through his natural senses, and by explaining it to the patient gives

---

101. Ibid., 175.
102. Ibid., 170, 171.
103. Ibid., 183.

another direction to the mind and the explanation is the science or cure.[104]

In Quimby's view, the origin of their false reasoning is their parents or public opinion (which he believed was stimulated by false religion and the thinking of doctors). "Disease is something made by belief or forced upon us by our parents or public opinion.... Now if you can face the error and argue it down then you can cure the sick."[105] What is disease? "It is false reasoning," he writes,[106] or again, "The cause of man's misery and trouble lies in our false reasoning."[107] "If I find no opinion, I find no disease, but if I find a disease I find an opinion."[108] "Diseases are in the mind, as much as ghosts, witchcraft, or evil spirits and the fruits of this belief are seen in almost every person."[109] Of course, Quimby, like all of the mind cure teachers that followed on from him, had to account for the apparent problem that if a person is in reality healthy, why do people think they are sick? Quimby was not the first or the last thinker to face this dilemma. Without realizing it, he was standing at a famous philosophical crossroads. On one side, objective idealism beckoned to the belief that matter is a form of the same ultimate reality that is expressed on a higher level in mind. On the other side, subjective idealism tempted with its restriction of reality to God and spirits emanating from Him or created by Him. Quimby, of course, without putting the problem in these philosophical terms, hesitated.[110] In response, he argued a form of metaphysical idealism as we have discussed already. In his view people were using their physical senses, which were not reliable, instead of believing a higher spiritual reality.

If you thought you were well, you were well, if you thought you were sick, your body became sick. Quimby called thoughts of health "knowledge" and thoughts of sickness "opinion."

3.3.2 Religion

Quimby's work was an implicit reproach to Calvinism. According to Roy M. Anker, Quimby identified Calvinism as a source of ills: "old-style Calvinism

---

104. Ibid., 180.
105. Ibid., 164.
106. Ibid., 275.
107. Ibid., 250.
108. Ibid., 352.
109. Ibid., 199.
110. Bates and Dittemore, *Mary Baker Eddy*, 83.

depressed people, its morality constricted their lives and bestowed on them large burdens of debilitating, disease-producing guilt."[111] Quimby lays much of the blame for peoples' illnesses at the feet of clergy, meaning mainly Calvinist thinking, and the medical profession, which was characterized by "heroic medicine." The two classes most dangerous to the happiness of man are priests and doctors:

> these two classes are the foundation of more misery than all other evils, for they have a strong hold on the minds of the people by their deception and cant. They claim all the virtue and wisdom of the nation, and have so deceived the people that their claims are acknowledged in war and peace. . . . Religion was what crucified Christ. Pilate's wisdom found no fault in him, but religion and the priests cried "crucify him."[112]

Calvinism was, in his view, the error that caused the sickness, and Quimby's approach was to convince the patient that the preachers were wrong. Consequently, many believed that he was undermining religion and attempting to destroy the Christian faith. Quimby writes,

> My object is to correct the false ideas and strengthen the truth. I make war with what comes in contact with health and happiness, believing that God made everything good, and if there is anything wrong it is the effect of ourselves, and that man is responsible for his acts and even his thoughts. Therefore, it is necessary that man should know himself so that he shall not communicate sin and error.[113]

Here, Quimby states his clear view that God made everything good and the problems of the sick are the result of their wrong acts and even their thoughts. The way to overcome this was, in his opinion, to show them that their misery (or depression) was the result of their wrong beliefs. When this was achieved, he believed that they rose to a higher state of Wisdom, which is not of this world but from the world of Science. Here, Science and Wisdom seem to mean "God" or God's thinking.

> If I can show that man's happiness is in his belief, and his misery is the effect of his belief, then I have done what never has been done before. Establish this and man rises to a higher state of wisdom, not of this world, but of that world of Science which sees that all the human misery can be corrected by this principle, as well

---

111. Anker, *Self-Help and Popular Religion in Early American Culture*, Vol. 1, 190.
112. Quimby, *The Quimby Manuscripts*, 306.
113. Ibid., 215.

as the evil effects of error. Then the Science of Life will take the place with other Sciences. Then in truth it can be said, "Oh, death, where is thy sting? Oh, grave, where is thy victory?" The sting of ignorance is death. But the Wisdom of Science is Life eternal.[114]

Quimby's theory was that the "real" world is the spiritual world which people are prevented from comprehending by ignorance or unbelief. Thinking from the perspective of this invisible spiritual world will cause people to understand themselves properly. The result of this should result in personal happiness and then the end of much suffering. He wrote,

is that there is no intelligence, no power or action in matter itself, that the spiritual world to which our eyes are closed by ignorance or unbelief is the real world, that in it lie all the causes for every effect visible in the natural world, and that if this spiritual life can be revealed to us, in other words, if we can understand ourselves, we shall then have our happiness or misery in our own hands; and of course much of the suffering of the world will be done away with.[115]

Here, he seems to be saying that there is a spiritual reality which is true or right; if people can rise to this higher level of wisdom they will realize the error of their beliefs about themselves, which will result in their healing.

3.3.3 Quimby's Theology

Quimby reveals a great deal of biblical knowledge. However, he interprets the Scriptures in an unorthodox way, similar to the approach of Emerson and Swedenborg before him. After his theories of healing were developed, he suggested that his own correct "spiritual" interpretation of Scripture confirmed his beliefs and practices, which were highly unorthodox, making a Gnostic distinction between "Jesus" and "the Christ," which he called Science. Quimby complained that if "you do not believe the Bible as they explain it then you are an infidel" in the eyes of traditional religion. "I do not throw the Bible away, but throw the explanation away, and apply Jesus' own words as he did and as he intended they should be applied, and let my works speak for themselves."[116]

Julius Dresser, a follower of Quimby, recalled that Quimby's discovery, "was not made from the Bible, but from the study of mental phenomena

---

114. Ibid., 227.
115. Ibid., 297.
116. Ibid., 159.

and as the result of searching investigations; and after the truth was discovered, he found his views portrayed and illustrated in Christ's teachings and works."[117] George Quimby said that his father "was a great reader of the Bible, but put a construction on it thoroughly in harmony with his train of thought."[118]

Though Swedenborg had set an example, the

> custom of interpreting the Bible in accordance with mental-healing principles began with Quimby. Many of his manuscripts are devoted to these efforts to bring out the inner or spiritual meaning of the Bible.[119]

In studying Jesus and his healings, Quimby came to quite different and "new conclusions concerning the mission of Jesus, the nature of sin, and the significance of the atonement"[120] to that of most of his religious contemporaries. Here, Braden makes his observation based on H. W. Dresser's notes in *Health and the Inner Life*:

> Fully one-half of Mr. Quimby's manuscripts abound in references to religious problems and to the Bible. The reason is not far to seek. Mr. Quimby found that the fears, emotions, and beliefs which were factors in producing the patient's disease were intimately connected with religious creeds and experiences.[121]

To Quimby, the "truth which shall set men free must explain both disease and sin . . . that the method of cure must apply both to the problems of disease and the problem of sin."[122] Both, he saw, were the products of ignorance, and if this were true, "The true cure is wisdom. This wisdom relates not alone to man's fleshly life, but to the life within, to his spiritual existence."[123] Quimby, as we have already observed, identifies Wisdom with God or God's thinking.

---

117. Dresser, *Health and the Inner Life*, 32.
118. Ibid., 47.
119. Dresser, *Handbook of the New Thought*, 69.
120. Braden, *Spirits in Rebellion*, 62–63.
121. Dresser, *Health and the Inner Life*, 226.
122. Ibid., 227.
123. Ibid.

3.3.4 God

Quimby was the originator of the term "divine mind," meaning God.[124] If people become properly attuned to this divine mind, they could be healed and even find prosperity and abundance.[125] Quimby sets out his understanding of the nature of God in the chapter "God and Man" in the manuscripts.[126] To him, God is invisible wisdom,

> which fills all space, and whose attributes are all light, all wisdom, all goodness and love, which is free from all selfishness and hypocrisy, which makes or breaks no laws, but lets man work out his own salvation; which has no laws and restrictions, and sanctions men's acts according to their belief, and holds them responsible for their beliefs right or wrong without respect to persons.[127]

God is not male or female, and is without form,[128] but God is still "he" to Quimby (most of the time), whereas God becomes "it" to later New Thought writers. Quimby takes the view that all people have an idea of God, but this idea is "a shadow of something that cannot be seen, worshipped by a man who knows not what it is."[129] He argues that God as most people know him has been invented by man, and has been "set up for the ignorant to worship."[130] He says, "As man's belief changes, so his God changes, but the true God never changes."[131] The true God, it seems, is Wisdom, but what is Wisdom, to Quimby? "It is an invisible Wisdom which can never be seen by the eye of opinion, any more than truth can be seen by error. . . . It is what never has been acknowledged to have an identity . . . it is God."[132]

3.3.5 Jesus

Quimby taught that "the Christ" was the spirit of God in all people. He understood "Jesus" to be just a human being, and that any teachings about him

---

124. Quimby, *The Quimby Manuscripts*, 59. And Simmons, "Christian Science and American Culture," 64.
125. Simmons, "Christian Science and American Culture," 64.
126. Quimby, *The Quimby Manuscripts*, 301.
127. Ibid., 305.
128. Ibid., 307: "Neither has he form, He is neither male nor female"
129. Ibid., 304.
130. Ibid., 302.
131. Ibid.
132. Ibid., 304.

in the Scriptures that suggest otherwise were invented by "the priests," or leaders of organized Christian religion.[133] To Quimby, Jesus "was as any other man,"[134] but he differentiated between "Jesus" and "the Christ." He said, "He [Christ] was the science that Jesus tried to teach."[135] "The Christ" was the wisdom or principles that Jesus taught.[136] In his view, the term "Christ" was never intended to be applied to the man Jesus, but to a "Truth superior to the natural man Jesus, and this Truth is what the prophets foretold."[137] Elsewhere, he wrote, "Christ is the God in us all. Do you deny that you have a particle of God in you?"[138] Also, "this Christ or God in us is the same that was in Jesus, only in greater degree in Him."[139] Jesus was "the natural man of flesh and blood, and Christ was the God manifested in the man Jesus."[140]

In an article dated January 1860, entitled "Another World,"[141] Quimby gives a fairly full description of the gospel as most Calvinists would have understood it. He talks about the idea that "man had wandered away from God . . . was so sinful that he was in danger of eternal banishment from the presence of God and unless he repented and returned to God, he would be banished from His presence forever." He then describes God's "only Son being given as a ransom for the redemption of the world" he "came into the world, suffered and died and rose again, to show us that we should all rise from the dead." Quimby then writes about life after death. He comments, "These beliefs embrace all the horrors of a separation from this world, and a doubt whether man will obtain that world beyond this life."[142] He continues,

> Jesus never taught one single idea of all the above, but condemned the whole as superstition and ignorance. He not only condemned the idea of a world independent of man, but proved there was none by all his sayings and doings. He looks upon all the above theories or beliefs as false and tending to make man unhappy.[143]

---

133. Quimby, "Jesus—His Belief or Wisdom."
134. Quimby, *The Quimby Manuscripts*, 254.
135. Ibid.
136. Ibid.
137. Ibid., 189.
138. Ibid., 282–83.
139. Ibid., 283.
140. Ibid., 282. The distinction dates, perhaps, from the first-century Gnostics.
141. Ibid., 181.
142. Ibid.
143. Quimby, *The Quimby Manuscripts*, 182.

He continues, Jesus "came to destroy these beliefs and establish the Kingdom of God or Truth in this world." He adds, "the embracing of the true Christ is the resurrection from the dead."[144]

In all of Quimby's writings, grace seems to be missing. Perhaps this was the fault of Calvinism and the way its predestination and electionism were taught.

3.3.6 Death

The above is all consistent with his view and denial of the bodily resurrection of Jesus. When Jesus spoke of his resurrection, according to Quimby, he did not mean that at all. He argues that his disciples misunderstood him, so they took his body from the tomb to "establish their belief that it rose from the dead."[145] Jesus did not mean that his body would rise but "his senses should rise from the dead."[146]

Quimby makes it quite clear that he does not actually believe in death. He writes, "Death is ignorance, and unless you are made to destroy it by your own belief [effort] you cannot *get* rid of it."[147] He adds, "You may ask me if I do not believe in what is called death. I answer, yes, if I did not I should not try to destroy it in others."[148]

In an article called "Parables," written in 1862, Quimby writes,

> It is like this: that the other world is only a state of mind and that Jesus never intended to teach the resurrection of the body and that heaven is not a place but a state of mind that will follow us after death.[149]

3.3.7 Jesus as the Exemplary Healer

Quimby understood Jesus to be the originator of the "science" of healing that he was now practicing. This, in his mind, had not been practiced by the church, when he writes,

---

144. Ibid.
145. Ibid., 343.
146. Ibid., 345.
147. Ibid., 369.
148. Ibid.
149. Quimby, "Parables."

> You ask if my practice belongs to any known Science. My answer is No, it belongs to Wisdom that is above man as man. The Science I try to practice is the Science that was taught eighteen hundred years ago, and has never had a place in the hearts of man since; but is in the world and the world knows it not.[150]

Again distinguishing between Jesus and Christ, he often speaks of Christ as Science and uses the term "Christian Science" long before Mary Baker Eddy apparently used it; he complains that Jesus's Science is never heard in the churches:

> So in the church the religion of Jesus' Science is never heard; for it would drive aristocracy out of the pulpit and scatter freedom among the people. Nevertheless, the religion of Christ is shown in the progress of Christian Science while the religion of society decays as the liberal principles are developed.[151]

So, according to Quimby, the Church would be very different if true Christian Science was taught.

When Quimby described the healing method of Jesus it sounded very much like his own method; in other words, Jesus healed people by changing their minds. "If a person was well," he wrote,

> it made no difference to Jesus what he believed, but he came to those who had been deceived. Well, how did he cure them? By changing their minds. For if he could not change their minds he could not cure them.[152]

It is obvious from what has been said so far about Quimby's theology that he did not believe in the Trinity in any traditional sense. However, he does have his own version of the Trinity that he calls P. P. Quimby's Trinity, which he describes as

> one living and true Wisdom called God, in Jesus (flesh and blood) a medium of this truth, and in the Holy Ghost, or explanation of God to man.... The Holy Ghost is the Science which will lead you into all truth; it will break the bond of error and triumph over the opinion of the world.

---

150. Quimby, *The Quimby Manuscripts*, 369.
151. Ibid., 359.
152. Ibid., 351.

3.3.8 Quimby's Understanding of Man

Quimby seems to be hinting at the divinity of man when he writes, "Every man is a part of God, just so far as he is wisdom."[153] However, this is only an assertion of man's potential for achieving divinity. In fact, Quimby distinguishes between "natural man" and "scientific man." Natural man is "indolent, brutish and wilfully stupid, content to live like a brute."[154] Scientific man rises above this, he is "man outside of matter."[155] He says of natural man that he "cannot see beyond matter, is in matter, but thinks he is outside it."[156] Natural man, it seems, has not achieved his potential; Quimby writes, "light of the body, or natural man is but the reflection of the scientific man."[157] The natural man is imprisoned in darkness until the "light of Wisdom bursts his bonds and sets the captive free."[158] The Christ's mission was to preach to the prisoners bound by error and set them free. Even here, in Quimby's thought, is the distinction that is made in later New Thought between man as he is and the "real" man. Quimby uses the term "real" to characterize "scientific man," saying, "Jesus taught that the real man is of wisdom."[159] All of this is highly Gnostic: wisdom is the *gnosis* that "scientific man" has, but "natural man" is lacking.

3.3.9 Mind and Matter

Quimby understands matter to be affected by the mind. In his introduction to a section of the *Quimby Manuscripts*, H. W. Dresser notes that Quimby "does not state his idea of matter very definitely, and often leaves the reader wondering how he distinguishes between matter and "spiritual matter" or the mind of opinions."[160] Quimby seems to be saying that mind or belief can result in physical chemical changes in the body. First of all, it is important to note his definition of "the mind": "you do not understand what is meant by the mind. It is this: all opinion, belief, reason, everything that

---

153. Ibid., 376.
154. Ibid., 222.
155. Ibid., 221.
156. Ibid., 220.
157. Ibid., 221.
158. Ibid.
159. Ibid., 220.
160. Ibid., 257.

can be changed."[161] To Quimby, "all disease is in the mind."[162] Matter can be changed by the mind; it can be "condensed into a solid by mind action"[163] and undergoes a "chemical change" as a result of mental changes.[164]

He suggests that fear of death and the afterlife causes people to invent all sorts "false ideas . . . all sorts of disease to torment himself."[165] These he describes as "the works of man: the God of Wisdom has never made anything to torment mankind."[166]

These false ideas he calls "error." "Wisdom is the true man and error the counterfeit. When Wisdom governs matter all goes well, but when error directs all goes wrong."[167] H. W. Dresser comments,

> The ordinary or external mind which is "spiritual matter" is the intermediate term. Above this mind is the real man with his spiritual senses, his clairvoyant and intuitive powers. The final term is Wisdom, making known its truths in so far as there is responsiveness and intelligence on man's part. This is said to possess a real identity. To find himself as an "identity" in every truth, man should know himself as the "scientific man," able through Wisdom's help to banish all errors from the world.[168]

Quimby gives an example in his approach to a person saying he or she has liver disease,

> For instance, to the person who believes it, liver complaint is a reality. To me it is imagination, as I define it, for I can make the same idea and know how I make it. But if I believe in disease, and make it so plain as to believe it is real disease, then my imagination is gone, and I am diseased. This is true.[169]

To Quimby, ideas are like "seeds." "Ideas are as separate as seeds. An apple seed will not produce a pear. Neither will the seed or idea of consumption produce liver complaint."[170]

---

161. Ibid., 266.
162. Ibid.
163. Ibid., 109.
164. Ibid., 245, 277.
165. Ibid., 258.
166. Ibid.
167. Ibid.
168. Ibid., 257.
169. Quimby, "Imagination II."
170. Quimby, *The Quimby Manuscripts*, 384.

In summary, Quimby's thought was a synthesis of mental suggestion, subjective idealism, Swedenborgianism's spiritual-material correspondence, and Unitarianism's emphasis on natural law. Many of those who developed the movement (modifying Quimby's theories) were his patients, most notably Warren Felt Evans, Mary Baker Eddy, and Julius and Anneta Dresser.

3.4 Other Key Metaphysical Teachers

3.4.1 Warren Felt Evans (1817–89)

When Evans came to Quimby in 1863 for healing, he already had a background as an Episcopal Methodist minister who had become interested in Swedenborg and was active as a leader in Swedenborgianism from 1864–69. What he found was that Quimby had been practicing what in effect was Swedenborg's theory. After Quimby healed him, Evans set up his own healing practice in Boston from 1867–69, and then in Salisbury.[171] Evans was a profound writer; he had already written books when he met Quimby, and he published his first book on mental healing in 1869. While Quimby had been writing his manuscripts since the late 1850s, none of them were published until 1895, so Evans was the first to widely publish views based on Quimby.[172] His view of healing was very close to Quimby's, though there were some notable additions. He more clearly based his thinking on Swedenborg's doctrine of correspondence, and he saw thought as a "creative principle" that produced material changes. In his view, wrong mental images resulted in sickness, and healing was the result of a change in consciousness. He wrote,

> I affirm that all bodily conditions are simply effects, of which some state of the spirit is the cause. Thus every diseased condition of the body is a wrong *thinking*. Change that false belief, that wrong state of the consciousness which is the inmost life, and the disease is cured from the root.[173]

---

171. Judah, *The History and Philosophy of the Metaphysical Movements in America*, 162–69; Braden, *Spirits in Rebellion*, 89–128. Evans started offering mental healing to others after he felt he was cured by Quimby of a long-term illness in 1863.

172. Parts of Quimby's manuscripts first appeared in print in Dresser, *The Philosophy of P. P. Quimby*. The full manuscripts were first published by Annetta Dresser's son H. W. Dresser. Warren Felt Evans's first book on mind-science was *The Mental Cure, 1870*; originally published 1869. So it can be seen that Evans "was the first American mental healer to publish his ideas extensively." See Teahan, "Warren Felt Evans and Mental Healing," 63.

173. Evans, *Soul and Body*, 48, 45.

Evans held "that thought was the creative principle of God and man, the power of mind over the appearance of matter." Unhealthy consciousness he called "fear"; "faith" was the remedy. However, this was not just expectation of change but a spoken affirmation of already being healthy.[174] He argues that "a spiritual idea . . . is acquired independently of the testimony of the external senses, and sometimes in direct conflict with their fallacious appearances. To think spiritually is to elevate the thoughts . . . above the sensuous degree of the mind."[175]

"You are not to get it [faith] in any way, but *use* it. We are looking for what we already possess. . . . Faith is only the action of the mind above the plane of sense, with its false and deceptive appearances."[176] Fear produces "the image which . . . becomes the seminal idea of the disease," but "faith is the spiritual principle of health. . . . It may exist as an expectation, that . . . recovery will be consummated. But the highest degree of faith is where there is a divinely inwrought conviction that we are saved [here he means healed], or being saved *now.*"[177] The concept of the power of spoken words, introduced by Evans, became a key element of mind science.

> To cure ourselves or others of disease we must rise in our conceptions out of the sphere of the senses to the realm of reality, to the spiritual perception of things that *are* and as they are.[178]

Evans said Jesus "comprehended the potential spiritual force of words. . . . He employed certain formulas or expressive sentences into which he concentrated and converged his whole mental force."[179] Here "appeared for the first time the prototypes of the positive formula prayers which have dominated the practice of all later New Thought healing groups. . . . With Evans begins the New Thought reliance upon affirmative prayer or positive thinking with the affirmation of the condition desired."[180] He believed he had rediscovered Jesus's method of healing, positive, verbal affirmation based on faith.

This faith that Evans spoke of was the same faith that God used in creating the universe. Humans could use this God-faith to change their own

---

174. Judah, *The History and Philosophy of the Metaphysical Movements in America*, 164–65.

175. Evans, *Soul and Body*, 12.

176. Evans, *The Primitive Mind-Cure*, 75.

177. Evans, *Soul and Body*, 24, 59, 69.

178. Ibid., 46.

179. Evans, *The Mental Cure*, 253.

180. Judah, *The History and Philosophy of the Metaphysical Movements in America*, 162, 167. See also Braden, *Spirits in Rebellion*, 89–90.

lives for the better. Evans, it seems, is the origin of the idea of having a God-like faith. He quotes scripture in the following way:

> We are told by Paul that it [faith] was an element in God's omnipotence, and that by it he created the worlds. (Heb. xi. 3) ... Christ commanded his disciples to "have the faith of God." (Mark xi. 22) ... For, as Solomon has said, "As a man thinketh in his heart, so is he." Such a faith is the *reality* of things, or, as Paul affirms, it "is the *substance* of things."[181]

Used to its full potential, it would result in profound changes for good in a person's life, even domination of his or her world. However, in essence, Evans held the same view as Quimby on healing. Wrong thinking caused disease, right thinking would bring a cure.

3.4.2 Mary Baker Eddy (1821–1910)

Quimby's faith cure attracted many women victims of neurasthenia,[182] many of them middle-class women chaffing against guilt and patriarchy and attracted by a more loving and maternal deity; middle-class women, banned from education and professions by prejudice. For many women, invalidism became an alternative career.[183] It was considered attractive, even fashionable.[184] One of these women, Mary Baker (Eddy), or Mrs Patterson as she was known at the time, was the daughter of a fire-and-brimstone preaching Calvinist farmer. She met Quimby in 1862.[185] In 1863, a very weak Eddy went to Quimby and was "cured." Eddy stayed for some time learning from him and reading his notes on healing. She was a devoted admirer of Quimby and his spiritual Science. In 1866, three years after her healing, Quimby died. According to some historians, she tried to deny her indebtedness to Quimby soon after his death, quickly announcing she had "discovered" Christian Science, effectively claiming his teachings as her own. Although it is often claimed that Eddy is indebted to Quimby for the phrase "Christian Science," Evans first used it in 1860 before meeting Quimby.[186]

By 1870, she had completed her first written work, *The Science of Man*, and gathered a small group of followers. By 1875, she had completed the

---

181. Evans, *Soul and Body*, 58–60.
182. See discussion of neurasthenia at section 3.5.
183. Ehrenreich, *Smile or Die*, 83.
184. Gill, *Mary Baker Eddy*, 33.
185. Ibid., 119.
186. Teahan, "Warren Felt Evans and Mental Healing," 77.

most famous of Christian Science books, *Science and Health*. After her excommunication from the Congregational Church in 1877, Eddy began holding Sunday services with small numbers attending in Lynn, Massachusetts, and formally set up the Church of Christ, Scientist in 1879. In 1881, she founded the Massachusetts Metaphysical College, and the *Christian Science Journal* was first published in 1883. She claims that she was the discoverer of mind over matter: "I discovered, in 1866, the momentous facts relating to Mind and its superiority over matter."[187]

There has been much debate on how indebted Eddy was to Quimby; indeed, much could be said about this, but there is not room for this in this present book. However, her version of Christian Science was quite distinctive. The most notable difference between her views and Quimby's was her belief in the unreality (non-existence) of matter. While Quimby and those who followed his teaching held to the provisional existence of matter as a product of mind, Eddy held the view that matter was an illusion of the mortal mind. She regularly contrasted her views with those of mind-curists, whom she sometimes called "mind-quacks." Stephen Gottschalk writes, "This question of the reality of matter constitutes a metaphysical dividing line between Mrs. Eddy's teaching and that of almost all New Thought writers. Where she declared that matter was completely unreal, the erroneous sense of true substance, they maintained that it was real but susceptible to thought control."[188] To her, the most significant reality was not material but based around thought, mind, goodness and love, or, as she termed it in almost economic terms, "supply." She calls God "a business God."[189] This idea may well have been an influence on H. Emilie Cady, a later New Thought writer who taught that the application of New Thought principles could result in wealth.

To Eddy, God or "divine mind" was the only reality, and the human mind needed to be subject to the divine mind. Matter was not God, so it had no true existence. Consequently, in Eddy's view of reality, the human body and its diseases did not exist. In her view,

> In Science, Mind is *one,* including noumenon and phenomena, God and His thoughts. . . . As Mind is immortal, the phrase *mortal mind* implies something untrue and therefore unreal . . . that which has no real existence . . . [Christian] Science shows

---

187. Baker Eddy, *Miscellaneous Writings,* 380. See Melton, *Biographical Dictionary of American Cult and Sect Leaders,* 80–81. On Baker Eddy's early organization Beasley records that, "In 1875, seldom more than twenty persons gathered for Sunday services in a small, rented hall in Lynn, Massachusetts," Beasley, *The Cross and the Crown,* v.

188. Gottschalk, *The Emergence of Christian Science in American Religious Life,* 121.

189. See "Supply." God is described here by Eddy as "a business God."

that what is termed matter is but the subjective state of what is termed by the author *mortal mind*.[190]

"If God is Spirit, and God is All, surely there can be no matter; for the divine All must be Spirit."[191] "Disease . . . is a human error, a constituent part of what comprise the whole of mortal existence — namely, material sensation and mental delusion."[192] She taught that illness was effectively an illusion of the senses, and so in order to be healthy the existence of illness must be denied. "Spirit is the only creator, and man, including the universe, is His spiritual concept."[193] Also, man is "God's spiritual idea, individual, perfect, eternal."[194] She adds:

> According to the evidence of the so-called physical senses, man is material, fallen, sick, depraved, mortal. Science and spiritual sense contradict this. . . . Health is the consciousness of the unreality of pain and disease; or, rather, the absolute consciousness of harmony and of nothing else. . . . The spiritual senses . . . deny the testimony of the material senses.[195]

To Baker Eddy, faith for those who felt ill was not asking God to intervene but realizing that they were already healthy. Trusting in the "divine mind" leads to triumph over the senses. As she argues, bondage will cease when humanity recognizes its "God-given dominion over the material senses. Mortals will some day . . . control their own bodies through the understanding of divine Science."[196]

In summary, Eddy, while insisting that matter does not exist and that the only reality is the divine mind, held to the essential principles of the mind cure: (1) When it comes to illness, the physical senses should not be believed. (2) A person needs to realize the practice of their spiritual identity and consequent perfection. (3) Faith for individuals was trusting in divine truth, believing they were completely well. (4) Like Quimby, the Bible should be interpreted in line with given metaphysical principles.

The principles behind the mind cure became even better known among ordinary Americans due to the growth of Eddy's Christian Science.

---

190. Baker Eddy, *Science and Health*, 114.
191. Baker Eddy, *Unity of Good*, 31.
192. Baker Eddy, *No and Yes*, 4.
193. Baker Eddy, *Unity of Good*, 32
194. Baker Eddy, *Science and Health*, 115.
195. Baker Eddy, *Rudimental Divine Science*, 7, 11, 5.
196. Baker Eddy, *Science and Health*, 228.

From the time of Quimby's death in 1866 until 1882, the only apparent mental healers were Evans and Eddy. Later the Dressers, who had followed other interests, returned to metaphysical healing. Boston was the geographical center of the mind cure at that time. Later the movement moved to New York and the mid-west of America.

The mind cure movement began to expand and diversify. A number of private healers appeared, and a number of Eddy's former students set up their own schools of healing, for example, Clara Choate. She moved from Boston to Chicago and founded the Institute of Christian Science in 1884. Others were A. J. Swartz, who started the Illinois Christian Science College, and George B. Charles, who founded the Illinois Metaphysical College.[197]

3.4.3 Emma Curtis Hopkins

Another keen student of Eddy and editor of the *Christian Science Journal* was Emma Curtis Hopkins. She parted company with Christian Science when she began to express too much independence of thought for Eddy's comfort. In 1886, Hopkins founded her own College of Christian Science, which was later known as the Christian Science Theological Seminary. Hopkins taught New Thought Science principles to many others, including Charles and Myrtle Fillmore, who founded the Unity School of Christianity, otherwise known as the Unity Church. Much more has been written about Unity than about many of the other groups discussed in this section.[198]

3.4.4 Prosperity Teachers

The early New Thought writers did not advocate the use of mind force to accumulate wealth, but it was not long before some did. One keen associate of the Fillmores and a widely read Unity writer was H. Emilie Cady. Cady had been converted to New Thought by reading Evans's books.[199] She was perhaps the most significant of the New Thought writers to teach that the application of New Thought principles could result in wealth. Like many of those who had been influenced by students of Eddy, she taught that God was "supply" and would provide anyone with what they dared to claim.[200]

---

197. See "The Developing Movement," in Braden, *Spirits in Rebellion*, 130–45.
198. See James Dillet Freeman, *The Story of Unity*, and D'Andrade, *Charles Fillmore*.
199. Albanese, *A Republic of Mind and Spirit*, 313.
200. Cady, *God a Present Help*, 74.

In teaching this, her two favorite biblical verses were Joshua 1:3 ("Every place that the sole of your foot shall rest upon, that I have given thee") and Mark 11:24, which she paraphrased as "All things whatsoever ye pray and ask for, believe (or claim and affirm) that ye receive them and ye shall have them."[201] This was an early example of "name it and claim it," a core idea in the HWPM.

As time passed, the Unity movement tended to focus less on the supplier than on what could be supplied, as evidenced by Unity books such as Charles Fillmore's *Prosperity* (1936), Ruthanna Schenck's *Be Ye Prosperous* (1928), and Georgina Tree's *Prosperity's Ten Commandments* (1946). Another writer who taught the use of the mind to secure prosperity was Ralph Waldo Trine who, we shall see, was almost certainly a tutor of E. W. Kenyon at the Emerson College of Oratory. Trine wrote,

> Suggest prosperity to your self. See yourself in a prosperous condition. Affirm that you will before long be in a prosperous condition. Affirm it calmly and quietly, but strongly and confidently. Believe it, believe it absolutely. Expect it—keep it continually watered with expectation. Thus you make yourself a magnet to attract the things that you desire. Don't be afraid to suggest, to affirm these things, for by so doing you put forth an ideal which will begin to clothe itself in material form. In this way you are utilizing agents among the most subtle and powerful in the universe.[202]

3.5 Why Has New Thought Persisted?

As far as sickness is concerned, New Thought might have remained obscure; it did not work for infectious diseases.[203] But it did work for slow, nameless, debilitating illness which included back problems, digestion problems, exhaustion, headache, insomnia, and melancholy, which became collectively known as neurasthenia[204]—all very similar, if not identical, to what we call today ME.

A key person who was sick in this way was George M. Beard, who later became a physician and was the originator of the term neurasthenia.[205] He

---

201. Cady, *Lessons in Truth*, 58–59. See also Cady, *Miscellaneous writings*, 58.
202. Trine, *In Tune With The Infinite*, 88.
203. Ehrenreich, *Smile or Die*, 80, 88.
204. Ibid., 80. See also Fuller, *Mesmerism*, 112.
205. Ehrenreich, *Smile or Die*, 81, 84.

believed this illness was due to the pressures of the new and changing world; in his view people were suffering from nerve strain that led to collapse.[206] One observation that seems to undermine Beard's reasoning is that it was not the highly stressed industrialists and bankers that became sick, but the genteel clergymen, academics, and middle-class women of leisure.[207]

In the Calvinist world, hard labor was the method of escape; if this was taken away, it often led to morbid introspection and neurasthenia.[208] In young men, it arose when undecided about their career, as in the cases of George Beard and William James.[209] The medical profession and its heroic medicine—for example, bleeding, the use of Calomel, bland foods and darkened rooms—made it worse.[210]

The invalidism had more to do with the old religion than the new challenges and struggles.[211] It was simply a continuation of the religious melancholy Robert Burton had studied around the time the Puritans set off for Plymouth.[212] A highly significant person, who lapsed into invalidism as a young man, was William James, a man of science and the first American psychologist.[213] He was perhaps the most influential convert to Quimby's New Thought. James sought help from Anna Dresser.[214] This must have worked, because James later praised the New Thought approach to healing.[215] It did not matter if it made sense or not. What mattered was that it worked, very much in line with James's pragmatism.[216] It healed the disease of Calvinism or, as James put it, "the morbidness associated with the old hell-fire theology."[217] James saw New Thought as healthy-mindedness.[218]

Quimby's New Thought attracted many women victims of neurasthenia, many of them middle-class women chaffing against guilt and patriarchy, and attracted by a more loving and maternal deity.[219] One of these

---

206. Ibid., 82.
207. Ibid., 83. See also Douglas, *The Feminization of American Culture*, 88.
208. Ehrenreich, *Smile or Die*, 84.
209. Ibid., 84. See also Richardson, *William James*, 86.
210. Ehrenreich, *Smile or Die*, 84–85.
211. Ibid., 82.
212. Ibid., 77, 82.
213. Ibid., 87.
214. Richardson, *William James*, 275.
215. James, *The Varieties of Religious Experience*, 95.
216. Ehrenreich, *Smile or Die*, 87.
217. James, *The Varieties of Religious Experience*, 91.
218. Ibid.
219. Ehrenreich, *Smile or Die*, 79.

was Mary Baker (Eddy).[220] She met Quimby in 1863 and was healed.[221] According to Barbara Ehrenreich many middle-class women became sick because they were banned from education and professions by prejudice. For many women, invalidism became fashionable and an alternative career. It was considered attractive.[222] Apparently, Baker and her sisters had access to magazines and so knew the fashions.[223]

As a child, Eddy agonized over Calvinist predestination to the point it made her sick:

> I was unwilling to be saved, if my brothers and sisters were to be numbered among those who were doomed to perpetual banishment from God. So perturbed was I by the thoughts aroused by this erroneous doctrine, that the family doctor was summoned, and pronounced me stricken with fever.[224]

The Calvinists and many early Americans understood their children as savages in need of discipline and correction. There was extreme religious pressure on children, for example, strict Calvinist preacher Lyman Beecher urged his children Catherine and George "[t]o agonize, agonize over the condition of their souls."[225] George Beard (a sufferer himself, and a son of another strict Calvinist preacher) later condemned religion for teaching children that "to be happy is to be doing wrong."[226]

Because so many of the views and beliefs of the transcendentalists and adherents of New Thought were at odds with evangelical revivalism, this phenomenon would probably have had very little influence on the nature of modern American evangelicalism if it had not been for the experience and subsequent distinctive teachings of one man, E. W. Kenyon (1867–1948).

As I have already mentioned in the literature review in chapter 1, D. R. McConnell, D. H. Simmons, R. M. Bowman and J. McIntyre all discuss Kenyon's attendance at the Emerson College of Oratory in 1892 at a time of spiritual crisis in his life.

Simmons, Bowman and others agree with McConnell's original thesis that, at the time, many of the teachers and students had New Thought inclinations, and that the atmosphere of the college had an influence on Kenyon.

220. Ibid.
221. Ibid., 79, 86.
222. Ibid., 83.
223. Gill, *Mary Baker Eddy*, 33.
224. Harrington, *The Cure Within*, 112.
225. Douglas, *The Feminization of American Culture*, 132.
226. Sicherman, "The Paradox of Prudence: Mental Health in the Gilded Age."

Of course, this is not just a "guilt by association" argument. It is very possible to encounter a view and not agree with it. However, if we point to the literary evidence of the similarity of Kenyon's writings in the years after his time at Emerson college with the teachings of mental healers, then the likelihood of Kenyon having learned these ideas from his tutors and fellow students is very high.

If we examine some of the published thoughts of tutors and students at Emerson while Kenyon was there, we should see a link.

3.6 Significant Tutors at Emerson College

3.6.1 Charles Wesley Emerson

During that time, C. W. Emerson, President of the college, gave individual attention to each of the students. Emerson was a former Congregationalist, Universalist, and Unitarian church leader, and, as Simmons notes, was definitely influenced by the idealism of Plato, Swedenborg, Delsarte, and Ralph Waldo Emerson.[227]

3.6.2 Ralph Waldo Trine

Another significant college tutor during Kenyon's time was R. W. Trine, author of *In Tune With the Infinite*,[228] a well-known and highly influential New Thought book.

He was clearly a believer in the power of positive thought to bring wealth to individuals when he wrote:

> this is the law of prosperity: When apparent adversity comes, be not cast down by it, and always look forward to better things, for conditions more prosperous. To hold yourself in this attitude of mind is to set into operation subtle, silent, and irresistible forces that sooner or later will actualize in material form that which is today merely an idea. But ideas have occult power, and ideas, when rightly planted and rightly tended, are the seeds that actualize material conditions.[229]

---

227. Simmons, *E. W. Kenyon*, 8.
228. Trine, *In Tune with the Infinite*.
229. Ibid., 88.

3.7 E. W. Kenyon's Return to Christian Ministry

As I noted at section 1.1 of this book, in the period before attending Emerson College Kenyon became disillusioned with Christianity and openly described himself as an agnostic.[230] He described these times,

> Years went by and I lost it and went back into sin; I dropped back deeper and deeper until I went into agnosticism. . . . I never left my bible behind me during those two or three years in which I was in darkness, but I never breathed a prayer to God Almighty.[231]

It was during those two or three years that Kenyon was at Emerson College being taught by recognized New Thought exponents, Charles Wesley Emerson and Ralph Waldo Trine.

During that time Kenyon married Evva Spurling on May 8th 1893. McIntyre comments,

> Evva admitted to being very bitter toward God due to sufferings and hardship she endured during her earlier days. She didn't go into details, but these experiences hardened her heart against believing in God. . . . Kenyon was just as hardened towards God.[232]

Simmons observes of the couple, "One of the things that had drawn the couple together was their mutual agnosticism."[233] What happened next in their lives was an amazing turn around. Simmons writes, "About a month after their wedding, however, the two skeptics made their way to a meeting at A. J. Gordon's Clarendon Street Church."[234]

Simmons continues,

> Upon returning home, Essek informed his bride that he had made the decision to give himself to the Lord "unreservedly and forever." Although she was "astonished and bewildered," Evva decided that for the sake of their marriage she had better join

---

230. See Simmons, *E. W. Kenyon*, 3, based on a report in the Quincy Daily Ledger 29th Jan. 1904, 1.

231. Kenyon "Justification,"133. Republished in *Kenyon's Herald of Life* July–September 2002, 3.

232. McIntyre, *E. W. Kenyon*, 23.

233. Simmons, *E. W. Kenyon*, 15.

234. The source of this information Simmons cites as, Evva Spurling Kenyon, "God's Leadings," 131.

with her husband. Accordingly she knelt beside him and gave herself "to that hard, indefinite God of [her] imagination." To her surprise, she was met by "the gentle, compassionate Jesus" who "bound me to himself forever."[235]

Kenyon immediately recommenced his evangelistic work. His original church was Methodist while Evva Kenyon's was Congregational. They decided to start afresh with the Free Will Baptists and early in 1894 Kenyon was ordained a Free Will Minister and took charge of a small church. In July the same year he was invited to be the pastor of a larger church in Springville New York. He was a very successful young minister, so three years later he was offered Wellington Street Church in Worcester, Massachusetts.[236]

During that time Kenyon became increasingly influenced by the writings of Higher Christian life advocates such as, George Muller, Charles Cullis and A. B. Simpson as well as the man whose preaching brought him back to faith A. J. Gordon.[237]

McConnell argues that Kenyon was exposed to New Thought during his time of agnosticism and especially during his time at Emerson College.[238] Bowman suggests that Kenyon may have picked up New Thought ideas through these Higher Life teachers who had already been influenced by New Thought.[239] This of course is a possible explanation, but it does not change our observation that somehow New Thought ideas had somehow been syncretized into the writings of Kenyon. McIntyre does not deny that Kenyon was exposed to metaphysical[240] writings during his time of agnosticism and they did affect his teaching. However, he argues that Kenyon later used his knowledge of the "cults"[241] to point out their weaknesses.[242] McIntyre then says, "The understanding he gained after recovering from this investigation into philosophy and metaphysics undergirded all his later teaching about sense knowledge and revelation knowledge."[243] What McIntyre fails to do is to see that Kenyon has taken on board a dualistic epistemology from the mind cults that has influenced his later teaching.

---

235. Simmons, E. W. Kenyon, 15.
236. Ibid., 15–17.
237. Ibid., 17–23.
238. McConnell, A Different Gospel, 34–51.
239. Robert M. Bowman, *The Word-Faith Controversy*, 82.
240. I.e., New Thought Metaphysics.
241. Meaning the metaphysical mind cults.
242. McIntyre, *E. W. Kenyon*, 13.
243. Ibid.

In 1899 Kenyon opened his own college the Bethel Bible Institute in Spencer, Massachusetts on a farm donated by one of his wealthy supporters.[244] The college remained on that site until 1923, with Kenyon as its president for nearly twenty-five years. The Bethel Bible Institute later moved to Providence, Rhode Island, and became Providence Bible Institute. Eventually it became Barrington College and merged with Gordon College, which was named after one of Kenyon's key mentors, A. J. Gordon.[245] Sadly, Evva Kenyon died in 1914.[246] Subsequently, Kenyon married Alice M. Whitney and had a son and a daughter with her.[247] Kenyon died in 1948.[248]

During his time at Bethel and in the years up to his death Kenyon wrote many books and articles, some of which are cited in this book as examples of beliefs influenced by New Thought and its background philosophy of subjective idealism and the dualistic epistemology that I've referred to above. These books are based on his sermons and what was taught at Bethel. Of course, the fact that many of his books were directly plagiarized[249] by Kenneth Hagin in the 1970s and 80s led to Kenyon's ideas being a primary influence on Word of Faith theology.

3.8 Some of Kenyon's Metaphysical Teachings

3.8.1 Creative Speech

Kenyon argues that God Himself had faith when he created the universe. He wrote, "Faith-filled words brought the universe into being, and faith-filled words are ruling the universe today."[250]

He argues God's words, "let there be,"[251] caused the creation to come into existence. He points to Hebrews 11:3 that says, "By faith we understand

---

244. Ibid, 28.
245. Ibid., 127.
246. Ibid., 337.
247. Ibid., 146.
248. Ibid., 168.
249. If for example you consider Hagin's book *The name of Jesus* (published 1979) and compare it to Kenyon's *The Wonderful Name of Jesus* (Originally published 1927) it is apparent that large portions of the text in Hagin's book is "borrowed" from Kenyon.
250. Kenyon, *The Two Kinds of Faith*, 20.
251. Kenyon, *New Creation Realities*, 21.

that the worlds have been framed by the word of God,"[252] and that from Hebrews 1:3 Christ is "upholding all things by the word of his power."[253]

3.8.2 Spiritual Laws or Principles that Bind God

The suggestion by Kenyon and those who have followed is that, instead of the universe being created directly by the will of God, He Himself spoke in faith, thus operating within some sort of spiritual laws that govern material reality along with the laws of physics. Kenyon describes these laws as "the great spiritual laws that govern the unseen forces of life. . . . They are to the spirit realm what iron, copper, gold and other metals are to the mechanical realm."[254]

3.8.3 Positive Confession

The creative/destructive speech, positive/negative thinking idea is widely known as the doctrine of positive confession. Although often thought to have originated with Hagin, it originally comes from Kenyon, and is the most widely used Faith Movement statement about the nature of faith: "What I Confess, I possess."[255] This formula is from Kenyon's book *The Hidden Man*,[256] in which he asserts, "Christianity is called 'the great confession.' The law of that confession is that I confess I have a thing before I consciously possess it."[257]

According to Kenyon, confession is the way that the spiritual laws are activated for good or ill in a person's life and determines how our life goes. He writes,

> Sooner or later we become what we confess . . . many people have a negative confession. They are always telling what they are not, telling of their weakness, of their failings, of their lack of money, their lack of ability, and their lack of health. Invariably they go to the level of their confession. A spiritual law that few of us have recognized is that our confessions rule us.[258]

252. Ibid., 5.
253. Ibid., 21.
254. Kenyon, *The Hidden Man*, 35.
255. Ibid., 98.
256. Kenyon, *The Hidden Man*.
257. Ibid., 98.
258. Kenyon, *The Two Kinds of Faith*, 66–67.

Kenyon teaches that, "You rise or fall to the level of your confession."[259] As I have indicated before, the Faith Movement's slogan "What you say is what you get," whether positive or negative, is derived directly from Kenyon. Kenyon writes,

> Our words are the coins of the Kingdom of faith. Our words snare us and hold us in captivity, or they set us free and become powerful in the lives of others. It is what we confess with our lips that dominates our inner being.[260]

3.8.4 Denial of Sensory Reality

A development of this thinking is what McConnell describes as the "Denial of Sensory Reality."[261] As McConnell says, "Based on his dualistic epistemology, Kenyon taught that in order to walk in Revelation Knowledge, the believer must often deny sense knowledge."[262] Kenyon writes, "There will always be a conflict between our senses and the Word."[263] He also comments, "God cannot communicate with you through your senses."[264]

This teaching is widespread in the Faith Movement; for example, Kenneth Hagin teaches in his book *Right and Wrong Thinking* that "one almost has to by-pass the brain and operate from the inner man (the heart or spirit) to really get into the things of God."[265] McConnell describes this view in both Kenyon and Hagin as a "strongly anti-intellectual bias";[266] this might be one reason why the above quote from Hagin has clearly been removed from the most recent version of his book.[267]

Sickness is a particular area where sensory denial is applied. As Kenyon teaches, "Confession always goes ahead of healing . . . don't watch the symptoms, watch the word. . . . Don't listen to the senses, give the word its place."[268] According to Kenyon, if people say that their faith has not healed

---

259. Kenyon, *The Hidden Man*, 147.
260. Kenyon, *The Two Kinds of Faith*, 72.
261. McConnell, *A Different Gospel*, 104.
262. Ibid.
263. Kenyon, *The Two Kinds of Knowledge*, 50.
264. Ibid., 18.
265. Hagin, *Right and Wrong Thinking*, 27.
266. McConnell, *A Different Gospel*, 104.
267. Compare Hagin, *Right and Wrong Thinking* (1982); 27. Hagin, *Right and Wrong Thinking* (2005), 63.
268. Kenyon, *Jesus the Healer*, 26.

them, "such people have Sense Knowledge Faith. They must have physical evidence or they do not believe."[269] He argues that this sense knowledge should be replaced by believing what the Word of God says, "that he has borne my sicknesses and carried my diseases," not relying on physical evidence. This teaching has caused people to give up their medication or medical help so as not to make a negative confession in the act of receiving it; this has, in some cases, caused their death.[270]

This sensory denial is similar to the teaching of metaphysical mind-science cults such as Christian Science; Mary Baker Eddy writes,

> All the evidence of the physical sense and all the knowledge from physical sense must yield to (Christian) Science, to the immortal truth of all things. . . . Mind must be found superior to all the beliefs of the five corporeal senses, and able to destroy all ills. Sickness is a belief, which must be annihilated by the divine mind. Disease is an experience of the so-called mortal mind.[271]

3.9 Those Who Have Followed on From Kenyon

I have given examples of the teaching of Kenneth Hagin, Don Gossett and Kenneth Copeland in chapter 1, (sections 1.3.2—1.3.4), so there is no need to repeat it here. As we shall see in chapter 5, Tommy Lee Osborn, who has been a key mentor to Michael Reid, is a devoted disciple of E. W. Kenyon, often reading Kenyon's books as his sermons during his worldwide ministry.[272] He is also highly dependent on the methods of William Branham.[273]

Conclusions

In conclusion, emulating H. Richard Niebuhr,[274] I have sought to demonstrate a flow of development of positive thinking and Unitarianism arising in response to the harsh asceticism of Calvinism; the arising of transcendentalism embracing the subjective idealism of Berkeley and the corre-

---

269. Kenyon, *The Two Kinds of Faith*, 23.
270. See, for example, Shawn Francis Peters, *When Prayer Fails*, 85, 133.
271. Baker Eddy, *Science and Health*, 493.
272. Simmons, *E. W. Kenyon*, 297.
273. Ibid., 296.
274. See Niebuhr's flow of religious thinking quoted at section 3.1.1.

spondence of Swedenborg in response to the dryness of Unitarianism; then through the New Thought of Quimby, Evans, Eddy, and their followers to E. W. Kenyon and his unwitting fusion of revivalism and New Thought, that has been absorbed into the background principles of a variety of twentieth- and twenty-first-century revivalists both in the United States and in the UK.[275]

The assumptions of this movement include:

1. changes in matter correspond to changes in the mind;
2. belief in laws that govern the spiritual world and affect the material world that need to be discovered and intuitively applied;
3. human intuition is aided by revelation knowledge, or truth by accessing the divine mind, or thinking God's thoughts, or thinking from God's perspective;
4. sickness is caused by wrong belief, false ideas, and wrong thinking;
5. "cure" is brought about by speaking "the truth," which critics may understand as denying reality;
6. healers should seek to change people's minds and their wrong thinking by positive verbal affirmation and encouraging positive confession; and
7. spiritual laws govern prosperity as well as healing.

Of course, all of these assumptions fit well within the instrumentality of an increasingly pragmatic culture.

275. See chapter 3.

Part Two:
Three Case Studies in England

Introduction

PART TWO IS ILLUSTRATIVE of influences of the movement in England at the end of the twentieth century. My intention is to move from theory and history to current practice. I intend to show that it is not just the teachings of my case studies that are influenced by pragmatism, New Thought, and neo-Gnosticism, but that their whole theological construction of reality occurs through their narrative and performance, which convinces adherents to believe that these leaders have special knowledge, resulting in a form of religion that works. All of the leaders' stories, which appear to be innocent testimonies, are actually laced theological tropes, paradigms in effect, which stick more in the memory than the principles do. People construct their realities through narrative; they encourage each other's faith by recounting the testimonies they read in books or hear on tapes and podcasts. The vast majority of the theological material of this sort of church, I argue, is carried in the stories.

In order to show how each of my three Faith teachers continue to have influence over significant audiences, I will focus on their performative rhetoric. Starting in chapter 4 with Colin Urquhart, I will first point to his own personal rhetorical qualities, and then examine the nature of his followers and audiences and their receptivity to his teaching. Thirdly, and most significantly, in the largest part of this chapter, I will examine his use of narrative, including stories, testimonies, and principles that he draws from or applies to Scripture. In chapters 5 and 6, I will consider Michael Reid and Jerry Savelle in a similar way.

One of the most significant elements of a preacher's rhetoric is his *ethos* or reputation, that is, how honest, reliable, and trustworthy the hearers perceive him to be. As rhetorical theorist James Andrews writes,

> The speaker may also bring to the speaking situation a public *character*. His or her past actions, not only those associated with the specific issue being discussed, will contribute to audiences' impressions of the speaker's sincerity, trustworthiness, judgment and ethical qualities.[276]

Andrews adds,

> As the critic attempts to reconstruct the public character of a speaker, much more is relevant than the speaker's identifiable stand on issues. The speaker's entire public life, as well as that part of his or her private life that is known or has been reported, is significant. A speaker's reputation is also made up, in part of the audience's beliefs about the speaker's *intelligence* and *experience*. It is apparent that for some listeners a speaker will be seen as someone who "knows what he's talking about." Aspects of the speaker's past will have established him or her as an authority on the question at hand. Simply being identified in an audience's mind as an expert can enhance a speaker's ethos.[277]

Kenneth Burke refers to this self-presentation as "portraiture." In referring to poets (although he could have equally been thinking about preachers), he writes, "We refer to the utterance as 'portraiture,' as the 'self-ex-pression' of an agent, as an act characteristic of the poet's 'personality' whether or not he so wills it"[278] Burke continues,

> Aristotle deals with this problem from the purely rhetorical point of view when discussing devices whereby the speakers can deliberately promote an audience's confidence in him simply as a person, regardless of the cause that is being advocated or of the speaker's true nature.[279]

---

276. Andrews, *The Practice of Rhetorical Criticism*, 39.
277. Ibid., 40.
278. Burke, *Essays Toward a Symbolic of Motives*, 41.
279. Ibid.

When he defines rhetorical criticism as "the systematic process of illuminating and evaluating the products of human activity,"[280] Andrews is clear that rhetoric is not just "talk," but "human activity." I understand this rhetoric, this human activity, to be something that is created and implicit within communities. As anthropologist Clifford Geertz believes with Max Weber, "man is an animal suspended in webs of significance he himself has spun."[281] So the rhetoric of an individual and associated movement can be something that is not wholly or deliberately created by the individual, but unintentionally and mutually created. The discourse community contributes to the rhetoric associated with its leader by the building of a reputation that is appreciated within the movement and is presented to those outside the movement. So a significant element of the rhetorical attractiveness of Colin Urquhart is his background, his family and his respectability, as I will now describe.

---

280. Andrews, *The Practice of Rhetorical Criticism*, 4.
281. Geertz, *The Interpretation of Cultures*, 5.

CHAPTER 4

The Rhetoric and Faith Theology of Colin Urquhart

4.1 Urquhart's Self-Presentation

THE REVEREND COLIN URQUHART is well known and widely respected as a leader among evangelicals in the United Kingdom. He started his training for ordination at King's College London in 1959 where he spent four years reading theology. In his first book, *When The Spirit Comes*,[1] Urquhart describes an incident that Peters[2] tells us took place during Urquhart's final year of ordination training at St. Boniface, Warminster, which was at that time a theological college attached to Kings College London.[3] Urquhart reveals that he could not believe that God wanted him to be ordained and he was fearful at the prospect. He tells us that God responded by baptizing him in the Holy Spirit.

> I started to breathe very heavily for a few minutes, and then suddenly was filled with a great peace. God was breathing his Holy Spirit into me. I found myself speaking strange words, a language I did not know. It never occurred to me that this was "speaking in tongues." I did not understand it.[4]

Peters comments that this baptism in the Holy Spirit was in response to Urquhart's crying out to God; that God would need to do something to convince Urquhart that ordination was right. This "Spirit baptism" gave

---

1. Urquhart, *When the Spirit Comes*.
2. Peters, *Colin Urquhart*.
3. Ibid., 9.
4. Urquhart, *When the Spirit Comes*, 11.

Urquhart confidence that his ministry was God-ordained.[5] In effect, this made Urquhart a pioneer of the charismatic renewal in England in the 1960s. Many of those who consider themselves to be charismatics at the present day appreciate Urquhart's long-term leadership in the movement.

The argument that his ministry is long-term is highly persuasive. Most of Urquhart's books point to how long he has been around to establish his credibility. Despite the fact that Urquhart had resigned his Anglican orders in the autumn of 1975, he is still well able to argue that he has been in ordained ministry for well over forty years.[6]

So Urquhart's life and especially his longevity suggest to those who read his books that he is reliable. The length of a preacher's ministry has often been used to support the reliability of the ministry. As Steven Pullum observes, this longevity of ministry was also something that was used by American Faith healer Aimee Semple McPherson to establish the reliability of her ministry.[7] She believed her techniques and their arguments had stood the test of time, and time had proved her miracles were authentic. Of course, this is just one factor in the establishment of the ministry's reliability. In the case of Colin Urquhart, as for many preachers, the role of his wife is highly significant. Peters tells us that Urquhart and his future wife, Caroline, met on a blind date in the first year of his curacy in Cheshunt, and they were married within a year.[8] Her role, and that of the family, is also a significant factor in establishing, to those who observe, that Urquhart is someone who has a stable family life.

This sort of seemingly mundane detail presents the preacher as someone that people can trust. It is a part of the rhetoric of his life. The canons of memory and organization are significant here: memory in the sense that Urquhart is presented as a normal married man, someone like them who they can trust; and organization in the sense that his life is a coherent argument for his own reliability. Caroline is seen very much as part of Urquhart's ministry; this is also true of the wives of the other two preachers that I am considering as we shall see later.

Urquhart's ministry of healing was established early in his curacy in Cheshunt. Peters informs us that, "a small but definite voice within him, kept urging him to "heal the sick.'" He tells us that God spoke to Urquhart directly, "whatever you believe, you will see happening." Peters also tells us

---

5. Peters, *Colin Urquhart*, 10.

6. Urquhart's *Having Confidence in God* tape set has written on the back of the packaging that Colin has been in ordained ministry for nearly forty years. This tape set (undated) was clearly made some years ago.

7. Pullum, *Foul Demons*, 17.

8. Peters, *Colin Urquhart*, 14–16.

that Urquhart saw the importance of believing all the Bible, "not just those parts predetermined by denominational bias."[9]

4.2 Urquhart's Humility and Compassion

Apparent humility, compassion, and disavowal of personal power are indispensable assets when appealing to those who would follow. In his first book *When the Spirit Comes*, Urquhart reveals that, during his time at theological college, he could not believe that God wanted him to be ordained and he was fearful at the prospect; he writes,

> One day in chapel I said: "Lord, I believe you want me to be ordained. You know I'm scared stiff. I cannot understand why you should want me to do this; I'm not the right sort of person. I freeze in the presence of others: I'm afraid to open my mouth at meetings. But Lord I am yours, I give myself to you. If you want me to do this you will have to provide all the power."[10]

This reveals a person who from beginning did not think of himself as capable but instead communicates his humility and reliance on God.

4.3 Urquhart's Followers

In Urquhart's biography, Peters reveals a number of significant things about Urquhart's audiences and followers. Peters quotes from a letter written to him by Lord Runcie, who was bishop of St. Albans during Urquhart's time as Vicar of St. Hughes Lewsey. Runcie comments, "I don't think Colin's ministry was very effective amongst the more intelligent and sophisticated; but then, 'not many wise, not many learned.'"[11] Runcie is portrayed by Peters and, indeed, Urquhart himself, as being sympathetic to Urquhart, but he obviously observed that, while many of Urquhart's followers were enthusiastic, not many were theologically sophisticated.

Peters describes that on Urquhart's Kingdom Faith missions (in 1979–80), team members were "confronted by the plea for basic Christian biblical teaching." The response to this was the Kingdom Faith Teaching Course. Peters continues,

---

9. Ibid., 14.
10. Urquhart, *When the Spirit Comes*, 10.
11. Peters, *Colin Urquhart*, 48.

> A limited number of advertisements were placed in the Christian press in the summer of 1980 with a view to beginning the course in September. The response was staggering: six hundred groups enrolled immediately, indicating the extent of the need for such teaching and the hunger in people's lives.[12]

Urquhart's audiences also contained a significant number who suffered from depression and emotional insecurity. Peters describes a person who came with depression being helped by the ministry of Charles Sibthorpe, who was a close co-worker with Urquhart in the 1980s. Peters writes,

> The person whose testimony I am quoting below (we shall call her "Janet") had previously suffered an acute depressive illness ... that same evening Charles spoke, and as he did, so I listened with a sense of anticipation that something was going to happen. I also felt nervous as I didn't want to cry again. He spoke about his own personal experience, the lack of power in his life, his fears and lack of faith until he asked the Lord to fill him with His holy spirit, and I knew that was what I needed to do. At the close of the meeting I went forward with a throbbing heart, various people laid their hands on me, and Charles prayed a beautiful prayer about God's Holy Spirit being a perfect gentleman, only going where he is asked, and that he was going to come into my life and heal me of all the past hurts.[13]

Peters also reveals that many of the students at Roffey place

> had unresolved issues in their lives—personal, emotional, spiritual, psychological—which required disciplined, skilful and regular counselling. This was simply not available to them ... men and women had come from a life of violence, or immorality, or drug addiction, or drunkenness.[14]

My own personal observation of the south-eastern English audiences of Urquhart (at Roffey Place) is that they are mostly middle-class, some coming with physical infirmities and emotional insecurities, but mainly with aspiration that God will give them hope through a more dynamic faith, rather than one that gives in to the skepticism of modernity. I observe them to be similar and indeed sometimes the same people who were participants in the Toronto Blessing phenomenon.

---

12. Ibid., 77–78.
13. Ibid., 78–80.
14. Ibid., 113.

David Hilborn, in his book *"Toronto" in Perspective* (2001), points to the work of Philip Richter, who

> draws on the work of Daniele Hervieu-Lèger to propose that TTB is a largely middle class phenomenon whose participants have found in it a way of responding to the increasing marginalisation of religious discourse in contemporary western culture.[15]

As Richter says,

> if intellectual middle-class Evangelicals are finding that the Gospel does not seem to be "speaking the same language" any more, one solution is to adopt the inarticulate meta-language of glossolalia, another is to embrace the non-verbal Toronto Blessing. Both solutions avoid head-on engagement with the language of modernity. In this way the Blessing can be seen as helping to mediate the acute contradiction between their religious "cultural capital" and the day-to-day realities of living and working in the 1990s.[16]

This increasing marginalization of religious discourse can be understood to be associated with the ongoing process of secularization. While this book will seek neither a full defense, refutation or elaboration of the theory of secularization, it notes that, as Bramadat writes, "this contentious theory forms part of the backdrop of virtually all contemporary discussions about the nature and role of religion in the modern world."[17]

While the resurgence of conservative Protestantism in the United States might be seen to be a striking refutation of the secularization thesis, as Berger suggests,[18] this hardly applies in the United Kingdom, where, despite the rise of a number of seemingly numerically successful evangelical ministries and fresh initiatives, there has been no halting of the sharp decline in overall church attendance throughout the twentieth century.[19]

In his ethnography of the IVCF (a Christian Union at McMaster University in southern Ontario, Canada), Bramadat rejects what he calls a "vulgar" or "positivistic form of secularization theory" that forecasts the end of

---

15. Hilborn, *"Toronto" in Perspective*, 244.
16. Richter, "God is Not a Gentleman," 34.
17. Bramadat, *The Church on the World's Turf*, 12.
18. Berger, *A Far Glory*.
19. Gilbert, *The Making of Post-Christian Britain*. See also Wolffe, *Evangelical Faith and Public Zeal*; Warner, *Reinventing English Evangelicalism*.

all religions in favor of a more modest approach to secularization.[20] Instead, he notes the suggestion of James D. Hunter that the apparent stability of American Christianity disguises a shift in its essence; that in order to attract members, evangelical churches have compromised with certain aspects of the dominant secular culture.[21] Bramadat asks, "are these groups growing because they have as it were, sold out to the non-Christian world?"[22]

As an alternative, he notes Weber's insight that organizations like this are resolute uprisings against the overwhelming disenchantment.[23] As Bramadat suggests, these groups are often the most vigorous because they are perceived by their membership "as being the least complicitous in the disenchantment cultivated by secularization."[24] He concludes that neither explanation is adequate. Instead, he suggests groups like the IVCF described in his book facilitate "both compromises and confrontations."[25]

Interestingly, commenting on evangelicals in the United Kingdom in the period 1966–2001, Warner states that "[a]nalysis reveals that pragmatic and acculturating entrepreneurs enjoyed more late 20th century growth than uncompromising conservatives."[26] So Urquhart's followers have tended to be mainly middle-class, but at the same time theologically unsophisticated, desiring basic and simple Christian biblical teaching. Many have been those with physical and emotional problems looking for pragmatic solutions in the face of rising secularization.

4.4 Urquhart's Use of Narrative and Testimony

We would all consider ourselves *Homo sapiens*—modern humans or modern man—but Walter Fisher[27] suggests we are more than that, we are also *Homo Narrans:* story-telling humans or story-telling man. He proposed that the way people explain and justify their behavior, whether in the past or the future, has more to do with telling a credible story than it does about producing evidence or constructing a logical argument. This is in contrast with the traditional paradigm of the rational world. John Niles in his book

20. Bramadat, *The Church on the World's Turf*, 14.
21. Hunter, "Conservative Protestantism," 159.
22. Ibid.
23. Weber, *From Max Weber*, 155.
24. Bramadat, *The Church on the World's Turf*, 14.
25. Ibid., 14.
26. Warner, "Fissured Resurgence," 2 (Abstract).
27. Fisher, "Narration as Human Communication Paradigm," 265–87.

Homo Narrans[28] explores how human beings shape their world through the stories they tell. All preachers do this in the way they re-tell biblical stories, and particularly in their use of illustrations—stories which in their telling interpret the passage considered. Like any other preacher, Urquhart's worldview is presented in the stories he tells.

As a preacher or any other storyteller tell their stories, listeners will have a gut reaction to the story and the conclusions made by those telling it; these reactions, Fisher explains, are how we discern between the truth and error in what we hear. The two ways that we make this distinction are by narrative probability and narrative fidelity. Narrative probability is whether a story seems coherent or that the events fit together without any holes. Narrative fidelity is whether the story represents accurate assertions about social reality or, in other words, that events do not seem to be contradictory to how a person views the world. If a listener has a negative feeling or discomfort as she listens to how the story unfolds, she does so because she feels the story is either not probable or lacks fidelity with how she views the world. Other listeners might feel intrigued, excited, or even vindicated by the story as it unfolds. This is because the events in the story did seem probable to them or they matched their view of how the world works.

Like many preachers, Urquhart uses stories from his own personal experiences to show to his readers that if something can work for him, it can also work for them. The stories he uses indicate key ideas in his worldview.

Narrative probability increases as people accept that the claims of his stories in their mind fit together in a seamless way. Narrative fidelity increases as people find that his stories are not contradictory and build a coherent understanding of reality. Of course, those who cannot accept the stories told by Urquhart and their coherence would find it difficult to support his ministry. Of course this also applies to Reid and Savelle's stories.

In the examples that follow from Urquhart's books, tapes, and his more recent radio broadcasts, the illustrations, testimonies and narrative act as lenses through which the passages of Scripture commented on are interpreted.

---

28. Niles, *Homo Narrans*.

4.5 Significant Stories and Narratives

4.5.1 Lead in the Eyes

At the beginning of his very popular book *Anything You Ask*,[29] Urquhart describes an event which took place when he was ministering in Cornwall.

Urquhart and his wife were staying with a couple, Charles and Joyce. He tell us, "On the previous evening I had been speaking about the prayer promises of Jesus and what it means to pray with faith, knowing that God is going to answer you."[30]

From the beginning of this illustration, he sets out his aim, to demonstrate how to pray with faith, knowing that God is going to answer.

The adults were drinking coffee together when one of the boys came rushing into the house to say there had been an accident. The children had been melting lead to put into molds to make gifts for Christmas. One of the children had dropped a piece of cold metal into the container causing some of the molten mixture to fly into Joanna's face.

When Charles carried ten year old Joanna into the room the adults were already praying. Prayer was the first thing on the agenda when it came to action, revealing the belief that prayer changes things and if the prayer is positive will result in healing of injuries. This belief in the likelihood of God healing immediately, in response to prayer, meant that instead of rushing Joanna to hospital, the prayer continued while her mother removed all the pieces of metal from her eyes. So it seems that prayer should be the first thing to do in the event of an accident, according to Urquhart. In any challenging situation, a person of faith should pray before acting.

Urquhart writes,

> it took her mother nearly forty minutes to remove all the pieces of metal. During that time we prayed, silently and aloud, with Joanna and for her. But all the time we thanked the Lord that there would be no damage to the eyes, and praised Him for His healing.[31]

This leads to the second thing this story reveals, the belief that thanking and praising God in advance will result in those praying getting what they ask for.

---

29. Urquhart, *Anything You Ask*, 15.
30. Ibid., 15.
31. Ibid.

4.5.2 St. Defeated

Another type of illustration that preachers use is the hypothetical story.

In his book, *The Truth That Sets You Free*,[32] Urquhart introduces the fictitious figure "St. Defeated." Urquhart tells us that "St. Defeated is confused because he wrongly believes facts to be the truth."

St. Defeated is obviously a "type" of Christian believer; he is given the label "St.," and Urquhart tells us that St. Defeated is a born-again believer as opposed to being just a churchgoer. This implies that St. Defeated has already put his faith in Christ in order to be born-again. However, by using the label "St. Defeated," Urquhart is suggesting that this person does not yet have enough faith to be victorious.

Urquhart then introduces the problem. St. Defeated is "told by his doctor that he has cancer and has only a short time to live. He is shown the X-rays which show clearly the existence of the tumor. He feels the symptoms in his body. Clearly the facts indicate he has cancer." Urquhart then says, "It would be foolish of him to deny these facts and claim the cancer didn't exist." But then he tells us, "These are the facts, but not the Truth!" He goes on to say that "[t]he Truth is that by the stripes of Jesus he is healed." He is here alluding to Isaiah 53:5 (RSV): "But he was wounded for our transgressions, he was bruised for our iniquities; upon him was the chastisement that made us whole, and with his stripes we are healed."

According to Urquhart, the facts state that St. Defeated has cancer, but the Truth says he is healed. The facts are natural; the Truth is supernatural. The supernatural is more powerful that the natural. So, Urquhart tells us, someone in this position needs to decide whether he puts his faith in the facts or the Truth. He says, "The Truth is able to change the facts but the facts can never change the Truth. So a believer can trust in the natural prognosis or the Truth." Urquhart says the Truth is a person, Jesus, because he said, "I am the Truth" (John 14:6). He argues that now St. Defeated is a new creation in Christ, he needs to concentrate on the spiritual supernatural truth that has changed the facts and made him a new creation. If he continues to concentrate and dwell on the facts, he will deny the Truth of what God has done for him in Christ.

Of course, what Urquhart is suggesting is that Christians who present symptoms of sickness are not actually sick because by Christ's stripes they are already healed. All they need to do is believe it.

---

32. Urquhart, *The Truth That Sets You Free*, 43.

4.5.3 Money for a Car

Another of Urquhart's stories illustrates his belief in divine provision of money.[33] His book *Faith for the Future*[34] describes a situation that had arisen about the time just after he had left St. Hugh's Lewsey in 1976. Just three months into his new itinerant ministry, Urquhart and his companions Vivienne and David were travelling to meetings by car all over the country. He introduces the illustration with the exclaimed prayer, "Lord, we don't have the money!" The problem, as Urquhart states it, is they needed a reliable car to arrive to meetings on time, and their present car had covered a high mileage. He does not say whether the current car had broken down or not, just that it had covered a high mileage.

Urquhart then says, "God had provided for our needs and we had kept our agreement with Him not to ask men for anything—even expenses. If we were asked "What are your expenses?" our reply was: "Nothing." This often produced reactions of surprise, or even annoyance, from treasurers until we explained." He tells us earlier in the book, "God had already assured us that this was His ministry and He would provide for it. If we had any need we were to ask Him, not men. We were not to contrive means of financial support or make any appeals for money: we simply had to trust Him."[35]

At that time, the ministry had a few hundred pounds in the bank and, along with the trade-in value of the old car, they had enough money to buy a reasonable second-hand car. When they went to showrooms to look, they found a good car and deal instantly. However, Urquhart decided to talk and pray with the others about whether this was the car God intended for them. He tells us that as they prayed, he realized that God was saying something he did not want to hear; he quotes what he felt God was saying to him: "I have led you to the kind of car you asked for, a good second-hand car. With the mileage you cover, you would need to replace that within a few months. You are to go out and buy a new car."

Urquhart tells us his response was, "Lord, we don't have the money." God's response, according to Urquhart, was that he had plenty of money, he had promised to supply all their needs, and they were to trust Him.

Urquhart acknowledges that he had heard of other people's foolish behavior, buying things without the necessary money, and that this was "dishonouring to the Lord if not initiated by Him." However, they agreed

---

33. Most evangelicals believe this, and most accept that God includes expenses from churches as a source of his provision. Urquhart rules expenses out and says that for God to give the money, gifts must be unsolicited.

34. Urquhart, *Faith for the Future*, 32.

35. Ibid., 19.

that God wanted them to act in faith; they ordered the car, and the necessary money came in.[36] He explains this approach to being sure of acting according to God's will earlier in the book. "I was now experiencing things daily that I did not know were possible. And one of the most important of these was the ability to hear God speak clearly." He goes on to say that people often ask if he hears an audible voice, and how he knows that he is not listening to his own thoughts or to "the enemy." Urquhart goes on to talk about great men of God who have spoken of "the witness of the Spirit" and adds that God speaks to him through the Bible, in times of prayer, sermons and in conversations with others. He says if it is not God he is hearing, he is not at peace in his thoughts.[37]

4.5.4 Reason Not as Important as the Bible

One of the most recent and concise summaries of Urquhart's teaching on the nature of faith was broadcast by Premier Radio as a series of five interviews on the subject of faith with Julia Fisher, one of Premier's presenters. These shows were broadcast in January 2008 as five daily editions of Premier's show, *Faith for Today*, in which Julia Fisher interviews Colin Urquhart on a variety of subjects. The first of the five interviews on faith, entitled "Faith for the Harvest," was broadcast on January 8th 2008. Subsequent editions were "Faith in Prayer" on January 9th, "The Centurion's Faith" on January 10th, "Speaking to the Mountains" on January 11th, and "Ask, Seek, Knock" on January 14th.[38] Each of the shows focuses mainly on interpreting one particular passage of scripture that is seen to be significant in his understanding of faith.

In the second of the shows, "Faith in Prayer," he comments that his book *Anything You Ask*[39] "came out of a real move of faith in my own life and ministry." In the book he comments,

> During the early years of my Christian life I was taught that our reason was as important as the Bible. You came to the words of Scripture and applied your powers of reasoning to it. As a result, you only believed what you could rationally accept as true and were free to discard the rest. The outcome was a relatively powerless life and ministry. Then I began to see the Word with

36. Ibid., 33–4.
37. Ibid., 11.
38. I downloaded all of these shows as webcasts from the Kingdom Faith website on 14th April 2008. See "Premier Radio Series."
39. Urquhart, *Anything you ask*.

the eyes of the Spirit. I began to believe it instead of criticise it! I began to accept it, instead of pull it apart so that I needn't believe it. And the outcome was a new life and a new ministry in which I have seen the power of God at work in ways that I never thought possible, but in ways that God promises in his word.[40]

I expect that it was during his theological training for ordination at King's College London that the use of reason was assumed in interpreting the Bible, although it may have been during the exploration of his vocation during which he was assigned a tutor, or during his A-level studies in religious knowledge. I have no doubt that he was taught about biblical criticism, but states that guided by the Spirit, he has rejected this rationalist approach to the Bible in favor of an acceptance of Scripture at face value as the Word of God, which has transformed a powerless life and ministry into a life in which he has seen God at work, fulfilling the promises of his Word.

Faith teachers suspend reason, as they argue that God's Word can actually contradict reason, encouraging their followers to deny their reasoning powers in order to see what they want to be the outcome in any given situation.

A classic example of this approach is from Kenneth Hagin, who writes,

> We cannot know God through our human knowledge, through our mind. God is only revealed to man through his spirit. It is the spirit of man that contacts God, for God is a Spirit. . . . We don't understand the Bible with our mind, it is spiritually understood. We understand it with our spirit, or our heart . . . as we meditate in this word, our assurance becomes deeper. This assurance in our spirit is independent of our human reasoning or of human knowledge. It may even contradict human reasoning or physical evidence.[41]

4.5.5 God Can Only Work in Response to Faith

In the first interview with Julia Fisher on the subject of faith, entitled *Faith for the Harvest*, Urquhart starts with a statement that he describes as a "truth." He says, "Whatever God does in our lives is a response to faith."

He is not quoting Scripture as we might expect him to, but is stating a summary of how Christian faith works in the form of a principle, spiritual

---

40. Ibid., 72–73.
41. Hagin, *New Thresholds in Faith*, 31–32.

law or secret. He comments that this truth is not widely liked because not all believers have a continuous faith-relationship with God.

This "truth" raises significant questions in itself. Does Urquhart mean that God can only act in a person's life while they have faith? The statement does seem to limit the sovereignty of God and his freedom to act in a person's life as he chooses. It also suggests a direct relationship between a person's faith and the activity of God, in which God seems to be controlled by one's faith.

4.5.6 Scripture is clear

In the second of his interviews with Julia Fisher, Urquhart deals with the subject of "Faith in Prayer." However, before he starts, Fisher raises a question from the previous day's interview. She asks, "What are these deeds, are they actually the things God has already planned for us to do?"

Urquhart replies, "Yes, the Scripture is clear, that he has planned good works for us and these are the works that can only be done by faith in God." Urquhart often uses this phrase—"the Scripture is clear"—in his talks and writings when it is very far from straightforward to interpret.

4.5.7 Have the Same Faith as God

In the fourth of his interviews with Julia Fisher, Urquhart introduces one of the most significant of the Faith Movement's texts: Mark 11:22–24. He notes that these verses are usually called the "prayer of faith." He says this reveals important "principles" in how to express "genuine faith" leading to "positive results" when we pray.

He observes of Jesus that "He healed with a word. Two thousand demons were cast out with one word: 'Go.'" He says we know that the lame were healed, Jesus said "pick up your bed and walk." Blind eyes were opened and deaf ears were opened, dumb mouths were opened just because he said "Be opened." He adds that while Jesus words produced extremely positive effects, they could also curse. "Woe to you, Chorazin! Woe to you, Bethsaida!" were curses, and he says both places are rubble nowadays. He concludes, "Whatever Jesus speaks for good or ill will come into being."

Urquhart then comments on the fig tree that the disciples were amazed how quickly it withered, so Jesus responded, "have faith in God."

At this point in the interview, Urquhart acknowledges that some teachers translate this as "have the faith of God," and that this is really stretching the Greek. Elsewhere in this book, I have noted that Hagin and other modern

Faith teachers have followed Kenyon's translation of this verse as "have the faith of God" and insist we should have a "God kind of faith." Urquhart is keen to distance himself from the carelessness of that translation in this interview; but this has not always been the case, as he wrote in 1978,

> Do we pray with Jesus' kind of faith ... Jesus wants to ... teach you to pray with His kind of faith. "Have faith in God" can be literally translated: "Have the faith of God." The Lord not only wants our trust to be in Him; He wants His own faith to be in us.[42]

Later in his ministry, Urquhart realizes the implications of embracing this attitude and distances himself from it. However, at the time of writing one of his best-known books, *Anything You Ask*, he is embracing a theology that implies that we should seek to have a faith like God's faith. The question then must be asked: Who or what does God have faith in?

4.5.8 Getting Airborne: See the Situation as God Sees It

Although Urquhart now distances himself from saying that we should have a "God kind of faith," it seems not from its meaning because he then encourages listeners to "look at the situation as God would see it," or, as he calls it, "getting airborne." Before talking about moving mountains, he describes flying over the Alps: how unmovable the mountains appear from the foot of the Alps, but how tiny they look from the aircraft. He says, "It's a matter of perspective, so what I believe this means is get God's perspective on your situation. How does God see your situation, have faith in God, see the situation as God sees it."

Now he does not give clear instruction how this is achieved but implies that a believer has to imagine that they are like God, or at least can see things from God's perspective. God sees things from his perspective as the creator of the universe and he sees our problems, and they are nothing for him. Now it seems to me that the only way we can do this is to imagine how God sees things—in other words, to use our minds, our imaginations, to see our problems smaller than they are and as easily dealt with by God.

Urquhart then goes on to describe a mountain as a thing that cannot be dealt with in the "natural" but needs the supernatural intervention of God. He quotes Jesus who said, "If anyone says to this mountain, go throw yourself into the sea." Urquhart observes that this is for anyone, not just those with enormous faith or a proven faith ministry, but observes this is

---

42. Urquhart, *Anything you ask*, 98.

not just about saying but also about not doubting. He recalls that Jesus says to the disciples, "Therefore I tell you, whatever you ask for in prayer, believe you have received it and it will be yours." Urquhart then tells us to pray in faith: "you do the business really before you ask. So you know you've sorted out what you believe, what you expect, what the outcome is going to be so you can be sure and certain."

Urquhart also comments on this text in his book *Receive Your Healing*.[43] Commenting on Mark 11:23, he says, "When praying the prayer of faith, stage one is to have faith in God. Stage two is to speak to the mountain and command it to move."

4.5.9 Speak to Your Problems

Then he commends the practice of speaking to your problems. He writes,

> How often do you speak to your problems? This is a question I often ask people, and the great majority admit they never speak to them. Yet this is what Jesus tells you to do. If you don't do things the way He directs, you can't have too many complaints if you don't obtain the results you want when praying to Him.[44]

He explains that when Jesus speaks of mountains, he is speaking about problems in a person's life. He says,

> You cannot move the problem, but God will when you speak to it in faith. *You are to speak to the mountain, not live with the problem.* Your responsibility is not to help people live with their mountains but to lead them to the kind of faith where they can speak to the problem and command it to move in the name of Jesus.[45]

Prayer, he argues, should be specific in detail. He writes,

> Nowhere does Jesus teach us to pray with vague hope that something will happen in the future; he teaches us to believe we have received the answer. "Therefore I tell you, whatever you ask for in prayer, believe that you have received it, and it will be yours" (Mark 11:24). *Vague prayers receive vague answers; specific prayers receive specific answers.*[46]

---

43. Urquhart, *Receive Your Healing*.
44. Ibid., 95.
45. Ibid., 97.
46. Ibid., 60.

Commenting on those who pray for someone who is seriously ill but who dies instead of being healed he says,

> Lovingly and gently they need to be shown that they were not in a place of faith. Faith doesn't say, "God will at some time in the future." Faith says, "God *has*." Faith knows the healing is accomplished. *Jesus bore your sicknesses on the cross. By His stripes you are healed. Your faith enables you to receive the benefit of what he has done. If He has done all that is necessary for your healing, do not give up. Persist in faith.*[47]

Urquhart seems to have developed in his understanding of this principle since the early days of his ministry.

4.5.10 Money for College

Mark 11:24 is to Urquhart not just an important promise about healing, but also about finance. In his book *The Positive Kingdom*,[48] he describes the time when the elders of his ministry, the Bethany Fellowship, felt led by God to open a college where people could be trained for various ministries. They soon heard of a college for sale nearby and after prayer it seemed right to them to make an offer of £570,000 plus £10,000 for the contents. They later heard their offer had been accepted, although there were higher offers, because their offer was in cash. Urquhart describes his initial problem in believing that God would provide £600,000. This, he tells us, happened just before he went on a ministry trip to the Far East. He says he knew that God could and would supply the money, but that is not faith. He writes,

> Faith says it has already happened, even if you have no visible evidence to substantiate your confidence. When Jesus taught his disciples to pray in faith, He told them: "Therefore I tell you, whatever you ask for in prayer, believe you have received it, and it will be yours." (Mark 11:24). . . . I believed that my heavenly father could supply the money, that he would do so; but I did not believe I had received it.[49]

Urquhart then tells us that you can take the view that this cannot be the will of God, or you can "seek Him for the faith you need." The first option is "actually unbelief." He tells us he began confessing his unbelief and

---

47. Ibid., 117.
48. Urquhart, *The Positive Kingdom*, 99–102.
49. Ibid., 100.

repenting. After two hours, he tells us, God said to Him, "Colin, I give you a million dollars." He returned to England to tell the others that the Lord had given him a million dollars, which, he tells us, encouraged them in their faith. In the following months, the Lord had only supplied £280,000. Just before the deal was due to be finalized, Urquhart had to go on a ministry visit to Australia. On the way back, he visited the city where God had promised him the million dollars. At a meal with some friends, he told them they needed £300,000 by the following Friday, and to his astonishment his friend said that he would wire the money from his bank to their bank so they would have it in time. He adds that £300,000 was a million dollars in their currency. He summarizes the attitude to faith when he writes, "Faith does not say you will receive, but that you have received."[50]

The real problem with this interpretation of the text is the assumption that there is a "spiritual law" of confession that implies all you have to do is to speak to your troubles in faith. This is very similar to the thinking of Kenneth Hagin described and critiqued at section 1.3.3 and both Copeland, Hagin and Savelle described and critiqued at section 6.9.

4.5.11 Rebuke the Germs

This speaking to your troubles is also recommended by Urquhart, as he writes,

> Many people pray about their problems: but not everyone talks to them! And yet that is what Jesus tells us to do. Speak to the mountain and tell it to move. When I feel the early symptoms of an attack of 'flu or a cold, I talk to the problem: "Cold germs, I utterly reject you in the name of Jesus Christ. My body is a temple of the Holy Spirit and you don't belong here."[51]

4.5.12 The Story of the Persistent Son

In his final interview on faith with Julia Fisher, Urquhart focuses on Luke 11:5–13 and Jesus's teaching about a person who goes at midnight to borrow three loaves of bread from a friend because the person has an unexpected visitor. The friend is already in bed and is reluctant, even though he is a friend, but he gets up and gives him what he needs because of his persistence

---

50. Urquhart, *True Faith*, 33.
51. Urquhart, *Anything You Ask*, 99–100.

and boldness. Urquhart observes that bold people (whether they are Christians or not) get what they want.

He then tells a story about his son (Clive) who has a high profile as Urquhart's heir-apparent in the ministry.

> Now one of the things that I have noticed is how bold people get what they want. I am not talking about Christians, I am not talking about prayer, I am talking about anybody. How when people are really bold, then it's amazing what they get. I can talk about my son now, not because of the anointing, not because of his faith, but he is one of these people who when he wants to buy anything, he is so bold in the way in which he negotiates a price. He doesn't even necessarily accept the price that is being asked, he will be bold, and I've heard him speak to people and I thought to myself, I would never even dare to expect the kind of deal that he is wanting, but you know that boldness gets rewarded. There was an occasion only last week where he was negotiating to buy a new car and the figure he started at, the salesman said, "That's totally impossible, we cannot come down to your price at all." But in the end, they came down to his price. It was through boldness and determination and just making it very clear I am not going to shift from this.

Urquhart observes from Luke 11:9–10 "that if we ask then we shall receive, because he says, for everyone who asks receives, everyone who asks in this way receives. He who seeks, and to him who knocks the door will be opened."

He goes on to suggest that Jesus is teaching that a believer's prayers should not be tentative but bold and determined, expecting answers. He observes that a lot of people pray tentatively; they would like the answer, but they do not go seeking for the answer.

Fisher says here, "Maybe they just don't feel that they deserve God to even listen to them." Urquhart acknowledges that no one deserves anything from the Lord and then, if we waited until we deserved anything, we would never ask. He then adds that we have been made sons of God through faith in Christ and we have a full inheritance. He says, "God wants to see that boldness and determination of faith that lays hold of what God says is ours."

4.5.13 Having Confidence in God

In Tape 1 of his tape series *Having Confidence in God*,[52] Urquhart brings together three ideas from Scripture that indicate with what attitude the life of faith should be lived. Urquhart refers his listeners to Matthew 21:22: "If you believe, you will receive whatever you ask for in prayer." He says, "Now that's a very simple statement by Jesus. . . . Many of us would say our experience argues against that. But it's not what Jesus says that's wrong, it's our experience that's wrong." Urquhart asks, "How are we to get confidence in the Lord like that?" He then refers to Proverbs 3:5, "Trust in the Lord with all your heart." He comments,

> Well, that's having confidence in Him, isn't it? That is having faith in Him so we can receive what we ask in prayer. Trust in the Lord with all your heart, so immediately we see it's not just a matter of prayer, but of the heart. We need trusting hearts, whatever that means and however we get them. Trust in the Lord with all your heart and lean not on your own understanding. So what is the greatest enemy of faith, of trust of confidence in God? Your own thinking! You see, the reason so many struggle with their walk of faith is because they believe their own thinking rather than trusting in the Lord with all their hearts. It's very easy to think your thoughts are right. But you see what God is saying to us in His word here is your own thoughts, your opinions, if you like, will undermine the life of faith, not enable the life of faith. This is why Paul says, "Let your minds be renewed that you will know the good acceptable and perfect will of God." So there's something that God needs to do in our hearts, and there's something that needs to happen in our minds. However, God won't interfere with your mind. It's for you to clear the rubbish out of your mind, the unbelief out of your mind, everything that contradicts what he says, and to fill your mind instead with the truth.

He continues,

> Verse 6 is equally important: "In all your ways acknowledge Him." You see what a lot of people try to do is have a life of faith, a life of confidence in God when they're only acknowledging the Lord in some of the things they do, and not in all of the things they do. Let me put this very simply. If I'm walking in my own way with my own ideas, with my opinions, my own

---

52. Date and place unspecified—Kingdom Faith Resources Ltd, PO Box 450, Horsham RH12 4YA

understanding, then I'm not acknowledging the Lord in all my ways, am I? But suddenly I want God to do a miracle in my life. I have a need and only God can do it, and I'm not on the right road, I'm walking down the way of my own understanding. I'm walking down the way of acknowledging what I choose to acknowledge.

Urquhart argues that in order to have true faith, true confidence in God that will result in believers getting what they ask for in prayer, not only do their hearts need to be changed by God, but also they need to replace their own thoughts with the truth (of Scripture). In order to see miracles, this needs to be applied to their whole lives.

4.6 Urquhart's Principles

The above stories reveal just a small selection of Urquhart's preaching narrative. From these stories, arguments, and narratives, a number of ideas or principles can be seen to be taught by Urquhart, by which the Scriptures and the life of true faith should be understood. These include:

1. In any challenging situation, danger, injury, sickness, or need, a person of faith should pray rather than take any action his or her own mind might suggest.

2. The belief that thanking and praising God in advance will result in those praying receiving what they ask for.

3. Belief in the supernatural truth that, in Christ, a person is healed already (because it is in the Bible), rather than material facts like a medical diagnosis (for example, an x-ray photograph).

4. Belief that God will provide all financial needs. This means waiting for money to come in the form of gifts, rather than claiming expenses.

5. The idea that people can hear God speaking to tell them to buy things before they have the money, and believing that God would provide the money.

6. Promises of God found in Scripture are to be believed more than reason. The Bible is not to be understood with a person's mind, but with his or her spirit; so in order to see God's promises fulfilled, believers should deny their reasoning powers.

7. Whatever God does in a person's life is a response to faith, implying that God can only work in response to faith.

8. Belief that Scripture is clear and straightforward in its interpretation.
9. Believers should have a faith like God's faith and see their situations from God's perspective.
10. Believers should speak to their situations using specific words, believing they have received what they ask.
11. If a person truly believes God wants them to buy something for His purposes, then they should make an offer even if they do not have the money.
12. If a person doubts that God will provide for their material needs, they should repent of their unbelief.
13. Believers should be bold and persistent, even daring, in their financial dealings and in their prayers to God.
14. In order to have confidence (true faith) in God and, consequently, receive what a person asks for in prayer, believers need to replace their own thoughts, ideas and opinions with what Urquhart calls the truth of Scripture.

CHAPTER 5

The Rhetoric and Faith Theology of Michael Reid

5.1 Introduction

BISHOP MICHAEL REID HAS been, until quite recently, a widely respected and successful leader among Pentecostal Christians in the United Kingdom, although there were many who had critical things to say about Reid's words and actions. For example, the Reachout Trust have a number of blogs where those critical of Bishop Reid's ministry have posted their comments.[1] There is also a site dedicated to complaints about Reid produced by former members of Peniel Church.[2] In 2008, Reid was voted out of leadership of his church after the discovery of an eight-year affair with the choir leader at Peniel.[3] However, in May 2010, with the support of his wife, Dr. Ruth Reid, he started a new church in a sports center in Ilford.[4] These seem to be hard times given that his congregation when I visited seemed to be about twenty people and, at the date of the meeting, Reid would have been aged sixty-seven.[5] The membership of the Peniel Church Brentwood (now renamed Trinity Church) had a regular attendance, at the height of Reid's ministry, of over 700. The church, now under the leadership of former assistant pastor

---

1. See "Reachout Trust, Peniel Church 2008" and "Reachout Trust, Bishop Michael Reid."
2. "Michael Reid Miseries." The website is now merged with "Controlling Churches." See also "Victims of Bishop Michael Reid."
3. "Allegation of Reid's admission of adultery."
4. I visited the new church with my wife at 2.00 pm on October 10th 2010. Afterwards, we spoke to the Reids.
5. Reid was born 15th May 1943. See Reid, *Strategic level Spiritual Warfare*, 348.

Peter Linnecar, has taken a significantly different direction.[6] There is now practically no upfront healing ministry for healing at the church, which is a significant contrast to the church under the leadership of Reid.

What is it about Reid and his ministry that gathered such a large congregation? In this chapter, I aim to demonstrate that Reid's rhetoric demanded attention. His belief in Christ and his own calling generated trust in many who went to Peniel looking for "a miracle." I will set out key points and significant influences in Reid's life, as described in his books and online videos, that chart the history of Peniel Church and Michael Reid Ministries before going on to consider his rhetoric.

In considering Michael Reid, at first look it is not easy to see in his writings and talks obvious Word of Faith teachings. Indeed, he is quite openly critical of certain aspects of Word of Faith teachings.[7] This is in stark contrast to what we discovered in examining the books and media of Colin Urquhart, where there are clear examples of teaching that seem to be similar to Kenyon and the mind curists before him. Urquhart's presentation is based around testimonies and stories in his books. There are fewer testimonies in Reid's books that he uses as the basis for his teaching, but there are some, which we will examine in this chapter. There are, however, some highly revealing comments in Reid's published DMin thesis, *Strategic Level Spiritual Warfare: A Modern Mythology?*,[8] and some interesting comments in his popular books that we will consider later in this chapter. More significant are the large number of videos in which we see Reid seemingly healing people and which reveal his indebtedness to his Faith teacher mentors. Those he holds up as his teachers and guides in ministry have more obvious connections to the "fathers" of the Word of Faith Movement. The two most notable of these are T. L. Osborn and Benson Idahosa, although a significant early mentor was Judson Cornwall. Other teachers he has studied that will be of significance in this book are Charles Finney and Smith Wigglesworth.

---

6. I first visited the church (soon after Reid's departure) on 13th April 2008. There I met Pastor Peter Linnecar, who was assistant pastor when Reid led the church. I subsequently met with Peter Linnecar at the church site on 12th June 2008. I have since attended the church on a number of occasions.

7. See, for example, Reid and Cornwall, *Whose Mind Is It Anyway*, 45. See also Reid, *It's So Easy*, 54–57, 79. See also his critique of seed faith gifts in Reid, *What God Can Do for You*, 38.

8. Reid, *Strategic Level Spiritual Warfare*.

5.2 Reid's Self-Presentation

It is important to realize from the outset the significance of not just Reid's written and spoken word, but the information, ideas, and influence that are presented incidentally through videos, advertising, and body language. Each of these is part of his overall rhetoric. In my own encounters with Reid (so far), I have always found him warm, welcoming, and, in fact, charming. This charm, I suggest, is part of the reason his ministry draws people and has been successful. I will discuss charm and charisma further in chapter 8.

When my wife and I visited his new small church in Ilford, we talked to Michael and Ruth Reid about our daughter Sophia, who has ME and is a deep concern to us. They showed us compassion and offered to meet with Sophia and to pray for her.[9]

Ruth Reid encouraged us to show Sophia the videos. It has become obvious that the Reids know that the videos raise expectation and faith. The videos about Peniel and Michael Reid that are available on YouTube and other websites all tell a story that I shall seek to understand as performative rhetoric and in terms of Reid's theological influences. Similar comments to those I made about Urquhart could be made about Reid's narrative by referring to Fisher[10] and Niles[11] and observing that Reid's world is similarly shaped by the stories he tells or are told about him. The difference is that, with Reid, these are more commonly in the form of videos. There are a number of things that made Reid and Peniel attractive to those who joined: Reid's personal appeal and charisma, the story of his conversion and calling, the way the church was set up and what it provided, that he was supported by his wife, the successful business-like way things were run, the church school, the international nature of Reid's ministry, his academic career, and the setting up of a university college. I will now examine those in a little more detail.

5.3 Reid's Appeal

As a young man Michael Reid was for nearly three years a police officer in the West End of London. He was very soon dealing with all sorts of crime and criminals. In a strange way, this contributes to Reid's credibility as a man who has had to face some of the harshest realities in life. In many ways,

---

9. Reid has been very successful in bringing healing to ME sufferers, as many of the videos from Peniel demonstrate.

10. Fisher, "Narration as Human Communication Paradigm."

11. Niles, *Homo Narrans*.

Reid's public image, as far as church members were concerned, was as a successful but ordinary man who enjoyed fly fishing, cooking, horse riding, and golf.[12]

5.4 Reid's Conversion and Calling

As a young police officer, Reid was an avowed atheist, but he encountered the American preacher, Demos Shakarian, at an evangelistic meeting.[13] After the meeting, there was an altar call, but Shakarian went straight over to Reid and said, "Come on, I've got people I want you to meet." Reid comments, "It was some years later he [Shakarian] told me God had spoken to him that night, pointed me out at the end of the meeting and said to him, 'Go get that man. I have a work for him to do.' He left everyone on the platform to come and find me."[14] It would appear that Reid had a special conversion and calling to God's work, a bit like St. Paul's Damascus Road experience. In a similar way to Urquhart, this gave Reid a confidence that he was called to a particular ministry by God. Later that evening, after dinner with Shakarian and others, they shared the gospel with him and he accepted Christ as his savior.[15] The following day, Reid was told that he needed to be filled with the Spirit; he was, and for the first time spoke in tongues.[16] In the week that followed, he spent time with Nicky Cruz, who was a member of Shakarian's team. Cruz was a former New York gang leader brought to faith through the ministry of David Wilkerson (author of *The Cross and the Switchblade*).[17] Cruz is well known to a whole generation of evangelical Christians who have read his best selling book *Run, Baby, Run*.[18] Mixing with people such as Cruz increased the credibility of what became Reid's early ministry.

---

12. From "The History of Peniel Church—Part Four," 0 mins 37 secs.
13. Demos Shakarian became the founder of the Full Gospel Businessmen's Fellowship International (FGBFI).
14. Reid, *It's So Easy*, 19–20.
15. Ibid., 20–22.
16. Shakarian, Reid, and so on, believe in a two-stage process typical of Pentecostals.
17. Reid, *It's So Easy*, 22–23.
18. Cruz, *Run, Baby, Run*.

5.5 Reid's Ministry

Reid left the police believing that God wanted to do something different with his life.[19] However, after Shakarian left the country, he found it impossible to find a church with the same life he had experienced with his American friends.[20] He had an early ministry in the north of England but found himself in dispute with other leaders. He writes, "They were also unhappy when I prayed for people, miracles happened so easily. They called me critical but it was actually nothing to do with criticism; I just wanted to preach the gospel."[21] This is a somewhat different account to that given by the leaders of the church concerned.[22] He left the ministry for a few years. During that time, he met his wife Ruth and moved to the south of England. Reid then went to work as a marketing director for a publishing company, and then as a salesman for the insurance company, Save and Prosper.[23] During this time, he visited Trevor Dearing,[24] who challenged him to start preaching again. Reid comments, "I knew at that moment God was speaking to me."[25] He had been discouraged by the division in the churches caused by "the discipleship movement." He writes,

> In the midst of this atmosphere, as I contemplated God's direction to start preaching again, God spoke to me. He clearly said, "You know what you don't want, now build what you do want." I knew at that point it was a call from The Most High to become a co-worker with Him in building His church.[26]

This raises questions about the sort of theological reality Reid wanted to construct, which we will consider later.

---

19. Reid, *It's So Easy*, 23.
20. Ibid., 27.
21. Ibid., 28.
22. Reid was excommunicated for "raillery"—a biblical term for slander—from Liverpool's Devonshire Road Christian Fellowship in 1969 and his "flesh was committed to Satan." See *The Guardian*, 31 December 2000.
23. Reid, *It's So Easy*, 37, 40.
24. Trevor Dearing was, at that time, an Anglican Vicar in Hainault and author of a number of books on healing and miracles. He was widely regarded as an authority on healing, especially among the early Charismatic movement in the UK.
25. Reid, *It's So Easy*, 40.
26. Ibid. See also See "The History of Peniel Church—Part Five," 2 mins 48 secs.

5.6 Church Set Up with His Wife

With his (by then) wife, Ruth, he set up a Bible study in their home in Ongar, Essex, and miracles apparently began to happen there, attracting more and more people.[27] This meeting became the Ongar Christian Fellowship, founded on 14th November 1976. Trevor Dearing, a well-known charismatic Anglican healer, spoke at the first meeting.[28] A few months after the church was formed, Reid became the pastor whilst keeping his full-time job for a further three years.[29] Eventually, the church moved to the Arts and Activity Centre on Ongar High Street.[30] Between 1978 and 1980, the church continued to grow with annual conferences and regular Bible teaching from Reid.[31]

5.7 Church Run like a Business

In 1979, the OCF moved to Budworth Hall and, at the request of the chairman of the Ongar Community Centre, began to manage it for the town.[32] Members of the church redecorated the place, and the church basically ended up running the cafe, the bar, a crèche, a playgroup, wedding banqueting services and the finance committee. The center returned a profit and the church grew in numbers.[33] The Reids and the Linnecars[34] sold their homes to buy Bell House, the seven-and-a-half acre site of a former private school and an adjoining market garden in Pilgrims Hatch, Brentwood.[35] This provided a church meeting place and a building that became a school for the children of church members. The church then changed its name from the Ongar Christian Fellowship to Peniel Bible Assembly.[36] The sale of their houses to set up the church was an act of capitalist asceticism and austerity, although it might also be viewed as entrepreneurship. From its earliest days,

---

27. See "The History of Peniel Church—Part Three," 3 mins 29 seconds.
28. Reid, *It's So Easy*, 41.
29. See "The History of Peniel Church—Part Three," 3 mins 50 seconds.
30. Ibid., 3 mins 59 seconds.
31. Ibid., 4 mins 30 seconds.
32. Ibid., 4 mins 35 secs.
33. Ibid., 4mins 48 secs.
34. Peter & Caroline Linnecar were assistants to Reid from the very early days of the Church and Peter Linnecar became assistant pastor. He took over as Pastor from Reid in 2008 when Reid was dismissed by the church.
35. Ibid., 5 mins 35 secs.
36. Why "Peniel"? "Peniel" means "face of God." See Genesis 32:30: "So Jacob called the place Peniel, saying, "It is because I saw God face to face, and yet my life was spared.""

Peniel seems to have been run like a business: when the OCF took on the running of Budworth Hall, they did things such as running the bar, which many evangelical Christians would shun. This, along with the sale of Reid and Linnecar's homes to purchase the site of the future Peniel Church, reveals a capitalist entrepreneurial approach. The church does appear (perhaps unwittingly) from the beginning to have been set up to grow as a financial enterprise. Perhaps this is not surprising, given Reid's background running a Christian bookshop business[37] and being an insurance salesman.[38] Selling for profit was instinctive for him. It has often been argued that there are significant links between the culture of Protestantism and the development of capitalist markets.[39] Reid's own study and appreciation of Puritan writers may have fostered in him an attitude of Protestant asceticism revealed in the investment of his own money and property, and encouraging the church to grow its portfolio of property over the years, investing many hours of work by church members in building and maintaining the church properties.[40]

5.8 Church School

Many people questioned whether it was possible to start a school, but Reid saw this as a challenge. First the church built the school hall that would also be used as the church meeting hall, which opened in 1982.[41] In January that year, Peniel Academy opened with just seventeen pupils and a handful of committed staff. Table tennis was introduced as the principal school sport, as the school was too small for team games; and within a year the first Peniel pupil had reached the national table tennis finals. Soon after, the school achieved full DfEE registration.[42] In 1985, a new classroom block was built on the Peniel site, including a new classroom, office, and

---

37. Reid sold his house to set up a Christian bookshop and printing business in Ripon Yorkshire, during the early 1970s. See "The History of Peniel Church—Part Three," 0 mins 20 seconds.

38. He was an insurance salesman with Save and Prosper in the early 1970s. See "The History of Peniel Church—Part Three," 2 mins 30 secs.

39. See Weber, *The Protestant Ethic and the Spirit of Capitalism*. See also Ward, *Selling Worship*, 11.

40. I have been told by former members of the church that church members not only built buildings free of charge, but worked many hours maintaining the site. This is also apparent on the videos. See "The History of Peniel Church—Part Three," 6 Mins 20 seconds onwards and 7 mins 50 secs onwards, but especially See "The History of Peniel Church—Part Five," 0 mins 32 secs.

41. See "The History of Peniel Church—Part Three," 6mins 35 secs.

42. "The History of Peniel Church—Part Three," 6 mins 40 secs.

dining and kitchen facilities.[43] In 1994, the church hall had to be extended to house the growing congregation, increasing the seating capacity to over 700.[44] In June 1998, Peniel Church acquired the beautiful seventy-four-acre site of Brizes Park in nearby Kelvedon Hatch.[45] This soon became the new site for Peniel Academy School. Twenty-one years after it had first opened, Peniel Academy was declared by the national press to be the best school in Essex, and the seventh best school in the country.[46] A brand new junior school block was opened by the local MP in May 2003.[47] The church provided an attractive package to those who joined, especially those who were drawn by its own elite school. As had always been the way, it had been built largely by church members who were encouraged to work on it, ensuring their children would grow up and be educated in a Christian environment.

5.9 Reid's Mentors

Other than Reid's early encounters with Demos Shakarian and Trevor Dearing, his first significant mentor was Judson Cornwall, who he met in the late 1970s.[48] Cornwall wrote a number of books with Reid and seems to be an early influence. The books he wrote with Reid are teachings based on an allegorical interpretation of the Old Testament. In Reid's later books, he is very critical of this approach to scripture.[49] Cornwall himself, like Reid, seems to be publicly quite critical of some of what might be thought of as characteristics of Word of Faith theology, particularly in his book *Unfeigned Faith*.[50] However, he is among those who endorse DeArteaga's book *Quenching the Spirit*,[51] which is a defense of Word of Faith teaching. Cornwall taught that miracles were often the result of praising God in all circumstances.[52] He is a figure who seems, even among contemporary charismatics, to be a person of significant prophetic vision.[53] It is very difficult, however, to see any clear

---

43. Ibid., 7 mins 48 secs.
44. See "The History of Peniel Church—Part Four," 1 min 38 secs.
45. Ibid., 4 mins 12 secs.
46. See "The History of Peniel Church—Part Five," 0 mins 16 secs.
47. Ibid., 0 mins 25 secs.
48. See "The History of Peniel—Part Three," 5 mins 4 secs.
49. Reid, *What God Can Do for You*, 67.
50. Cornwall, *Unfeigned Faith*.
51. DeArteaga, *Quenching the Spirit*.
52. Cornwall, *Let us Praise*.
53. See Ponsonby, *More*, 89.

evidence in Cornwall's writings of definite Word of Faith ideas. It seems that Reid moved on from this sort of approach.

Perhaps the most influential person in Reid's development was Archbishop Benson Idahosa, who he met in 1985 at a convention in Minehead. Reid and Idahosa undertook missions around the world together and through Idahosa, Reid got to know T. L. Osborn and Oral and Richard Roberts.[54] In 1990, Michael and Ruth Reid visited Idahosa's church in Benin City, Nigeria. They returned inspired by the experience, and started holding regular music and miracle services at Peniel modeled on Idahosa's church.[55]

In 1995, Peniel Church Belgium opened; this seems to have been a church that opened with Reid's support.[56] In 1997, Reid was appointed European director of Idahosa World Outreach.[57] In 1998, Reid's other major influence, T. L. Osborn, made his first visit to Peniel Church.[58] Reid openly describes Osborn as a key mentor.[59] Through Osborn, Reid was being influenced by a first-generation Word of Faith teacher. Osborn was directly influenced by E. W. Kenyon's writings, openly preaching directly from them throughout his ministry.[60] Indeed, in his book *Healing the Sick and Casting Out Devils*, Osborn says that he would have considered it an injustice if he had changed the meaning of Kenyon's writings, "seeing they were penned by a divinely inspired hand."[61] Osborn's books reveal how much he absorbed of Kenyon's teaching and built his own highly pragmatic approach to Word of Faith teaching, based on Kenyon's books.[62]

Osborn encouraged Reid to set up the Global Gospel Fellowship (GGF) in order to mentor other ministries throughout the world; I assume Osborn supported Reid in this, knowing they shared similar ideas.[63]

The last two mentors I am going to mention in this section are Oral and Richard Roberts.

---

54. See "The History of Peniel Church—Part Three," 7 mins 25 secs.
55. "The History of Peniel Church—Part Four," 0 mins 15 secs.
56. See "Peniel Belgium." and "The History of Peniel Church—Part Four," 2mins 0 secs.
57. See "The History of Peniel Church—Part Four," 3 mins 26 secs.
58. Ibid., 4 mins 5 secs.
59. Reid, *Faith: It's God Given*, 10 and Reid, *Its So Easy*, 6.
60. Simmons, *E. W. Kenyon*, 297.
61. Osborn, *Healing the Sick and Casting Out Devils, Vol. 3*, 130.
62. See, for example, Osborn, *The Message That Works*.
63. See "The History of Peniel Church—Part Four," 4 mins 58 secs.

In 2002, Reid was elected to the board of trustees of the International Charismatic Bible Ministries organization established by Oral Roberts.[64] Reid undertook degrees of MA and DMin through Oral Roberts University. However, it seems that Reid is not in sympathy with everything originating with Oral Roberts. In his book *What God Can Do for You*, Reid is openly critical of seed faith gifts,[65] an idea that originated with Oral Roberts.[66]

5.10 Peniel Choir

In 1989, the Peniel Choir was formed, starting with just twenty-three members, but swelling to over one hundred members within six to seven years. The choir was a key element in the success of Peniel and continues to this day in Trinity Church. For an amateur choir, it has a very high standard and, it seems clear to me, is a very significant social group within the church. My observation of the choir is of a group of spiritually engaged people, taking notes and listening intently to sermons. The choir has toured with Reid internationally.[67] This was a very attractive element of Reid's ministry. I also think that the rhythm of their music and how the church would often sway from side to side to the beat may result in heightened suggestibility among worshipers.

William Sargant suggests that mystical experiences can,

> be induced by a wide range of stresses to the brain. What is more, feelings of divine possession and subsequent conversion to a religious faith can be helped on by the use of many types of physiological stimuli . . . electrical recordings of the brain show that it is particularly sensitive to rhythmic stimulation by percussion.[68]

He further, states that, "Belief in divine possession is very common at such times, and so is the mystical trance . . . "[69]

Judith Becker writes of the rhythm of charismatic worship putting worshipers into a trance like state, a state in which they are highly suggestible.[70]

Margaret Paloma writes that,

---

64. Ibid., 5 mins 8 secs.
65. Reid, *What God Can Do for You*, 38.
66. Schmidt and Kess, *Television Advertising and Televangelism*, 54.
67. "The History of Peniel—Part Four," 0 mins 5 secs.
68. See Sargant *Battle for the Mind*, 88
69. Ibid., 89.
70. Becker, *Deep Listeners*, 13–54.

music appears to be related to the altered states of consciousness (ASC) experienced by many who attend the P/C [Pentecostal-Charismatic] renewal services. Revival experiences have been noted to commonly include one or more of the following: an alteration in thinking or in perception of time, a loss of control, a change in emotional expression, dissociation between mind and body, perceptual changes, feelings of profound insight, a sense of the ineffable, feelings of rejuvenation, and hypersuggestability.[71]

So it may well be the case that the choir and music ministry play a part in bringing people to a state of trancelike suggestibility, in which "miracles" resulting from suggestion are more likely.

5.11 Publicity

In 1986, the church's newspaper, *Trumpet Call*, was launched with an initial circulation of 20,000, quickly rising to 70,000.[72] This was certainly more than a normal church publicity drive and was a way of advertising the miracle ministry of the church. In May 2002, Peniel TV was launched with the weekly show, *What God Can Do for You*, televised on religious television channels and the internet, reaching audiences not just in Britain but Europe, Africa and across the world.[73]

I had thought that another good example of Reid's self-presentation in his time at Peniel was his use of billboards. In the year before the Reids left Peniel, I noticed a large billboard advertising Peniel on the Commercial Road in North London. I understand that the church placed large billboards advertising the ministry as far away as Edinburgh. I had thought that this advertising was aimed at the aspiring middle-class, for example, adherents of black Pentecostal churches in the Commercial Road area; but on further investigation, it seems that these boards were placed where there was a Gay Pride march (Edinburgh) and near a gay club in Commercial Road, London. I can only interpret these as anti-gay propaganda.[74]

In the 1990s, there were legal challenges by the media and individuals to the church's claims of miracles.[75] In the end, this only served to in-

---

71. Poloma, Main Street Mystics, 43.
72. See "The History of Peniel Church—Part Three," 7 mins 58 secs.
73. See "The History of Peniel Church—Part Four," 5 mins 23 secs.
74. Reid founded the Christian Congress for Traditional Values who suggested gays were aiming to abolish the family. See *The Guardian*, Wednesday 6 February 2008.
75. "The History of Peniel Church—Part Four," 0 mins 55 secs.

crease the church's national and international presence, and led to stronger relationships with other churches and ministries around the country. Someone once said, "there's no such thing as bad publicity," and in the case of Peniel this is certainly true: the controversy resulted in even greater attendance and growth.

5.12 Study and Theology

From the beginning of his Christian life, Reid became a student. He writes, "I avidly read the Bible, as well as many books written by men and women who were inspired of God through the centuries."[76] In his book, *Faith: It's God Given*,[77] he reveals,

> I was . . . greatly influenced by the first generation of Quaker writings of George Fox, William Penn, James Naylor, Robert Barclay and Isaac Pennington; enriched by the Wesley brothers, George Whitfield and other Puritan writers; blessed by the books of Finney, Spurgeon, Count Zinzendorf and the Moravians and inspired by the works of the Marechale, Smith Wigglesworth, Maria Woodworth-Etter, Aimee Semple Macpherson and Kathryn Kuhlman. I enjoyed many years of rich fellowship and ministry with the late Archbishop Benson Idahosa, who was truly an outstanding apostle of faith of the twentieth century, a man who believed God and did exploits. My life has been challenged by the work and writings of both Oral and Richard Roberts and I am honoured to count Dr. T. L. Osborn as a friend and father in the faith. I am grateful to Dr. Judson Cornwall, for his wisdom, encouragement and friendship over many years. He also has been part of my shaping in God.[78]

This list of course reveals that Reid's theological influences come from the Puritan and revivalist traditions but also, significantly, from Word of Faith teachers.

Early in the church's life, in 1980, the Reids, assisted by Peter and Caroline Linnecar, set up the first church Bible school, with Bible study meetings held twice a week at Great Stony School in Ongar.[79] Lectures were given by Michael and Ruth Reid and Peter and Caroline Linnecar. In 1994, the Peniel Bible School was started, linked to Friends University in the USA

76. Reid, *It's So Easy*, 27.
77. Reid, *Faith: It's God Given*.
78. Ibid., 10.
79. See "The History of Peniel Church—Part Three," 5 mins 22 secs.

(Friends International Christian University).[80] This seems to be the start of the church's involvement with universities. In 1996, this continued when Peniel Bible School sought affiliation with Oral Roberts University.[81] This was supported by Idahosa, and in less than a year full ORU accreditation had been achieved for Peniel church's academic courses. Also, in 1996, Reid was made an associate "regent" of ORU.

In 2000, the Peniel College of Higher Education (PCHE) was officially opened by Richard Roberts.[82] In preparation for teaching at PCHE, Reid had, in 1998, obtained a Master's degree in practical theology at ORU, and then gained a doctorate in practical theology in May 2002.[83] Reid then started studying for a PhD with the Open University in England on "The Whole Man Ministry of Oral Roberts."[84] In May 2002, Reid received his DMin at the ORU graduation ceremony in Tulsa, Oklahoma.[85] He took the whole Peniel Choir to this event. Later in 2002, Reid published his doctoral thesis, "Strategic Level Spiritual Warfare: A Modern Mythology?," hereafter known as SLSW.[86] In May 2003, Reid was granted an honorary Doctor of Divinity degree by ORU in recognition of a lifetime of service to the Kingdom of God; he was sixty.[87] This academic emphasis by Reid persuaded many visitors to Peniel that Reid was qualified to teach. The College attracted students from other churches, further widening Peniel's sphere of influence.

5.13 Reid Made a Bishop

In 1996, Reid was made a bishop of the International Communion of Charismatic Churches in a ceremony hosted by Benson Idahosa in Benin City, Nigeria.[88] It ought to be noted at this point that Reid was consecrated as a bishop in a denomination with a very large world membership.[89] No one should underestimate the significance of this; according to the ICCC's

---

80. See "The History of Peniel Church—Part Four," 1 min 46 secs.

81. Ibid., 2 mins 03 secs.

82. Ibid., 4 mins 38 secs.

83. Ibid., 4 mins 44 secs.

84. Ibid., 5 mins 18 secs. To date I can find no evidence that Reid has completed this degree.

85. Ibid., 7 mins 50 secs.

86. See "The History of Peniel Church—Part Five," 0 mins 1 sec.

87. Ibid., 0 mins 40 secs.

88. See "The History of Peniel Church—Part Four," 2 mins 15secs.

89. See "letter from Archbishop David Huskins." Huskins, presiding bishop of the ICCC, confirms that Reid was consecrated by Idahosa.

website,⁹⁰ their episcopate was recognized by Pope Paul VI in 1978. The website history comments,

> the pope saw it as a gesture of genuine desire to identify with the historical church and he defended the actions of the three Pentecostals and called for McAlister and DuPlessis to be brought before him for commissioning as bishops of special recognition and rights thereby establishing them both as direct descendants of apostolic succession.

Robert McAlister consecrated Benson Idahosa, and Idahosa consecrated Reid. So Reid became, it seems, a genuine bishop in the apostolic succession. This was a significant part of Reid's public self-presentation and rhetoric. I must add that I can find no independent evidence that the Pope recognized McAlister and DuPlessis as bishops, however the photograph of McAlister, DuPlessis, and other Pentecostal leaders with Pope Paul VI and other Vatican leaders on I.C.C.C.'s website reveals there was a relationship. David DuPlessis was a key figure in ecumenical dialogue between Pentecostals and the Roman Catholics between the second Vatican council and his death in 1987.⁹¹

5.14 Faith Teaching in Reid's Books

An initial look at Reid's books, which are in the main simple, popular works,⁹² seems to reveal very little evidence of direct Word of Faith teaching. In SLSW, he does quote Kenyon on a number of occasions, so he is clearly aware of Kenyon's theology. However, a closer look reveals distinctive ideas about faith, some of which seem very much in line with Word of Faith teaching.

Some of his writing seems to suggest that miracles are brought about, not by a person's direct faith in God or Jesus Christ, but by having faith in God's faith.

For example, he writes,

> I don't look at the problem, I look at the wonderful source of all life—Jesus my Lord! In simplicity I lay myself at His feet and say,

---

90. See ICCC website.
91. See Gros, et al. *Growth in Agreement II*.
92. Except his published DMin thesis, which is a sophisticated critique of third wave charismatic Christianity.

"Lord, you are the source who never fails!" It's not my believing, it's His believing that creates life.[93]

It might well be asked, who or what is Jesus believing in? This quotation seems very much in line with the Faith teaching's denial of sensory reality, and that God's faith creates. Reid confirms his belief that God has faith when he describes a healing; he writes,

> She leapt to her feet and began to run across the front of the meeting hall, leaping and jumping and raising both arms above her head, as she shouted, "I'm healed, I'm healed, I'm healed!" God had come . . . she did not even have the faith to ask. But His faith performed the impossible. . . . When it's God's faith it works.[94]

Elsewhere he writes,

> So often we fight to muster up faith and like the disciples we fail miserably. People are told, "If you really believe for your healing, you'll be healed." But I say, Not so. Believe him who is able. Believe Him who believes. He never doubts. He never fears. He never loses faith. All things are possible to Him. All we have to do is believe in Him who can do everything. He is the Answer.[95]

Reid also seems to put belief in God's word before sensory reality; to Reid belief in the power of God's word transcends human experience:

> Very often, when God speaks a word to us we take it so lightly, we forget so easily. When circumstances seem to contradict it, we believe the circumstances rather than the living word of the living God. Disaster strikes and we abandon faith in the word that was given to us, the sure promise.[96]

Reid seems to suggest that a believer's personal faith is useless, when it comes to the miraculous. What Reid is asking people to do is to have faith in Christ's faith. Jesus believes on our behalf, that is, he has faith, he is a faith God. It appears that this idea of God having faith has come directly from Kenyon; Reid quotes him in SLSW. Kenyon writes, "He is not only in the Word, but He breathes His very life through it as it is unfolded . . . it is His word that gives birth to faith. . . . It is God's faith expressed."[97]

93. Reid, *Faith: It's God Given*, 31.
94. Ibid., 18–19.
95. Ibid., 39.
96. Ibid., 98.
97. Reid, SLSW, 276, quoting E. W. Kenyon, *New Creation Realities*, 6.

Denial of sensory reality is also taught by Reid. He writes, "In reality, the scriptures are the only measure by which to evaluate any spiritual experience; thus if the experience does not accord with the word, the experience is false."[98]

Reid also reveals his belief that spiritual laws exist alongside and distinct from natural laws, and writes,

> There are many who understand God's principles. Many who have learned that if you have faith in the principles they will operate just as they did for the centurion. God has set laws both in the natural and the spiritual realm and those laws are immutable. But causing laws to operate is very different from openly desiring to know Jesus for Himself.[99]

Reid is being critical of others here but he reveals his own belief in spiritual principles or laws.

He suggests that in order for miracles to occur, a person should look beyond the natural world: "The eyes of faith look beyond the natural realm with all its problems and impossibilities and are fixed on the One who cannot fail, the One whose name is Love."[100]

So Reid teaches that in order for miracles to occur, a person should have faith in Jesus/God's faith. As a consequence, he also teaches that if miracles do not occur in a church, then Jesus/God is not there and so the place cannot be a church. This in turn makes him seem to have a neo-Gnostic approach and to suggest that only his church and churches like it have the "secret."

For example, he writes,

> It is so important to get the best ministers gifted in the things of God to come and share with the people to plant eternal things in their lives . . . find "fathers in the faith" who have succeeded and proved their ministry . . . without that demonstration of power, we merely have another philosophy. What separates Christianity from everything else is that we have a Jesus who is alive and does miracles. I often tell people, "No miracles, no Jesus!" Wherever Jesus is, and the gospel is preached in the power of the Spirit, there will always be miracles. If you go to a church where you do not see miracles regularly, you have not really found a church yet.[101]

98. Ibid., 268.
99. Reid, *Faith: It's God Given*, 83.
100. Ibid., 97.
101. Reid, *What God Can Do for You*, 61.

He reiterates this throughout his books. "My desire wasn't to bring people into a religion but to bring them to Christ. The Church began with the simple occurrence of miracles because that's the way Jesus advertised his church. 'No miracles, . . . No Jesus!'"[102] Also, "I tell people, 'If you go to a church where you don't see miracles: blind eyes opening, deaf ears unstopping, cripples running, then you haven't found a church yet.' . . . [N]o miracles, . . . No Jesus."[103] And, "He spoke to me and said, 'You know what you don't want, now build what you do want.' . . . From the earliest meetings God did such beautiful miracles because wherever the gospel is preached miracles happen. No miracles, No Jesus!"[104]

Reid teaches that miracles only occur when Jesus is present in some special way. He writes,

> In the early years of my Christian life, I moved in power ministry. People in need would come and I prayed with them. Sometimes nothing I did worked. I tried in every possible way. I prayed, I struggled and I prayed again. I knew that God could do it, but I also knew that He wasn't doing it! There were other times when the miracles happened straightaway—because Jesus was there.[105]

Reid's teaching on right and wrong, or positive and negative, thinking is also remarkably similar to Word of Faith teachers in that he seems to suggest a person's problems are in his or her mind. He writes,

> Often when I hold seminars for pastors and church leaders, I ask them if they would like to get all their problems in the palm of their hand and just crush them to get rid of them. They always say, "Yes!" So I tell them to hold out their right hand in front of them and then put it on top of their heads. Their problems are between their ears![106]

He says that "so many sincere people become trapped in bondage because of ignorance or wrong teaching that leads to wrong thinking."[107]

Christ's work, according to Reid, was to destroy the works of the devil through positive thinking. "The Bible says that Jesus was manifested to destroy the works of the devil. He has come to turn the negatives into

---

102. Reid, *It's So Easy*, 45.
103. Ibid., 77.
104. Reid, *What God Can Do for You*, 36.
105. Reid, *Faith: It's God Given*, 36.
106. Reid, *What God Can Do for You*, 33.
107. Reid, *Strategic Level Spiritual Warfare*, 268.

positives."[108] Elsewhere, he writes, "So many people lack real faith and the ability to see beyond the present. They live with a defeatist attitude and think small."[109]

Alongside a low regard for the efficacy of human faith, Reid suggests that human effort and the commitment of a person's life has no value to God. He writes, "I tell people, 'He doesn't want your stinking life. He wants to give you His life.'"[110] He amplifies this when he says,

> One of the prevalent practices in evangelical circles is to ask people to come and "give their lives to the Lord," to "lay down their lives,"... and many other phrases which can only be interpreted as God needing us. People are told that you have natural gifts that God can use and God cannot accomplish His purposes without you. It all seems so right but unfortunately it is all so wrong. The emphasis on what I can do for God is very false.... Often in a meeting I will tell people, "God does not want your stinking life. You were born totally perverse and reprobate. The human heart is deceitfully wicked above all things. He doesn't want your heart." Then I pause. You can see the shock on people's faces. Only then do I qualify by saying, "He doesn't want your rotten life. He comes to give you His life. He wants you to be a partaker in his nature. Christ in you the hope of glory. It's not what you can do for God. It's what God has done for you!"[111]

In this teaching, he suggests that we can do nothing for God; he wants us to let go of human effort and become partakers of the divine nature. He writes,

> In the New Covenant we have better promises and a better hope. We not only have forgiveness of sins, but we have a transformed life when the power of the Holy Spirit comes within, to transform our natures; and we become partakers of the Divine nature.[112]

This might sound panentheistic, similar to Word of Faith and mind cure teachings originating in Swedenborg's ideas, where believers become "little gods" and in which man is deified.[113] Others, however, might argue

108. Reid, *What God Can Do For You*, 34.
109. Ibid., 57.
110. Ibid., 44.
111. Ibid., 49.
112. Ibid., 81.
113. See chapter 3 of this book. See also Hank Hanegraff, *Christianity in Crisis*, 107–27.

that there are overtones of what is regarded as the more orthodox doctrine of *theosis* here in Reid's teaching, which may well be the case. *Theosis* i.e. becoming divine transformed by Divine grace. Among revivalists *Theosis* as a doctrine developed distinctively direction among Wesleyan Methodists Methodists, and elsewhere in the holiness movement. This teaching sometimes implies the doctrine of *entire sanctification* which teaches that in becoming more and more like God that it is the Christian's goal, to live without any (voluntary) sin, i.e. *Christian perfectionism*.[114] It may be the case that Reid's distinctive teaching owes something to both his Word of Faith mentors and the more orthodox holiness movement.

Reid seems, as I have mentioned already, to have a tendency towards Gnosticism. He suggests that he knows the "secret" to spiritual success revealed in miracles, suspending the mind and drinking of the heavenly source. He writes,

> I've learned a secret—it's better not to ask questions, but to wait for Him. Pray, yes and wait until He comes. The miracle of life happens at the point when the living reality of His presence is there. Then we can drink of that heavenly Source—and that which seems impossible is done in a moment.[115]

Elsewhere, he suggests the "secret" is trusting in God's faith:

> That is the secret. It is His love and grace which reaches out. His faith can transform that which seems to be "unfathomable"! All we have to do is open our hearts to his coming. He does the rest.[116]

Reid also reveals an almost legalistic approach to his belief that God will perform according to perceived promises of his spoken words in Scripture. He writes, "The gospel is so simple, so sure, because it is based on the covenant word of our unchangeable God. The fact is that all God has promised He will perform."[117] He also says, "Many Christians have such a puny understanding of the power contained within the words which God speaks."[118]

This seems very similar to the idea of the power of the spoken word in Kenyon and Hagin's teachings. To Reid, God's spoken words in the

---

114. See Christensen "John Wesley."
115. Reid, *Faith: It's God Given*, 30.
116. Ibid., 88.
117. Ibid., 118.
118. Ibid., 91.

Scriptures have an eternal significance and can be applied to any situation. He writes,

> You know you can return to any word of promise which God speaks to you, again and again and again. The circumstances are irrelevant, the impossibilities don't matter at all because within each and every promise spoken by the Creator God is the power for an eternal work.[119]

Again here is a suggestion of denial of sensory reality. In Reid's teaching, God seems almost bound by a literalistic appeal to apparent "promises" in scripture: "He cannot deny His name and He cannot deny His word and He will fulfil his promises without fail." [120] These promises, according to Reid, can be applied to any need,

> When God speaks a word it has to be. Sometimes we find the circumstances seem to say it's impossible, it cannot be! But when God speaks it's impossible for it not to be! He is able to reach in and meet the deepest need of any life, whether physical or spiritual.[121]

In summary, Reid's teaching seems to have many of the marks of Word of Faith theology:

1. belief in a God who himself has faith;
2. the denial of sensory reality;
3. the importance of positive or right thinking over negative or wrong thinking;
4. an almost Gnostic suggestion that he is teaching "secrets" that others do not have;
5. a refusal to believe that human commitment and gifts have any significance compared to God's grace; and
6. a mechanistic approach to the promises of God in Scripture.

---

119. Ibid., 100.
120. Ibid., 101.
121. Ibid., 105.

5.15 Comment on Miracles

In this section, I want to examine videos of Reid's ministry to demonstrate distinctive practices that may have links with Word of Faith theology or nineteenth-century revivalism.

Much of what Michael Reid does and says as he prays for people to be healed, or reflects on their healing, reveals a distinctive theology and cultural influences. I will examine key examples from videos that are widely available on the internet, videos that are viewed by many before they seek the healing ministry of Dr. Reid. This is something that the Reids have realized attracts new people and in a way raises their faith.[122]

I will examine a series of video clips (which, perhaps, once were parts of one longer film) entitled *No Miracles No Jesus*. On the first video,[123] the commentator introduces the film by saying, "This remarkable church sees miracles every week, Peniel Pentecostal Church in Brentwood. Jesus Christ saves and heals today as he did 2,000 years ago. This film makes you a witness." It might be asked, a witness of what? The miracles are presented as evidence to anyone watching that Christ does indeed heal those who come to Peniel Church.

There is considerable disagreement whether miracles occur or not, both from without and within the worldwide church. Those who argue against the possibility tend to follow the arguments of Spinoza and Hume: for example, David Jenkins[124] from a liberal moral perspective, or B. B. Warfield[125] from a Reformed perspective. Others have found no evidence that any miracle can be shown to have occurred, for example, Peter May[126] and James Randi.[127] Others who critique Hume and come to different conclusions are J. Houston[128] and J. Rodman Williams.[129] To come to a conclusion on this is beyond the scope of this book, but a question that surely needs to be asked is how do these "miracles" compare with the miracles of the New Testament?

The comparison to the New Testament is striking. Jesus met sick people as he travelled along. Generally, people come to Peniel or one of

---

122. On a visit to Ilford Sports Centre, I talked to Dr. Ruth Reid about our daughter Sophia who suffers from ME. She helpfully suggested that I show Sophia the videos.

123. "No Miracles No Jesus—Part One."

124. Jenkins, *God, Miracle and the Church of England*.

125. Warfield, *Counterfeit Miracles*.

126. May, "The Faith Healing Claims of Morris Cerullo."

127. Randi, *The Faith Healers*.

128. Houston, *Reported Miracles: A Critique of Hume*.

129. Williams, *Renewal Theology*.

THE RHETORIC AND FAITH THEOLOGY OF MICHAEL REID 171

Reid's meetings; they come to him. In the videos of Peniel, "sick" people who arrived on two feet were offered wheelchairs.[130] This might give the impression that they are wheelchair-bound when they are just resting.

Most, if not all, of the miracles on Reid's websites are not miracles of compassion for the poor, as in the New Testament, but miracles for the middle-classes. Almost all of the sicknesses or conditions healed could be seen to be open to the suggestion that the sickness is somehow linked to the person's mind or psychological condition, and that Reid helps the person to somehow control their mind and therefore their body. What is happening is not the same as the New Testament exemplified in the miracles of Jesus.

The sort of illnesses that are healed are ME, rheumatism, arthritis, trapped nerves, and perceived back and walking problems. When objectively assessed these do not sound like any condition that Jesus healed, which were usually conditions that were a threat to life and livelihood.[131]

ME is still an illness in need of an explanation. Some suggest a virus; others suggest it is to do with digestion and so try special diets, alternative and Chinese medicine, and acupuncture; still others suggest it is to do with the mind so can be treated with cognitive therapy and hypnosis. Whatever it is, Reid seems to have a great deal of success with ME and similar debilitating illnesses.

5.16 Video Miracles

The videos on YouTube posted by Babypears,[132] and on Michael Reid's website,[133] give rich information on what sort of miracles took place at Peniel during Reid's years as Pastor. I have looked at seventeen of the miracles; I have detailed these in the Appendix. There are many more videos of Peniel on the internet, but these are perhaps among the most obvious to anyone looking. Some of the videos give more detail; often Reid's prayers can be heard, and what he does with each of the people can be clearly seen, so it is possible to discuss Reid's "methods."

---

130. This is clearly to be seen on some of the videos. This practice is widespread among faith healers—for example, Benny Hinn.

131. Percy, *Power and the Church*, 29–30.

132. A large number of videos concerning Michael Reid and Peniel can be found at http://www.youtube.com/user/BABYPEARS.

133. Miracle videos can be found at http://www.whatgodcandoministries.com/#/miracles.

The videos cover a significant time period from the late 1980s up to 2008 (Reid looks very much younger in some of them so they are possibly from the 1980s and early 1990s).

The miracles fall into two broad categories. First, those where the sick people suffer from issues that affect their mobility (their ability to walk, stretch or bend their body), or because they are weak: those suffering from ME, for example, or from arthritis, rheumatism, back problems or trapped nerves. The second are other problems: for example, arthritis in the hands, severe pancreatitis, a kidney stone, a blocked kidney tube, blindness (in the three cases I found, blindness in one eye only) and one example of terminal cancer.

Some of those who have come for prayer can be heard to say that they have seen miracles at the church before, or that they have seen videos of miracles online and have come for healing because of what they have seen. This is significant, because these videos are a form of performative rhetoric that causes people to believe they can be healed. The availability of these miracles on the internet in recent years has drawn others to seek out Reid's ministry.

Before I make further comment, it should be said that most of the people in the videos were in very real trouble when they went to Peniel, and all felt that they had been truly healed. I intend to group the miracles/sicknesses/injuries into types.

Three of the healings are people who went to Reid with ME (Myalgic Encephalomyelitis), otherwise known as CFS (Chronic fatigue syndrome).[134] These are Carol Groom,[135] Joan Wentworth[136] and Jo Wilkinson.[137] Although there is considerable debate in the medical community over the causes of ME, that is, whether it is psychological or linked with viral illness or both, there is no doubt that this condition is very real, and devastating, to the person concerned.

---

[134]. I understand there others who have been healed of this condition; the name Brian Hunt is mentioned in the video on Joan Wentworth. Brian had suffered with ME for seven years.

[135]. This incident is from "Jesus Heals the Sick—Part Two."

[136]. This video is entitled "No Miracles No Jesus—Part Two."

[137]. Found at a video entitled "Expect a Miracle—Part Two." 2 mins 12 secs.

5.17 Reflections on Reid's Healing Methods

5.17.1 Reid's Walking Talking (or Just Talking) Cure

In several of the videos, Reid walks the sick person back and forth on the carpet at the front of church in the full view of everyone in the congregation. As he walks, he talks persuasively to the person.[138] Probably the best example of this in the videos is the healing of Joan Wentworth (Appendix: Miracle B).

First Reid helps Joan out of her wheelchair.[139] There is incidental evidence in the videos that some people did not arrive in wheelchairs, for example, unnamed woman two (Appendix: Miracle F), who talks about walking into the church but is clearly in a wheelchair at the beginning of the video. Providing of wheelchairs for sick people, a common practice among Word of Faith teachers,[140] creates the illusion that they are worse that they actually are. It also creates the illusion that something miraculous is taking place when the person is lifted out of the wheelchair.[141]

Reid says to Joan, "Look at me," requesting her full attention; this reminded me of a hypnosis induction technique. Reid prays for Joan, during which a man is standing behind her in case she falls (being "slain the Spirit"). This is a common practice among charismatics, but could be a phenomenon that is socially constructed[142] or the result of suggestion. Whatever the case, the twentieth century "falling back" is somewhat different to the eighteenth century "falling down on faces."[143]

Reid does this walking up and down in several of the videos. In the healing of Carol Groom, Reid walks her up and down on the carpet, he asks her how her leg is feeling, and then he says, "I just want you to know, it's the end." He already told her at the beginning of her healing, "Ok, time for it to

---

138. In many of the videos, Reid tells the sick person that this is a special piece of carpet, reminding them that others have been healed in this way, and thus raising their faith.

139. In the healing of Carol Groom (Appendix: Miracle A), Reid helps her out of a lounger at the front. In the healing of unnamed woman two (Appendix: Miracle F), Reid helps her out of a wheelchair.

140. For example, this is a common practice at Benny Hinn missions. See the videos critiquing Hinn at http://topdocumentaryfilms.com/question-of-miracles-faith-healing.

141. Any of the healing videos show the sick people placed on the front row of the congregation at Peniel, often in a wheelchair or a lounger provided by the church.

142. People may feel pressure to fall back to please the preacher or their friends. In the past I have been pushed to fall backward by leaders.

143. Percy, *Power and the Church*, 37.

end." Idahosa says something similar, "It's done" in (Appendix: Miracle J). This could be a suggestive strategy. In the healing of unnamed woman one (Appendix: Miracle D), he walks her up and down, he tells her to kick her shoes off, he gets her to bend her knees right up. In the healing of unnamed woman two (Appendix: Miracle F), Reid walks her up and down, but she reminds him that she cannot bend—so he gets her to bend down and touch her toes. In Joan Wentworth's healing, and a number of others, he gets her to break into a jog and flex her arms over her body and in a circular motion, and to run up a flight of stairs in the hall. Flexing of the body seems to be a common element of the healing practice; for example, in the healing of Shân Brown (Appendix: Miracle I), Reid gets her to move her head from side to side; and in the healing of Merle (Appendix: Miracle J), Idahosa gets her to twist her body, something she could not do before the healing. All of this reminded me of the pragmatism of Charles Finney and his "new measures," that is, doing something to affirm God's activity.

5.17.2 Cursing, Exorcism, and Talking to the Sickness

Videos of Reid's healing ministry reveal that when praying for some sick individuals, he "curses" the sickness. In the healing of Claire of Reading, he talks to the problem (like Urquhart suggests). He says, "In the name of Jesus, I curse this foul affliction. You've no power to hold this woman bound anymore. Lord Jesus, release this back, release this body, Lord, break the tyranny of this disease in Jesus's name. Amen."

As well as talking to the problem or affliction with the words, "You've no power to hold this woman bound anymore," Reid curses the disease with the intention of causing it to wither. This is compared by those who employ this method to Jesus's cursing of the fig tree.[144] Reid uses this method on a number of occasions on videos and, therefore, I assume it was—and is—a regular practice. Other examples include the healing of:

1. Unnamed woman two, who has problems with her back and with walking (Appendix: Miracle F), where Reid prays, "Father, I just curse this foul disease in the name of Jesus which has [. . .] this body, in the name of Jesus, and break its power over this being. Lord, from this day I command life and liberty into this back and this spine. Lord, set her free in Jesus's name."

---

144. That is, by those who justify cursing disease!

2. Carol Groom with ME (Appendix: Miracle A). Reid prays, "I curse this filthy disease, I break your power over this life, in the name of Jesus. I command you from this day, you're going to release this body."

3. Joan Wentworth with ME (Appendix: Miracle B). Reid prays, "In the name of Jesus, I command you to come out of this body, come out of this body, come out of this body."

4. Jo Wilkinson with ME (Appendix: Miracle C).Reid prays, "I loose these fetters forever, come of your life, come off your body, come of your [. . .]"

5. A young woman with a blind eye (Appendix: Miracle K). Reid prays, "Father, I thank you that you came to open blind eyes. In the name of Jesus, I curse this affliction. Lord, cause life to come into this whole being."

6. Udmillah with cancer of the breast, lungs and spine (Appendix: Miracle Q). Reid says, "In the name of Jesus, I curse this disease. Lord, let that mighty healing power flow through every part of this being right now, go on, disease, you're going to go from this body, you're going to loose this woman completely, you've no power to hold her, hallelujah, hallelujah, hallelujah, that's the end of your disease, that's the end of your sickness. . . . Devil, you're gonna loose this right now in Jesus's name." He says to the congregation, "You know, sickness has a personality, the personality of the devil, it's destructive, Jesus came to make you whole."

When I first observed these prayers, I thought what a strange thing for a Christian preacher to do, to curse something. My mind instantly went to Romans 12:14 (NRSV): "Bless those who persecute you; bless and do not curse them." However, Reid is not cursing the person, but the disease.

Read speaks to the disease like Urquhart and Word of Faith healers. It could be that, in Reid's opinion, the ME is the result of an evil spirit that he seeks to exorcise, or that he just talks to the problem.

In trying to find others who used this method, I found a number of American preachers in the Word of Faith stream who do so.[145] But in terms of key figures in revivalist evangelicalism and the Word of Faith stream, I could find only two: William Branham and Smith Wigglesworth. Reid says

---

145. See for example, Eldridge, "Healing Confessions." The preacher says, "As Jesus cursed the fig tree and it withered, I curse, in the name of Jesus, the disease or sickness, and it shall also wither." There are many other examples of this among healing preachers.

that he studied the writings of Smith Wigglesworth, but does not mention Branham. However, there may be links to Branham and his methods. Reid's mentor, Benson Idahosa, studied at Christ for the Nations Institute, Dallas, Texas, in 1971. This college was founded in 1970 by James "Gordon" Lindsay, who was Branham's campaign manager in the 1940s. It may well be the case that Idahosa learned this practice from Lindsay and passed it on to Reid.

Another connection with Branham is Reid's first mentor, Demos Shakarian. Branham was a friend of Shakarian and helped him with his tent campaigns. For example, when Shakarian held meetings in Fresno, Branham was the evangelist for one week of his campaign.[146] Again, it may be the case that the young Michael Reid picked up this practice from Shakarian, who in turn learned it as he watched Branham healing in his campaigns.

Examples of Branham's practice of cursing sickness can be found in his sermons, many of which are available on the internet both as mp3s and in transcription. For example, at the end of his sermon *Elijah and Elisha*,[147] Branham prays for someone, a "lady," who cannot speak English, who has kidney trouble. He says, "Heavenly Father, I cursed this disease with this stomach, and may she be made well in Christ's name."[148] Another example is in Branham's sermon *Faith Without Works is Dead*,[149] where he prays for a woman who is hard of hearing. He says, "Almighty God, author of life, giver of every good gift, bless this woman. I curse this disease, this deaf spirit. Leave her in the name of Jesus Christ."[150]

Smith Wigglesworth's sermons are also available in books and online; he, too, curses sickness. An example is found in his book *Ever Increasing Faith*.[151] Wigglesworth tells of an incident when he was in Bergen, Norway. A young woman, who had a big cancer growth on her nose, came out for prayer; he asked her what her condition was and she said, "I dare not touch my nose, it gives me so much pain." Wigglesworth said to the congregation, "I want you to look at this nurse and notice her terrible condition. . . . I am going to curse this disease in the all powerful name of Jesus. . . . I laid my

---

146. Shakarian, *The Happiest People on Earth*, 122.
147. Branham, *Elijah and Elisha*.
148. Ibid., section E-73 of the Sermon.
149. Branham, *Faith Without Works is Dead*.
150. Ibid., section E-52 of the sermon.
151. Wigglesworth, *Ever Increasing Faith*. Also found in the sermon *The Words of this Life*.

hands on the nose of that suffering nurse and cursed the evil power that was causing her such distress."[152]

5.17.3 Congregational Participation

When Reid prays for the unnamed woman who has problems with her back and with walking (Appendix: Miracle F), many in the congregation raise their hands in prayer and blessing. When Darren Smith is healed (Appendix: Miracle L), Reid tells the congregation to give God a clap offering. There is a sense here that those prayed for are in an atmosphere, an occasion where the public are with them, an environment of social expectation of healing. The raising of hands reminded me of the gathered clergy raising their hands during the ordination of priests.[153]

5.17.4 People Responding to Publicity

Unnamed woman 2 (Appendix: Miracle F) tells Reid during her healing that she has seen the film (meaning the videos of healings). Janet Wragg says on the video about her healing (Appendix: Miracle H) that "Something said to me, you've got the Peniel newspaper (*The Trumpet Call*), so I got up and went." In the healing of John (Appendix: Miracle P), John's wife, Lilly, says that she used to say lots of prayers that John would be healed but nothing happened. But when she saw the *Trumpet Call*, she thought this might be the answer. It seems both the internet films and the church newspaper were a wider public form of rhetoric, encouraging people to believe in Reid's miracle ministry.

5.18 Conclusions

There are a number of reasons why Reid's ministry over the years has been persuasive. First of all, we would have to point to who Reid is as a person. To many who meet him, particularly the sick, he is charming and compassionate. However, it is not his personality that caused people to stay with the

---

152. Ibid., 61.

153. At many Anglican ordinations the robed priests present will either lay hands on the ordination candidates or raise their hands towards the person being ordained. Their silent prayer is that God will bless the person being ordained. In a similar way the congregation at Peniel prayed with their hands raised towards individuals seeking healing.

church when they felt he had abused them. It was the success of the church, a church in which Reid had led them to invest. It was their spiritual and social home, a place of security that provided many of their needs, such as the elite school for their children and activities like the Peniel Choir. Reid himself was viewed, in some ways, as an ordinary family man but one who had experienced the harsher side of life during his time in the Metropolitan Police. A number of factors made his ministry attractive. Good examples are his conversion and early mentoring by Demos Shakarian and his encounter with Nicki Cruz, and the support throughout his ministry from his very capable wife. Also, the fact that the church was run in a business-like way, a factor that would have been very attractive to those committed to capitalist values. The church that Reid built was well publicized and made attractive by its multimedia presentation of its message. Reid's standing was enhanced by the fame and high profile of his mentors in world charismatic circles. His credibility was enhanced by his higher academic qualifications and his published writings, which was further enhanced when he was made a bishop. Finally, the miracles in Reid's ministry seemed to work; this suited the pragmatic people who wanted a religion with results. Many people came to the church with deep perceived needs, which Reid met with his miracle ministry and his persuasive rhetorical skills and use of suggestion.

CHAPTER 6

The Rhetoric and Faith Theology of Jerry Savelle

6.1 Introduction

Unlike my two previous case studies, Jerry Savelle is an American. As a key ministry associate of Kenneth Copeland, Savelle represents typical Word of Faith teaching and practice. Like my two English case studies, he has an international ministry working in countries across the world. Over the years, the UK has been a significant part of this international ministry, having offices in the UK.[1]

My first encounter with the ministry of Jerry Savelle was in 2005, when I was given a tape of his preaching by a former member of the King's Church in Medway who was a spiritual refugee at the Anglican Church of which I was Vicar. As I listened to the tape, it became clear that Savelle had a significant influence on the thinking and teaching of the King's Church leader, Grant Gill. Before a visit to hear Savelle preach at Hillsongs church in London during 2007, it became apparent[2] that he has a large following in key independent Pentecostal churches in the UK.[3] In 2012, he was due to preach at a number of growing churches in London and South Wales.[4]

---

1. See "Details of Savelle's international offices." Savelle's European headquarters are in Chepstow, Monmouthshire, Wales.

2. When researching his preaching dates in the UK.

3. The leader of Hillsongs in London said, as he introduced Savelle to a congregation of approximately 3,000 at the Dominion Theatre, that Savelle had been a key influence in his life. This would also be true of a number of other leading Pentecostals in the UK. Savelle has since revisited Hillsongs in London on at least one occasion. See "Savelle's visit to Hillsongs, London on 13th September 2009."

4. I was informed of these venues in a flyer from his UK offices, which were sent

Although Savelle's teaching reveals that he believes in healing miracles, his major focus is the area of prosperity. Like Urquhart, Savelle is a "storytelling man," using many little stories, illustrations and insights into his experience to frame his message. Like Urquhart, Savelle uses stories from his own personal experiences to convince those listening, watching or reading that if something can work for him, it can also work for them. While Reid, at the height of his ministry, depended heavily on the public visual presentation of miraculous healings, Savelle has presented his message verbally through public preaching, books, tapes, CDs, internet videos, and so on. Most of his illustrative stories are those of God's provision of money, property or possessions. I use some significant points from the two talks he gave at King's Church, Medway, in 1999.[5] Throughout the tape of these addresses, Pastor Grant Gill (who I know personally) can be heard in the background saying "yes" in agreement as each point is made. Savelle uses much repetition for rhetorical effect. I will add further material from his webcasts and books to reveal the internal consistency of his teaching.

As with Urquhart and Reid, in this chapter I will focus on Savelle's performative rhetoric and examine the key interpretive principles at the heart of his teaching.

Also, like Urquhart and Reid, a huge part of the attractiveness of Savelle is his background, his family and his respectability, as I will now describe.

6.2 Savelle's Self-Presentation

Jerry Savelle was brought up in a devout Southern Baptist family, initially in Vicksburg, Mississippi,[6] and then from five years of age in Shreveport, Louisiana.[7] He tells of how his family and church taught him the Christian faith and how, as a teenager, he was "saved" and baptized in water.[8] However, his faith waned when he went off to college in 1964, and he started smoking and drinking.[9] Savelle tells his life story with considerable humor: of how he was an ordinary man who did not want to be religious, but how his life changed,

---

me as a "mission partner" because I had a bought a book from his website. The venues were 1) 18th March: Destiny Christian Centre, London; 2) 19th March: Cornerstone Church, London; 3) 21st March: Newport City Church, South Wales; 4) 22nd March: London Miracle Centre, London; and 5) 23rd March: Praise Chapel, London.

5. Savelle, tape of sermon at King's Church, Medway, Bible week 8th November 1999.

6. Savelle, *Receive God's Best*, 13.

7. Ibid.

8. Ibid., 15.

9. Ibid., 19.

influenced by his wife Carolyn, his future mentor Kenneth Copeland, and his belief that God had taken hold of his life for a purpose.

In the early years of his marriage, it became apparent that while everything in Carolyn's life revolved around church, all that Savelle wanted to do was fulfill his ambition of having his own car paint and body shop, and to race cars. He says, "That's what I lived for."[10] He did not want to meet the latest preacher from the church; he says that when he got home from his garage, "All I wanted to do was to take a shower, put on a clean "Jerry's Paint and Body Shop" uniform and watch TV."[11] In those days, Savelle was a keen drag racer: "I had a 1965 Pontiac GTO, 389" that he describes as a "hot rod."[12]

An essential element of Savelle's life rhetoric is his passion for motorcycles and classic cars. He starts one of his *Chariots of Light* TV shows[13] with scenes of him dusting a beautiful old red sports car (a 1961 Chevrolet Corvette) and then driving it around. He says,

> You know I've been a car enthusiast and motorcycle enthusiast all my life. I grew up around this. My dad was a hot rodder and that was my passion before coming to Christ, before going into the ministry. And now God's allowed me to turn this into a tool of evangelism. When I was growing up I always wanted a Corvette. My dad worked on Corvettes and he just couldn't afford to buy me one. But I always wanted one. I always said, you know when I grow up I'm going to be a Corvette man. Well, I drive new Corvettes and I have for many years but I still love these old ones. This is a '61 and God's been so good to me, he has blessed me, he caused every dream I've ever had to be fulfilled. That's why I want to talk to you about how to receive God's best.[14]

6.3 Savelle's Appeal

Savelle's subsequent spiritual transformation, and working for (and then in partnership with) Kenneth Copeland, have been affected by his love of motorcycles and cars, so much so that a large part of his worldwide ministry runs around his Christian motorcycle and classic car club called Chariots

---

10. Savelle, *In the Footsteps of a Prophet*, 26.
11. Ibid., 30.
12. Ibid.
13. "Chariots of Light broadcast 044."
14. Ibid., 1 min 20 secs–2mins 20secs. The book *Receive God's Best* is a condensation of material from these TV shows.

of Light. Many of his TV shows that I have recorded streamed from the internet are simply called *Chariots of Light*. In these broadcasts, Savelle talks about his love of bikes and classic cars, and at the same time preaches that God has apparently given him the prosperity to indulge his passion. This sort of presentation is highly attractive to those, both male and female, who are keen on bikes and cars, and those drawn to a pragmatic and materialist American culture. In many of the videos, Jerry is pictured with his classic cars and high-powered touring bikes, and he can be seen going on motorcycle preaching tours with various chapters of the Chariots of Light club. He is every bit a man's man, making friends through his shows with all sorts of people who might not be initially interested in his religion. In his other shows, and in preaching in churches, Savelle presents as a prosperous business-like preacher, wearing either fine suits, or broadcasting from his lovely home. He seems, on all levels, to be a successful man.

6.4 Early Influences of His Future Wife

A significant story in Savelle's autobiography,[15] in a chapter entitled "The Girl Who Changed Everything," is how he met his wife Carolyn, and the impact she had on his life and faith. This is a significant part of Savelle's self-presentation. His wife, as we shall see, effectively led him into God's purposes for his life. She was the one who was brought up in a family influenced by Word of Faith theology. She grew up attending the revivals of Oral Roberts, T. L. Osborn and William Branham.[16] She would be his future partner in ministry (that is, other than Copeland). It is unlikely that Savelle would have encountered Word of Faith teaching at any serious level if it had not been for his relationship with Carolyn. His later sharing of ministry with her, and later their daughter Terri Savelle-Foy, communicates that Savelle has a stable and happy family life. His anecdotes about their life together and the enjoyment and fun he seems to have all contribute to his apparent trustworthiness.

Virtually all of the preachers in this stream of the church seem to make their wives pastors: for example, Kenneth and Gloria Copeland (and in Chatham, Grant and Philippa Gill). They also tend to create a spiritual dynasty—usually a son, but in the case of Savelle, a daughter is gradually introduced as a leader in the ministry to take it over when the father retires.[17] This practice has been embraced by Urquhart, as we saw in chapter 4.

15. Savelle, *In the Footsteps of a Prophet*.
16. Ibid., 39.
17. In this case, it is Terri Savelle-Foy. Savelle-Foy now has her own ministry and

The story of how they came to be together presents, to anyone reading, that God is in control and can make a success out of anyone. One year after graduation from high school, Savelle returned to Shreveport for a weekend reunion with some friends. He was cleaning his 1957 Chevy at a carwash when he recognized a girl he had grown up with, Carolyn Screech. He talked with her because he remembered her from school. She left in her car and he followed her; they turned left into a sideroad and she said, "Are you following me?" She was going to a prayer meeting at a friend's house and invited him. He did not want to do that, so they went for a milkshake instead. She told him that she was "filled with the Holy Ghost when she was eight years old, and she had a vision and a call from God that she was going to preach the gospel. She said as soon as she got out of high school, she was going to Bible school in San Antonio, Texas." Then she said, "And I'm going to marry a man who is born again and filled with the Holy Ghost, called to preach, and we'll go to Africa."[18] Savelle comments that his first thought was "I will never turn left again as long as I live!" He could not wait to get rid of her and went to meet his friends at a bar. However, he could not get her out of his mind. He started to go out with Carolyn, but found that his new student lifestyle of drinking, swearing, smoking and dancing were challenged by Carolyn, who told him that he was not brought up like that and his parents were not like that. He did not want to be with her because all she would talk about were spiritual things. However, he could not stay away from her and found himself skipping college classes in order to be with her.

On one of their dates, she took him to a Pentecostal youth revival, where there was speaking in tongues and casting out of devils; it was loud. He says, "I liked my Baptist church. It was quiet. Only one person prayed at a time. Nobody lifted their hands."[19]

In May 1966, they were engaged to be married. She reminded him that she had made a promise to God when she "got filled with the Holy Ghost, that the man I marry will be born again, filled with the Holy Ghost, preach the Gospel and go to Africa." He replied, "You're marrying the wrong man." She replied, "No, you're *it*. The first time I ever saw you . . . you were eleven years old . . . I told my mother, 'Mom, there's the boy I will marry.'"[20] Savelle comments, "I loved her. I knew I loved her and I wanted to be with her. I just thought, Well, I'll go ahead and marry her, and I can talk her out

---

website. See "Terri."

18. Savelle, *In the Footsteps of a Prophet*, 20–21.

19. Ibid., 22–25.

20. Ibid., 26.

of all this 'preaching' stuff later."[21] In the early years of their marriage, he was somewhat resentful of Carolyn apparently giving their money away to preachers and preparing meals for them. However, that all changed because of two significant events in his life.[22]

6.5 Conversion and Calling

As a young man, Savelle had made a profession of faith in Jesus and been baptized in his home church in Shreveport.[23] He seems to have strayed significantly from this during his college years, becoming a regular gambler, smoker, and drinker.[24] However, sometime after his marriage, he records that on February 11th 1969, he was baptized in the Holy Ghost and called to the ministry. Carolyn had persuaded him to go to hear a preacher called Brian Rudd, a Canadian and former drug addict and dealer who had been converted in prison. She managed to persuade Savelle not to go in one of his paint and body shop uniforms and to leave his cigarettes in the car.[25]

During the meeting, as Rudd was speaking, he said, "There is somebody in this room tonight that's going to get delivered of smoking." He got off the platform and walked up to Savelle and said, "Tonight is your night, young man, to be delivered from smoking."

The rest of his story illustrates Savelle's present-day beliefs about the power of words. Rudd asked Savelle if he had his cigarettes. He said, "No. She wouldn't let me bring them in."[26] Rudd found someone else in the room who smoked the same brand as Savelle, gave him the package and told him to take them out, break them in half and throw them on the floor. Rudd then told him to "point at them and say, 'In the name of Jesus, I have authority over you, and I'll never smoke again.'"[27] He told Savelle that he was delivered. Savelle went to sit down, but Rudd called him back and told him that he was called to preach. Savelle was not convinced. Authority over life events and circumstances is a gift from God that Faith teachers suggest all people of true faith should have.[28]

---

21. Ibid.
22. Ibid., 29–32.
23. Ibid., 14–15.
24. Ibid., 19.
25. Ibid., 33.
26. Ibid., 35.
27. Ibid.
28. For example, Hagin, *The Believer's Authority*.

The following day at work he was strongly tempted to smoke. He also reflected on the suggestion from Rudd that he was called to preach. He thought, "I was doing what I wanted to do, working on cars, building hot rods, racing. This preaching's going to foul up everything . . . I fought it with everything that was in me."

He continues the story by saying there was a young man at Rudd's meeting who had been delivered from drug addiction. He knew this person and saw the change in his life. On February 11th 1969, the young man came up to Savelle in his works yard and shared his testimony with him. Savelle acknowledged the difference in his life. He says, "I couldn't deny this miracle that was standing right in front of me. I knew it was real." Savelle went home, went to bed, but he could not sleep. At three o'clock in the morning, he finally said to God, "I heard you call me into the ministry when I was eleven years old in my grandmother's home in Oklahoma City. I've run from you, and I have fought this most of my life. I don't know if you still want me or even need me. But if you do here I am." He continues, "I lifted both hands and said, 'Jesus, come into my life. I surrender it to You.'" He then spoke in tongues for four hours.[29]

6.6 Savelle's Encounter with Copeland

The second significant event came soon afterwards, his first encounter with Kenneth Copeland. Carolyn had been to hear him preach on successive nights at Life Tabernacle in their hometown. Each night, she came home and made statements such as, "Jerry, I've grown up with this all my life, but I've never heard the Word preached like this before." She arranged for Savelle to meet Copeland at her parent's house. Carolyn's father introduced him to Copeland. The first thing Copeland said to him was "God is going to prosper you beyond your widest imaginations." Immediately, without another word, Copeland returned to his bedroom. Savelle was left thinking that Carolyn must have told him about his business and his debts. Then he thought perhaps she had not and that God was speaking through him, telling him that he was going to prosper and would not have to go into the ministry. Savelle writes, "I had never associated prosperity with preaching."[30]

He went with Carolyn to the service that night and was immediately brought to attention by Copeland, who was picking the verses of a song apart and showing the congregation how they did not "line up with the Word of

---

29. Savelle, *In the Footsteps of a Prophet*, 37.
30. Ibid., 41.

God."[31] Savelle describes the sermon that followed as "[t]he message that changed my life." Copeland simply gave it the title "The Word of Faith."[32]

Savelle writes, "I went home with a new outlook." The following day, he went into work and sent his helpers home. He went into his office and locked the door; he searched the Bible all day trying to find the scriptures that Copeland had used the night before.[33] (As we shall see, Savelle's theology revolves around the interpretation of key biblical texts through Word of Faith principles.)

Savelle felt that he was a complete failure. He asked God what he could do with a failure, and heard God say, "Son, don't worry. I am a Master at making champions out of failures." Savelle continues, "by the end of the day I was a new man." He regretted not hearing everything that Copeland has said. The following day a friend of Carolyn brought him seven reel tapes of the Copeland meetings and a huge tape player.[34] Savelle took notes and outlined every sermon. He says, "I wrote down the key points that Brother Copeland made in his messages, and then I would endeavor to put them to work in my own life."[35]

6.7 Savelle's Ministry

Sometime later in 1969, Copeland returned to Shreveport. During one of his talks, he got Savelle to stand up and said, "God showed me that you and I will be a team and we'll spend the rest of our lives preaching the gospel around the world together. It will be your responsibility to believe God for the perfect time for the team to begin."[36]

Nine months later, he went to work for Copeland. After a couple of years, he felt led by the Spirit of God to launch his own ministry. He felt worried that this would mean the team splitting up, but believed that God had said to him, "No, the team will not split up; the team will cover twice as much territory with the same message." Savelle continues, "I said, Okay Lord, if that's what you want, but I am not making one move until you reveal it to Brother Copeland, and he brings it up in conversation."[37]

---

31. Ibid., 43.
32. Ibid., 45.
33. Ibid., 46.
34. Ibid., 47.
35. Ibid., 48.
36. Savelle, *Receive God's Best*, 41–42.
37. Ibid., 42.

Sometime later, in October 1973, Copeland asked him, "When are you leaving and going into your own ministry?" Savelle told Copeland that he was supposed to work for him until December 31st that year and then, on January 1st 1974, launch out into his own ministry.[38] Copeland said, "I know some pastors that would love to have you and when we get back home, I'll start writing some letters and call and tell people that you're out in your own ministry."[39] Savelle replied, "Excuse me sir, I really appreciate that, but please don't. He said, Why not?" Savelle said, "Because I don't want to spend the rest of my life wondering if it was only through Kenneth Copeland's influence that got me meetings." He continues,

> Brother Copeland, I have raised my hand to God. He's my source of supply and I'm asking God to honor his Word that says my gift will make room for me. If God's put a gift in me for the body of Christ then that gift has got to make room for me . . . I've got to know that God is my source.[40]

This response displays, to those listening and reading, Savelle's honorable nature and his trust in God. He worked for Copeland for five years or so until January 1st 1974.[41] Savelle writes,

> I walked into my fully furnished office on January 1st. That very day I got a phone call from a businessman in Georgia. . . . Did you catch that he was a businessman not a preacher, not a pastor. During those two weeks that I was in Georgia, I booked meetings for the next six months![42]

In fact, we discover in another book[43] that this businessman was none other than Charles Capps, who, although a businessman (a farmer), had already started a Word of Faith preaching ministry of his own. Capps is now a preacher and author who teaches positive confession exactly like Savelle.[44]

Savelle observes,

> Now, 37 years later, I have never had to ask for a place to preach. I can't even go to all the places that I am invited to preach. I

---

38. Ibid., 43.
39. Ibid.
40. Ibid., 43–44.
41. Ibid., 43.
42. Ibid., 44.
43. Savelle, *In the Footsteps of a Prophet*, 258–59.
44. See, for example, Capps, *Faith and Confession*.

can truly say that no man made Jerry Savelle a success in the ministry but Almighty God.[45]

6.8 Ministry Run like a Business

From the beginning, Savelle's ministry seems to have been run like a business, with his own fully furnished office and meeting set up by the businessman, Charles Capps.

Many of his practices and choices give the impression of business-like behavior. For example, if anyone buys a book (or anything) from his website, he or she becomes a ministry partner and receives Savelle's newsletter with his or her own number and Savelle's glossy magazine, *Adventures in Faith*. Savelle's hope is that, encouraged by his teaching, people will sow money into his ministry.

This reminds me so much of my wife's brief experiences with the pyramid selling practices of Kleeneze in the mid-1990s. Despite being a trained nurse, my wife wanted to work at home, because of our small children. So she signed up to have a Kleeneze franchise, selling their household products. New Kleeneze representatives had to sign up through someone else who was already in Kleeneze, and part of their profit was paid to them. If they, in turn, recruited people, part of their profit was paid to them. The more people they recruited, the more profit they made. Kleeneze held area and national meetings, where successful Kleeneze sellers gave motivational talks on success, telling their stories about how their lifestyle had been transformed beyond their wildest dreams—quite like the stories of Savelle. For successful Kleeneze franchise holders, there were rewards of luxury cruises that doubled as business meetings, all paid for by the company. At one seminar, a highly successful Kleeneze area leader showed photographs of the brand new luxury house he was having built. His comment was, "If I can do it, so can you." That is, unfortunately, only possible for a few. People who try soon find there is a limit to how many people they can recruit who will pass on profit to them.

Savelle, as a successful Faith preacher, has now introduced his daughter, Terri Savelle-Foy, to his ministry. She often appears in his TV shows and videos, and has recently written her own books. She is working for her dad and seems a natural successor to him. Interestingly, in the UK, Colin Urquhart has introduced his son, Clive, into his Kingdom Faith ministry, and Clive has now taken over as the official leader.

---

45. Savelle, *Receive God's Best*, 45.

Businesses passed on through families are, of course, a common feature of capitalism. For example, I recently internet-searched someone I know who I thought was a car salesman to find out from his website that he was the managing director. The large car business was originally set up in 1947 by his father. In the late 1960s, my friend and his brother went to work as salesmen for the business. When their father retired, they took over as joint managing directors. Now my friend's nephew is working as a car salesman for the same business. Presumably one day he will take over the business.

These practices are just examples of how Savelle's ministry is run like a pyramid selling business. This sort of success story may well be appealing to those who think that God blesses late-capitalist practices.

6.9 Savelle's Mentors

Jerry Savelle was originally inspired by and is a devoted disciple and imitator of Kenneth Copeland.[46] Copeland was, in turn, influenced by a tape of Kenneth Hagin in 1967 and holds many of the same teachings as Hagin, but with an emphasis on prosperity.[47] Hagin himself is recognized by many as the "father of the Faith Movement," who throughout the 1970s popularized the teaching of positive confession.[48] As Dan McConnell writes, "The founding father of the Faith Movement is commonly held to be Kenneth Erwin Hagin, the man termed by *Charisma* magazine as, 'the granddaddy of the Faith teachers' and, 'the father of the Faith Movement.'"[49] Andrew Walker, Nigel Wright, and Tom Smail recognize that Hagin, Copeland, and Fred Price were the acknowledged leaders of the Faith Movement at the time of writing *The Love of Power or the Power of Love* in 1994. They also recognize there are "strong echos" of the Faith teaching in Britain in the so-called new churches and in the ministry of evangelists such as Don Double and Colin Urquhart.[50] Walker, Wright, and Smail acknowledge their indebtedness to D. R. McConnell and his book *A Different Gospel*[51] for their understanding of Hagin and his revelation knowledge.[52]

---

46. But see also Hummel, *Fire in the Fireplace*, 222, and Hanegraff, *Christianity in Crisis*, 37.
47. Hummel, *Fire in the Fireplace*, 221.
48. Ibid.
49. McConnell, *A Different Gospel*, 3.
50. Smail et al., *The Love of Power or the Power of Love*, 75.
51. McConnell, *A Different Gospel*.
52. Smail, et al., *The Love of Power or the Power of Love*, 79.

6.10 Publicity

Jerry Savelle's publicity is of the highest quality. His website (jerrysavelle.org) gives details of his international offices and pages to purchase his books and DVDs, and to stream his TV shows. His magazine *Adventures in Faith*, which is distributed to anyone who shows an interest, is a quality product. This magazine has large glossy photos of the Savelles demonstrating their wealthy lifestyle and Jerry's success. The website and the magazine are examples of performative rhetoric at its best.

6.11 Savelle's Theology

6.11.1 Study

Savelle started studying the Scriptures aided by tapes of Copeland right from the beginning. He has no earned academic theological qualifications, although he is called "Dr. Savelle" by himself and by others.[53] His early study and apprentice-like working for Copeland could be seen as a "degree" in the theology of Word of Faith.

In his sermon at King's Church, Medway, he describes his early encounter with Copeland. His experience of Copeland's preaching caused him to immediately, the following day, study the Bible himself. He said, "I wanted to read it for myself and see if he said it the way the Bible said it." After a struggle, he surrendered his life to God. He said,

> I was filled with the Holy Spirit, answered the call of God, and it became my quest immediately not to become religious but to find out the knowledge of God; to understand the principles that God had written in his word that man could live by and prove that it could work because that's what I saw Kenneth Copeland doing.[54]

Here, Savelle demonstrates that he picked up the idea of "the knowledge of God," otherwise known as "revelation knowledge," from Copeland. This knowledge consists of principles that, if applied by believers, can work,

---

53. See "Biographical page" and Savelle, "One of Savelle's visits to London in 2012." Savelle is on the executive committee of Oral Roberts University and presumably has an honorary doctorate from that institution as most of the others seem to. See "Savelle a 'Regent' of Oral Roberts University and on Its Executive Committee."

54. Savelle, tape of sermon at King's Church, Medway, Bible week 8th November 1999.

resulting in prosperity and health. As such, they are an example of pragmatic religion.

Following on from Copeland, Hagin, and ultimately Kenyon, Savelle clearly believes and teaches that following spiritual laws can bring prosperity and health. Jerry Savelle's theology is very simple, with similar and often identical basic points made in each book, talk and broadcast that he gives. He presents these ideas with a variety of personal anecdotes and observations for rhetorical effect.

6.11.2 Success is Achieved by Control of the Mind

Savelle claims that Christians in general today are limiting God by what he describes as "small thinking."[55] Success in Savelle's theology is about prosperity and, to a small extent, healing, and is achieved by "thinking big" and positively rather than negatively.

Savelle teaches that these limited, small-thinking Christians need a revelation of God's Word to change their thinking so they think like God and think God's thoughts.

This revelation of God's Word is made by anointed men of God who teach revelation knowledge, which, from what Savelle believes, is a Spirit-led interpretation of the Scriptures. These preachers preach with power; they are not religious but different, like Christ. Savelle argues that every time Jesus healed, people thought bigger thoughts, and their possibility levels were raised. The revelation these anointed Faith preachers preach consists of "principles God has written in his word, his book, for men to live by."[56]

At the heart of Savelle's strategy for success is the need for the believer to choose to believe and do God's word. However, the believer is asked to believe and act upon the scriptures interpreted through the principles or laws of positive confession.

6.11.3 Priority of God's Word

At the very beginning of Savelle's ministry, he resolved to put the Word of God first. He writes, "I told the Lord I was going to get up in the morning at 6 o'clock to spend the first hour of my day in the Word. I was serious."[57] To Savelle, belief in "the Word" is of primary importance; he writes, "The Word

---

55. Ibid.
56. Ibid.
57. Savelle, *Receive God's Best*, 21.

says that with God all things are possible. You just have to choose to believe his Word and choose to do his Word. If you do that, then He will take care of the rest."[58] To most Christians, this would be highly commendable; but it should be realized that Savelle's study of the Scriptures was molded significantly by the teaching of Kenneth Copeland. Savelle's theology revolves around the interpretation of key texts through Word of Faith principles.

6.11.4 Preaching with Power

In Savelle's sermon at King's Church, Medway, he refers to Luke 4: where Jesus is teaching in Capernaum. He points to 4:32: "And they were astonished at his doctrine: for his word was with power," and concludes that they had not heard teaching like this before. He continues by likening this astonishment to the experience of his wife, Carolyn, and himself of the preaching and ministry of Kenneth Copeland. Savelle says, "I heard the gospel like I'd never heard it before, and I was astonished because his word was with power."[59] The listener is left with the impression that Copeland is almost on a level with Christ, certainly as far as Savelle is concerned. He views Copeland as a prophet, as is clear from his book *In the Footsteps of a Prophet*.[60]

6.11.5 Determined Positive Thinking

Savelle teaches that material wealth and physical well-being result from positive thinking and claiming God's promises as he perceives them.

For Savelle, the first step to success is to "believe that God wants you to have His best,"[61] and then "to decide you truly want it."[62] At the beginning of a series of televised talks entitled "How to Receive God's Best," he says,

> You have to make the decision, if you're gonna have God's best, you have to decide. As for me, I'm gonna have it and Satan is not gonna stop me. I'm telling you now, when you make this decision you've gotta be unwavering, you've gotta be firm, you've

---

58. Ibid., 10.

59. Savelle, tape of sermon at King's Church, Medway, Bible week 8th November 1999.

60. Savelle, *In the Footsteps of a Prophet*.

61. Savelle, *Receive God's Best*, 15.

62. Ibid.

gotta be serious. You can't play church with this and expect to have God's best. You have to make a firm decision.[63]

The power is totally in the believer's hands; Savelle writes, "My point is this, if you want to have God's best, then it's up to you. You must make the choice. Nobody else can do it for you, not even God."[64] He adds, "God leaves the choice up to you. He has already made His decision. Now, you just have to make your decision. Do you choose to have God's best?"[65] He recommends visualizing this thought as often as possible. He says, "put on a card "as for me, I choose to have God's best in my life." Place it on the refrigerator door, the dash of your car, on your mirror the office or wherever you can see it often."[66]

This sort of attitude is very similar to the thinking of Norman Vincent Peale, who, for example, wrote, "One thing every one must learn is how to have what it takes to take it—and better still overcome."[67] Being an overcomer or winner or big thinker is stressed by Savelle and other Faith teachers.[68]

Savelle's teaching is full of motivational material; for example, "Say 'I'm a winner, I'm called to win, it's my destiny.' God has called you to be a winner in life. No one is interested in following a loser."[69] Ultimately, success all depends on a person's attitude. Savelle says, "my motto became—If it is to be, then it is up to me."[70] Savelle (and other Faith teachers) often use mottos like this to make their interpretive principles more memorable; as such, they are significant rhetorical devices.

According to Savelle, most Christian believers need to have their mind changed. The remedy for this negativity, he suggests, is "a revelation of God's

---

63. "Chariots of light broadcast 044."
64. Savelle, *Receive God's Best*, 17.
65. Ibid., 19.
66. Ibid., 21–22.
67. Peale, *Positive Thinking for a Time Like This*. This is a revision and condensation of *The Tough Minded Optimist* by the same author.
68. For example, the song that introduces the webcasts of Joel Osteen (a young rising star among American Faith teachers) says this: "You're an overcomer, more than a conqueror today, discover the champion in you." See "Osteen Webpage." This, of course, is a motivational jingle that conflates thoughts about Christian victory from various New Testament verses, such as Romans 8:37 (NIV) "No, in all these things we are more than conquerors through him who loved us," and 1 John 5:4 (NIV) "for everyone born of God overcomes the world. This is the victory that has overcome the world, even our faith."
69. Savelle, sermon at Hillsongs London, 25/02/2007, 11.00 am service.
70. Savelle, *Receive God's Best*, 16.

word that will change your thinking—so you think like God." Savelle says the Apostle Paul calls this change of thinking, the renewing of the mind, referring to Romans 12:2: "Do not be conformed to this world, but be transformed by the renewing of your minds." Savelle argues that this revelation thinking can only be imparted by "anointed men of God." Savelle is saying that Christians need to be taught revelation knowledge that comes from what he believes to be a Spirit-led interpretation of the Word. Most of the Faith teachers talk about revelation knowledge or taking on board revelation thinking. But this distinction between sense knowledge and revelation knowledge originates from the writings of E. W. Kenyon, especially in his book *The Two Kinds of Knowledge*.[71] According to Kenyon, sense knowledge is all that can be known through the physical senses.[72] To answer the great spiritual questions of life, a different type of knowledge is needed, revelation knowledge, that transcends sensory and scientific knowledge; as he says, "Revelation or Faith Knowledge is in the realm above Sense Knowledge."[73] Savelle also makes this distinction, talking of sense knowledge and revelation knowledge, following on from Copeland, Hagin, and Kenyon.[74]

6.12 Spiritual Laws

6.12.1 The Law of Seedtime and Harvest, and the Law of Hundredfold Return

As we shall see, Savelle sees this as the most important spiritual law he ever learned;[75] nearly all of the stories in his materials are illustrations of this. The key scriptural passage for Savelle from which this law is understood is Mark 4:1–20, the parable of the sower, and more specifically, its interpretation by Kenneth Copeland and Oral Roberts. The concept of "seed faith" was popularized by Oral Roberts.[76] Savelle writes,

> If you get a revelation on this parable, then all of a sudden the entire Bible begins to make sense. You begin to understand God's system of operation. Once I understood this, then I studied the

---

71. Copeland and Copeland, *One Word from God Can Change Your Family*, 88; Hagin, "The Resurrection," 6; Kenyon, *The Two Kinds of Knowledge*.

72. Ibid., 11–13.

73. Ibid., 20.

74. Savelle, *Receive God's Best*, 109; Savelle, *Called to Battle Destined to Win*, 72; Savelle, *If Satan Can't Steal Your Dreams He Can't Control Your Destiny*, 20.

75. Savelle, *Receive God's Best*, 57.

76. Hummel, *Fire in the Fireplace*, 228.

Word day and night endeavoring to learn how I could take charge of my destiny through the seeds I would sow.[77]

Here, Savelle, Copeland, and Roberts understand money, possessions, and in fact anything a person owns, as "seed," which, when sown by giving it away, will result in a harvest of return to the giver. Giving is not motivated by gratitude for salvation but to receive God's blessing. Savelle often uses a motto that he learned from Roberts; he writes, "Oral Roberts taught me this many years ago. Giving is not a debt you owe, but it's seed you sow."[78] This interpretation is expressed by Savelle and Copeland as being a spiritual law. As I have said, Savelle says this is the most important spiritual law he ever learned. He writes, "Everything on this planet revolves around the law of seedtime and harvest."[79]

Savelle suggests that he first understood this as he was listening to Copeland preaching at a believers' convention in England. He writes, "As I am listening the Spirit of God asked me a question. He said, 'After creating man what were the first two gifts I gave him?'"[80] The Spirit, he says, led him to look at Genesis 1. There, he observed that "Gift number one was dominion and authority."[81] The second gift he observed to be "I have given thee every herb bearing seed."[82] He says, "from the very beginning in the mind of God, He intended for man to be a sower of seed."[83]

The Savelles seem to have practiced this law right from the beginning of Jerry's ministry, even if they did not think in terms of giving to do with this particular law at the time. When Savelle first went to work for Copeland, the family moved into a house in Fort Worth. When the cost of the house and other items had been paid, and he went on his first ministry trip with Copeland, all he could leave Carolyn was $3. She thought that was not very much, so she put it in the collection at church; when she got home, she found a $50 bill that someone at church had slipped into her pocket[84] (in another account of the incident, she received a $20 bill).[85]

Savelle writes,

---

77. Savelle, *Receive God's Best*, 63.
78. Ibid., 39.
79. Ibid., 57.
80. Ibid., 58.
81. Ibid., 59.
82. Ibid., 59.
83. Ibid., 59.
84. Ibid., 143–4.
85. Savelle, *In the Footsteps of a Prophet*, 137.

> The first thing I learned about seeds was this: My thoughts were seeds. I realized that everything in life began as a thought. Everything in your life began as a thought. That makes it a seed. Your thoughts are seeds. If you will change the way you think, then you will change the way you live.[86]

For Savelle, thoughts change your life materially, not just your attitude, as we shall see. Claiming material things with your thoughts is an example of the subjective idealism described in chapter 3 of this book.

Savelle continues,

> The second thing I began working on was my words. I began to recognize that my words, just like my thoughts, were seeds. Jesus said in Matthew 12:35, *A good man out of the good treasure of the heart bringeth forth good things and an evil man out of the evil treasure bringeth forth evil things.* Simply said: positive words produce positive results. Negative words produce negative results.[87]

Savelle tells of how he realized the significance of positive and negative words: "shortly after I had first received Christ, I had asked God to meet a need that I had, but I wasn't seeing any results. God gave me supernatural recall of everything that had come out of my mouth from the time I had asked Him to meet the need. One moment it was positive, the next moment it was negative. . . . He said, 'Son, you are sowing the wrong seeds and because of your negative words, I can't help you.'"[88] Here, God seems powerless to help people who are adversely affected by their own words. God, it seems, has put spiritual laws into place and is unable to override them.

Savelle then applies his seed teaching to attitudes. He writes, "If you don't expect anything good to happen to you, it's because you don't really believe God's Word yet."[89] He adds, "If you are not convinced that God can be depended upon, your attitude will reveal it. And that makes your attitude a seed."[90] He goes even further. "I also discovered that everything I have in the way of material possessions are seeds. My finances are seeds. Everything I have is a seed."[91]

---

86. Savelle, *Receive God's Best*, 64.
87. Ibid., 64.
88. Ibid., 65.
89. Ibid.
90. Ibid.
91. Ibid., 67.

He says that he started out unable to sow anything but prayer into Kenneth Copeland's ministry, but he could eventually sow $1000, then $10,000, then $100,000. He is now working on a million dollars. His prayer is that God will give church members raises, promotions, and clever inventions to raise their income so they can give more and be a greater blessing to the church.[92]

In his talk at King's Church, Medway, he illustrated sowing possessions by talking about his airplane. He says, "I only know one way to get 'em. Give the one I got away. And I remember when I said to my wife we're going to sow this airplane into another ministry."[93] He said that was eight airplanes ago! God, he claims, has raised his thinking. Now he flies internationally in his own plane.[94] God, he says, has caused him to think big. A key text associated with the "seed faith" idea is Mark 10:29–30 where Jesus says

> Verily I say unto you, There is no man that hath left house, or brethren, or sisters, or father, or mother, or wife, or children, or lands, for my sake, and the gospel's, But he shall receive an hundredfold now in this time, houses, and brethren, and sisters, and mothers, and children, and lands, with persecutions; and in the world to come eternal life. (KJV)

This passage is said to teach the spiritual law of the "hundredfold return." As Gloria Copeland explains,

> You give $1 for the Gospel's sake and $100 belongs to you; give $10 and receive $1000; give $1000 and receive $100,000. I know that you can multiply, but I want you to see it in black and white and see how tremendous the hundredfold return is. . . . Give one house and receive one hundred houses or one house worth one hundred times as much. Give one airplane and receive one hundred times the value of the airplane. Give one car and the return would furnish you a lifetime of cars. In short, Mark 10:30 is a very good deal.[95]

---

92. Savelle, tape of sermon at King's Church, Medway, Bible week 8th November 1999.

93. Ibid.

94. See also Savelle, *Receive God's Best*, 48, and Savelle, *Expect the Extraordinary*, 150–60.

95. Copeland, *God's Will is Prosperity*, 54.

This seems to work very well for Savelle—almost too well. As he writes, "I have given motorcycles away. Carolyn told me to never do that again because they come back to me in fleets."[96]

Commenting on the careers of believers, he uses another motto.

> We have turned it into what we do to earn a living. God considers your job as what you do to earn a giving. In other words, your job is nothing more than a means for you to have seed to sow.[97]

Savelle comments,

> When God calls a person a sower, He is saying this is what they live 24 hours a day, 7 days a week. They understand the law of seedtime and harvest. They understand their thoughts, their words, their attitude, their actions, and everything they possess are seeds. That is a sower.[98]

To illustrate this, he tells the story of how the Savelles received their first house. He writes,

> We had to have a place to live, so we rented for a while and then we realized we could be paying the same amount for a house that would eventually belong to us. We bought our first house and had a mortgage on it, and we believed that God could pay the mortgage off. What God did was send us a buyer who offered us twice what we had put into that house. That enabled us to pay the debt off and then have the same amount left over to put into another house. And we did it. We had a mortgage on it. But then God sent us another buyer, and he offered us twice what we had put into that house. And that eventually enabled us to build our dream and it's free of debt. It was all because we sowed seed.[99]

In support of the seed idea, he quotes 2 Corinthians 9:10 in the Amplified Bible: "And [God] Who provides seed for the sower . . . will also provide and multiply your [resources for] sowing."[100] He concludes that God promises sowers two things: they will never be without seed, and He will increase their resources for sowing.

---

96. Savelle, *Receive God's Best*, 150.
97. Ibid., 60.
98. Ibid., 62.
99. Ibid., 67.
100. Ibid., 68.

In order to help people to remember the principle for success, he uses another of his memorable mottos: "The seeds you sow determine how far you will go."[101]

In order to be successful in this, Savelle argues, a person must not hold onto money. He says, "My giving to God is a seed I sow. It is a seed of love."[102] He points to the Scripture and says that *the love of money is the root of all evil*, not money itself (1 Tim 6:10). He comments, "The bottom line is if people won't give to God, they are in love with their money."[103]

> If you refuse to give to God, then the bottom line is that you don't have money, it's got you. The quickest way that you can find out if something has you or you have it, is to ask yourself: Can I give it away? If you can't it's got you. If you can you've got it.[104]

He illustrates with another story about his airplane. "I learned that, with the first airplane that God blessed this ministry with."[105] After he had received delivery of the plane he put it in the hanger, but later went back with Carolyn to lay hands on the plane and say, "'God, I just want you to know that if You tell me to give this airplane away tonight, I will gladly do it.' . . . He said, 'Thank you. Use it for now. I'll talk to you about it later.'"[106] He comments,

> then about a year and a half or two years later, I found out about two ministries that were going under because of financial pressure, and the Lord said, "if you were to sell the airplane and divide the money between those two, you will save two ministries." So I sold it . . . then later, God blessed me with another debt-free airplane.[107]

In an attempt to preempt those who question that Christians should accumulate wealth, Savelle comments, "it's okay to have a lot of money."[108] To justify this, he writes about the wealth of Abraham, Isaac, and Jacob, and says,

---

101. Ibid., 57.
102. Ibid., 45.
103. Ibid., 47.
104. Ibid., 48.
105. Ibid.
106. Ibid., 48–49.
107. Ibid., 49.
108. Ibid., 50.

All these men developed a right view of money. It did not control them. They controlled it. They practiced what God later told Moses to tell the children of Israel in Deuteronomy 8:18, *But thou shalt remember the Lord thy God: for it is He that giveth thee the power to get wealth.*[109]

6.12.2 The Law of Sevenfold Return

Savelle teaches that God told him that if "the devil couldn't get his joy, he couldn't hold onto his possessions." Based on Proverbs 6:30-31, "*Men* do not despise a thief, if he steal to satisfy his soul when he is hungry; 31 But *if* he be found, he shall restore sevenfold; he shall give all the substance of his house." The devil, being a thief, has to pay back seven times to those he takes things from. Savelle illustrates this with a story.[110] They bought a house and it needed renovation. The trees and shrubs in the garden were in a poor state. They got a man to look at the trees and he concluded that the trees were being eaten by insects. Savelle agreed that he could treat the trees for $500. After the work was completed, the man said the trees needed to be trimmed at a cost of $5,000. The Savelles had other things to spend money on, so they said no. They went away to Florida, but on their return they found the man and his workmen trimming the trees. They told him that they had not agreed to this, but he said that they had already done $3,000 dollars worth of work. Savelle's initial response was to contact his attorney. However, he felt that God was saying to him "walk in love" and "pay the man . . . love never fails. I'll get it back to you." Savelle understood that his money had been stolen by the devil and kept saying to the devil, "you're going to have to pay me back seven times the amount." As time passed, Savelle forgot about it, but one morning he got a call from a man he met a couple of weeks before who wanted to meet him for breakfast. This man told Savelle, "God spoke to me about the $3,000 the devil stole from you. My wife and I have been instructed by the Lord to give it back to you sevenfold." He gave Savelle $21,000 in cash. Savelle comments, "since then Carolyn and I have been working on the devil to give back all he has stolen from us—and he has been bringing it in sevenfold."

---

109. Ibid., 51.
110. Savelle, *If Satan Can't Steal Your Joy He Can't Keep Your Goods*, 47–56.

6.12.3 Planting Extraordinary Seed for an Uncommon Harvest

Savelle writes of sowing $10,000 into a project run by Kenneth Copeland, and within a few days received a check for $50,000 from another ministry.[111] The usual practice would have been to tithe this to the ministry's "tithe account" to be given away. But on this occasion, he felt God say to him, "Plant an uncommon seed." So Savelle sowed the whole $50,000 into other ministries. This produced two checks for $100,000 each.

6.12.4 The Law of Faith

Savelle states, in a similar way to all Faith teachers (based on Mark 11:23), "if you believe those things which you say shall come to pass; and do not doubt in your heart, you shall have them." He argues that if, with the mouth, confession is made unto salvation (based on Romans 10:10), then it stands to reason that your words can change other situations in your life. He says, "If words are powerful enough to change your eternal destiny, then surely they can change the power of your checkbook."[112] This has been passed on from Hagin and Kenyon.

6.12.5 The Law of Reciprocity (Financial Partnership)

Another of the spiritual laws that the Faith Movement teaches is what Savelle calls the "Law of Reciprocity."[113] He teaches this in his book *Biblical Partnership*, in which he argues that it is a spiritual law that Christians should support, financially, ministers who have taught and mentored them.[114] In his case, he mentions his mentors, Oral Roberts, Kenneth Copeland, and Kenneth Hagin. To not support them would, in Savelle's opinion, be a violation of spiritual law and cutting himself off from the anointing of their ministries; and for those who have received from Savelle's ministry, not to support him is a violation of the same spiritual law.[115]

---

111. Savelle, *Expect the Extraordinary*, 67.
112. Savelle, *Receive God's Best*, 93.
113. Jerry Savelle, *Biblical Partnership*, 9.
114. Ibid.
115. Ibid., 12, 15.

He says that this spiritual law is to be seen in the Word of God, but the Body of Christ has very little knowledge of it. He says, "it's something that each and every one of us should have a revelation of."[116] Of course, here we have another incidence of a spiritual law that we need to be made aware of by revelation. Based on Galatians 6:6 in the Amplified Bible, Savelle argues that those who receive instruction in the Word should contribute to his support.[117] As to the level of financial support that he expects, Savelle is not really clear. But he talks about tithing being a command of God, and a failure to tithe is rebellion.[118] He argues, as so many people do, that the tithe belongs to God, and to withhold it will result in financial problems; to give the tithe shows God that a person can be trusted with their money.[119] He argues that over and above the tithe, the Bible speaks about "tithes and offerings"; giving is not limited to a simple tenth, but multiples are required in order to receive greater blessing.[120] Many critics of the movement (and teaching about tithing in general) argue that, in the New Testament, the giving of tithes to churches or ministries is not binding on Christians, and this teaching is often applied in an abusive way.[121] Savelle mentions the concept of sowing seed into others' ministries; in his particular case, he mentions Kenneth Copeland.[122] The implication is that people should be sowing money into his ministry. This whole practice reminds me of pyramid selling. He pays to those who have brought him into the movement; those he is bringing into the movement pay him. The more he gets paid, the more he can pass on to Kenneth Copeland—but he still has a very good living himself.[123]

6.12.6 Poverty and Sickness Defeated by the Atonement

The result of studying Copeland was that he made up his mind to live a victorious Christian life by faith with no sickness and no poverty, but prosperity and health. He then argues, "if God says, "I wish above all things that

---

116. Ibid., 10.
117. Ibid., 13–14.
118. Ibid., 16.
119. Ibid., 16–17.
120. Ibid., 19.
121. Kelly, *Should the Church Teach Tithing?*, summarized in Kelly, "Tithing is Not a Christian Doctrine."
122. Ibid., 21–3.
123. See my reflections earlier regarding Kleeneze.

thou mayest prosper and be in health even as your soul prospers,"[124] then that's what I'm going for. My attitude was, God if you didn't intend for that to be in my life you shouldn't have put it in my copy of the book, cause I'm going for it."[125] Here Savelle introduces what is the key scripture text of the Faith and prosperity teachers, 3 John 2 (KJV). Presumably he had heard this expounded by Copeland on the night before his conversion. Commenting on this text, Copeland says, "John writes that we should prosper and be in health."[126] We might well ask, is this really what the text means? Of course not! See Gordon Fee's comments at section 1.2.1 of this book.

Savelle denies that he has or should have any sickness; for example, he writes,

> A short time ago he [Satan] tried to put symptoms of the flu on me. My nose and my eye started to run. I began to sneeze and ache all over. I haven't had the flu since 1969, and I'm not going to have it now. I'm redeemed from the flu! Immediately I began to confess God's Word that I'm healed by the stripes of Jesus. I rebuked Satan and refused his lying symptoms. I wasn't trying to get something I didn't have; I was keeping something I already have. I am healed. Those symptoms were an intimidation of the adversary. The thief was trying to steal one of my possessions—my health. I have health and I stand protective over what is already mine.[127]

Healing, although seemingly a small part of Savelle's experience, is evidenced by a few of his testimonies, the most remarkable of which is the story of the healing of his daughter, Terri, whose fingertips were cut of in nursery accident when she was a baby.[128]

Savelle and his family were at a meeting where Copeland was preaching. The baby was brought to Savelle with blood pouring from her fingers. Copeland came over to them, laid his hands on baby Terri and said, "In the name of Jesus, I command the blood to stop and the pain to cease." Savelle writes, "The bleeding stopped instantly." When he examined her more carefully, he saw that two of her fingers had been cut of behind the first joint. Later the nursery attendant brought him the fingertips. Savelle is not clear which side of the joint was cut, which is of key importance in claiming a

124. 3 John 2 (KJV).

125. Jerry Savelle, tape of sermon at King's Church, Medway, Bible week 8th November 1999.

126. Copeland, *The Laws of Prosperity*, 14.

127. Savelle, *If Satan Can't Steal Your Joy He Can't Keep Your Goods*, 4.

128. Savelle, *If Satan Can't Steal Your Dreams He Can't Control Your Destiny*, 101–7.

miracle.[129] The Savelles were told the fingertips were inoperable and would never grow back; although she could have a skin graft, she would never have finger nails. Savelle insisted, "You don't understand. My God will restore my baby's fingers." Again, they were told that was medically impossible. Three weeks later, they returned to the hospital, the bandages were removed, and the fingers were totally restored. In another version of the story,[130] Savelle reveals that the scars are still there on the fingers of the now adult Terri underneath the nails, so in front of the first joint.

In another healing of a baby claimed by Savelle, he tells of finding a man in a parking lot crying and saying that his baby was dying. Savelle went back to the house of the parents, who were living in terrible poverty. He laid his hands on the baby and shouted, "The baby will live and not die in the name of Jesus! According the Mark 11:23, I can have what I say." He continues,

> The anointing of God absolutely consumed the place. They started crying, and I led them both to the Lord. The baby started getting better right there in our presence. Years later I got a picture from that couple, and that baby was about four or five years old, doing well, and never had another problem. I saw the Word work right before my eyes.[131]

6.12.7 The Need to Change One's Mind to Think like God

In his address at King's Church, Medway, Savelle described his study of the ministry of Jesus. He argued that the underlying theme in everything Jesus taught was "dare to be different." According to Savelle, everything about Jesus was different. He referred to Luke 4:33ff and the amazement of the crowd at Jesus's deliverance of a man possessed by an evil spirit and concludes, "Apparently, they had never seen deliverance." He acknowledged that God provided healing under the old covenant but he argued that by the time of Jesus, "religion had removed healing, religion had removed prosperity, religion had removed the blessings of Abraham." He then turns to the woman

---

129. See Illingworth, "Trapped Fingers and Amputated Finger Tips in Children," 853: Illingworth writes, "We now know that spontaneous regeneration and excellent cosmetic and functional results can be obtained in guillotine amputations of finger tips in young children."

130. Savelle, *In the Footsteps of a Prophet*, 103–15.

131. Ibid., 70–71.

bowed over for eighteen years. He suggests, "Religion had taken away the blessings of Abraham." Savelle continues by arguing that every time Jesus healed someone, the people began to think bigger thoughts about God. He introduces what he says is a brand new concept from Jesus: "All things are possible to him that believeth" (Mark 9:23). Again, says Savelle, this further removed people's limitations.

He argues that as people are taught truths from Scripture by anointed men of God, then their minds will be renewed.

Savelle then turns to Luke 5:17: "And it came to pass on a certain day, as he was teaching, that there were Pharisees and doctors of the law sitting by, which were come out of every town of Galilee, and Judaea, and Jerusalem: and the power of the Lord was present to heal them." He argues that the power of the Lord was present to heal the Pharisees and doctors of the law but none of them received it, adding that the Bible says, "you have to mix faith with the word that is preached and then it will profit you."[132] Savelle recalls the paralytic who was lowered by his friends into Jesus's presence. Savelle says, "When Jesus saw their faith, he said to the man your sins are forgiven and he was restored and made whole." He points to the fact that they were again amazed and said, "we have seen strange things today." Savelle argues that this would have caused observers to think, "If he could do that for him, he could do that for me." Experience like this, he argues, causes, "possibility thinking . . . God is not what religion told me. God can do what religion said he can't do."

Savelle recalled that when he first encountered Kenneth Copeland, he felt called to shut down his business for three months to study the Bible all day, every day. He tells us that at the end of three months, he was thinking differently and the process of renewing of his mind had begun. He said,

> I am now thinking in terms of possibilities, you understand what I'm saying? I'm thinking in terms of there is a way to live debt free. I didn't know there was that kind of existence prior to that. I'm thinking there is a way to live in divine health. I didn't know there was that kind of existence prior to that. I got sick just like everybody else did.

His mind, he argues, was thinking bigger thoughts because he had spent time studying God's Word. He said, "God's word is designed to do just that, take you from the unthinkable to the thinkable . . . you cannot hang around God and remain a small thinker."

---

132. Elsewhere, he says something very similar: "you must mix faith with what God says in order to give his Word substance." Savelle, *If Satan Can't Steal Your Dreams He Can't Control Your Destiny*, 15.

He says that when God says, "Come let us reason together,"[133] he does not want Christians to think on their level but God's. Savelle observes there are a lot of big thinkers in the body of Christ today, more than in the past. He remembers how difficult it was for him and Copeland to preach their message in the UK in the 1980s but now they have an army of supporters.

Savelle then says that religion thinks small; the average church size in the UK is thirty-two members. But some are thinking big. He refers to Pastor Grant's vision to turn the current church building into a youth church and build a much bigger one for the church. He then starts thinking big about God providing material things. He remembered the days when he just used a Ford station wagon to drive all over America to preach. Then, he says, God started to talk to him about airplanes and that he would not be able to fulfill his ministry without one. So they started praying for one. He claims that God told him he should never be in debt to buy an airplane, but to believe for it.

He said, "I don't ever go up to somebody and say, we're believing God for an airplane, is God talking to you?" Eventually, he got his first plane and flew it all over America. But then he needed a bigger and faster one.

He turns to Isaiah 55:8: "For my thoughts are not your thoughts, neither are your ways my ways, saith the LORD." He argues that the people to whom this was written were old covenant people who were not born again, not filled with the Holy Spirit, and who did not have access to what Paul calls the mind of Christ.[134] But Christians do. Savelle then asked the congregation to think about people who have big thoughts; he recalls his friendship with Oral Roberts, who had a plaque on his desk that said "no small thoughts here," and Kenneth Copeland, whose thinking stretched Savelle.[135] He then thinks about God saying, "For my thoughts are not your thoughts, neither are your ways my ways, saith the LORD."

> But then in verse 11, he shows us how he's gonna change that. ... He said my thoughts are higher that your thoughts but here's what I'm gonna do for you. So shall my word be that goeth forth out of my mouth. It shall not return to me void, but accomplish that which I please and it shall prosper in the thing in which I have sent it."

Savelle argues that God has sent his word to us to bring us up to God's way of thinking. He says,

---

133. Savelle's version of Isa 1:18.

134. 1 Cor 2:16.

135. Actually, Oral Roberts's favorite saying was "make no small plans here"; he had it inscribed on a plaque on his desk. See Cook, "Make No Small Plans."

this is the mind of God in a book ... so we could think like him, talk like him, get the results that he gets ... this is a manual ... you could put on the front of this how to live successfully like God in the earth.

But it is more than just the Bible; he suggests that in order to think like God,

We've got to clear our minds. We've got to keep hearing the instructions of the Holy Spirit. We've got to keep flowing with God. As we keep doing these things, we're going to see what God sees. We're going to have the mind of God.[136]

There are many parallels in the preceding teaching with that of E. W. Kenyon and, indeed, Kenneth Hagin.

Savelle describes his interest in fast cars and motorcycles and magazines he read with tips to improve performance. He argues that the Bible is like that and recalls Paul's statement, "All things are lawful unto me, but all things are not expedient."[137] Savelle explains, "In other words what he's saying is there are things in my life that are not necessarily sinful but they're no longer profitable. So he started peeling them away, why? Maximum performance."

He argues if you read the books of Churchill every day you will end up thinking like him. If you read the Bible you will end up thinking like God. He claims that as we think like God we will give more and more and, as we give, God will give us more.

6.13 Conclusions

Like Urquhart, Savelle's performative rhetoric depends heavily on his narratives, his story-telling. His reputation and self-presentation are also highly significant.

Before his conversion to Word of Faith and his call to preach, he was a religious skeptic whose life passion was motorcycles and cars. This passion has not been quenched but assimilated into his ministry as Chariots of Light, a tool for evangelism. This communicates that God does not always stop you doing what you enjoy. You can be a biker or a car enthusiast and live a life of faith.

Savelle's life was changed by his girlfriend and now wife, who is a key figure in his life; her influence has effectively reconstructed him. Their

136. Savelle, *Called to Battle Destined to Win*, 45.
137. 1 Cor 6:12.

loving successful and fulfilled family shows that Savelle's message works and is highly attractive to pragmatists. Stable family life makes Savelle an attractive preacher of credible integrity to many potential adherents of this stream of Pentecostalism.

Another persuasive element of his rhetoric is the professionalism of his publicity, that is, his website and magazine, and the quality of his TV shows and books. Savelle's professional, organized, business-like manner and his entrepreneurial pragmatism is also an attractive feature. Like Urquhart's teaching, Savelle's material is all very simple; it does not challenge the mind too much. He uses mottos to make his ideas more memorable; these are often rhyming couplets, a well-recognized rhetorical technique. Despite this, Savelle sounds learned, calling himself and being called Dr. Savelle. Like other Word of Faith teachers, most of his teaching is presented as spiritual laws, laws that if followed result in success.

Part Three:
The Effect of Word of Faith on Some English Revivalist Churches

Introduction

THE STUDY OF THESE ministries and their methods and principles left me with some further significant questions (see after I introduce the case studies in the introduction to the book). It became clear that further thinking and further methodology was necessary in order to unearth possible answers to some of these questions.

In order to attempt to address these questions I decided, in this part of the book, to consider and apply to my case studies methodologies from congregational studies, organizational theory, and Maussian analysis in chapter 7; and then in chapter 8 to look at the nature of the charisma of my case studies and the concepts of enchantment, disenchantment and *habitus*. I also briefly consider the theory of cognitive dissonance, the nature of neo-Gnosticism evident in these ministries, and the relationship between attraction to these ministries and social class.

CHAPTER 7

Using Insights from Congregational Studies, Organizational Theory, and Anthropology

7.1 Insights from James Hopewell's Congregation

IN CONSIDERATION OF MY case studies, I intend to glean insights from the discipline of congregational studies and particularly Hopewell's reflection on churches.[1]

Hopewell investigates the sort of outlook or mindset churches are set up with, and the influences that affect their development. When studying churches, Hopewell utilizes the sort of approach that a family might make in choosing a dwelling; he calls this "househunting." Hopewell points to four approaches to househunting: contextual, mechanistic, organic, and symbolic. He analyses and categorizes churches in these terms.[2] While in every church, all four of these are in play, one of them usually dominates. However, more than one of these approaches might have a significant influence on the nature of an individual church.[3] In what follows, I seek to explore some of the material Hopewell cites to gain a better impression of each category. I then reflect on how these approaches are helpful in the reading of the rhetoric of my case studies.

1. Hopewell, *Congregation*.
2. Ibid., 21–39.
3. Ibid., 19.

Contextual

In choosing a home, a primary consideration for many would be the dwellings context. In a similar way, for some leaders, a contextual rationale for a ministry or congregation might be a significant or even the most significant factor. Hopewell notes the reports of working groups of the World Council of Churches in the 1960s suggesting radical new forms of church to be developed in the secular context. The suggestion was made that, "Instead of starting from the *church* and the problem of, 'what is the true church?,' why not start our investigation in the *world*, especially where attempts are being made to respond to the agenda of the world?"[4] Another report noted that what was envisaged was "not so much a missionary structure for a congregation, but . . . structures for missionary congregations."[5] The form of these missionary congregations were to be determined by the needs of the world; through them, churches should serve "their neighbors in crisis." The aim was not necessarily to convert people and make new church members but to participate in the *missio Dei*,[6] God's mission to a struggling world, addressing their social needs.

We might well ask what specific examples of contextually driven churches are cited by Hopewell, illustrating what he understands this sort of church to be. A significant book that points to the contextual sort of congregations that Hopewell envisages is that by theologian and social reformer George Webber, *God's Colony in Man's World*.[7] Webber, as one of the leaders of East Harlem Protestant Parish, and a theologian at Union Theological Seminary, describes their radical approach to setting up storefront churches in one of New York's most socially challenging environments. As a theologian, Webber developed a successful program to open the study of theology to black and Hispanic people, to women, and to the socially disenfranchised such as inmates at Sing Sing Prison just north of New York.[8] The parish was set up by four Protestant denominations, and soon joined by another four. The central aim was to "confront" the people of East Harlem with the good news that Jesus is both Lord and Christ.[9] In so doing, they were driven to

---

4. World Council of Churches, *The Church for Others and the Church for the World*, 61. Cited by Hopewell, *Congregation*, 21.

5. World Council of Churches Department on Studies in Evangelism, *Planning for Mission*, 26.

6. Hopewell, *Congregation*, 22.

7. George Webber, *God's Colony in Man's World*. Cited by Hopewell, *Congregation*, 22.

8. Obituary of George Webber from the *New York Times*, 13th July 2010.

9. Webber, *God's Colony in Man's World*, 13.

rethink the nature of the church and the gospel, and the realization that methods successful among the middle classes, such as proclamation and visitation programs, would not work in East Harlem.[10] They realized that while the gospel remains the same, new wineskins were needed to achieve their aim. In the view of the leadership, the church must offer Christ's love to those in need, participating in the community, and thus gaining the right to speak directly of the meaning of the gospel. The major challenge was the experience of people in East Harlem of depersonalization resulting from poor and overcrowded housing, and the lack of healthcare provision, poor education, racial discrimination, and so on. The church sought to win the trust of local people by giving advice and involving themselves in political protest on their behalf.[11] Webber writes about the irrelevance of evangelistic campaigns to people who have long since stopped listening to the jargon of ministers. These methods net only people who have already been in the orbit of the Christian faith.[12] At the heart of Webber's approach was biblical teaching pointing to the radical nature of the gospel, in which members of the church in Harlem were called to submit to the lordship of Christ and truly live as the body of Christ, an incarnational community serving each other and anyone in need.[13] The church was to be a colony of heaven in a world in need of salvation. Webber speaks of vertical, circular and horizontal dimensions of the gospel. The vertical dimension is always first. Jesus, he argued, did not leave behind a code of ethics or a set of principles but people bound together by the knowledge that he was their Lord and Savior. Human beings are made one because Christ is their Lord, and then driven to the "circular dimension"—their quality of life together as a result of realizing that they should recognize each other as those for whom Christ died. This should lead to the horizontal dimension because the church exists for its mission to the world.[14] It is a fellowship where there is no place for exclusiveness among those who have been transformed by their confession of Christ. God's colony is open to people of every station and color, but closed to those who do not accept Jesus Christ as Lord.

Webber is critical of many churches in America where the radical nature of the gospel has been compromised,[15] where preachers are "peddlers of the gospel" and are acting like life insurance salesmen selling a product,

---

10. Ibid., 23.
11. Ibid., 94.
12. Ibid., 38.
13. Ibid., 43.
14. Ibid., 47.
15. Ibid., 48.

which is in fact a distorted gospel aimed primarily at getting people into the institutional life of the church by meeting only their natural needs and demanding no real renewal of their nature.[16]

Other examples of contextual church cited by Hopewell are described in a book, *Models of Metropolitan Ministry* (1979),[17] edited by B. Carlisle Driggers. This is a collection of accounts of social ministries of twenty churches written by their ministers. The vast majority are Baptist, with one Episcopal, one Methodist, and two Presbyterian. There are a variety of approaches and theologies represented in this book but the majority are evangelical. Some are certainly mechanistic and positivist/pragmatist but with contextual elements.

Other specific examples of contextual churches cited by Hopewell are described by authors such as Goodman.[18] Goodman considers churches that seem to be much more driven by a need for social action, and so are highly contextual.

All of my case study churches are of the more mechanistic, positivist/pragmatist forms of church observed by Driggers. I suspect that Webber would view all three as churches where the true nature of the gospel has been compromised. While I am sure each ministry considered would point to their aim of challenging and bringing spiritual transformation to the lives of their adherents, there is a clear sense in which each of the ministries are selling a product. Their CDs, DVDs, streamed videos, and mp3s are all saleable products.

However, each of my case studies could be considered to have a contextual element to their ministry. Peniel, under the leadership of Reid, I am reliably informed,[19] never engaged in social action and activity outside the Peniel site, except for publicity. If we introduce a similar categorization to that of Wallis, who suggests that New Religious Movements can be categorized into three groups—the world-affirming, the world-rejecting, and the world-accommodating (see chapter 2)—this further refines Hopewell's categorization.[20]

In Wallis's categorization, Peniel would tend towards the world-rejecting end; people had to come in and embrace their values and theology in order for God to act in their lives. This has changed since Peniel has become Trinity Church, which has started outreach programs. This world-rejecting

---

16. Ibid., 124.
17. Driggers, *Models of Metropolitan Ministry*.
18. Goodman, *Rocking the Ark*.
19. By various ex-members of Peniel.
20. Wallis, *The Elementary Forms of the New Religious Life*.

category would also apply, in my opinion, to Urquhart's Roffey Place College. However, Urquhart's Kingdom Faith has always had soup kitchens and street work, so in this respect its ministry has been more contextual and world-accommodating, even world-affirming. At first glance, Savelle seems to have very little contextuality in his ministry's blend; but when we consider his Chariots of Light ministry, in which he relates directly to the biker and "petrol head" communities, we might think differently. When we consider the churches he influences, such as King's Church, Medway, there is a strong contextual, world-accommodating and world-affirming element with its Caring Hands hostel that engages local prostitutes and drug users, and its pregnancy crisis center and debt advice unit.

Now there needs to be a certain amount of provisionality when it comes to observing these ministries as contextual. Mainstream Word of Faith churches flowing out of the Rhema churches, associated with Kenneth Hagin, Copeland, and Savelle, all seem to have built into their blueprint a ministry of social outreach and social care. But there is always the question, is this a major priority of the church? While it may well be for enthusiasts working in each ministry, I suspect that as far as the leadership is concerned, the major priority is the recruitment of new members to be financial partners and the purpose of the social ministry is to attract and increase the "narrative probability" of the ministry's integrity to those considering joining. In my observation of these ministries, I suspect the most genuinely motivated contextual ministry comes from Urquhart's Kingdom Faith.

Mechanistic

Another important approach in choosing a home, or, indeed, in structuring an ecclesial environment, is to ask how effectively does the house or church function? Hopewell comments that as contextual approaches to church receded, a new focus on the internal workings of churches came to prominence.[21] These mechanistic approaches, observed in the initiatives of the church growth movement, measured their effectiveness by the judged success of their programs of activity. The church growth envisaged here is in terms of numbers of adherents, as opposed to maturity and relationships implied by an organic vision of church that we will consider later. Growth in terms of numbers reveals that faith in God works, but it also provides the personnel and gifts to provide polished worship and effective ministry. The church here works like a machine which is either efficient or not.

---

21. Hopewell, *Congregation*, 23.

Mechanistic approaches to church operate in line with rational principles.[22] Hopewell gives an as example of a mechanistic approach ministry the work of C. Peter Wagner and his "seven vital signs" of a healthy church.[23]

Each of his signs are powered by mechanistic images: dynamics, catalysis, mobilization, size, range, balance, unit, priority, and order. While the contextual movement aimed to meet the social and justice needs of the world at large, the church growth movement used formulas to bring individuals to personal salvation. Wagner saw church growth principles as a major scientific discovery that would maximize numerical increase; he regarded it as consecrated pragmatism. Hopewell understood church growth science as just one approach among many that see the congregation in mechanistic terms. He gives the further examples of the parish report, with its analysis of data, specifically of attendance and finance measuring the efficiency of the parish, as a mechanistic approach, and also the intervention and planning approach of Lyle Shaller. Hopewell could have included Wagner's work on the identification and utilization of spiritual gifts to facilitate church growth.[24] If he had been writing after 1984, Hopewell could have included Rick Warren's *The Purpose Driven Church*[25] and Willow Creek Community Church's *Network*,[26] both of which have a very similar approach to Wagner's work on spiritual gifts, but which concentrate on more practical rather than supernatural gifts.

As described earlier in this book, all three of my ministries have highly mechanistic approaches. All three ministries are led by pragmatic, positive, possibility thinkers, men of vision, whose primary aim was to mobilize their churches to bring numerical increase by conversion to faith in Christ. However, all three of the ministries aim at more than just making converts and numerical growth, for they aim at personal fulfillment through healing and God's provision of money and even wealth. Each of the ministries have mechanistic approaches to church that operate in line with rational principles.

---

22. Ibid., 24.

23. Wagner, *Your Church Can Grow*, 159. See also Wagner's summary article in Hoge and Roozen, *Understanding Church Growth*, 270–87.

24. Wagner, *Your Spiritual Gifts Can Help Your Church Grow*.

25. Warren, *The Purpose Driven Church*.

26. Bruce et al., *Network*.

Organic

In sketching the organic approach to leading and developing a church, Hopewell asks the same questions as someone might ask about a house having the potential to result in the fulfillment of the family: Is the place conducive to good relationships? Did it aid the development of a happy home?[27]

He writes, "Organic approaches recognize the heterogeneity of members and their deep need to be reconciled in a common, if complicated, life." Hopewell cites Robert Worley,[28]

> Our current lack of common definitions has led to frustration, bitterness, and even withdrawal from the church by both clergy and laity. The absence of commonly accepted definitions means that people do not feel they have a place, do not know who they are in the congregation. It means that they are not established as persons in the church. In the turbulence of contemporary congregational life, diverse definitions of behavior, attitudes and interests exist. Church members have great difficulty dealing with this diversity. In the midst of competing and conflicting ideas and expectations, they suffer an identity crisis.[29]

Worley describes institutional churches where people may not be encouraged to have a role and ministry and, consequently, are frustrated and unfulfilled. These people do not feel included in the family and mission of the church; they feel they do not have a place. An organic attitude, when it comes to leading a church, means building a family church with good social relationships, a place where each person has a role, a church where people work together towards a common goal.

In this way of thinking about church, a congregation is envisaged as a living organism. Distinct from the mechanistic approach that stresses the importance of church as an efficient producer of converts, the organic approach is less concerned about whether the church works efficiently and is more concerned about household sensitivity and maturation, and the development of vitality and style. Just as one might choose a house to bring style and fulfillment to life, one might set up a church or choose to join a church with these priorities. Organic approaches to church recognize that church members are often alienated from each other and are in need of reconciliation. The organic approach views a congregation as a community and

---

27. Hopewell, *Congregation*, 26.
28. Ibid., 27.
29. Worley, *A Gathering of Strangers*, 18.

more than just the sum of its parts, where the parts work together towards wholeness and where everyone participates.

This approach is not usually associated with churches such as my case studies, who are clearly highly biased towards the mechanistic. Indeed, Hopewell contrasts the organic approach which, in his view, tends towards a democratic approach to decision-making, as opposed to the singular authority given to leaders of mechanistic churches.[30]

However, all of my case studies have organic elements, more so than many institutional churches.

Reid's Peniel had the highest organic element, being a "one stop shop," aiming to offer fulfillment in every area of life: spiritual, social, educational and financial. Everyone had a role, be it as a steward in the church or car park, being a teacher in the school, singing in the very large choir, being a musician or a technician, or delivering the *Trumpet Call* newspaper; and everyone was encouraged to give time, effort and money towards building new parts of the site and maintaining the buildings.

In Reid's healings, the church participated in healing prayer; many individuals raised their hands to share in the prayer. Presumably this had been taught by Reid. Social activity was largely catered for within the fellowship; in fact, outside social relationships were discouraged. People were encouraged to send their children to the fee-paying church school, which had an excellent reputation and an ethos guaranteed to be in line with the beliefs of the church members. Also, Reid and Linnecar ran a financial services company to meet the insurance and mortgage requirements of congregation members.

Urquhart's Kingdom Faith has elements of this, but I perceive much less than that of Reid's church. Certainly, an every-member ministry is aimed at, with people using their gifts widely in the church.

Savelle's ministry wants to bring spiritual, psychological, and financial well-being to its adherents, so it could be considered to have an organic slant. When we consider King's Church, Medway (influenced by Savelle, Rhema, WOF, and so on), then there is undeniably an organic element evidenced by large social events such as their annual bandstand barbecue and a church family café known as King's Kitchen.

Symbolic

The symbolic perspective on the local church is less frequently advanced, but is the focus of most of Hopewell's book. In the same way that, as Hopewell

30. Hopewell, *Congregation*, 28.

says, "it is frequently the image projected by a house that first attracts or repels prospective occupants"—"This house is us!," cry some "househunters" when they find their choice, referring to its symbolic identity—the identity or image of a church is highly significant for many people, who might well say "This church is us!," or "Following this leader is us!" In this approach, a congregation is viewed as a discourse and focuses on a church's identity, its views, values and motivations. It is how well it conveys meaning through narratives, stories, and ways of speaking about itself that cause potential members to be attracted.

All three of my case studies are capable of being read symbolically; all three have a symbolic element, I think, of varying intensity. All three have a definite ethos or even ethnos about them. There was a definite family-like feel to members of Reid's church, who could be called "Peniel people"; this is also true, I feel, of Urquhart's church and "Kingdom Faith people," and to those "chapter members" of Savelle's Chariots of Light. All identify with observable values and motivations.

The image of the leader is a key element. The ministry with the highest level of personal "success" symbolism is surely Savelle's, with his jet airplane, his classic car collection, his lovely house with extensive grounds,[31] his model-image daughter. The pictures of Savelle and his family in his very glossy *Adventures in Faith* magazine give him an almost film star image. There is a very real sense of an anthropology of clothing and ambiance.[32] What he wears in videos, in photographs and in public creates an impression. People are likely to relate to him influenced these impressions. When Savelle is on stage in a large church or venue, he is most often dressed in an expensive suit with a neat flat top haircut; he presents a professional successful businessman made good—in the God business. This suggests that those who follow and learn from him can have the same results. When he is recording his *Chariots of Light* program, he is either dressed in dungarees and a checked shirt or in leathers, identifying with his mechanical and biker supporters who see him as one of them. When recording programs with Copeland or his daughter, he is often smart-casually dressed and in a room or an environment that suggests comfortable prosperity.

The ministry with the next highest level of personal success symbolism is that of Michael Reid. Reid's luxury house, his obvious comfortable lifestyle, his big car, and his higher academic degrees all point to success, a ministry that was worth following and heeding.

---

31. Observable on Savelle's Chariots of Light videos.

32. See comments on the significance of Reid's clothing etc. in section 8.2.4 of this book.

As far as the anthropology of clothing and ambiance are concerned, Reid nearly always wore very smart suits and paraded himself in front of the congregation. The church building itself was more like a television studio than a traditional church, with its lighting and cameras, and its recording and broadcasting programs on television and the internet. Reid was backed by the uniformly dressed Peniel choir, and he presided over meetings with his wife, Dr. Ruth Reid, and his Assistant Pastor, Peter Linnecar, seated on large comfortable armchairs to one side of the stage, seemingly overseeing and approving everything that went on. Another part of Reid's symbolism was the placing of billboard posters, announcing that his was a ministry that, although in suburban Essex, was worth travelling to, as indeed many people did.

Finally, Urquhart still has a significant success symbolism. His flagship church in Horsham is called the National Revival Centre, making a clear claim that his ministry is of at least national significance. His Faith Camp each year attracts thousands of delegates who are drawn by his reputation as an authoritative leader in the charismatic movement. Leaders, or those who see themselves as future leaders, want to be associated with him and come under his "covering"—his network. Another significant symbol of his success is his college at Roffey Place that attracts a large student body each year, often recruited at Faith Camp. The symbolic nature of Urquhart's ministry has been enhanced over the years by the publishing and marketing of his books by Hodder and Stoughton. Significantly, on most of these books, his name was in larger print than the title, suggesting that if it is by him, it must be worth reading.[33] In my observation, his dress was usually casual, cords, check shirt, Hush Puppies type shoes, presenting a comfortable, trustworthy "grandfather-of-the-movement" type image.

Conclusion

If we represent the househunting approach pictorially as a square with "mechanistic," "contextual," "organic," and "symbolic" located towards the four vertices, then my case studies are definitely all located in the "mechanistic" corner. But each vary in their level of especially "contextual," but also, I think, "organic" and "symbolic."

---

33. Of course there is a similar principle at work in secular publishing, too.

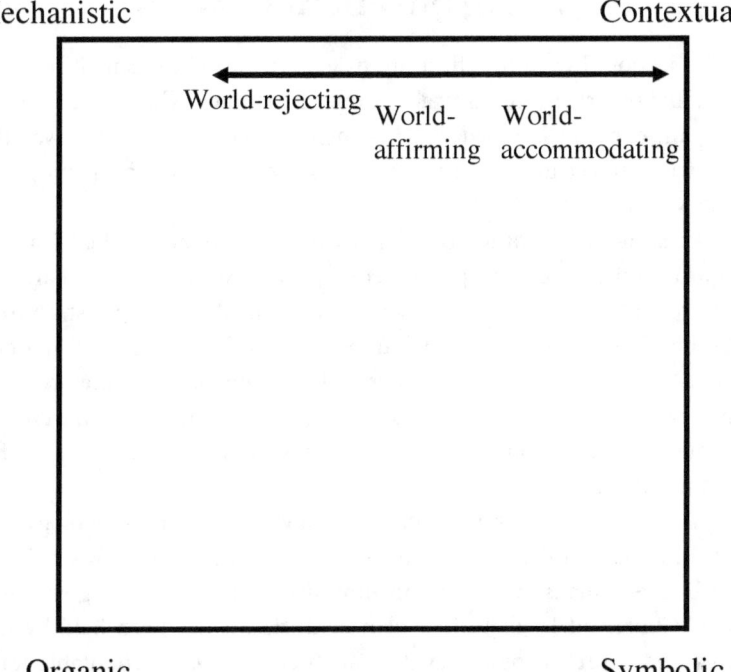

Of course, it is not really possible to plot these four (or even five) variables graphically on a 2D graph, but the reader can understand that while all three case studies have a similar (high) level of "mechanistic," they have varying levels of "contextual," "organic" and "symbolic" in their makeup.

All of these ministries being highly mechanistic would appeal to those who prefer a more pragmatic approach to church, however the image, context and what the ministry offers to prospective adherents are also significant.

7.2 Organisational Theory

In this section, I want to reflect on insights that can be gleaned from organizational theory. In thinking about my case studies, what sort of churches and ministries am I considering? Is there something about the way these ministries are set up that makes them more attractive and persuasive to those who join?

First of all, I want to consider my own experience as the Vicar of an Anglican church, albeit deeply embedded in the evangelical and charismatic traditions. St. Philip and St. James, Chatham is an Anglican parish church; it uses the official liturgies of the Church of England. As vicar, I was under the authority of the Bishop of Rochester and accountable to the hierarchy. This is my starting point in thinking about those who left us to join the churches and ministries I am considering, and those who came to us as refugees from other ministries.

As an Anglican incumbent, I have always held an ecclesiology at the heart of which was the notion of the parish. The term "parish" was originally used by the Romans to describe an administrative unit of local government. In the Church of England in recent centuries, it has been held by many clergy and church people that the parish church was accountable for the spiritual well-being of the entire community living in the parish, whether the residents were Anglicans or not.[34] During my time in Walderslade, I became acutely aware of other churches—for example, the local Baptist church—that viewed itself as having a ministry to an area, similar to a parish. Giles Ecclestone and his core group from the Grubb Institute write of two models of the local church, "parish" or "associational." They note that in the past, in England, the Anglican Church has come closest to exemplifying the parish model, with other denominations tending to the associational pattern; but their view is that "the distinction exists within most denominations and . . . the processes we shall describe express a more universal tension between two modes of engagement of Church and Society."[35] Before I discuss these more fully and apply them to my case studies, I want to say that these two "models" or "modes" are ideal types, and most churches are on a continuous spectrum between the two. Ecclestone speaks of the parish model as being "contextual church" or "communal church" because it is concerned with its community environment.[36] This, it seems, is based on earlier sociological research summarized most helpfully by Geoffrey K. Nelson in

---

34. Ecclestone, *The Parish Church*, 4–5.
35. Ibid., 6.
36. Ibid., 7.

his essay "Communal and Associational Churches."[37] This is a very similar, if not identical, typology to that postulated by Philip Selznick, with his distinction between "institutions" and "organizations."[38]

So a spectrum of modes of church exists between institutional (parish, contextual, or communal) and organizational (associational).

Institutional
(Parish,
Contextual or
Communal)

Organizational
(Associational)

In the Section that follows, I will examine these two "types."

Institutional Churches

What sort of definition can be made of an institutional ideal? Percy[39] celebrates sociologist David Martin's "eloquent *apologia* for the parish church."

> [M]any of the networks of charity, of voluntary work and of the arts, especially music, link up with the social network of the parish. . . . [T]hen there is latent "folk" religion which . . . does have some kind of focus in the parish church [but also] offers some kind of meaning which is embodied architecturally. . . . [I]t [is] often the only non-utilitarian building in certain areas. It is *there*, . . . [suggesting that] people are still in some ways located, whatever social or geographical mobility does to them, . . . [enabling] them to retain a sense of place, a sense of origin, a sense of continuity. . . . [This] goes back several hundred years.[40]

In seeking to develop a model for the classification of churches, Nelson points to the concepts of community and association defined by MacIver,[41] and derived ultimately from the concepts of *Gemeinschaft* ("community") and *Gesellschaft* ("society"), formulated by Tönnies.[42]

---

37. Nelson, "Communal and Associational Churches," 102–10.
38. Selznick, *Leadership in Administration*, 5–21.
39. Percy, "Confirming the Rumour of God." See also Percy, *Engaging with Contemporary Culture*, 77.
40. Martin, "A Cross-Bench View of Associational Religion," 51.
41. MacIver and Page, *Society*.
42. Tönnies, *Community and Society*.

Nelson seems to be saying something very similar to Martin when he lists the characteristics of the ideal type communal church (that is, institutional) thus:

1. It recruits its members from a given and clearly defined territorial area, which may for instance be a single village or a neighborhood within a wider urban area.
2. It exercises, either *de jure* or *de facto*, a monopoly of religious provision within the community.
3. Such a church is viewed by the members of the community as providing the center for the religious activities of the community.
4. Such a church is seen as the center of the symbolic as well as the religious life of the community.[43]

Nelson also notes N. J. Demerath's relating of the communal type to the church-sect typology.[44] Demerath says that sects demand complete commitment from their members, whereas a church recognizes outside groups as legitimate and sees itself as one among many organizations which serve meaningful purposes.[45] He is influenced by Philip Selznick's distinction between organizations that some are of the type of which their members are only segmentally involved,[46] whereas others have an organic commitment.[47] Selznick writes of institutions and those who are segmentally involved:

> In its most obvious sense, segmental participation refers to the partial commitment a man may give to organizations in which he has a limited interest and which do not affect him deeply. In extreme but not unusual cases, membership is of the "paper" variety, and the members themselves are easily manipulated by a small core of leaders and their supporting cliques.[48]

Elsewhere he writes,

> Such membership is *segmental*; that is, it affects only a small part, or segment, of the member's life. Most members of large organizations, including universities, trade unions, and cooperatives,

---

43. Nelson, "Communal and Associational Churches," 105.
44. Ibid.
45. Demerath, *Social Class in American Protestantism*, 66.
46. Selznick, *The Moral Commonwealth*, 6.
47. Selznick, *The Organizational Weapon* (1960), ix, xvi, 153.
48. Selznick, *The Organizational Weapon* (1952), 286.

invest only a limited part of themselves in organizational activities . . . the cost to the individual is minimal.[49]

Demerath concludes,

> In short, the churchlike parishioner should be *segmentally* involved in his religion, while sectlike parishioners are *organically* involved. As Philip Selznick uses the terms, a segmental commitment claims only part of the individual and shares his allegiance with other groups. Organic commitment is enveloping.[50]

So institutional church membership tends to be segmental with partial commitment whereas organizational, associational sectlike membership is organic and demands an enveloping life-embracing commitment.

Organizational Churches

In describing organizational or associational churches, Nelson points to MacIver's definition of an association as "a group organized for the pursuit of an interest or group of interests in common."[51] This sort of church has been stripped of the wider societal functions of the institutional (communal) church. So it is not like the parish—it is a group of people with common religious interests and beliefs with a distinct type of worship, or teaching or ritual practice. People choose to join it rather than be (in the extreme) parishioners by default (as in the case of the English parish church as envisioned by Ecclestone and his core group).[52] Organizational or associational churches can be seen to be in a "market situation."[53] Berger points especially to high potential middle-class suburban areas, where these organizational churches are successful, which are "inhabited by a population that is highly mobile, highly literate, and highly selective in its pattern of consumption."[54] In choosing a church, people "approach the matter with all the sophistication of the higher-level consumer in an affluent economy." So churches find themselves competing with each other to recruit members in a similar way that supermarkets compete for customers. They are, in a very real sense,

---

49. Broom and Selznick, *Essentials of Sociology*, 223.
50. Demerath, *Social Class in American Protestantism*, 66.
51. Nelson, "Communal and Associational Churches," 105.
52. Ecclestone, *The Parish Church*, 5.
53. Berger, "A Market Model for the Analysis of Ecumenicity."
54. Ibid., 82.

competitive businesses in an environment of "inflation . . . an enormous rise in costs for every conceivable aspect of church activity."[55]

Nelson summarizes the associational church as an ideal type in the following way:[56]

1. It does not of necessity recruit its members from a given and clearly defined geographical area, but is composed by those who have *chosen* to join that church, although they may reside in a widely dispersed area.

2. It makes no claim of monopolizing the religious provision within a community.

3. Such a church is viewed by its members and by the general public as an association established for the purpose of providing for the religious needs of its members.

Conclusion

In response to my first question under the heading of insights from organizational theory (What sort of churches am I considering?), it ought to be clear that my case studies (and St. Philip and St. James, Walderslade) are, relative to all churches, firmly at the organizational end of the spectrum (though some are more institutional than others). Obviously, being an Anglican parish, St. Philip and St. James is the most institutional, but at least one of the case studies has, arguably, a hint of institutionalism. I suspect that Urquhart would, subliminally, influenced by his very English, Anglican, King's College London background, still have an institutional bias some distance from admitting he was running a business. Savelle clearly is running a business with clear fiscal aims, with Reid only slightly less so.

Finally, is there something about the way these ministries are set up that makes them more attractive and persuasive to those who join?

Clearly my case study churches seem to answer the specific needs and wants of adherents in a way that institutional churches normally do not. They resort to radical, spectacular, innovative and modern methods to attract members. Instead of broad theologies, liturgies and other formalized practices of institutional churches, they have narrow, focused and definite visions. In a similar way to earlier innovative and pragmatic church

---

55. Ibid., 83.
56. Nelson, "Communal and Associational Churches," 106.

movements,[57] there is an emphasis on free expression of religious feelings and popularization of religion among those who would not feel comfortable in the more formalized institutional form of church. The appeal to those who want religion to work both for their own benefit, to assure them that their God is real and the church they've attached themselves to is not in decline like institutional churches.

7.3 Giving and Receiving: Maussian Analysis

Any study of the Faith Movement must account for its economy of giving and receiving. All three of my case studies testify that they, or people who have had contact with them through their ministries, have received money, possessions, or healings from God because of their faith.

An important question to ask is, where do these things come from? What do those who receive these things have to do in order to receive them? How does it all work? At first sight, these are obvious questions to ask about the prosperity oriented ministry of Savelle, where people are taught by example to give in order to receive a hundred-fold return. However, insights into the ministries of Reid and Urquhart can also be discovered. For example, members of Peniel church gave their time and energies to work on a number of building projects in the church complex in order to receive a secure Christian context in which to bring up and educate their children. One of Urquhart's books on healing is simply entitled *Receive Your Healing*; the question might be, what is it that you have to give in order to receive your healing? Could it be obedience, application of Urquhart's faith principles, and compliance to his suggestions?[58]

In seeking to explain the success in terms of prosperity in my case studies, and how money and possessions change hands, insights from exchange theory, particularly Maussian analysis, are enlightening. Others have used this methodological tool in this sort of study. Simon Coleman utilizes Mauss in his work on Ulf Ekman's Livets Ord Word Faith Church in Sweden; he comments, "the use of both language and money in a charismatic

---

57. For example, see the early Salvation Army in Canada and its distinctiveness from the more institutional Methodist Church, from which it sprang. But note also the eventual institutionalization of the Salvation Army. See Clark "The Methodist Church and the Salvation Army."

58. See chapter 8, section 8.2.2.5, where Urquhart is seen to say at Faith Camp 2007 in the Faith Camp 2008 promotional video, "You have to admit that when I preach you can understand what I'm saying, so you've got no excuses for *disobeying* . . . no, no it's very simple."

context can be reconsidered in the light of Maussian analysis."[59] Also, Martyn Percy uses Maussian analysis in his work on blessing in the Toronto Airport Christian Fellowship.[60]

The groundbreaking anthropological study of gift-giving in Polynesian, Melanesian, and North Western Native American societies by Mauss, resulting in his book *The Gift*,[61] is of profound importance in my study. While there are huge differences between a modern/postmodern twentieth-/twenty-first-century late capitalist context and the "archaic" contexts of Mauss's study, Mauss himself draws parallels with gift giving in his early twentieth-century context.[62] For example, he comments,

> We contend that the same morality and economy are at work, albeit less noticeably, in our own societies, and we believe that in them we have uncovered one of the bases of social life; and thus we may draw conclusions of a moral nature about some of the problems confronting us in our present economic crisis.[63]

E. E. Evans-Pritchard writes in his introduction to *The Gift* that Mauss

> reveals not only the meaning of certain customs of North American Indians and of Melanesians but at the same time the meaning of customs in early phases of historical civilizations; and what is more, the significance of practices in our own society at the present time. . . . He is asking not only how we can understand these archaic institutions but how an understanding of them helps us the better to understand our own, and perhaps improve them.[64]

It is clear from Mauss's study that gift cultures are identifiable in ancient cultures across the globe; his observations are not limited to Melanesian and North West American contexts but are expanded to make observations about giving and receiving in ancient Scandinavian, Roman, Hindu, Germanic, and Chinese cultures.[65] So this is not just a study of the distant past and uncivilized cultures; many of the observations that Mauss makes about

---

59. Coleman, *The Globalisation of Charismatic Christianity*, 198.

60. Percy, *Power and the Church*, 106.

61. Marcel Mauss, *The Gift: Forms and Functions of Exchange in Archaic Societies*, (1966).

62. Ibid.

63. Ibid., 2.

64. Ibid., ix.

65. Ibid., 1, 47, 53, 59, 62.

gifts and relationships of reciprocity rise above historical and cultural settings. They are human traits.

Of course, since the publication of *The Gift*, those who have followed Mauss have developed and modified his approach. Anthropologist James G. Carrier writes in his book *Gifts and Commodities*[66] that his own research in Papua New Guinea, part of Melanesia, led him to ideas of anthropologists that drew on the work of Marcel Mauss. For Carrier, the most important exponent of this new Maussian approach was C. A. Gregory and his work, also called *Gifts and Commodities*,[67] and an earlier article, "Gifts to Men and Gifts to God: Gift Exchange and Capital Accumulation in Contemporary Papua."[68] Carrier observes that Gregory and others like him drew heavily on *The Gift*, which Mauss finished in 1925. However, he observes that "what they wrote was not simply a recapitulation of what Mauss had said about social organization and exchange in pre-capitalist societies. Instead, they extended Mauss with a strong mix of Marx."[69]

Important for this study is Coleman's observation that

> a Maussian perspective can be used to encourage reflection not only on processes of circulation in any given context, but also on the nature of relationships that might exist between human participants in relations of exchange.[70]

As I say, this is not just a study of the past. We have inherited many of the practices of our cultural ancestors into our modern commodity societies. There might well be two different economic spheres of life for us, our work life and our home/friends/family life. Social rules that originate from our ancestors play a significant part in our practices of giving, receiving and reciprocating.

A likely complication in considering my Faith ministry case studies is that they can be considered to have two overlapping spheres of economic activity. They have a decidedly capitalistic commodity-like sphere; that is, they market their ministries through the sale of conference places, books, and media of their messages. But they also have a gift culture economic sphere. It is that gift culture that Mauss and Maussian insights might well help us to understand. In a similar way to Niles's *Homo narrans* (or storytelling man), we are in many ways *Homo donum* (or gift-giving man).

---

66. Carrier, *Gifts and Commodities*, vi–vii.
67. Gregory, *Gifts and Commodities*.
68. Gregory, "Gifts to Men and Gifts to God."
69. Carrier, *Gifts and Commodities*, vii.
70. Coleman, *The Globalisation of Charismatic Christianity*, 198.

In exploring how insights from Mauss might illuminate understanding of the complex web of relationships in the Faith Movement, I have been informed by a number of more recent scholars.

A doorway into understanding the usefulness of this complex but valuable interpretive tool was an essay by Tim Woods,[71] exploring Nuruddin Farah's novel *Gifts*.[72] Woods observes,[73] Farah's acknowledgement of his debt of insight to Mauss. He also notes the view of Claude Levi-Strauss that, as a study of gift giving, *The Gift* inaugurated a new era for the social sciences, reaching beyond empirically observed behavior, demonstrating how unconscious rules of exchange manifest the deeper realities of society's composition.[74] Woods notes "that where empirical observation sees only giving, receiving and returning, Mauss sees a whole series of social relationships concealed in this process."[75]

Mauss distinguishes gift societies from commodity societies. Gift societies are dominated by kin relations that define individuals and their relations with, and obligations to, each other. Commodity societies are not defined by kin relationships but are made up of independent individuals who transact alienated commodities freely with each other, separating the giver from the recipient.[76]

Both of these definitions are more like "ideal types."[77] The commodity system of the modern west is observably affected by a veneer of relationships of giving and receiving that set up hierarchies, governed by rules that have their origin in conventions and relationships that developed in more primitive societies.

In my observation, the practices of giving and receiving in Word of Faith are comparable in many respects to Mauss's primitive gift societies.

Before we proceed, it would be helpful to give a brief description of some of the archaic practices of giving and receiving observed by Mauss.

First of all, for Mauss a significant term was the "potlatch." In the editorial note at the beginning of W. D. Hall's Translation of Mauss's *The Gift*,[78] the following statement of the meaning of the potlatch is made:

71. Woods, "Giving and Receiving."
72. Farah, *Gifts*.
73. Woods, "Giving and Receiving," 93.
74. Levi-Strauss, *Introduction to the Work of Marcel Mauss*, 46.
75. Woods, "Giving and Receiving," 93.
76. Ibid., 93–94.
77. See the Weberian concept of ideal types.
78. Mauss, *The Gift: The Form and Reason for Exchange in Archaic Societies* (2011).

The North American Indian term "potlatch" has been retained in the translation. Various definitions of it are given in the text: "system for the exchange of gifts," (as a verb) "to feed, to consume," "a place of being satiated" [Boas]. As elaborated by Mauss, it consists of a festival where goods and services of all kinds are exchanged. Gifts are made and reciprocated with interest. There is a dominant idea of rivalry and competition between the tribe or tribes assembled for the festival, coupled occasionally with conspicuous consumption.[79]

Mauss himself tells us that "potlatch" is a Chinook word. He says that the Tlingit and Haida tribes of North West America, being very rich, passed their winters in constant festival, during which marriages, initiations, shamanistic séances and cults of the great gods took place. He writes, "These are all accompanied by ritual and by prestations by whose means political rank within sub-groups tribes, tribal confederations and nations is settled." Ian Cunnison, translator of *The Gift* (1954), informs us that the French word "prestation" is used by Mauss "to mean any thing or series of things given freely or obligatorily as a gift or in exchange; and include services, entertainments, etc., as well as material things."[80] So the tribal leaders that Mauss describes demonstrate their wealth and therefore their status by being more and more conspicuously generous.

I am reminded of one of Savelle's stories of a poor family, just mother and children who had driven in an old car across America from Boston to Augusta, Georgia, to hear Savelle and Jesse Duplantis speak at a conference. The car had broken down right in front of the hotel where Savelle and Duplantis were staying. A little girl in the family prayed that God would send Brother Jerry to fix the car. When she saw him, she ran over to him and told him that she prayed for God to send him to them. Savelle offered to get the car towed to a garage and have it repaired, saying that he would pay for it. He also offered to pay for them to stay in the hotel, and to pay for whatever they wanted to eat from the hotel menu. Duplantis was there with Savelle. Duplantis said, "You're not getting all that blessing. I'm paying for half of this." Savelle writes, "Well, we got their car repaired, and Jesse and I paid for it. We paid for the room, and we loaded them up with tapes and books and gave them some money to get back home."[81] Here, Savelle and Duplantis exhibit competitiveness in giving so they may both receive a blessing. They display their wealth, and this no doubt increased their status within the movement, certainly as the story is published in Savelle's book. At

---

79. Ibid., vii.
80. Mauss, *The Gift: Forms and Functions of Exchange in Archaic Societies* (1966), xi.
81. Savelle, *Expect the Extraordinary*, 96–101.

conferences and gatherings of this sort within the Faith Movement, people will see opportunities to sow money by giving to others in order to receive a blessing from God. In doing this, they may well increase their reputation among their friends and acquaintances as being people of faith, and those who have a known ministry are obvious targets for people to give to so they may receive a blessing from God in return. None of this requires God to exist in order to operate; it is about sowing and reaping and building reputation. Of course, there will be those who give, perhaps not conspicuously enough or who are not known by anyone, and so they are unlikely to be noticed and receive any blessing or return from those who might give to those perceived to be giving and therefore deserving blessing.

This leads on to the second significant concept I want to highlight from *The Gift*, which is the hau. The motive for reciprocity is explained by Mauss using the mysterious Maori concept of the "hau." The detail of the origins of this term are helpfully explained by Lewis Hyde; he writes

> The Maori have a word, *hau*, which translates as "spirit," particularly the spirit of the gift and the spirit of the forest which gives food. In these tribes, when hunters return from the forest with birds they have killed, they give a portion of the kill to the priests, who, in turn cook the birds at a sacred fire. The priests eat a few of them and then prepare a sort of talisman, the *mauri*, which is a physical embodiment of the forest *hau*. This *mauri* is a gift the priests give back to the forest, where, as a Marori sage once explained to an Englishman, it "causes the birds to be abundant . . . , that they may be slain and taken by man." There are three gifts in this hunting ritual; the forest gives to the hunters, the hunters to the priests, and the priests to the forest. At the end, the gift moves from the third party back to the first.[82]

Hyde adds the following comments:

> With a simple give-and-take, the hunters may begin to think of the forest as a place to turn a profit. But with the priests involved, the gift must leave the hunters' sight before it returns to the woods. The priests take on or incarnate the position of the third thing to avoid the binary relation of the hunters and the forest which by itself would not be abundant. The priests, by their presence alone, feed the spirit. . . . The return gift, the "nourishing *hau*," is literally feedback. . . . We all know that it isn't "really" the *mauri* placed in the forest that causes the birds

---

82. Hyde, *The Gift*, 18.

to be abundant. . . . The forest's abundance is in fact a consequence of man's treating its wealth as a gift.[83]

Woods, in his essay, describes Mauss's theory of why gifts are reciprocated.[84] Mauss suggests that a spirit of power resides in the thing that compels the recipient to return it. The circulation of gifts is explained by the mysterious Maori concept of *hau*, a spiritual power invested in the gift which causes reciprocation.[85] Woods prefers Farah's explanation of the circulation of gifts to the metaphysical explanation of Mauss. Farah's novel seems to suggest that the giver himself is bound into a cycle, responding with counter-presentation: the donor is already implicated as a receiver before a gift is given.

This strikes me as having relevance to the sort of mechanism that might well be at work in the Word of Faith law of seedtime and harvest. God is paralleled by the forest, the priests are the Faith teachers who receive gifts on behalf of God, and the hunters are those who make gifts to others, and especially to preachers in Word of Faith contexts. Just as the tribesmen sow a portion of their catch as an offering back to the forest via the priests, so Word of Faith adherents sow their money expecting a return from God. If they are known as faithful sowers in the Faith discourse community, they may well sooner or later receive a return. Simon Coleman illustrates this sort of activity, citing a story that appeared in the Livets Ord *Word of Life Newsletter*:

> At a meeting there was a sermon about God as the God of plenty. Two collections were taken up. On the second one I felt that I should give my last money. I needed it. In any case I put 50 crowns [about 4 pounds sterling] in and thought I had 10 left. When I came out I had the 50-crown note left and must have put the tenner in instead. But in my heart I had given the 50-crown note away. The same day I went into a video shop. As I stood there a man came in and said: "Lucky that you're here. You see my wife and I decided this morning to give you 5000 crowns!!!" I was so happy at this 100-fold harvest that I witnessed about Jesus to everybody standing around me and on the way out. God is good!

Coleman comments,

---

83. Ibid., 18–19.
84. Woods, "Giving and Receiving," 99.
85. Mauss, *The Gift* (2011), 13–14.

> We see here how a sermon leads to inner conviction, followed by action. The motivation of the person is not only tested, it is also measured—and found to be worth "50" rather than "10." Giving is rewarded by receiving, not from the original recipient (in this case, the group itself) but from two people who may or may not be strangers to the narrator but who themselves feel an urge to give to him. The reward is an impressive return on the original.[86]

In this case the couple probably did know the person who received the gift. Had they observed his giving at Livets Ord and decided to bless him? So, again, this mechanism does not need a spiritual explanation.

Another important concept from *The Gift* is that of "the big man."[87] Milbank picks this up; he writes

> In the case of the archaic societies described by Malinowski and Mauss, one finds a great accentuation of all the traits of gift exchange which survive spasmodically in our society: *obligation* to give, obligation *to receive,* and obligation to *give back.*[88]

Milbank notes from Mauss that in "certain archaic cultures there is an obligation *to give back more.*"[89] Milbank draws from Mauss and more recent anthropologists that "big men" gave gifts to retain their place of domination in kinship groups.[90] There was an obligation to be always more generous than your rivals, so that the out-given other remains more in your debt than you in his. In support of this, Milbank cites Gregory.[91] He notes that "Gregory appears to stress only the self-interested aspect of "giving back more" and to deny the social obligation to be ever-more-generous in big man societies." However, Milbank counters this by pointing to "Andrew Strathern, *The Rope of Moka* for an account of a 'big man' urging the underlings to give more at a gift-giving ceremony."[92]

If we turn again to my case studies, the Maussian concept of the "big man" might well be helpful. If we consider Urquhart's Kingdom Faith, Reid's Peniel, and associates of Jerry Savelle's ministry as ecclesiastical tribes, then Urquhart, Reid, and Savelle might well be considered as the "big men," who

---

86. Coleman, *The Globalisation of Charismatic Christianity*, 194–95.
87. Mauss, *The Gift* (1966), 12.
88. Milbank, "Can a Gift be Given?" 126–27.
89. Ibid., 127.
90. Ibid.
91. Gregory, *Gifts and Commodities*, 9, 53.
92. Milbank, "Can a Gift be Given?" 155.

are seen as givers—either, as in Savelle's case, as a financial sower, or as someone who sows teaching as a gift to their adherents attracting abundant gifts in return. Their approach suggests that the more you give in partnership to their ministry, the more you will receive from God—or so you think.

In a footnote, Coleman observes that

> Percy . . . reiterates the Weberian point that charismatic leaders can act as obligatory passages through which the best blessings flow. "Certain people become key points or agents in a distributive power circuit. . . . Charisma is a dominating nodal point in a circuit of power, which is also a place of limited exchange for believers. They must be willing to shed material or ideological baggage and suspend belief above reality, but in return for this they receive power themselves, and feel blessed. The more you give, the more you get."[93]

Those who want to bless you actually share in your blessing. Reputation and the discourse community enhance this.

---

93. Coleman, *The Globalisation of Charismatic Christianity*, 207.

CHAPTER 8

The Charisma of Leaders

8.1 Introduction

IN THIS FINAL CHAPTER, I want to examine some of the underlying factors that account for the rise and success of my case study ministries before making final conclusions.

There has always been a special relationship between English and American evangelicals, with a regular flow of ideas in both directions across the Atlantic. However, throughout the later half of the twentieth century, English evangelicals became accustomed to the arrival of regular innovations from the United States with fresh ideas for evangelism, worship, and church growth.[1] What many evangelicals did not realize is they had settled

---

1. My own experience of this from 1974 onwards is illustrative. My early encounters with American evangelicalism were with the worship songs of Betty Pulkingham's Fisherfolk, the Christian rock music of Larry Norman, and Jimmy and Carol Owens's musical *Come Together*. However, 1984 saw the arrival of John Wimber, his teaching and demonstrations of healing in London, and his books *Power Evangelism* and *Power Healing*, which were key influences on me. This led, in my experience, to an ongoing relationship with Vineyard through St. Andrew's Chorleywood, led by Bishop David Pytches, and, later, the New Wine conference, which hosted a number of American preachers and worship leaders—for example, James Ryle and Bill Johnson. Another key figure for me in the 1990s particularly was Derek Prince, who, although born in India to British parents, emigrated to the United States in 1963 and based initially in Seattle and then, from 1968, in Fort Lauderdale, Florida. Through Pytches and St. Andrew's Chorleywood, I encountered the Kansas City Prophets and, more latterly, Mike Bickle and the "prophetic movement." In 1994, I encountered a different form of American Church (non-charismatic, seeker-friendly) through a conference held in Cardiff by the Willow Creek Community Church. From 1994 onwards, I became increasingly aware of the Toronto Blessing, attending Toronto in January 1996, and then the Pensacola and Lakeland revivals. To this list could be added a number of other influential international leaders and speakers, although not from America, who have themselves been

for a form of religion that was uneventful, even boring; and with the steady rise of secularization,[2] there was an unspoken anxiety. As Paul Bramadat points out regarding secularization, "this contentious theory forms part of the backdrop of virtually all contemporary discussions about the nature and role of religion in the modern world."[3]

The response of entrepreneurial evangelicals throughout the 1990s in particular was, in the words of Rob Warner, "a collective amnesia about past disappointments." As they hastened "from one mission initiative to the next," they exhibited,

> a late modern preoccupation with mechanical techniques . . . allegedly guaranteed to deliver immanent growth; and an inclination to "vision inflation" that anticipates success in inverse proportion to the impact of secularization.[4]

That anxiety was relieved, in part, by these largely American innovations. English churches and ministries that welcomed these initiatives were led by their own lively entrepreneurial leaders who were all too ready to welcome new things.

Those bringing the ideas were selling something, something that appeared to work. From the nation where pragmatism developed as a philosophy and attitude, it is not surprising that this was the case. The problem for most of those attracted to these ideas was that while they initially embraced them with enthusiasm and vigor, they were always looking for something better. People became addicted to new teaching and new and powerful manifestations.[5] Many of those who came from America were openly offering secret insights into Christian truth that had not yet been discovered.[6] For me, John Wimber was, in the 1980s, a key figure in what

---

significantly influenced by American teaching: Bill Subritsky, Paul Yongi Cho, Brian Houston, Carlos Annacondia, and Ed Silvoso. Finally, Colin Urquhart's books were a draw to me through the 1980s and 1990s.

2. See Brown, *The Death of Christian Britain*, and Bruce, *God is Dead*.

3. Bramadat, *The Church on the World's Turf*, 12.

4. Warner, *Secularization and its Discontents*, 148.

5. Andrew Walker notes the religious addiction traits of fundamentalists; see Osborn and Walker, *Harmful Religion*, 3–5.

6. In contrast to the understanding of grace as being the unmerited favor of God, James Ryle (founder and president of Truthworks, and leading speaker on behalf of the Promise Keepers in the United States) taught at New Wine (1997) that grace is "the empowering presence of God." To those interested in power, this was an exciting prospect, that with this fresh revelation they could now start to live in hope. Evangelicals also embraced the innovative teaching of American Brian McLaren and his books—for example, *The Secret Message of Jesus*.

was a significant change in the charismatic renewal. He really introduced and developed the miraculous in an accessible way, but also brought with him charisma, charm, and an image that people were comfortable with. His Vineyard church, although eventually setting up congregations in the UK, became, from the 1980s onwards, a source of new worship and new experiences of the power of God.[7] The Vineyard "brand" was influential on both Anglican and New Church evangelicals.[8] This branding of religion led to an increasing commodification of renewal. Although free gifts of the miraculous and empowering presence of God were on offer, there were also products, books, tapes, CDs, videos, and DVDs for sale. Wimber was doing what was common among other evangelists in the United States at the time.

Wimber's bringing of power changed the charismatic renewal in mainstream denominations. Pentecostals realized that charismatics were becoming more like them, so they began to interact extensively, realizing that they had much in common.

Some went further; rather than embracing Wimber, they wanted even more power. For example, Colin Urquhart, although not critical of Wimber, embraced a different style and took on insights from Pentecostal and Word of Faith teachers, such as Benson Idahosa (see chapter 4).[9]

Evangelicals associated with the Pentecostal tradition knew of an older generation of American revivalists of whom great stories were told. These revivalists had, in post-war America, almost legendary tent campaigns with claims of great miracles.[10] To some in the new churches of the late twentieth century, both leaders and ordinary church members, the spiritual descendants of those American revivalists offered something extra, not only principles that would result in power to heal, but also, in some cases, power to overcome in life so that followers could have lives characterized by health and material prosperity. To those who were sick or struggling with their health, and those living from pay day to pay day—in other words, those of a certain social class[11]—stories of healing and God's miraculous provision, and suggestions of how to tap into these things, were highly attractive.

7. See Percy, *Words, Wonders and Power*.

8. Percy observes in *Words, Wonders and Power* the comfortable American father-like image of Wimber. The staged presentation of ideas remind me of the presentation of Apple iPhones and other products by Steve Jobs. Charisma of this sort I would suggest is highly marketable.

9. It ought to be noted that my other English case study, Michael Reid (a Pentecostal), is highly critical of Wimber and strategic-level spiritual warfare.

10. Revivalists such as William Branham and Kathryn Khulman. See Pullum, *Foul Demons, Come Out*.

11. Mainly the aspirational working-class and lower middle-class.

It is the persuasive teachings and principles of these preachers and their origin that this book has been exploring. More than that, I have been seeking to unearth clues in order to answer my principal research questions. What social and theological construction of reality, and what factors or reasons, make these ministries appealing to people, and what is the true nature of what these ministries offer?

I intend to examine my case studies further by looking at a number of factors that help in understanding the susceptibility of the adherents of my case study ministries, the persuasiveness of the leaders, and any possible American cultural influences.

8.2 Charisma

8.2.1 Charismatic Authority and Persuasion

In any study of the persuasion of religious leaders, there must be consideration of their charismatic authority. In observing my case studies, we shall see that charismatic authority is a significant factor in their ability to persuade and create the world they inhabit. In explaining the social significance of "charisma," the most important academic authority to turn to is Max Weber, who effectively introduced the term to sociological methods. He used the term in his classification of types of authority: rational-legal, traditional, and charismatic authority. He distinguished the charismatic leader from "ordinary men" and argued that they should be "treated as endowed with supernatural, superhuman, or at least specifically exceptional powers or qualities."[12] In his view, common leaders do not have what is seemingly a divinely given authority. This supernatural charisma is recognized and validated by followers who find evidence in the actions, the oratory and the presence or image of the leader. Weber acknowledges the inherent instability of charisma in which the charismatic leader "gains and maintains authority solely by proving his strength." If the leader cannot "perform miracles" or "heroic deeds," then the followers will eventually evaporate.

Charismatic leaders are different to others, tending to be revolutionary, and continually requiring followers to reject "all ties to any external order" and to break with "traditional or rational norms" in order to maintain their charismatic authority. Although Weber notes that charismatic authority tends to be subversive, criticizing or transcending established structures, there is the possibility that charismatic influence may result in

---

12. Weber, *The Theory of Social and Economic Organization*, 328, 358–59; Weber, *On Charisma and Institution Building*, 22, 24.

a stable movement in itself, especially if there is continuity and succession of leadership, resulting in the routinization of charisma and the continuing arrival of new phenomena. Charismatic leaders continually maintain the recognition of their supernatural gift by providing an ongoing flow of miracles or works of power.[13]

In this section, I intend to follow the pattern of Percy's analysis[14] of the dimensions and process of charisma that reveal "the integral interrelationships that exist between leader and led." Alluding to these relationships, Thomas Dow states that "obviously, people must recognize, accept, and follow the pretender before he can be spoken of as truly charismatic. The question is why do they do so?"[15]

There are a number of elements that contribute to the overall charisma of the leader as recognized by followers, which we now consider.

8.2.2 Charismatic Message Elements

The message has a number of possible characteristics.

8.2.2.1 A Strikingly Revolutionary Message

The revolutionary message seems to be the best way for followers to find a way out from the present perceived crisis.

If we first consider Colin Urquhart, he proclaims a radical revolutionary message that claims to be able to change the whole fabric of British society and rescue the church in England from numerical decline by bringing in revival. His own flagship church in Horsham, West Sussex, is called the National Revival Centre, almost implying that revival, as far as the whole of the UK is concerned, might well be significantly enabled by his ministry.[16] It has long been known that Urquhart believes that his ministry exists to prepare and equip leaders for a revival that will result in "a true turning back of this country to God." His "vision" for this is set out in *The Coming Revival: Colin Urquhart's Vision* by Melanie Symonds. More recently, this vision is usually voiced by his son and successor Clive, suggesting a likely routinization of charisma.[17]

---

13. Arthur Schweitzer, "Theory and Political Charisma."
14. Percy, *Words, Wonders and Power*, 53–59.
15. Dow, "The Theory of Charisma."
16. See "Urquhart's National Revival Centre."
17. Clive Urquhart says, "I live for revival. . . . It's the church living in the power of

If we consider Michael Reid, an essential focus of his ministry is his miraculous healings. The major revolutionary aspect of his message is that if you do not see miracles like those at Peniel in your church, then you have not found a true church where Jesus is at work. Reid frequently states "no miracles, no Jesus," as we have seen in chapter 5.

Finally, in the case of Jerry Savelle, his continually stated aim is to "talk people out of poverty and sickness." According to Savelle, full acceptance of his argument will result in divine life transformation for those who are poor or sick. It will turn people from losers to winners.

8.2.2.2 The Message Must Be Simple.

Charismatic leaders frequently use simple straightforward language. For example, the grammatical and linguistic simplicity of Urquhart's writings and broadcasts are obvious.[18] However, people are aware of a background of study, particularly his use of biblical Greek in hermeneutics. While followers perceive in his teaching "truths" that are clear "insights" into the working of the created order and the kingdom of God,[19] the simplicity of his message leads to a reduction in the likelihood of selecting alternative, more complex explanations.

Michael Reid's books, with titles such as *It's So Easy*, and his sermons are in general very simple in their linguistic style. An exception would be his published DMin book as mentioned in chapter 5.[20] Again, people have an awareness that Reid has a capable mind but that he expresses truths in simple terms for ordinary followers.

---

the gospel, it's seeing a nation turn back to God. I can see the very fabric of society being changed, areas of government, law and even policy being shaped again by the truth of God's word. I see households of whole families coming to God from the toughest estates to the most rural areas." See "Revival."

18. As I noted in chapter 4, Peters reveals in Urquhart's biography a number of significant things about Urquhart's audiences and followers. Peters quotes from a letter written to him by Lord Runcie, who was Bishop of St. Albans during Urquhart's time as vicar of St. Hughes Lewsey. Runcie comments, "I don't think Colin's ministry was very effective amongst the more intelligent and sophisticated; but then, 'not many learned' . . . ." See Peters, *Colin Urquhart*, 48. Runcie is portrayed by Peters and, indeed, Urquhart himself, as being sympathetic to Urquhart, but he obviously observed that while many of Urquhart's followers were enthusiastic, not many were theologically sophisticated.

19. Peters notes that "[l]ots of students come to the college [Roffey Place] precisely because Colin is there. They are eager to learn from him principles of faith, holiness and healing, three fundamental emphases of his ministry" See Peters, *Colin Urquhart*, 2.

20. Reid, SLSW.

Jerry Savelle's output in terms of books and television shows is, by nature, highly simplistic. However, the perception of readers and viewers who "buy into" his message is that he is no fool, who has well-reasoned arguments. But because of the speed and persistence of his delivery,[21] there is a tendency not to question his narrative and resulting principles.

8.2.2.3 Charismatic Messages Often Have Inherent Presence

Charismatic persuasion often relies on the "presence" of the leader and their "aura of pertinency." Louise Karon, in her essay on *The New Rhetoric*, highlights the effects of presence in charismatic persuasion:

> First, it [presence] is a felt quality in the audience's consciousness. This quality, created by the rhetor's "verbal magic," enables him to impress upon the audience whatever he deems important. Second, presence fixes the audience's attention while alerting its perceptions and perspectives. Third, its strongest agent is the imagination. Fourth, its purpose is judgement. Fifth, it is created chiefly through techniques traditionally studied under the headings of style, delivery, and disposition.[22]

Certainly, all three of my case studies have "presence." For example, videos of Reid preaching at Peniel reveal a congregation often spellbound by his addresses, with a packed auditorium and many people taking notes. Reid seems to choose titles for many of his sermons that directly address the perceived problems of the followers, dealing with their possible fears and troubles, and especially countering the likelihood of people making mistakes and experiencing failure because of their lack of faith. Reid's sermons have a challenging edge, and as he delivers them, he is seen to walk back and forth on the stage, microphone in hand, engaging the congregation. Because of his size and his deep strong voice, he has a commanding presence. Challenging titles of his sermons include "Bitter or Blessed,"[23] "Faith or Fatalism,"[24] "Attitudes that Destroy,"[25] and "Avoiding Foolishness."[26] Similar observations can be made of Urquhart and Savelle.

---

21. In Savelle's television programs, his presentation is often relentless in its pace.
22. Karon, "Presence in *The New Rhetoric*," 97.
23. "Bitter or Blessed."
24. Reid, "Faith or Fatalism."
25. Reid, "Attitudes that Destroy."
26. Reid, "Avoiding Foolishness."

8.2.2.4 A Charismatic Message is Dependent on the Promulgation (Formally Proclaiming or Declaring) of Collective Identity.

In other words, this means agreeing to sign up to the movement or organization and identifying with the leader. Eric Hoffer points out that the true charismatic leader must evoke "the enthusiasm of the communion—the sense of liberation from a petty and meaningless individual existence."[27]

Martin Spencer adds the insight that the articulated message must say "what people want to hear, but do not know how to say themselves."[28] Shared identity in the charismatic situation is vital if the audience is to be persuaded, and not just thrilled.

In my contacts with Savelle's ministry in order to buy books, I have received, with the book, a magazine and a letter informing me that I am now a "partner" with Jerry Savelle; they even gave me a number. I am sure there are many who give offerings to this ministry who choose to join the collective identity associated with Savelle.

This becoming a partner idea is also employed by Urquhart's Kingdom Faith.[29] Joining the collective identity of Reid's Peniel seems to have been much more comprehensive. As well as tithing their income to the church, members were encouraged to send their children to the church's fee paying school, and to buy mortgages and insurance products from companies owned by the leaders and advertised in the church's newspaper.[30]

8.2.2.5 Charismatic Messages are Often Characterized by "Polarized Aggression"

Irvine Schiffer[31] uses this term to point to the charismatic communicator's ability to argue for something, against something. This requires a characterization of opposing viewpoints.

Urquhart is sometimes seen to dismiss implicitly those who might have psychological explanations of spiritual phenomena. For example, in his biography by John Peters, it is revealed that when Urquhart first experienced

---

27. Hoffer, *The True Believer*, 105.
28. Martin Spencer, "What is Charisma?" 348.
29. See "Becoming a Kingdom Faith Partner."
30. See Sarah Jones, *Call Me Evil, Let Me Go*, plus the personal account of a number former members of Peniel who have identified Sarah Jones as Caroline Green, a former member of Peniel.
31. Schiffer, *Charisma*, 37.

glossolalia, while he was at St. Boniface Training College, Warminster, he did not understand what was happening. So he consulted a member of staff, who did not understand Colin's experience either, and offered a psychological explanation of what had happened, something that Urquhart rejected as unhelpful.[32] Similarly, there is an implied criticism of those whose preaching is complex and therefore deemed as unintelligible. For example, in the promotion video for his 2008 Faith Camp, Urquhart says,

> You have to admit that when I preach you can understand what I'm saying, so you've got no excuses for disobeying. . . . I mean you can't say, well, I couldn't understand what he was talking about. What was he talking about? I don't know what he was talking about, all this high-faluting language, no, no, it's very simple.[33]

Here, Urquhart compares his teaching with those who use complex language.

In an address to church leaders in the UK, Reid says that people who are not seeing miracles cannot be teaching right.[34] Approaches of this sort often caricature those who the leader opposes. The leader distinguishes between those who are "dead" and those who are "alive" (in their spiritual vitality).

Sometimes, Satan is humanized as a personal adversary who constantly seeks to lie about, undermine, and destroy the work of the charismatic leader and the followers.[35] All three of my case studies believe and warn their followers to be aware of Satan. Urquhart, for example, produced a whole set of addresses on his *Faith for Today* program entitled "Overcoming the Enemy,"[36] with individual talks entitled "Knowing Your Enemy," "Names of Satan," How the Enemy Operates," "How to Overcome the Enemy," and "Getting Free from Bondage." Other teaching about believers struggling with Satan is to be found in Urquhart's book *Explaining Deception*.[37] His talks reveal his views that Satan binds and hinders the faith of believers. However, there is no explicit claim that Satan should be blamed for failure to heal.

Reid is similar. Although he believes in the existence of Satan, he warns people about the undue attention given to Satan and the demonic through the methods of strategic-level spiritual warfare espoused by John Wimber,

---

32. Peters, *Colin Urquhart*, 10.

33. "Faith08 promo video." I am sure certain leaders from mainstream denominations are envisaged here.

34. See "How to Recognise True Annointings."

35. Savelle especially talks about Satan as if he is virtually an incarnate being.

36. All broadcast in the week 11th -15th January 2010.

37. Urquhart, *Explaining Deception*, 26, 27, 41.

C. Peter Wagner, and others[38]—though sometimes he himself seems to give too much attention to Satan. At the beginning of a talk about God's authority, he says, "I want to talk about Satan's dominion and God's,"[39] almost as if God is an afterthought.

As with Urquhart, there is no evidence that I have seen that Reid blames Satan[40] for an individual's spiritual failure in terms of healing, or that he excuses his own inability to heal by blaming Satan.

Savelle, on the other hand, seems to blame Satan for everything that goes wrong. Even the titles of his books suggest that it is giving in to Satan and not applying faith principles that leads to poverty in terms of material goods and failure to achieve your ambitions.[41] This is inevitable in the rhetoric of a charismatic leader who needs someone or something to blame when their message appears to fail. If followers are faithfully applying the teachings of the leader, there must be another explanation for failure. Usually, in the case of these sort of ministries, the intervention of Satan or unconfessed sin are often the cause.

The above factors are not the only possible ingredients, but they are often present in the teachings and approaches of charismatic leaders. Their presence increases the likelihood of people following.

8.2.3 Personality Elements

Weber's work highlights the importance of personality in charisma. Although charismatic leaders can have widely differing social and cultural backgrounds and address varying crises and needs, common personality traits are identifiable. All of them are not essential but the more a leader has, the more persuasive they tend to be.

The first is perceived "high status." This is achieved by appointment to a position or role, or through the ability to produce results in the form of miracles, or both. In either process, "routinization of charisma" takes place, which moves the leader to a position that is exalted above that of the group.[42]

Another trait is a "stranger quality," or an air of aloofness from the group, although too much of this could be counterproductive and alienating. As Percy says, "Perhaps the proverb 'familiarity breeds contempt' has a

---

38. Reid, *Strategic Level Spiritual Warfare*, 14–23.
39. "God's authority." 1 min 39 secs–1 min 43 secs.
40. At least in public addresses.
41. Savelle, *If Satan Can't Steal Your Dreams He Can't Control Your Destiny* and *If Satan Can't Steal Your Joy He Can't Keep Your Goods*.
42. See sections 8.2.1 and 8.2.2.1 of this book.

corollary: something strange yet familiar breeds charisma."[43] Certainly, in all of my three case studies, both of these traits are present.

Although Urquhart has handed on succession to his son, Clive, he seems to have no less authority at major events such as Faith Camp. Pastor Colin, as he is known, has taken on the role of the "Apostle" who oversees and "covers" Kingdom Faith.[44] In the day to day running of Kingdom Faith and Roffey Place College, Colin Urquhart is still involved, but most leadership tasks are delegated to others, and he keeps some distance from the mundane. This increases his mystique and charisma.[45]

As we have seen in chapter 5, in 1996, Reid was consecrated as a bishop in the International Communion of Charismatic Churches. Despite the criticism of some that this appointment is not the equivalent of bishops in the established Church of England, Reid was consecrated by Idahosa, who was respected by a huge following in Nigeria, into a denomination whose bishops were recognized by Pope Paul VI in 1978.[46] This status has since been a prominent part of Reid's self-presentation.

In my observation of Reid, while he was at Peniel, he was nearly always the preacher, certainly at main morning worship and through the church's media of television and DVDs. He also seems to be the only person at Peniel who could "heal" (or was allowed to heal). In all of the videos, he is the one who seemingly is the focus of Christ's power to heal. So Reid was viewed as the only one who was worth listening to, and the only one who could produce results, building in an inherent indispensability.

Savelle's status seems to be the result of his partnership with Copeland, who is viewed by many as the leader of Word of Faith worldwide. Although Savelle was ordained by Copeland, he has no special title except "Doctor," which, as we have discussed in chapter 6, appears to be the result of having an honorary degree from Oral Roberts University.

In contrast to these remarks, a third trait is the exhibition of "conquerable imperfection." While all three of my case studies have worked hard to put over a strong charismatic image, they all are keen to stress their ordinariness. Urquhart, for example, right from the beginning of his ministry, has expressed his own feelings of inability to lead and teach others.[47]

---

43. Percy, *Words, Wonders and Power*, 56.

44. Some insights into the phenomenon of twentieth-century apostles and the process of recognition of "apostolic anointing" are to be found in Kay, *Apostolic Networks* and Wagner, *Apostles Today*, 68–70.

45. In a visit to Roffey Place, I could not fail to notice the awe of a student who told me excitedly, "Pastor Colin is lecturing us this morning."

46. See chapter 5.

47. See Urquhart, *When the Spirit Comes*, 10.

Reid's public image was, as far as many church members were concerned (as we noted in chapter 5), of a successful but ordinary man who enjoyed fly fishing, cooking, horse riding and golf.[48] Savelle, as we noted in chapter 6, tells his life story, with considerable humor, of how he was an ordinary man who did not want to be religious, but how his life changed, influenced by his wife Carolyn, his future mentor Kenneth Copeland, and his belief that God had taken hold of his life for a purpose. He describes himself as a failure before he met Copeland.[49]

This trait can be further endorsed by a fourth, namely sexual mystique. As Percy notes, Jimmy Bakker and Jimmy Swaggart have both shown this; that the sexuality of the charismatic leader is of absorbing interest to immediate followers, not just the general media.[50] As far as I am aware, there is no suggestion of sexual impropriety with regard to Urquhart or Savelle. However, Reid is of particular interest in this respect. He still has a significant following and faithful supporters despite his alleged affair with the choir leader at Peniel and another woman.[51]

8.2.4 Delivery Elements

Ann R. Willner claims that

> nearly all leaders for whom charisma has been claimed have also been described as eloquent, or spell-binding orators. Charismatic appeal involves investigating not so much what a leader says, as how he says it, i.e., the style of his verbal communication.[52]

The three categories of speech delivery considered here represent elements that many theorists have mentioned as aiding charismatic perception. Each category has sub-characteristics that have been observed in speech delivery amongst charismatic leaders. The three to be discussed are vocal force, vocal inflexion, and non-verbal language—"body language" and other gestures.

First, vocal force is a general term that describes such delivery techniques as volume variety, pitch variables, stress on words, and so on. Erwin

---

48. "The History of Peniel Church—Part Four," 0 mins 37 secs.
49. Savelle, *In the Footsteps of a Prophet*, 46.
50. Percy, *Words, Wonders and Power*, 56.
51. Report of the testimony of Peniel church trustee Meidre Cleminson at an employment tribunal, where Reid argued that he had been unfairly dismissed: *Daily Express*, 1st December 2009.
52. Wilner, *Charismatic Political Leadership*, 103–4.

Bettinghaus's study of political campaigners and revivalists in *Persuasive Communication*[53] notes that a bond is often developed between audience and leader by means of vocal cues. Speaking softly, in a concerned voice, invites the audience to listen more attentively, and share the concern. Shouting or ranting can often be a vocal cue that suggests imminent action, outrage, or condemnation. The vocal force of the leader has an impact on the reception of the words that are being spoken, facilitating the charismatic process.

In this respect, all three of my case studies have remarkable rhetorical gifts. All three seem to preach without visible notes.

Second, Reid preaches holding a microphone in his hand; he starts at a podium, but walks to and fro in front of the congregation, looking directly at people while asserting his points. He regularly points his finger at people saying things such as, "If you think, then . . ." He raises his voice, almost shouting, to emphasize a point. However, when healing, he teaches the congregation while he speaks to the person in a much more gentle and sympathetic way.

Urquhart also walks to and fro on the stage. He tends to use a lot of hand gestures like Tony Blair and other political leaders: pointing to God above, but with his hand flat, lowering it, suggesting God's power coming down.

Savelle also walks around and holds his floppy Bible in one hand. He also points at the congregation to make a point, but it is not clear who he is pointing to, as if to say, if this speaks to you, receive what I am saying.

Third, situational non-verbal cues can arouse emotional responses as well. Audiences seeking a charismatic figure respond to the "body-language" of leader-communicators. For example, physical attractiveness can aid charismatic perception. Mark Knapp states that "it is not at all unusual to find physically attractive persons outstripping unattractive ones on a wide range of socially desirable evaluations, such as success, personality, popularity, sociability, sexuality, persuasiveness."[54]

Assessing attractiveness can be a highly subjective process. What is attractive to one person might not be to another.

At the time of much of the material considered in this book (for example, his miracles displayed on YouTube), Reid was a balding man with grey hair and increasingly overweight. To many, however, he was and is a large, tall, strong, comforting presence. He is also imposing in the sense he looks strong enough to deal with those who might aggressively disagree with him. At the same time, there is a gentleness about him; he is often

---

53. Bettinghaus, *Persuasive Communication*, 113.

54. Knapp, *Non-Verbal Communication in Human Interaction*, 158.

pictured holding the sick and vulnerable to his chest in a hug while praying for them. As a charismatic figure, Reid is typical in often using punches, wagging his finger, and pacing up and down while preaching, linked with sometimes exaggerated facial expressions and significant body posture.

Clothes can also make a statement about the charismatic leader. Rosenfeld and Civikly note that "we select fabric and color to help us conform to our self-image."[55] Reid nearly always wears expensive looking suits. He looks professional, even wealthy. Some of the socially aspirational working- or lower-middle-class in the congregation at Peniel may well have thought that if they could have the same faith as Reid, they may well be blessed with the same material success. I could not help but notice his car when he arrived to lead a church meeting in Ilford; it was a large, expensive-looking Land Rover as chunky and solid as the man driving it.

When I first went to Peniel, there seemed to be an abundance of men in suits or, at the very least, in jacket and trousers, and all wearing ties. Dressed in casual wear, I felt significantly underdressed.

Touch is also part of the process of non-verbal communication, and is often a vital element in the charismatic persuasion process. Touch is the "language of love and acceptance," according to Sidney Jourard,[56] in which intimate mutual identification can take place. In the charismatic situation, this can be especially so. Throngs of people yearned to touch Jesus Christ, so that miracles of healing might "flow" from him. This phenomenon is widespread today in Pentecostal circles, or in "faith healing" services. However, some are reluctant to touch while praying for a person to avoid the accusation of pushing people over, which is often made of healing evangelists such as Benny Hinn.

Much of what I have said about Reid could also be said about Savelle. Although he is short, he is, I am sure, in the eyes of many people, a handsome man. His hair, although grey now, is cut very cleanly in an American flat-top style, and he has shining white teeth. He tends to wear expensive suits at large preaching engagements, something that communicates his wealth and success, and which is common practice in Word of Faith churches nowadays, although in his television shows he is often casually dressed. If he is in his home environment while filming, he wears smart casual, very similar to Urquhart, putting over an image that is comforting, homely and successful. In his *Chariots of Light* videos, he is sometimes dressed in motorcycling "leathers," or in a way that looks like he has just been tinkering with his large collection of bikes and cars, but without getting dirty. This is

---

55. Rosenfeld and Civikly, *With Words Unspoken*, 71.
56. Journard, "An Exploratory Study of Body-Accessibility."

especially appealing to those who are motor enthusiasts themselves, and it identifies Savelle as an ordinary man. Savelle projects the image of a home-loving man; for example, in his magazine *Adventures in Faith*, he is often pictured with his wife and family, expensively dressed, and exuding an image of success.

It should be repeated that these messages, personality, and delivery characteristics of the charismatic communication situation are not prescriptive for every charismatic occasion. All sorts of variables in cultural settings and environmental crises create unique exhibitions of charismatic phenomena. But charismatic impact and persuasion are increased with the presence of each identifiable characteristic.

8.3 Enchantment, Disenchantment, Charisma, and *Habitus*

My initial encounter with each of the case study ministries was through a few individuals who had been or were still involved with these ministries, and who had a link with my church. In interviewing these people, it was clear there was or had been a real enchantment with the ministries concerned. The concepts of enchantment, disenchantment and charisma are famously associated with the work of Max Weber.

Weber defines charisma as

> a certain quality of an individual personality by virtue of which he is considered extraordinary and treated as endowed with supernatural, superhuman, or at least specifically exceptional powers or qualities. These are such as are not accessible to the ordinary person, but are regarded as of divine origin or as exemplary.[57]

Weber suggests that charisma is "guaranteed by what is held to be a proof, originally always a miracle."[58] The leader "gains and retains it solely by proving his powers in practice. He must work miracles if he wants to be a prophet."[59]

Weber's concept of rationalization is related directly to charisma; this is a complex term about which much is written. Talcott Parsons explains

---

57. Weber, *Economy and Society*, Vol. 1, 241.
58. Ibid., 242.
59. Ibid., 1114.

that, "Rationalization comprises first the intellectual clarification, specification and systematization of ideas."[60]

Among the many effects of rationalization is "the elimination of magic from the world."[61] Weber recognized that an effect of rationalization was "the disenchantment of the world."[62] S. N. Eistenstadt explains that this is "a concept which denotes the demystification and secularization of the world, the attenuation of charisma."[63]

However, although the longstanding sociological view of modernity, following Weber, is that it is characterized by disenchantment, Michael Saler summarizes the view of many that there is a resurgence of enchantment today evidenced by "a mélange of marvels once thought to have been exorcised by the rational and secular processes of modernity."[64] Indeed, a significant challenge to the classical Weberian account of disenchantment as a unidirectional and universalizing tendency of modernity is made by scholars such as Richard Jenkins.[65]

Claudia Währisch-Oblau, in her essay on material salvation in African migrant churches in Germany, writes of the "'enchanted' worldview in which outcomes in the material world are determined by events in the spiritual realm."[66] It is this sort of enchantment that is associated with a worldview that is constructed by the performative rhetoric of my case study ministries. In citing Fisher's narrative paradigm and John D. Niles *Homo narrans* in chapter 4, I argue that the stories and images in books and videos construct the enchanted worldview that attracts people to these ministries.[67]

In some adherents of my case studies, this led to disenchantment when it was realized that the claims made in terms of healing miracles and/or financial abundance did not materialize for them. However, adherents of my case study ministries even revealed a sense of addiction to the forms of worship and the atmosphere of meetings put on by the leaders concerned and their associates.[68] In interview, it was clear with refugees from King's

---

60. Parsons, "Introduction," xxxii.

61. Weber, *The Protestant Ethic and the Spirit of Capitalism*, 105.

62. Weber adopted this phrase from Friedrich Schiller. See Gerth and Wright Mills, "Bureaucracy and Charisma," 11.

63. Eisenstadt, *Max Weber on Charisma and Institution Building*, liv.

64. See Saler, "Modernity and Enchantment," also Saler, *As If*. Also Landy and Saler, *The Re-Enchantment of the World*.

65. Jenkins, "Disenchantment, Enchantment and Re-Enchantment."

66. Währisch-Oblau, "Material Salvation."

67. See this book chapter 4 and Fisher, "Narration as Human Communication Paradigm." See also Niles, *Homo Narrans*.

68. See Walker's comments on an addiction-model understanding of abuse in

Church, Medway, and from Peniel Church that, despite a feeling of unease, there was a real devotion to what was on offer. One of the King's Church people, when speaking about Savelle and others, told me, "We loved those guys; we couldn't miss their Bible week each year." Similarly, and to my initial surprise, one of the Peniel people told me his favorite teacher (because he was so "sound") was T. L. Osborn, and that he had many of his tapes.

Some of those I had interviewed had been at a number of churches, moving from one to another, attracted by what they considered to be a "fresh move of God." In thinking about this, I have come to realize that their behavior was most likely stimulated by, and in reaction to, an unwitting sense of the rise of secularization.[69]

As I have already explored in chapter 8, Reid, Urquhart, and Savelle all have significant charisma that attracts adherents. But each of them are subtly different. Closely linked to the charisma and enchantment surrounding these ministries is the concept of *habitus*. In seeking to gain a deeper understanding of enchantment from a sociological perspective, I was drawn to Kieran Flanagan's *The Enchantment of Sociology*.[70] Writing from a Catholic perspective, Flanagan states the aim of his study as "to give expression to a sociological habitus and to link reflexivity to theological reflection in understandings of culture."[71] The *habitus* of which he speaks is that of the distinctively cultural nature of Catholicism. Flanagan sees the monastery as the exemplary site for this *habitus*, but it also exemplifies the ideal field for re-enchantment and resistance to postmodernity.[72] I would argue, in a similar way, that the somewhat isolationist environments of Peniel and Roffey Place are fields ideal for an enchanting Word of Faith/charismatic *habitus*. As I noted in chapter 1, in his reflection on the Swedish charismatic church Livets Ord, Simon Coleman describes something like Bourdieu's *habitus*:[73] learned attitudes, habits, style, taste, body language, and so on, through which particular groups structure their lives.[74]

As a term in contemporary usage, *habitus* was introduced by Mauss.[75] The idea was significantly developed by Bourdieu.[76] Although the concept of

---

Osborn and Walker, *Harmful Religion*, 3–5.
69. See my chapter 8 and Warner, *Secularization and Its Discontents*, 148.
70. Flanagan, *The Enchantment of Sociology*.
71. Ibid., xi.
72. Ibid., x.
73. Coleman, *The Globalisation of Charismatic Christianity*, 62–64.
74. Ibid., 140–41.
75. Mauss, "Techniques of the Body."
76. Bourdieu, *Distinction*.

habitus is widely used, it is not always well understood. Bourdieu's language and explanation of concepts are often complex as he struggles with social realities.[77] In order to utilize his thinking, it is necessary to deconstruct and clarify his terms. Key concepts from Bourdieu's theory or practice are "agency," "field," "capital" and "*habitus*."[78]

When he refers to an "agent," he is talking about a person within a structure, such as a doctor in a hospital, a pupil in a school or a person involved in one of my Faith ministries. In a capital-based society, "cultural capital" refers to objects or things that possess value, money, possessions, or attributes such as education. An example of this might be the scholastic capital of a medical degree or a higher theological degree for Michael Reid and other leaders at Peniel. These objects can have value and directly affect relationships in the field. The field might be a hospital in the case of a doctor, or a church in the case of a church leader—although the field might be wider, such as a medical field in which a doctor might specialize, or, in the case of a church leader such as Michael Reid, associated faith and healing ministries in the south-east of England, or even a wider group of interested people around the world.

The self is understood as an "embodied history" where the body is a site in which social structures are internalized over a length of time. Social customs and conventions are "written" on the body, and this *habitus* determines our response to the situation in which we are placed. What is learned by the body, Bourdieu comments, is not something that one has, but something one is.[79] Agents behave in ways that are influenced by "history objectified in the form of structures and history incarnated in bodies in the form of habitus."[80]

Bourdieu's attempts to define *habitus* are often extremely complex; for example, a definition of *habitus* common in his writings refers to

> systems of durable, transposable dispositions, structured structures predisposed to function as structuring structures, that is, as principles which generate and organize practices and representations that can be objectively adapted to their outcomes without presupposing a conscious aiming at ends or an express mastery of the operations necessary in order to attain them. Objectively "regulated" and "regular" without being in any way

---

77. Bourdieu's writing approach is, in his own words, a "permanent struggle against ordinary language." See Bourdieu, *Homo Academicus*, 149.

78. This is not a thorough study of Bourdieu, just a clarification of his use of terms.

79. Bourdieu, *The Logic of Practice*, 73.

80. Bourdieu, *Pascalian Meditations*, 152.

the product of obedience to rules, they can be collectively orchestrated without being the product of the organizing action of a conductor.[81]

He says a lot in this definition and it needs to be broken down for a clear understanding. The term "disposition" or "dispositions" is explained by Bourdieu:

It expresses first the result of an organizing action, with a meaning close to that of words such as structure; it also designates a way of being, a habitual state (especially of the body) and, in particular, a predisposition, tendency, propensity or inclination.[82]

He comments further that these dispositions, that is, these tendencies or outlooks, are durable in that they last over time, and are transposable in the sense that they can become active in a variety of social fields.[83]

Habitus does not work in isolation. Bourdieu is not suggesting that agents are in some way unable to resist the way they have been programed by their past experiences. Instead, their behavior results from what he describes as, "an obscure and double relation"[84] or "an unconscious relationship"[85] between their *habitus* and any particular field. So their behavior is not simply due to their *habitus* alone, but affected by their capital and their field, that is, by their current circumstances.

A more concise and lucid definition of *habitus* is provided by Loïc Wacquant, Bourdieu's former student, and one of his main interpreters. *Habitus* is

the way society becomes deposited in persons in the form of lasting dispositions, or trained capacities and structured propensities to think, feel and act in determinant ways, which then guide them.[86]

Faith/charismatic *habitus* can be learned by participation in services and classes; Coleman observes that "preachers and those who stand closest to the stage, as well as ushers who stand at the end of each row, tend to be the most practised exponents and therefore act as exemplars for others."[87] Par-

---

81. Bourdieu, *Outline of a Theory of Practice*, 72.
82. Ibid., 214.
83. Bourdieu, *Sociology in Question*, 87.
84. Bourdieu and Wacquant, *An Invitation to Reflexive Sociology*, 126.
85. Bourdieu, *Sociology in Question*, 76.
86. Wacquant, "Habitus."
87. Coleman, *The Globalisation of Charismatic Christianity*, 140.

ticipation in the ritual acts of such meetings result in further enchantment. For example, Coleman notes[88] the phenomenon (without naming it) of being "slain in the Spirit" and cites Csordas's observation that the act of falling is spontaneously co-ordinated in such a way that, following Bourdieu, it can be described as a disposition within the charismatic ritual *habitus*.[89]

I would further argue that a Faith/charismatic *habitus* is cultivated in agents by sustained exposure to the wider field of the Faith/charismatic world. Reid's academic degrees (albeit through Oral Roberts University), Savelle's airplane and classic car collection, and Urquhart's large number of successfully marketed faith-building books are all examples of the cultural capital that works together with the *habitus* in the three fields of my case studies and the wider field of the Faith/charismatic world. Exposure to events such as Urquhart's Faith Camp, attending one of Reid's healing services, or participating in Savelle's Thunder Over Texas[90] may well result in an enchanted *habitus* that is taken back to the visitor's normal church.

8.4 Cognitive Dissonance

The concept of "cognitive dissonance" arose out of a study by Leon Festinger, Henry W. Riecken and Stanley Schachter of a 1950s UFO cult that predicted the end of the world, an end which did not materialize.[91] The theory was further developed and stated by Festinger.[92] The usefulness of this theory is not limited to millennial disappointment but can be applied to any area where supernatural claims are made without good evidence to support those claims. It is directly applicable to my case study ministries in discussing why people continue to be influenced by these ministries when they might suspect what is claimed in terms of the miraculous is not actually true and why some people come to their senses and leave.

In simple terms, cognitive dissonance is a tension that occurs in individuals when their belief is not matched by their experience. Festinger suggested that people who experience this tension attempt to reduce it by changing their beliefs or their behavior by replacing them with new

---

88. Ibid., 135.
89. Csordas, *The Sacred Self*, 233.
90. Thunder over Texas is a yearly gathering of members of the Chariots of Light motorcycle club in Granbury, Texas at which Savelle, Copeland, and DuPlantis preach.
91. Festinger et. al. *When Prophecy Fails.*
92. Festinger, *A Theory of Cognitive Dissonance.*

information or beliefs. Or they seek to forget or reduce in some way the thoughts (cognitions) that have led to the dissonance.[93]

8.5 Neo-Gnosticism

My case study ministries' leaders all make claim to have special knowledge and therefore extraordinary authority. For example, in the promotion video for his 2008 Faith Camp, Urquhart says, "You have to admit that when I preach, you can understand what I'm saying, so you've got no excuses for disobeying . . . no, no it's very simple."[94] Urquhart has an engaging preaching style, easily comprehended, and, as we have seen in chapter 3, presents with narratives that illustrate the pragmatic principles that he teaches. Interestingly, in the same video, a man attending the previous conference (2007) says, "It's definitely spending a good time with God and is a very good investment." I was struck by the neo-capitalist tone of this throwaway comment. I will comment on capitalism later in this chapter.

As we saw in chapter 5, Reid writes,

> It is so important to get the best ministers gifted in the things of God to come and share with the people to plant eternal things in their lives . . . find "fathers in the faith" who have succeeded and proved their ministry . . . without that demonstration of power, we merely have another philosophy. What separates Christianity from everything else is that we have a Jesus who is alive and does miracles. I often tell people, "No miracles, no Jesus!" Wherever Jesus is, and the gospel is preached in the power of the Spirit, there will always be miracles. If you go to a church where you do not see miracles regularly, you have not really found a church yet.[95]

He reiterates this throughout his books: "My desire wasn't to bring people into a religion but to bring them to Christ. The Church began with the simple occurrence of miracles because that's the way Jesus advertised his church. No miracles, . . . No Jesus!"[96] Also, "I tell people, if you go to a church where you don't see miracles: blind eyes opening, deaf ears unstopping, cripples running, then you haven't found a church yet . . . no miracles,

---

93. Festinger et. al. *When Prophecy Fails*, 25–26.
94. "Faith08 promo video."
95. Reid, *What God Can Do For You*, 61.
96. Reid, *It's So Easy*, 45.

... No Jesus."[97] Reid sees himself as an exceptional leader, a gifted father in the faith. His church is the place where you will find authentic Christianity as opposed to almost anywhere else. Former members of Peniel have told me that he frequently criticized other local leaders as failing to have Jesus at work in their churches.

Savelle, as we saw in chapter 6, suggests that the church needs preachers who preach with power and teach revelation knowledge (like Copeland and himself). He argues that this revelation of God's Word is made by anointed men of God who teach revelation knowledge, which comes from what Savelle believes is a Spirit-led interpretation of the scriptures. These preachers preach with power; they are not religious, they are different—like Christ. Savelle argues that every time Jesus healed, people thought bigger thoughts and their possibility levels were raised. The revelation these anointed Faith preachers preach consists of "principles God has written in his Word (his book) for men to live by."[98] There is a certain neo-Gnosticism about all of this, as described in Philip Lee's book *Against The Protestant Gnostics*.[99] I am not saying that my case studies are teaching the errors of the early Gnostics, but their claim to what approaches an exclusive access to power has a tendency towards the attitude of Gnosticism.

8.6 Class, Money, Evangelicals, and Revivalists

The early Christians, while they had the rich among them who had surrendered to their message, had a large majority of the poor. As H. Richard Niebuhr comments,

It began as a religion of the poor, of those who had been denied a stake in contemporary civilization. He cites Origen and Tertullian, along with opponents of Christianity such as Celsus, that, "the uneducated are always in a majority with us."[100]

New movements within the church though tended to reflect Jesus saying, "It will be hard for a rich person to enter the kingdom of heaven."[101] The poor found it easy to respond to the Christian gospel, with its offer to the poor of a share in the life to come, of a share in Christ's inheritance. They

---

97. Ibid., 77.
98. Savelle, tape of sermon at King's Church, Medway, Bible week 8th November 1999.
99. Lee, *Against The Protestant Gnostics*.
100. Niebuhr, *The Social Sources of Denominationalism*, 32.
101. Matt 19:23 (NRSV).

were also attracted by the suggestion of the gospel that the rich should share their wealth with them, and the practice of the apostles of sharing money raised by liquidation of the property of the wealthy among the poor. The vision that among the early Christians, "[a]ll who believed were together and had all things in common,"[102] was attractive to those in need. So while there was a promise of justice in the life to come, there was also hope of "abundant life" in the here and now. However, as Niebuhr comments,

> the new faith became the religion of the cultured, of the rulers, of the sophisticated; it lost its spontaneous energy amid the quibbling of abstract theologies; it sacrificed its ethical rigorousness in compromise with the policies of governments and nobilities; it abandoned its apocalyptic hopes as irrelevant to the well being of a successful church.[103]

While the Roman Church "supplied to the unsophisticated groups a type of religion which largely satisfied their longings, . . . Montanism, the Franciscan movement, Lollardy, Waldesianism, and many other similar tendencies are intelligible only as efforts of the religiously disinherited to discover again the sources of effective faith."[104]

Pre-Reformation Catholicism was a religion which, like all institutional churches, blessed the rich and kept the poor in their place; the institutions of the church had become based on the dominant feudalism of the period. Fourteenth-century reform movements such as Lollardy, inspired by Wycliffe and his "poor preachers," looked to a church that returned to a more equitable sharing of wealth.[105]

The Reformation, with its Bible in the languages of the masses, was a source of hope to the disinherited, a hope that was soon to be shattered when it became clear, despite the offer of salvation to all, that money was still firmly in the control of aristocratic church leaders and those they recruited as priests from among the poor, who became comfortable with their new positions of relative wealth. This soon led to frustration and the appearance of the churches of the disinherited—Anabaptism and similar—that promised, and were condemned as heretics for, a sort of communism. Condemnation for reinstitution of the New Testament idea of holding all things in common was widespread among the new "princes" of Protestantism. For example, the Church of England's Thirty-Nine Articles have, as Article 38,

---

102. Acts 2:44 (NRSV).
103. Niebuhr, *The Social Sources of Denominationalism*, 32–33.
104. Ibid., 33.
105. Aston, *Lollards and Reformers*, 160.

Of Christian men's Goods, which are not common. The riches and goods of Christians are not common, as touching the right, title, and possession of the same, as certain Anabaptists do falsely boast. Not withstanding, every man ought, of such things that he possesseth, liberally to give alms to the poor, according to his ability.

So while there were changes in doctrine, there was no real change materially. The poor remained poor, and the church maintained social structure and hierarchy.

Into the age of revolution came the Wesleys and their Methodists. Although the main leaders were highly educated, their new "lay preachers" were from among the poor.[106] The greatest success of their preaching was among the poor, although some of their converts were aristocrats.[107] Niebuhr notes that the Methodist movement was as significant for England as the Revolution had been for France.[108]

Along with their message of salvation came a message of holiness which was, in effect, living frugally and saving money by abstinence from drink and gambling, along with a commitment to hard work. For many, this asceticism led (as Weber, Tawney, and so on famously argued) to an accumulation of wealth among the Methodists. This led to a new class of wealthy people who endowed the churches with new buildings, but the poor still remained poor. New waves of hope arose among the Quakers, but they too soon had their wealthy industrialists.

The final denomination of hope for the poor was Booth's Salvation Army,[109] flowing out of the Methodist movement. It too encouraged Protestant asceticism, but later some of its members generated significant wealth.

It was into this Protestant world that came the American prosperity teachers, who taught the principle that giving from the poor would result in financial abundance. This pragmatic principle was seductive, and those who heard the message for the first time saw that the leaders, who faithfully applied the principles they taught, became wealthy.

Of course, those who followed their message needed to have, to an extent, some disposable income in the first place. However, even those who have little, as we have seen with Savelle, if they show faith, encourage others to give them money. As they continue to sow their money, they become richer and richer.

---

106. Niebuhr, *The Social Sources of Denominationalism*, 60.
107. Ibid., 61.
108. Ibid., 64.
109. Ibid., 75.

In our time, this message not only inspires the poor, but also the aspiring middle-classes—those who are not poor, but who want to live in "abundance." The wealth of the Faith teachers seduces them away from pure motives towards, perhaps unwittingly, more selfish ones.

Summary

My initial approach in chapter 1 was to examine the various confessional critiques of Word of Faith teachings. However, stimulated by the approach of the more scholarly treatments of Word of Faith, particularly Simon Coleman's work and my early methodology of rhetorical analysis, I became aware that there were significant social and cultural forces at work in my case study ministries. People had been persuaded, not just by the oratory of leaders, but by their whole performance.

Over the course of this study, I came to understand that the task was to unearth how these ministries might be successful in persuading people, by the use of insights from rhetorical studies, sociology, anthropology, psychology, congregational studies, and organizational theory. In order to shed light on the significance of the performative rhetoric of my case studies and, in particular, the American origins of much of their attitudes, behavior and theology, I developed two cultural "tools" or "resources" in chapters 2 and 3.

Early in chapter 2, I set out my initial background methodology of rhetorical analysis to be applied to my case studies. In this, I noted the subtle but significant differences in the rhetoric of my Faith ministries, but also their similarities—particularly their social and theological construction of reality, and that this rhetoric is unintentionally and mutually created between the leader and the discourse community who build the leader's reputation.[1] I was particularly influenced by the work of Stephen Pullum on the rhetoric of faith healers, but also the work of Annabel Mooney on the rhetoric of religious cults, and Roy Wallis's distinction between new religious movements. I noted the importance of the ability of the leaders of

---

1. See my material on John M. Swales and his concept of the discourse community.

Faith ministries to persuade adherents using their own credibility, character and perceived reliability, as well as their use of narrative, emotion, knowledge, language, and their self-presentation. I further noted the importance of mental suggestion for healers,[2] but also the possibility of suggestibility characterizing those who claim to be healed.

I proceeded in chapter 2 by developing the first of my cultural resources, arguing that in my case studies, there has been a significant importing of American cultural ideas. In order to do this, I argued that there is a general cultural difference between English and American evangelicalism, and that this is an example of a wider American exceptionalism. While I agreed with Bebbington that evangelicalism is, in its entirety, not something distinctively American, I disagreed with his assertion that American and British evangelicalisms are in essence identical. Instead, building on Marsden's comparison of American fundamentalism with English evangelicalism, I pointed to considerable differences between English and American evangelicalisms going back to the time of the first Great Awakening. In plotting the historical trajectory of the distinctive characteristics of American evangelicalism, I asserted that it is this attitude and mindset from their American contacts that has influenced leaders and adherents of my case studies in England.

I concluded that American revivalist evangelicals tend to see themselves as a special, God-chosen people who, influenced by commonsense philosophy, believe that sufficient theology can be simply comprehended by ordinary people, and as such tend towards anti-intellectualism. This simple way of presenting their faith charms or enchants some English evangelicals, particularly when they present a mechanistic, innovative, pragmatic approach to religion that flows out America's home-grown philosophy of pragmatism. I also noted the American tendency to run churches like businesses, flowing out of their Calvinist Puritan ascetic heritage and its associated spirit of capitalism, with a tendency towards neo-Gnosticism in claiming special, even "secret," insights into authentic Christianity they have discovered. Early in my study, I became aware that people were looking for a pragmatic religion that, in their perception, definitely "worked," as opposed to the less decisive, perhaps more skeptical, approach characterized by more mainstream English churches.

In tracing the religious family tree of my case study ministries in chapter 3, I realized they were all associated with, or influenced by, an American form of Pentecostalism, sometimes coming to the UK via Africa, or even Australia and the Far East. This form of Pentecostalism was influenced by

---

2. Particularly in my case studies for Michael Reid.

New Thought, which, in turn, was influenced by American transcendentalism and, ultimately, subjective idealism.

I could summarize this in a similar way to Niebuhr: a single line of development leads from the pragmatism of early American Puritans such as Franklin, through the half-way covenant of Edwards and then the new measures of Finney, along with the transcendentalism and neo-Gnosticism of Swedenborg and Emerson, and then New Thought and the mind cure to late nineteenth-century revivalists, especially E. W. Kenyon and his unwitting syncretism of transcendentalist principles with revivalism, continuing with Hagin and Copeland to contemporary revivalists.[3] As such, what was happening was a globalization of this Pentecostal/charismatic form of religion known as the Health, Wealth, and Prosperity Movement (HWPM).[4]

I was initially influenced in my study of the origins of ideas of this sort by D. R. McConnell's book *Another Gospel*[5] and those who critiqued his work.[6] His assertion that ideas or principles taught by Word of Faith preachers most likely had their origins in New Thought metaphysics that had unwittingly been syncretized or absorbed into late nineteenth-century revivalism by E. W. Kenyon seemed to be a reasonable explanation for their presence in this form of religion. Some who have critiqued McConnell have suggested that these ideas were just "in the air" of nineteenth-century American culture and, therefore, generally influenced some American revivalists. I tend to side with McConnell, but whether he was right or not about the process of their arrival, we see in modern charismatic religion ideas that seem to originate from American transcendentalism and subjective idealism.

In order to illustrate the arrival of these cultural and religious imports, I undertook a subordinate but vital analysis of key insights into the performative rhetoric of the case studies in chapters 4, 5, and 6.

In both of my cultural chapters, I noted the significance of the influence of American pragmatism and its instrumentality. The evidence of a pragmatic attitude can be seen in each of my case studies with principles and methods that will generate success.

I noted the similarity of Michael Reid's walking, talking method of healing to Quimby's talking cure, and at the same time that this was another manifestation of the sort of phenomenon observable in the "new measures"

---

3. See Niebuhr's summary early in chapter 3.

4. Similar to the observation by Simon Coleman in his study of Livets Ord in Sweden.

5. McConnell, *A Different Gospel*.

6. See chapter 1.

of Charles Finney's pragmatic revivalism. I noted that Reid himself seems to have been strongly influenced by American T. L. Osborn (author of *The Message that Works*,[7] and a keen follower of Kenyon) and American-trained Benson Idahosa (who trained at Christ for the Nations Institute, Dallas, Texas commonly associated with the HWPM).

The origin of Colin Urquhart's principles seemed less clear, but he too was influenced by Idahosa, while asserting that Idahosa does not preach the prosperity gospel. (As an aside, this seems to be a clear example of cognitive dissonance, something that is characteristic of both the leaders and adherents of these ministries, as I discussed in chapter 8.) Savelle, of course, is a clear descendant from Kenneth Hagin, who was extremely indebted to Kenyon. His teaching, his methods, and particularly his spiritual laws are highly pragmatic.

At the center of the thinking of pragmatists[8] is the question: Does it work? Or more exactly, does it work well? As far as those enchanted by the movement are concerned, the miracles and the financial provision work if the principles taught by Faith teachers are followed. It works if you use the special principles they teach; as such, this is a form of neo-Gnosticism.

Throughout the book, I have noted that these ministries and their claims of miracles appeal to certain sorts of people; the suggestible,[9] and the pragmatic people who want a simple, mechanistic ordered approach to faith. In trying to understand this further, in chapter 7, I noted observations from congregational studies and organizational studies. I noted that all three of my ministries were organizational, associational, demanding an organic life with life-embracing commitment distinct from more mainstream, institutional, contextually driven community churches represented by denominational churches such as Anglicanism, which only require a segmental commitment. In terms of Hopewell's househunting classification, all three of my case studies are highly mechanistic, that is, pragmatic and symbolic. However, they all seem to have what could be regarded as organic elements, offering life solutions to adherents, serving the poor, and so on, although the motives of leaders in encouraging this approach could be questioned: is this not just a way to improve their public relations? In terms of Wallis's classification, certainly Reid and, to an extent, Urquhart could be seen to have a world-rejecting element. However, all three have significant elements of world-accommodating behavior.

---

7. A prime example of the pragmatism I have been pointing to.
8. See chapter 2, particularly the section on Benjamin Franklin.
9. See chapter 2.

SUMMARY

In trying to understand how this religious system works, I have sought explanation for the miracles claimed by my case studies. I can imagine the incredulity of some of my former church members to my questioning of the idea that some miracles might not have their origin in God but are socially constructed. One former church member once said to me, "They work, don't they, so it must be God." Of course, an important question is, do they work or not?

The miracles that are claimed by Reid, Urquhart and Savelle are quite different to New Testament miracles. Peter May argues that, apart from exorcisms, Jesus's healings in the New Testament were of incurable diseases; these were not psychosomatic healings.[10] May adds that these conditions were non-remitting, instantaneous and complete, a big contrast to the "healings" claimed by Faith teachers.

The miracles claimed by Reid, Urquhart, and so on are very difficult to verify. Generally, only non-visible and internal problems are cured.[11] Obesity is not cured; this seems odd, given that it is the biggest killer in USA and increasingly so in the UK. Also, there are no miracles similar to Jesus walking on water and turning water into wine. So here again, people may well suppress their awareness that the miracles claimed by my case studies are not the same as those of Christ, again exhibiting a form of cognitive dissonance.

The question arises how these miracles might appear to happen. In considering the healing miracles of Michael Reid, I suggested in chapter 2 that these might be the result of mental suggestion, following Quimby and later mind cure healers. People who are particularly suggestible may well be more attracted to these forms of church. Enchanted people can be persuaded that the miraculous is at work and exhibit a form of "collective amnesia" about failures to heal or receive material blessing; as such, they exhibit a form of cognitive dissonance.

Much of my analysis of the case studies centers on the concept of the discourse community.[12] Enchanted adherents of each ministry, through their conversations, testimonies and behavior, produce a narrative that increases the credibility of the ministries to potential new members.[13] My argument is further enhanced in chapter 7 by use of Maussian analysis.[14] I observed that each of my case study ministries might well have two overlap-

10. May, "Claimed Contemporary Miracles."
11. Percy, *Power and the Church*, 22.
12. Swales, *Genre Analysis*.
13. See Fisher's narrative paradigm.
14. See chapter 7 of this book.

ping economic spheres in operation, a more capitalistic marketing of the ministry on one hand, and a gift economy, with rules that have their origins in our human past, on the other. I suggested that each of the ministries had what could be described as a tribal nature and used the Maussian concepts of the "potlatch," the "hau," and the "big man" in considering the giving behavior of leaders and adherents of the ministries. Using Savelle as an example, I pointed to the practice of competitive giving, which might take place at a gathering of the tribe, which increases the reputation of a person of faith in the discourse community, and stimulating others to give to them in the hope they would share their blessing. If people are seen to be faithful "sowers," then others will notice and give to them, resulting in prosperity for their faithfulness. Leaders like Savelle, Reid and Urquhart could be considered to be "big men" who people want to bless by giving, in order that they may share in their blessing. An example would be Savelle's plane. He does not say, "I'm believing that God will give me a plane"; but the fact that he needs one (or wants one) is known in the discourse community. This results in a social and theological construction of reality that depends on significant webs of relationships.[15]

Throughout the book, I have noted how the case study ministries are heavily marketed against a background of increasing commodification of religion and thinking in terms of material success representing God's blessing.[16] This is precisely the sort of approach that those who genuinely seek to proclaim the good news to the poor reject as the peddling of religion.[17] As Niebuhr and others have noted, this form of religion appeals to people of a certain class who want material blessing—perhaps the upwardly mobile working- and middle-classes.

This book has not set out to question whether the miracles of Jesus are authentic or whether miracles still happen today. However, I take the view that much of what is on offer in my case studies and similar ministries is something quite different to the miracles of Jesus. Many of the claimed miracles are, I think, illusory; some may be the result of the power of suggestion from leaders with significant charisma.

As I have suggested throughout this book, pragmatism and its fusion with revivalism accounts for the appeal of this form of religion. I would go as far as saying that faith—true and unconditional faith—has been seduced by pragmatism. When the principles taught by Faith teachers are found not to work, mainstream churches find disenchanted refugees in their midst.

15. Geertz, *The Interpretation of Cultures*, 5.
16. See Pattison, *The Faith of the Managers*.
17. See Webber, *God's Colony*, 234.

Final Conclusions

In final conclusion, I would say that I take note of and agree with many of the conclusions of the confessional critiques that say that Word of Faith teachings are not biblically or theologically correct. However, this book has taken a totally different approach by explaining how people are persuaded and enchanted by the performative rhetoric of Faith teachers, using a sociological and anthropological methodology that utilizes insights from congregational studies and organizational theory.

My initial research questions were: What social and theological construction of reality, and what factors or reasons, make these ministries appealing to people, and what is the true nature of what these ministries offer?

My main conclusions are:

1. The understanding of imported faith considered in this book is a distinctively American neo-Gnosticism that is offered by those, who, in line with their puritan heritage, view themselves as a special God chosen people who offer "secret" insights they have received.
2. The philosophical background to this epistemology is subjective idealism and Scottish common-sense, in contrast to European rationalist skepticism.
3. This results in a pragmatic, mechanistic, associational form of religion that is perceived to "work," in contrast to institutional religion that is viewed as powerless and ineffective.
4. This is received by suggestible people who, as a discourse community, mutually create an enchanted illusory world that builds the reputation of leaders.

The heart of my argument is that this form of religion appeals to those who embrace, or have a tendency towards, pragmatism and want to be involved in churches that effectively "work" as a mechanism for their benefit. These people are confirmed in their beliefs by their participation in a discourse community that builds the reputation of leaders in conjunction with the performative life rhetoric of leaders and the theological construction of reality that results, aided by faith-building narratives.

It is my observation that, in the UK, this is currently a much smaller proportion of the population than in the United States. In the UK, the majority are more influenced by the dominant European skepticism, but there is the possibility that this form of religion will increase here if the tide of pragmatism continues to rise as a manifestation of the globalization of American culture.

This epistemology, I argue, causes people to believe that giving money will result in receiving more back in return. It also causes people to believe in what appear to be miracles, but I argue that these are not the same as the miracles of Jesus; they operate in those whose illnesses are psychosomatic and can be cured by suggestion according to principles that originate in subjective idealism, American transcendentalism and mind-healing praxis. The principles taught and marketed by my case studies represent a capitalistic form of pragmatic religion which is an expressive neo-Gnosticism for the twentieth and twenty-first centuries.

APPENDIX
Videos of Peniel Miracles

Mobility illnesses

A. Carol Groom

Carol had suffered with ME for eighteen months when she went for prayer at Peniel. The video informs us that Carol was a senior neuro-technologist and was devastated by the illness, which devoured every ounce of her energy.

She describes her illness on the video: "I can remember it was a real effort just to walk five or six yards from one room in the house to another, and I was limited to one trip downstairs and one trip back up again a day. I didn't leave the house, and many things that I eat used to produce the most awful feelings, unwell, burning hands, sickness and dreadful upset stomachs all the time." She continues, "I couldn't concentrate properly, I couldn't read properly, I hadn't got the energy to write. It was very distressing for me to be not able to look after my children, and it was distressing for my husband to be not able to help me. He so much wanted me to be well, and yet there just didn't seem to be an answer." In the healing video, Reid helps Carol out of the lounger and says, "You haven't stood very easily. Okay, time for it to end." He says to her, "Relax." He prays for her (holding her close to his chest, his hand around the back of her head as he speaks into the handheld microphone) and says, "I curse this filthy disease, I break your power over this life, in the name of Jesus. I command you from this day you're going to release this body." He then takes Carol by the hand and walks her up and down on the carpet in Peniel. He says, "Okay, here, you just come with me. Come with me. Okay, you're going to start walking, how's your leg feeling? Wobbly, it's alright . . . just walking that's all. I just want you to know, it's the end. The Devil doesn't have control, Jesus has control. Doctors might not cure ME, Jesus does."

B. Joan Wentworth

Joan had suffered with ME for five years. She says, "I was diagnosed with severe ME in 1990. The ME affected me with everything. Um, most of the day I spent in bed, in pain. On my better days, I could get up for a few hours. But I wasn't able to watch television, read, or listen to the radio. I found talking to people, even to my children, a strain. I couldn't manage to walk up the stairs to have a shower, my eldest son had to carry me up and the same with coming back down again. The doctor said there was nothing that they could do, it was just a matter of time hopefully, but they couldn't help me in any way." She continues: "At one time, things got on top of me so much with the illness, I felt so ill that I tried to take my own life at one point. Thank God I didn't manage it, but I'd reached such a low, and I was in such pain." In the healing video, first of all Reid helps her out of her wheelchair and walks her back and forth on the carpet in front of the congregation. He says to her, "Look at me", requesting her full attention. She explains, "When he came over for me and walked me up and down, I just felt as if I was dragging myself along. And I felt as if he was willing me to get better and I couldn't get better." Reid then stops and prays for her. There is a man standing behind her (in case she falls, being "slain in the Spirit"). Reid says, "In the name of Jesus, I command you to come out of this body, come out of this body, come out of this body." (She falls back into the man's arms.) Reid continues, "In Jesus's name. Okay?" He helps her up and says, "Still a bit wheezy, that's okay. Now start walking, smile."

Joan tells him she does not feel like smiling, and he tells her about Jesus's encounter with the man with a withered arm, and that Jesus asks him to stretch forth his arm. Reid then tells Joan that Jesus often asks us to do things, to participate. He prays for her again, as Joan remembers, "to let the illness leave my body", and then says, "I just felt a big smile on my face . . . it was just amazing." He then walks her up and down on the carpet again, encourages her to flex arms over her body and in a circular motion, and then he gets her to break into a jog. He asks her if she feels different, she says, "I feel a bit stronger . . . yes, it does feel different." He replies: "Now it'll remain different, too, Jesus came to heal you, Jesus came to set you free, but you weren't half stubborn"—to which Joan and the congregation laugh. He then runs her up a flight of stairs and says, "That's nice and easy, isn't it? Your legs are together, aren't they?"

C. Jo Wilkinson

Jo had to give up work because of ME in 1990; she was often feverish and bedbound. This got worse in 1994 just before she went to Peniel. The healing video starts with Reid walking Jo back and forth on the carpet in front of the congregation. Reid tells her, "Jesus came to open a prison." He pulls her head close to his chest and prays, "I loose these fetters forever, come off your life, come off your body, come of your [...]." He then commands (shouts at) her to run to the door and back, to applause from the congregation.

Four of the video miracles are of people suffering with arthritis, back problems and similar problems.

D. Unnamed Woman One

In one of the videos,[1] Reid helps an unnamed woman to her feet. She tells him she has polymyalgia rheumatica. She explains this is rheumatism in all her muscles, she has to take steroids, and she is sick of it. And she has also got arthritis in her knees so she cannot get up the stairs. In the healing video, Reid at first walks the woman up and down the carpet in front of the congregation, speaking into the handheld microphone as he leads her so she can be heard as well. The commentator on the video says that Reid makes a simple prayer. He then walks her up and down on the carpet. Again, he comments that she seems to be enjoying it and "it's easy." He tells her to kick her shoes off and to walk quicker. He asks her how she feels and she replies that she is okay. Then he encourages, even commands her, to bend her legs right up and to lift her knees right up as she walks. She has doubts about this, but Reid tells her they will come right up. She leads her to a flight of stairs in the meeting hall and gets her to run up them. He concludes, "Well, that was easy."

E. Clair of Reading

In another video,[2] Reid meets Clair, who has arthritis in her back and legs, and a trapped nerve in her back. She tells him it is painful. The friends who brought her explained the arthritis caused her to be bent double. Reid takes her hands and prays for her. He says, "In the name of Jesus, I curse this foul affliction, you've no power to hold this woman bound anymore. Lord

---

1. "No Miracles No Jesus—Part One."
2. "No Miracles No Jesus—Part Four."

Jesus, just release this back, release this body. Lord, break the tyranny of this disease in Jesus's name. Amen?" (Nearly all of the congregation have their hands up and pointing towards Clair.) He then takes her by the hand again and encourages her to walk along the carpet in front of the congregation, and they continue walking back and forth. He asks her how she is doing, and she replies that this is the first time she has walked straight for eighteen months. He then tells her that this is a special piece of carpet, and she laughs. He gets her to bend her knees up to her chest and then asks her, "Where's the pain in your back?" She tells him it has gone. Clair smiles. He walks her up the stairs into the congregation and gets her to swivel her hips and touch her toes.

F. Unnamed Woman Two

In another significant video, Reid meets another unnamed woman who has problems with her back and with walking. We are not told much about this woman, but she is in a wheelchair at the beginning of the video. Reid takes her hands and helps her out of her wheelchair. He suggests prayer, and many in the congregation raise their hands towards the woman. Reid says, "Father, I just curse this foul disease in the name of Jesus which has [. . .] this body, in the name of Jesus, and break its power over this being. Lord, from this day, I command life and liberty into this back and this spine. Lord, set her free in Jesus's name." He walks her back and forth on the carpet in front of the congregation; Reid again in this case tells her it is a special piece of carpet. He asks her how she is feeling. She says something about her back and then that she is walking easier (unclear on video). She then says, "I'm walking better than when I walked in" (so she did not come in a wheelchair). She adds that she has not been able to walk like this for years. He asks her what she cannot do and she says, "I can't bend", and she has not been able to do that for years. He asks her, "Are you sure?" (The congregation laughs.) She tells him that she has seen the film (meaning the videos of healings). He gets her to bend down and touch her toes and then gets her to walk up and down some more. She says she is worn out at this point, but Reid tells her Jesus gave us a body to use and that he came to heal the sick, deliver the captive, and that he loves her. He then gets her to bend her knees right up one after another. She tells him she could not do that but she can now.

G. Katy Medland

In another video,[3] Reid heals Katy, who has hereditary arthritis. Katy was a sporting sixteen year old. Her arthritis had got to the stage that she could not even manage to walk far, run, or sit. She says, "I went up for prayer and came out and I felt perfect, totally, totally healed." There is no hint of what Reid does in this video. She says, "I came out of the meeting and it had completely gone, and we had some friends for lunch and they said to me well prove it, you know what couldn't you do. So I sat down on the floor and got up with ease, which I hadn't been able to do for months. It had been impossible, I had to sort of gradually lower myself down and I had to have help getting up. And I went up the Peniel and I played hockey, which again I hadn't done for months."

H. Janet Wragg

In another video,[4] Janet is interviewed. She was suffering from back pains and arthritis. She says on the video, "Something said to me, you've got the Peniel newspaper (*The Trumpet Call*) so I got up and went." On the video she is prayed for by Benson Idahosa (only momentarily, no audio on the video). As days passed, she got better.

I. Shân Brown

On the same video,[5] Shân testifies to being healed from a severe whiplash injury resulting from a car accident. Her physiotherapist is interviewed on the video and says that this whiplash injury was one of the worst she had seen. The video shows Shân being healed by Reid in a church meeting. He gets her to move her head from side to side at the end of the meeting. Her pain had disappeared.

---

3. This is in the same video as the healing of Carol Groom: "Jesus Heals the Sick—Part Two" at 3 mins into the video.
4. "Expect a Miracle—Part Three."
5. Ibid., 1 min 27 secs.

J. Merle

In the video, "Healed from Osteoarthritis and Cancer by Jesus Christ!!",[6] Merle tells her story. She had osteoarthritis: she could not twist, she could not bend, she could hardly go up and down stairs, she had dreadful pain. She was prayed for by Idahosa, who says to her, "It's done in Jesus's name" (we do not hear what he said before). One thing she could not do was twist her body, and the first thing he got her to do was to twist. She knew she had been healed because she could twist (seen on the video). Later in the video, Merle reveals that doctors were planning an operation on her spine—now not necessary.

Other problems and illnesses

Three of the miracles were the curing of blindness in *one eye only*.

A. Young Woman with Blind Eye

In one of the videos, Reid prays for a young woman with one blind eye.[7] He holds her head in his hands and says, "Father, I thank you came to open blind eyes. In the name of Jesus, I curse this affliction. Lord, cause life to come into this whole being." At this point, the young woman falls back; she is caught by someone, a catcher, standing behind her. She immediately gets up and Reid takes her by the hand. He says to her, "Felt that, didn't you?" The camera moves to a scene with her hand over her right eye. Reid then says, "Now blink tight, now open. Now blink again, now open. Just relax, relax. God does it." The girl is audibly crying at this point. Reid asks, "What can you see now?" The girl tells him she can see him and cries with Joy. Reid holds her to his chest and says "Isn't that lovely?" to applause from the congregation, and further tears of joy from the girl.

B. Darren Smith

In another three videos,[8] Reid heals a young man called Darren Smith. This took place quite a long time ago with a very much younger Reid. Reid

---

6. "Healed from Osteoarthritis and Cancer by Jesus Christ!!" Starting at 20 mins 40 secs.
7. "Miracle of Blind Eye Opening!"
8. "Miracle Caught on Camera—Part One."

is talking to a young man who has come forward for prayer. Revealed to be called Darren in an interview with Dr. Juan Escobel on video "Miracle caught on camera—Part Two",[9] and Darren Smith on the YouTube notes for this video. The notes say:

The operation in 1972 to remove a cyst from six-month old Darren Smith's left eye didn't work; instead he lost vision in it all together. We recorded on camera (in 1991) God's restoration of his sight here in Brentwood (Essex) on 2nd April 1991. Before praying for him, Rev. (Bishop) Michael Reid had preached specially for people with a need to be healed, including those who would like to understand first. This two part video on You Tube includes Darren Smiths testimony, and interview with a doctor to confirm Darren's recovery.

On the video, Reid asks Darren what's wrong with him. He replies that he lost the sight of his left eye when he was young. Reid then prays for him and says, "Father, I just pray that in your mercy and your grace that you'll restore that was lost, in the name of Jesus, hallelujah." Darren falls backwards, that is, he was slain in the Spirit. Reid continues to pray for him while he is on the ground—inaudibly—and then lifts him up.

Reid tells Darren to cover his good eye with his hand. Reid then says, "Now look, open it. Lord Jesus, thank you, hallelujah. Can you see a shadow?" At this point, Reid is waving his hand over the eye. Darren says something almost inaudible on the video, possibly, "It's half gone."

Reid then says, "It's gonna open. Blind eye, you're gonna open. You can feel all the movement in the nerves, can't you?" Darren nods in agreement.

Reid then tells the congregation, "You know he can feel it stinging, it's never stung like it before, but it's stinging in his eye. The Holy Ghost will rebuild the whole of this nervous system. Hallelujah. That's what he's come to do, he's gonna create that which wasn't there."

Again, he says to Darren, "Your eye's gonna open, hallelujah. Holy Ghost, thank you, you're the healer. Thank you, you're the one who opens blind eyes. Lord, all we know is once we were blind, now we see." Reid then speaks in tongues. The congregation starts singing in worship, getting louder and louder, and apparently more excited by what's happening before them. Reid waves his hand before Darren's eye. He says to Darren, "You'll find your sight is gonna come back. It's gonna open, gonna open." Loud worship continues. Reid then stops the worship and waves his hand before Darren's eye and says, "Now you can see that, can't you?"

Darren replies he can. Reid then says, "You were totally blind, weren't you?" Darren replies he was and then says he can see the light of the screen

---

9. "Miracle Caught on Camera—Part Two."

(on which the words for the worship are projected). At this point, there is loud applause from the congregation. Reid then tells him, "Well, you're gonna see everything. You're gonna see everything. It just takes time." Reid then explains to the congregation, "See, first he got a stinging in his eye, which has been totally blind. Now he began to see shadows, and now he can see the screen, but he'll see everything, that's what God does."

Reid repeatedly prays for Darren. After a while, he tells Darren that his eyes look better, to which Darren replies they feel better. Reid says, "Something's happened, hasn't it? Sight's come back, hasn't it?" Daren says, "It's a bit watery." Reid says, "Yes, it's watering, it's just watering. Well, the blurredness is gonna go. Okay, in the name of Jesus, come on, blurredness, you go. Lord, let him see clearly, let this be totally healed, hallelujah. Now go on, look up there." Reid points to the projector screen. He tells him to keep blinking. Reid says, "It's no good being open and blurred." He speaks to the eye, "You're gonna see, eye, do you understand me, eye?" Reid then says, "I command this blurredness in this vision and this blind spirit, you get out of this eye completely now." Darren falls back again, slain in the Spirit.

Reid then explains, "Do you know there's an angel in there busily working way at every optic nerve?" Darren replies, "Yes, yes." Reid continues, "He may have got a wire or two crossed, but he's gonna uncross them." Reid prays, "Father, remove all the scar tissue, oh, Holy Ghost, in your mercy and love, I thank you for sight, oh Lord. Lord Jesus, Lord Jesus, Lord Jesus." Darren falls back yet again.

The healing continues in the second video.[10]

Darren's eye improves, and Reid says to the congregation, "Hallelujah, come, let's give God a clap offering", and shouts, "Glory to his name." The congregation and Darren clap and praise God.

The video continues with Dr. Juan Escobel (a member of the congregation) interviewing Darren. In the interview, he learns from Darren that he had some cysts in his eye when he was just six months old. In removing the cysts, the doctors said they had scarred the eye, and he has been unable to see out of the eye since. He could only see if the sun was out through that eye, and could not recognize any objects. Darren tells Escobel that he saw a specialist about three or four years ago.

Darren tells him that when he was prayed for by Reid, he could eventually see colors and make out shadows. He says, "I nearly fell over again, after I stood up it was such a surprise, I nearly fell flat on my back again, it was really strange. I mean, it's sort of hard to describe."

---

10. "Miracle Caught on Camera—Part Two."

Escobel then examines his eyes. In the third video,[11] Reid interviews Escobel, who tells him that Darren could only faintly see light through the eye before he was prayed for, and now he has almost 100 percent vision to that eye. Darren can see shapes, he can recognize faces, he can see fairly small details. Any shortfall Escobel attributes to an adjustment problem between the two eyes.

Reid asks him if he would have any explanation apart from the fact that when Darren was prayed for, the healing happened? Escobel says, "No, that's very difficult to explain, especially because what he describes seems to have been a problem of the retina of the eye, which has to do with the perception of light more than the lens in itself, which is what usually can have a surgical treatment, and what he had, obviously, the way that he describes it, is more a retinal problem." Reid asks, "So there was no hope of him ever re-establishing sight?" Escobel replies, "No, I think he, pretty much since when he was born it was diagnosed, he had been seen by several specialist consultants and they didn't give him any hope for recovering vision." Reid asks, "So you'd call it a miracle?"

Escobel replies, "Definitely a miracle as far as I can tell. Yes . . . this is definitely an amazing miracle."

C. Linda King

In another video,[12] Linda is interviewed by Ruth and Michael Reid about the healing of her hands that occurred at Peniel about twenty years ago (early 1990s). Linda had arthritis in her hands and thumbs (she was a seamstress). She received her healing where she was sitting without any prayer. There was burning in her hands on the way home and for two days or so, but her hands were healed as a result. Linda was expectant having seen other miracles at the church when she had previously visited.

D. John Healed from Kidney Stone

In another video, the Reids are interviewing John, who was healed from a kidney stone.[13] John had severe pains in his side; his doctor thought he had renal colic and sent him to the hospital where a kidney stone was confirmed. It was a bank holiday weekend, so he could not be treated until a later date.

---

11. "Miracle Caught on Camera—Final Part."
12. "Linda King's Testimony of Miracle from God."
13. "John Healed from Kidney Stone—Bishop Michael Reid—Part {2}."

He later visited the specialist, who tried to retrieve the stone by putting a probe up inside John. This did not succeed—he pushed the stone further into the kidney, so they left it to see if it would pass naturally in the urine, which would have been painful. In a church meeting after this, Reid picked John out and prayed for him and said, "It's over, do you believe it?" John replied, "Yes." He went back to the specialist, who took an x-ray but could not find the stone. He was told if he had passed the kidney stone, he would have felt it. He believed it was a miracle.

E. Rob Whitaker

In another video,[14] Reid prays for Rob. He had been diagnosed with a blocked kidney tube. Rob says that he discovered that he was passing blood with his urine. He went for some medical tests with a specialist, and amongst those there were x-rays of the kidney. The video shows an x-ray transparency of Rob's kidney; he points with a pen to the affected area. He points to a lump just circled there, and this caused the specialist concern. He was prayed for by Reid at church about a week later. The next week, he went in for investigative surgery to see what there actually was in the kidney. The new x-ray paelagrams (shown on the video) from the second investigation revealed no lump. The specialist had marked on the slide where he expected to see something, and there is nothing at all. And what had been there before had gone completely. Whitaker believed this was due to God's miraculous intervention through the Bishop's prayer.

F. John: After-Effects of Heart Attack

In another video,[15] John is healed of the effects of a heart attack. John explains that he could not walk far, he could not breathe easily, and that he was yellow. Ruth Reid asks his wife Lilly what she felt about his sickness. She replied that she has always believed, and that she used to say lots of prayers that John would be healed, but nothing happened. But when she saw the *Trumpet Call*, she thought this might be the answer. She had been going to the Spiritualist Church. John reveals that he was an atheist and did not believe in this stuff. He went to Peniel because Lilly kept moaning at him, but he knows different now. He was prayed for (no hint at the prayer is given

---

14. "Expect a Miracle—Final Part."
15. "Healed from Osteoarthritis and Cancer by Jesus Christ!!"

in the video), and after the service he was able to walk up the stairs of the church, without realizing the change, which continued at home.

G. Udmillah: Cancer of the Breast, Lungs, and Spine

On the same video,[16] Reid prays for Udmillah, a Hindu woman who had breast cancer that had spread to her lungs and spine. In an interview with Reid, Dr. Juan Escobel reveals that Udmillah had already started chemotherapy when she realized that the cancer had spread to her lungs. He says when she came to the church she was terminal and had not eaten for weeks (Reid says two months). In the service, Reid says, "I'm going to touch you, and the power is going to flow, and when that power flows that miracle is there for you, the cancer's gonna go, the chains are gonna snap, believe God." He goes to pray for Udmillah and says, "In the name of Jesus, I curse this disease, Lord, let that mighty healing power flow through every part of this being right now, go on disease, you're going to go from this body, you're going to loose this woman completely, you've no power to hold her, hallelujah, hallelujah, hallelujah, that's the end of your disease, that's the end of your sickness. . . . Devil, you're gonna loose this right now in Jesus name." He says to the congregation, "You know sickness has a personality, the personality of the devil, it's destructive, Jesus came to make you whole." Afterward, Escobel reveals that Udmillah's appetite returned and she put weight back on. Escobel reveals that two months after being prayed for, she was given a follow-up scan, and there was no trace of the cancer. She was dismissed from the hospital.

H. Ian Veal: Acid Reflux

In another video,[17] Ian claims he is healed from acid reflux, which had been a problem for him for ten years or so. It meant that he had to be very careful what he ate. He was not prayed for, just sitting at the back of the church. He has had no problems since.

---

16. Ibid.
17. "Expect a Miracle—Part Three."

I. John Cope: Severe Pancreatitis

In the same video, the story of John Cope[18] is told. John was rushed to hospital with severe pancreatitis. The video commentator tells John's story. His wife had been a Christian for twenty-five years, and she had been a member of Peniel for seventeen years. John was an atheist, who had no need for God. He only attended church for special occasions, for example, his daughter's wedding. John says he was very frightened when he became ill and was rushed into Broomfield hospital in Chelmsford. John's story continues on the final video in the series.[19]

Reid interviews him in front of the congregation and says, "The first thing I told him was that he couldn't afford to die because he was on his way to hell." He continues,

"You see, what I said to John was quite plain and simple, its time to turn. And when you've got someone on a sickbed, the last thing you want to do is tell them lies. If its their last day this side of eternity, you'd better tell them the truth." Reid says to him, "So I was fairly plain with you, wasn't I, John?" He replies, "You told me the truth, Michael." Reid then says, "Yes, I did, and I also told him you won't die . . . you can't die, because you'll go to the other place [points down]. So you'd better fight for life, boy."

Reid then says that they prayed, though he does not say what the prayer was.

John got better, to the surprise of the doctors who were treating him. The final part of the video is an interview with John's surgeon, Joseph Mathai (a surgeon at Broomfield Hospital). He says, "John probably came into the category of 15 percent of patients with pancreatitis who are at serious risk of damage to not just the pancreas itself, but other organs as well. When I studied John's case notes, it was very obvious that he was categorized as at grievous risk to both life and health, and, at one stage, surgery was being contemplated as an immediate possibility. That was the morning that Pastor Reid came to pray for him. His recovery was quite tremendous. He was on the Sunday being considered for surgery; on the Monday, he looked so much better, so much brighter. We do see recovery, but it's over a period of time. This happened quite rapidly. So one would have to accept that something other than his treatment and his own resources had intervened to bring about the change in John."

---

18. "No Miracles No Jesus—Part Four." Starts at 4 mins 24 secs.
19. "No Miracles No Jesus—Final Part."

Bibliography

Ahlstrom, Sydney. *A Religious History of the American People*. New Haven: Yale University Press, 1972.

———. *A Religious History of the American People*. 2nd ed. New Haven: Yale University Press, 2004.

Albanese, Catharine L. *A Republic of Mind and Spirit: A Cultural History of American Metaphysical Religion*. New Haven: Yale University Press, 2007.

"Allegation of Reid's Admission of Adultery." The *Daily Mail* webpage that alleges Reid's admission of adultery. Online: http://www.dailymail.co.uk/news/article-558365/Bishop-preached-family-values-finally-admits-I-adulterer.html [accessed 5.12.2008].

Anderson, C. Alan, and Deborah G. Whitehouse. *New Thought: A Practical American Spirituality*. 2nd ed. Fairfield, CA: 1st Books, 2003.

Andrews, James R. *The Practice of Rhetorical Criticism*. New York: Macmillan, 1983.

Anker, Roy M. *Self-Help and Popular Religion in Early American Culture: An Interpretive Guide, Volume 1*. Westport, CT: Greenwood, 1999.

Aristotle. *Rhetoric*. Translated by W. Rhys Roberts, 1954. Reprint. Stilwell, KS: Digireads.com, 2005.

Aston, Margaret. *Lollards and Reformers: Images and Literacy in Late Medieval Religion*. London: Hambledon, 1984.

Atkins, Gaius Glenn. *Modern Religious Cults and Movements*. New York: Revell, 1923.

"Avoiding Foolishness." Online: http://www.youtube.com/watch?v=DYp2IGSDFSY [accessed 12.2.2012].

Ayer, A. J. *Language, Truth and Logic*. London: Penguin 1971.

Baker Eddy, Mary. *Miscellaneous Writings*. Boston: Trustees under the Will of Mary Baker G. Eddy, 1896.

———. *No and Yes*. 1898. Reprint. Boston: Trustees under the Will of Mary Baker G. Eddy, 1915.

———. *Rudimental Divine Science*. 1891. Reprint. Boston: Trustees under the Will of Mary Baker G. Eddy, 1936.

———. *Science and Health: With Key to the Scriptures*, 1875. Reprint. Boston: The Writings of Mary Baker Eddy, 2000.

———. *Unity of Good.* 1887. Reprint. Boston: Trustees under the Will of Mary Baker G. Eddy, 1936.
Baker, Robert A. *They Call It Hypnosis.* Amherst, NY: Prometheus, 1990.
Bates, Ernest S., and John V. Dittemore. *Mary Baker Eddy: The Truth and Tradition.* New York: Knopf, 1932.
Beasley, Norman. *The Cross and the Crown: The History of Christian Science.* New York: Duell, Sloan and Pearce, 1952.
Bebbington, David. *Evangelicalism in Modern Britain.* London: Unwin Hyman, 1989.
———. "Evangelicalism in Modern Britain and America—A Comparison." In *Amazing Grace: Evangelicalism in Australia, Britain, Canada and the United States,* edited by George A. Rawlyk and Mark A. Noll, 183–85. Montreal: McGill-Queens University Press, 1994.
———. "Not so Exceptional After All—American Evangelicalism Reassessed." Online: http://www.christianitytoday.com/bc/2007/003/5.16.html [accessed 9.10.2008].
Becker, Judith. *Deep Listeners: Music, Emotion and Trancing.* Bloomington, IN: Indiana University Press, 2004.
"Becoming a Kingdom Faith Partner." Online: http://www.kingdomfaith.com/AboutUs/Gift.aspx [accessed 8.2.2012].
Beit-Hallahmi, Benjamin, and Michael Argyle. *The Psychology of Religious Behaviour, Belief and Experience.* London: Routledge, 1997.
Bender, Courtney. *Heaven's Kitchen: Living Religion at God's Love We Deliver.* Chicago: University of Chicago Press, 2003.
Bercovitch, Sacvan. *The Puritan Origins of the American Self.* New Haven: Yale University Press, 1975.
Berger, Peter. *A Far Glory: The Quest for Faith in an Age of Credulity.* New York: Free, 1992.
———. "A Market Model for the Analysis of Ecumenicity." *Social Research* 30 (1963) 77–93.
Berger, Peter, and Thomas Luckmann. *The Social Construction of Reality.* 1966. Reprint. London: Penguin, 1991.
Berkin, Carol, et al. *Making America, Volume 2: Since 1865: A History of the United States.* Boston: Wadsworth, 2010.
Bettinghaus, Erwin. *Persuasive Communication.* New York: Holt, Rinehart & Winston, 1980.
Billig, Michael. *Arguing and Thinking: A Rhetorical Approach to Social Psychology.* Cambridge: Cambridge University Press, 1987.
"Biographical page." Online: http://www.jerrysavelle.org/about/jerrybio.html [accessed 14.1.2012].
Black, Edwin. *Rhetorical Criticism: A Study in Method,* 1965. Reprint. Madison, WI: University of Wisconsin Press, 1978.
Bloch, George. *Mesmerism.* Los Altos, CA: Kaufmann, 1980.
Boles, John. *The Great Revival: Beginnings of the Bible Belt.* Lexington, KY: University Press of Kentucky, 1972.
Bosco, Ronald A., and Joel Myerson, eds. *The Later Lectures of Ralph Waldo Emerson 1843–1871, Volume 1: 1843–1854.* Athens, GA: University of Georgia Press, 2001.
Bourdieu, Pierre. *Distinction: A Social Critique of the Judgement of Taste.* Translated by R. Nice. Cambridge: Harvard University Press, 1984.
———. *Homo Academicus.* Stanford: Stanford University Press, 1988.

———. *The Logic of Practice*. Translated by R. Nice. Cambridge: Cambridge University Press, 1995.
———. *Outline of a Theory of Practice*. Translated by R. Nice. Cambridge: Cambridge University Press, 1977.
———. *Pascalian Meditations*. Translated by R. Nice. Cambridge, UK: Polity, 2000.
———. *Sociology in Question*. Translated by R. Nice. London: Sage, 1993.
Bourdieu, Pierre, and Loïc Wacquant. *An Invitation to Reflexive Sociology*. Translated by L. Wacquant. Cambridge: Polity, 1992.
Bowman, Robert M. *The Word-Faith Controversy: Understanding the Health and Wealth Gospel*. Eugene, OR: Wipf & Stock, 2001.
Braden, Charles. *Spirits in Rebellion: The Rise and Development of New Thought*. Dallas: Southern Methodist University Press, 1963.
———. *These Also Believe*. New York: Macmillan, 1960.
Braid, James. *Neurypnology*. London: Churchill, 1943.
Bramadat, Paul A. *The Church on the World's Turf*. New York: Oxford University Press, 2000.
Branham, William. "Elijah and Elisha." Audio sermon. Online: http://www.nathan.co.za/message.asp?sermonum=162 [accessed 21.09.2010].
———. "Faith without Works is Dead." Audio sermon. Online: http://www.nathan.co.za/message.asp?sermonum=126 [accessed 21.09.2010].
Bremer, Francis J. "William Winthrop." In *Puritans and Puritanism in Europe and America Vol 1.*, edited by Francis J. Bremer and Tom Webster, 285–86. Santa Barbara, CA: ABC-CLIO, 2006.
Brierley, Peter. *God's Questions: Vision Strategy and Growth*. Tonbridge, UK: ADBC, 2010.
Brock, Bernard L., Robert L. Scott, and James W. Chesebro, eds. *Methods of Rhetorical Criticism: A Twentieth-Century Perspective*. 3rd ed. Detroit: Wayne State University Press, 1989.
Broom, Leonard, and Philip Selznick. *Essentials of Sociology: From Sociology—A Text with Adapted Readings*. 6th ed. New York: Harper & Row, 1979.
Brown, Callum G. *The Death of Christian Britain: Understanding Secularization 1800–2000*. Oxford: Routledge, 2001.
Browning, Don S. *A Fundamental Practical Theology: Descriptive and Strategic Proposals*. Minneapolis: Fortress, 1996.
Bruce, Steve. *God is Dead: Secularization in the West*. Oxford: Blackwell, 2002.
Bugbee, Bruce, et al. *Network: The Right People, in The Right Places, for the Right Reasons*. Grand Rapids: Zondervan, 1994.
Bultmann, Rudolf. "Ginōskō." Translated by G. W. Bromily. In *Theological Dictionary of the New Testament*, edited by Gerhard Kittel and Gerhard Friedrich, 1:692–96. Grand Rapids: Eerdmanns, 1964.
Burke, Kenneth. *Essays Toward a Symbolic of Motives 1950–55*. West Lafayette IN: Parlor, 2006.
Burton, Robert. *The Anatomy of Melancholy—Vol. II*. Philadelphia: Wardle, 1836.
Cady, H. Emilie. *God a Present Help*. Kansas City, MO: Unity School of Christianity, 1942.
———. *Lessons in Truth: A Course of Twelve Lessons in Practical Christianity*. Lees Summit, MO: Unity School of Christianity, 1962.
———. *Miscellaneous writings*. Kansas City, MO: Unity School of Christianity, 1933.

Cameron, Helen, Philip Richter, Douglas Davies, and Frances Ward, eds. *Studying local Churches: A Handbook*. London: SCM, 2005.

Campbel, Karlyn Kohrs, and Kathleen Hall Jamieson, eds. *Form and Genre: Shaping Rhetorical Action*. Falls Church, VA: Speech Communication Association, 1978.

Campbell, James. "The Pragmatism of Benjamin Franklin." *Transactions of the Charles S. Peirce Society* 31 (1995) 745–92.

———. *Recovering Benjamin Franklin*. La Salle, IL: Open Court, 1999.

Capps, Charles. *Faith and Confession: How to Activate the Power of God in Your Life*. Tulsa, OK: Harrison House, 1987.

Carrier, James G. *Gifts and Commodities: Exchange and Western Capitalism since 1700*. London: Routledge, 1995.

"Chariots of Light Broadcast 044." Online: http://jsmiwm.webcastcenter.com/jsmi/col_044.wmv [accessed 18.3.2007].

Christensen, Michael J., and Jeffery A. Wittung, eds. *Partakers of the Divine Nature: The History and Development of Deification in the Christian Traditions*. Grand Rapids: Baker Academic, 2007.

Christensen, Michael J. "John Wesley: Christian Perfection as Faith Filled with the Energy of Love." In *Partakers of the Divine Nature: The History and Development of Deification in the Christian Traditions*, edited by Michael J. Christensen and Jeffery A. Wittung, 219–27. Grand Rapids: Baker Academic, 2007.

Clark, S. D. "The Methodist Church and the Salvation Army." In *Sociology: A Text with Adapted Readings*, 3rd ed., edited by Leonard Broom and Philip Selznick, 430–34. New York: Harper & Row, 1963.

Cloer, Edie. "Profiles in Evangelistic Persuasion: A Descriptive Analysis of the Persuasion Techniques of Seven Preachers of the Churches of Christ." D.Min thesis, Harding Graduate School of Religion, Memphis, Tennessee, 1991.

Coleman, Simon. *The Globalisation of Charismatic Christianity: Spreading the Gospel of Prosperity*. Cambridge: Cambridge University Press, 2000.

Conkin, Paul K. *Puritans and Pragmatists: Eight Eminent American Thinkers*. Waco, TX: Baylor University Press 2005.

"Controlling Churches." Online: http://www.controllingchurches.com/ [accessed 14.12.2010].

Cooke, George W. *Unitarianism in America: A History of Its Origin and Development*. Boston: American Unitarian Association, 1902.

Cook, Phil. "Make No Small Plans." Online: http://philcooke.com/Oral_Roberts [accessed 16.1.12].

Copeland, Gloria. *God's Will is Prosperity*. Tulsa, OK: Harrison House, 1978.

Copeland, Kenneth, and Gloria Copeland. *One Word from God Can Change Your family*. Tulsa, OK: Harrison House, 1999.

Copeland, Kenneth. *The Laws of Prosperity*. Fort Worth, TX: Kenneth Copeland, 1974.

Cornwall, Judson. *Let us Praise*. Alachua, FL: Bridge-Logos, 1973.

———. *Unfeigned Faith*. Old Tappan, NJ: Fleming H. Revell, 1981.

Cotton, John. "Letter to Lord Say and Seal." In *Puritanism in Early America*, edited by M. Waller, 11–14. Lexington, MA: Heath, 1973.

Cruz, Nicky (with Jamie Buckingham). *Run Baby Run*. 1968. Reprint. London: Hodder & Stoughton, 2003.

Csordas, Thomas J. *The Sacred Self: A Cultural Phenomenology of Charismatic Healing*. Berkeley: University of California Press, 1994.

D'Andrade, Hugh. *Charles Fillmore: Herald of the New Age*. New York: Harper and Row, 1974.
DeArteaga, William. *Quenching the Spirit*. Lake Mary, FL: Creation House, 1992.
De Tocqueville, Alexis. Translated by A. Goldhammer. *Democracy in America*. The Library of America, 2004.
Demerath, N. J. *Social Class in American Protestantism*. Chicago: McNally, 1965.
Denzin, Norman K. *The Research Act: Theoretical introduction to Sociological Methods*. 3rd ed. Englewood Cliffs NJ: Prentice Hall, 1988.
"Details of Savelle's International Offices." Online: http://www.jerrysavelle.org/ministries/international-offices/ [accessed 12.11.2007]. His European Headquarters are in Chepstow, Monmouthshire, Wales.
Douglas, Ann. *The Feminization of American Culture*. London: Papermac, 1996.
Dow, Thomas E. Jr. "The Theory of Charisma." Sociological Quarterly 10 (1969) 306–18.
Dresser, Annetta G. *The Philosophy of P. P. Quimby*. Boston: Ellis, 1895.
Dresser, Horatio W. *Handbook of the New Thought*. New York: Crowell, 1917.
———. *Health and the Inner Life: An Account of the Life and Teachings of P. P. Quimby*. New York: Putnam's Sons, 1906.
———. *Health and the Inner Life*. 1906. Online: http://www.freehealingbooks.com/user/image/health_and_the_inner_life_horatio_dresser.pdf) [accessed 17.5.2010].
———. "The New Thought and the New Church." *The Helper* 71, February, 1923, 3–17.
Driggers, B. Carlisle, ed. *Models of Metropolitan Ministry: How Twenty Churches Are Ministering Successfully in Areas of Rapid Social Change*. Nashville: Broadman, 1979.
Dyton, Simon. "Anabaptists." In *Puritans and Puritanism in Europe and America Vol. 1*, edited by Francis J. Bremer and Tom Webster, 298–301. Santa Barbara, CA: ABC-CLIO, 2006.
Ecclestone, Giles, ed. *The Parish Church? Explorations in the Relationship of the Church and the World*. Oxford: Mowbray's, 1988.
Ehrenreich, Barbara. *Smile or Die: How Positive Thinking Fooled America & the World*. London: Granta, 2010.
Eisenstadt, S. N. *Max Weber on Charisma and Institution Building*. Chicago, IL: University of Chicago Press, 1968.
El-Faizy, Monique. *God and Country*. New York: Bloomsbury, 2006.
Emerson, Ralph Waldo. "Compensation." In *Essays and Lectures*, 147–57. Digireads.com, 2009.
———. The Complete Works of Ralph Waldo Emerson. New York: Sully and Kleinteich, 1883.
———. "Humanity and the Over-Soul." In *Natural Abundance: Ralph Waldo Emerson's Guide to Prosperity*, edited by Ruth Miller, 57–72. New York: Atria, Beyond Words, 2011.
———. *The Later Lectures of Ralph Waldo Emerson, 1843–1871, Volume 1: 1843–1854*. Edited by Ronald A. Bosco and Joel Myerson. Athens, GA: University of Georgia Press, 2001.
———. *Nature*. Boston: Munro, 1849.
———. "Nature." In *Essays and Lectures*, 278–86. Digireads.com, 2009.
———. "The Over-Soul." In *Essays and Lectures*, 199–208. Digireads.com, 2009.

———. "Poetry and Imagination." In *The American Transcendentalists: Their Prose and Poetry*, edited by Perry Miller, 196–219. New York: Doubleday, 1957.

———. "Spiritual Laws." In *Essays and Lectures*, 158–69. Digireads.com, 2009.

Evans, Warren Felt. *The Divine Law of Cure*. Boston: Carter, 1884.

———. *The Mental Cure: Illustrating the Influence of the Mind on the Body, Both in Health and Disease, and the Psychological Method of Treatment*. Glasgow: M'Geachy, 1870.

———. *The Primitive Mind-Cure. The Nature and Power of Faith, or, Elementary Lessons in Christian Philosophy and Transcendental Medicine*. Boston: Carter, 1885.

———. *Soul and Body*. Boston: Carter, 1876.

"Expect a Miracle—Part Two." Online: http://www.youtube.com/user/BABYPEARS #p/u/250/Rv4pxAn7avs [accessed 15.11.2010].

"Expect a Miracle—Part Three." Online: http://www.youtube.com/user/BABYPEARS #p/u/249/3lnRIeXFy9c [accessed 7.11.2010].

"Expect a Miracle—Final Part." Online: http://www.youtube.com/user/BABYPEARS #p/u/134/SDQuOJqPTqQ [accessed 16.11.2010].

"Faith08 Promo Video." Online: http://www.youtube.com/watch?v=nMK-rfnGsow&feature=related [accessed 9.4.2008].

Farah, Nuruddin. *Gifts*. New York: Penguin, 2000.

Fee, Gordon. *The Disease of the Health and Wealth Gospels*. Vancouver: Regents College, 1985.

Festinger, Leon. *A Theory of Cognitive Dissonance*. 1957. Reprint. Stanford, CA: Stanford University Press, 2001.

Festinger, Leon, et al. *When Prophecy Fails*. 1956. Reprint. Minneapolis: University of Minnesota Press, 2011.

Finney, Charles G. *Finney on Revival*, arranged by E. E. Shelhammer. London: Marshall, Morgan & Scott, 1939.

Fisher, Walter R. "Narration as Human Communication Paradigm: The Case of Public Moral Argument." In *Contemporary Rhetorical Theory: A Reader*, edited by J. L. Lucaites et al., 265–87. New York: Guildford, 1999.

Flanagan, Kieran. *The Enchantment of Sociology*. London: Macmillan, 1996.

Freeman, James Dillet. *The Story of Unity*. Lee's Summit, MO: Unity School of Christianity, 1954.

Freud, Sigmund. "Lines of Advance in Psychoanalytic Therapy." In *The Standard Edition of the Complete Works of Sigmund Freud, Vol. 17*, 157–68. London: Hogarth and the Institute of Psycho-Analysis, 1958.

Fuller, Robert C. *Mesmerism and the American Cure of Souls*. Philadelphia: University of Pennsylvania Press, 1982.

Gay, Peter, ed. *Deism: An Anthology*. London: Van Nostrand, 1968.

Geertz, Clifford. *Available Light: Anthropological Reflections on Philosophical Topics*. Princeton: Princeton University Press, 2000.

———. *The Interpretation of Cultures*. New York: Basic, 1973.

Gerth, H. H., and C. Wright Mills. "Bureaucracy and Charisma: A Philosophy of History." In *Charisma, History and Social Structure*, edited by Ronald M. Glassman and William H. Swatos Jr., 11–24. New York: Greenwood, 1986.

Gilbert, Alan D. *The Making of Post-Christian Britain: A History of the Secularization of Modern Society*. London: Longman, 1980.

Gill, Gillian. *Mary Baker Eddy*. Cambridge, MA: Perseus, 1998.

"God's authority." Online: http://www.youtube.com/watch?v=u8t2Q-5EE70 [accessed 12.1.2012].

Goodman, Grace Ann. *Rocking the Ark: Nine Case Studies of Traditional Churches in the Process of Change*. New York: United Presbyterian Church USA, 1968.

Gossett, Don, and E. W. Kenyon. *The Power of Spoken Faith*. New Kensington, PA: Whitaker House, 2003.

———. *The Power of Your Words*. New Kensington, PA: Whitaker House, 1977.

Gossett, Don. *What You Say Is What You Get*. Springdale, PA: Whitaker House 1976.

Gottschalk, Stephen. *The Emergence of Christian Science in American Religious Life*. Berkeley: University of California Press, 1973.

Gregory, C. A. *Gifts and Commodities*. London: Academic, 1982.

———. "Gifts to Men and Gifts to God: Gift Exchange and Capital Accumulation in Contemporary Papua." *Man* New Series 15.4 (1980) 626–52.

Grenz, Stanley. "What Does Hollywood Have to Do with Wheaton? The Place of Pop Culture in Theological Reflection." *Journal of the Evangelical Theological Society* 43.2 (2000) 303–14.

Gros, Jeffrey, et al. *Growth in Agreement II: Reports and Agreed Statements of Ecumenical Conversations on a World Level 1982–1998*. Geneva: WCC, 2000.

Guest, Matthew, et al. *Congregational Studies in the UK: Christianity in a Post-Christian Context*. Aldershot, UK: Ashgate, 2004.

Guinness, Os. *Fit Bodies Fat Minds: Why Evangelicals Don't Think & What to Do About It*. London: Hodder and Stoughton, 1995.

Hagin, Kenneth E. *The Believer's Authority*. Tulsa, OK: Faith Library, 1986.

———. *How To Write Your Own Ticket With God*. Broken Arrow, OK: Rhema Bible Church, 1979.

———. "The Law of Faith." *Word of Faith Magazine*, November 1974.

———. *The Name of Jesus*. Tulsa, OK: Kenneth Hagin Ministries 1979.

———. *New Thresholds in Faith*. Tulsa, OK: Kenneth Hagin Ministries, 1972.

———. "The Resurrection." *Word of Faith Magazine*, April 1977.

———. *Right and Wrong Thinking*. Broken Arrow, OK: Rhema Bible Church, 1982.

———. *Right and Wrong Thinking*. Tulsa, OK: Kenneth Hagin Ministries, 2005.

Hall, James A. *Hypnosis: A Jungian Perspective*. New York: Guildford, 1989.

Hamner, Gail. *American Pragmatism*. New York: Oxford University Press, 2003.

Hanegraaff, Hank. *Christianity in Crisis*. Eugene, OR: Harvest House, 1997.

Hankins, Barry. *The Second Great Awakening and the Transcendentalists*. Westport, CT: Greenwood, 2004.

Harrington, Ann. *The Cure Within: A History of Mind-Body Medicine*. New York: Norton, 2008.

Harrison, Milmon. *Righteous Riches*. New York: Oxford University Press, 2005.

Hatch, Nathan O. "Evangelicalism as a Democratic Movement." In *Evangelicalism and Modern America*, edited by George Marsden, 78–79. Grand Rapids: Eerdmans, 1984.

Haykin, Michael A. G., et al. *The Emergence of Evangelicalism: Exploring Historical Continuities*. Nottingham, UK: IVP, 2008.

"Healed from Osteoarthritis and Cancer by Jesus Christ!!" Online: http://www.youtube.com/watch?v=VMnO-X7H6y8&feature=channel_video_title [accessed 7.11.2010].

"Healing confessions." Pastor Don Eldridge at Victory Life Church, Folsom, CA, U.S.A. Online: http://www.victorylifechurch.org/pdf/healing_confessions.pdf [accessed 13.12.2010].

Heimert, Alan, and Andrew Delbanco. *The Puritans in America: A Narrative Anthology.* Cambridge. Harvard University Press, 1985.

Helm, Paul. "Calvin, A. M. Toplady and the Bebbington Thesis." In *The Emergence of Evangelicalism: Exploring Historical Continuities*, edited by Michael A. G. Haykin and Kenneth J. Stewart, 200–208. Nottingham, UK: IVP, 2008.

Herskovitz, Melvin. *Man and His Works.* New York: Knopf, 1948.

Hilborn, David, et al. *Toronto in Perspective.* Carlisle, UK: Paternoster, 2001.

"The History of Peniel Church—Part Three" Online: http://www.tangle.com/view_video?viewkey=07872fd6f286c4c06655 [accessed 4.1.2011].

"The History of Peniel Church—Part Four" Online: http://www.godtube.com/watch/?v=7D766PNX [accessed 17.12.2010].

"The History of Peniel Church—Part Five" Online: http://www.godtube.com/watch/?v=9J9M2JNU [accessed 4.1.2011].

Hoffer, Eric. *The True Believer.* New York: Harper & Row, 1965.

Hofstadter, Richard. *Anti-Intellectualism in American Life.* New York: Knopf, 1963.

Hoge, David A., and Dean R. Roozen, eds. *Understanding Church Growth.* New York: Pilgrim, 1979.

Hopewell, James. *Congregation: Stories and Structures.* Philadelphia: Fortress, 1987.

Houston, J. *Reported Miracles: A Critique of Hume.* Cambridge: Cambridge University Press, 1994.

"How to Recognise True Annointings." Video of Reid teaching that church leaders not experiencing miracles are not teaching correctly. Online: http://www.youtube.com/watch?v=dgZIMUrVx-k&feature=related [accessed 12.1.2012].

Hummel, Charles E. *Fire in the Fireplace.* 2nd ed. Downers Grove, IL: IVP, 1993.

Hunter, James D. "Conservative Protestantism." In *The Sacred in a Secular Age: Toward Revision in the Scientific Study of Religion*, edited by Phillip Hammond, 150–66. Berkeley: University of California Press, 1985.

Hyde, Lewis. *The Gift—How the Creative Spirit Transforms the World.* Edinburgh: Canongate, 2007.

"ICCC Website." Showing ICCC leaders with the pope and claiming that their episcopate was recognized by Pope Paul VI in 1978. Online: http://www.theiccc.com/aboutUs.html [accessed 7.1.2011].

Illingworth, Cynthia M. "Trapped Fingers and Amputated Finger Tips in Children." *Journal of Pediatric Surgery* 9 (1974) 853–58.

James, William. "Pragmatism: A New Name for Some Old Ways of Thinking." In *Pragmatism and Other Writings*, 1–132. New York: Penguin, 2000.

———. *Pragmatism and Other Writings.* New York: Penguin, 2000.

———. *The Varieties of Religious Experience.* New York: Penguin, 1985.

Jenkins, David. *God Miracle and the Church of England.* London: SCM, 1987.

Jenkins, Richard. "Disenchantment, Enchantment and Re-Enchantment: Max Weber at the Millennium." *Max Weber Studies* 1 (2000) 11–32.

"Jesus Heals the Sick—Part Two." Online: http://www.youtube.com/watch?v=uo8XWuayNmc [accessed 4.11.2010].

"John Healed from Kidney Stone—Bishop Michael Reid—Part {2}." Online: http://www.youtube.com/user/BABYPEARS#p/u/142/Fz_3mxvL-zs [accessed 19.1.2012].

Jones, Sarah. *Call Me Evil, Let Me Go: A Mother's Struggle to Save Her Children from a Brutal Religious Cult*. London: Harper Element, 2011.
Journard, Sidney. "An Exploratory Study of Body-Accessibility." *British Journal of Social and Clinic Psychology* 5 (1966) 221–31.
Judah, J. Stillson. *The History and Philosophy of the Metaphysical Movements in America*. Philadelphia: Westminster, 1967.
Karon, Louise. "Presence in The New Rhetoric." *Philosophy and Rhetoric* 9 (1976) 96–111.
Kay, William. *Apostolic Networks: New Ways of Being Church*. Milton Keynes, UK: Paternoster, 2007.
Kelly, Russel Earl. *Should the Church Teach Tithing?* New York: Writers Club, 2000.
———. "Tithing is not a Christian Doctrine." Online: http://freebelievers.com/article/tithing-is-not-a-christian-doctrine [accessed 15.1.12].
Kenyon, Essek. W. *The Hidden Man: An Unveiling of the Subconscious Mind*. Lynnwood, WA: Kenyon's Gospel Publishing, 1998.
———. *Jesus the Healer*. 1943. Reprint. Lynnwood, WA: Kenyon's Gospel Publishing, 1981.
———. "Justification." *Reality*, November 1909, 133. Republished in *Kenyon's Herald of Life* July–September 2002.
———. *New Creation Realities*. Online: www.scribd.com/doc/50305759/NewCreationRealities [accessed 28.8.2011].
———. *The Two Kinds of Faith*. 1942. Reprint. Lynnwood, WA: Kenyon's Gospel Publishing, 1998.
———. *The Two Kinds of Knowledge*. 1938. Reprint. Lynnwood, WA: Kenyon's Gospel Publishing, 2004.
———. *The Wonderful Name of Jesus*. 1927. Reprint. Lynnwood, WA: Kenyon's Gospel Publishing, 1998.
Kenyon, Evva Spurling. "God's Leadings." *Tabernacle Trumpet*, January 1901, 131–36.
Klyn, Mark S. "Toward a Pluralistic Rhetorical Criticism." In *Essays on Rhetorical Criticism*, edited by Thomas R. Nilsen, 146–57. New York: Random House, 1968.
Knapp, Mark. *Non-Verbal Communication in Human Interaction*. New York: Holt, Reinhart and Winston, 1978.
Kyle, Richard. *Evangelicalism: An Americanized Christianity*. New Brunswick: Transaction, 2006.
Landy, Joshua, and Michael Saler, eds. *The Re-Enchantment of the World: Secular Magic in a Rational Age*. Stanford CA: Stanford University Press, 2009.
Larsen, Timothy. "The Reception Given *Evangelicalism in Modern Britain* since Its Publication in 1989." In *The Emergence of Evangelicalism: Exploring Historical Continuities*, edited by Michael A. G. Haykin and Kenneth J. Stewart, 21–36. Nottingham, UK: IVP, 2008.
Lee, Philip J. *Against the Protestant Gnostics*. New York: Oxford University Press, 1987.
———. "Protestant Gnosticism Reconsidered." *Modern Reformation* 17.3 (2008) 37–40.
Lessnoff, Michael. *The Spirit of Capitalism and the Protestant Ethic*. Aldershot, UK. Elgar, 1994.
"Letter from Archbishop David Huskins." Huskins, presiding bishop of the ICCC confirms that Reid was consecrated by Idahosa. Online: http://www.

beforeiforget.co.uk/2008/hypocrisy-is-the-greatest-luxury/#comment-18239 [accessed 7.1.2011].

Levi-Strauss, Claude. *Introduction to the Work of Marcel Mauss*. 1950. Reprint. London: Routledge and Kegan Paul, 1987.

Lewis, Todd V. "Charismatic Communication and Faith Healers: A Critical Study of Rhetorical Behavior." PhD thesis, Louisiana State University, 1980.

"Linda King's Testimony of Miracle from God." Online: http://www.youtube.com/user/BABYPEARS#p/u/106/wh3_3gXYggo [accessed 19.1.2012].

Lindsey, Hal. *The Late Great Planet Earth*. Grand Rapids: Zondervan, 1970.

MacArthur, John F. *Charismatic Chaos*. Grand Rapids: Zondervan, 1992.

MacIver, R. M. and Charles. M. Page. *Society: An Introductory Analysis*. London: Macmillan, 1955.

Macquarrie, John. *Twentieth-Century Religious Thought*. London: SCM, 1971.

Marsden, George. "America's 'Christian' Origins: Puritan New England as a Case Study." In *John Calvin: His Influence in the Western World*, edited by W. Stanford Reid, 244–49. Grand Rapids: Zondervan, 1982.

———. *Fundamentalism and American Culture*. 2nd ed. New York: Oxford University Press, 2006.

———. "Fundamentalism as an American Phenomenon: A Comparison with English Evangelicalism." *Church History* 46.2 (1977) 215–32.

———. *Jonathan Edwards: A Life*. New Haven: Yale University Press, 2004.

———. *Religion and American Culture*. Belmont, CA: Wadsworth Thompson, 2001.

———. *Understanding Fundamentalism and Evangelicalism*. Grand Rapids: Eerdmans, 1991.

Martin, David. "A Cross-Bench View of Associational Religion." In *The Parish Church? Explorations in the Relationship of the Church and the World*, edited by Giles Ecclestone, 43–51. Oxford: Mowbray's, 1988.

Martin, Jim. "A Rhetorical Analysis of the Illustrative Technique of Clovis G. Chappell, Batsell Barrett Baxter, and Lynn Anderson." D.Min thesis, Harding Graduate School of Religion, Memphis, Tennessee, 1987.

Mauss, Marcel. *The Gift: Forms and Functions of Exchange in Archaic Societies*. Translated by Ian Cunnison. London: Cohen & West, 1966.

———. *The Gift: The Form and Reason for Exchange in Archaic Societies*. Translated by W. D. Halls. 1990. Reprint. London: Routledge, 2011.

———. "Techniques of the Body." *Economy and Society* 2.1 (1973) 70–88. Translation of his 1934 essay "Les Techniques du Corps" by Ben Brewster.

May, Peter. "Claimed Contemporary Miracles." Unpublished paper dated June 2010.

———. "The Faith Healing Claims of Morris Cerullo." *Free Inquiry Magazine* 14.1 (1993) 5–7.

McConnell, Dan. R. *A Different Gospel*. Peabody, MA: Hendrickson, 1995.

———. *The Promise of Health and Wealth: A Historical and Biblical Analysis of the Modern Faith Movement*. Sevenoaks, UK: Hodder & Stoughton, 1990.

McGrath, Alister. *Evangelicalism and the Future of Christianity*. London: Hodder and Stoughton, 1994.

McIntyre, Joe. *E. W. Kenyon: The True Story*. Lake Mary, FL: Charisma House, 1997.

McLaren, Brian. *The Secret Message of Jesus*. Nashville, Tennessee: W, 2006.

McLoughlin, William G. *Modern Revivalism*. New York: Ronald, 1959.

Melton, Gordon J. *Biographical Dictionary of American Cult and Sect Leaders*. New York: Garland, 1986.
Meyer, Donald. *The Positive Thinkers: Popular Religious Psychology from Mary Baker Eddy to Norman Vincent Peale and Ronald Reagan*. Middletown, CT: Wesleyan University Press, 1988.
"Michael Reid Miseries." Online: http://www.michaelreidmiseries.org/general/about_michael_reid_miseries.html [accessed 14.7.2008].
Milbank, John. "Can a Gift be Given? Prolegomena to a Future Trinitarian Metaphysic." *Modern Theology* 11.1 (1995) 119–61.
Miller, Perry, ed. *The American Transcendentalists: Their Prose and Poetry*. New York: Doubleday, 1957.
Miller, Perry, ed. *The American Puritans: Their Prose and Poetry*. New York: Doubleday Anchor, 1956.
———. "The Puritan Way of Life." In *Puritanism in Early America*, edited by George M. Waller, 35–54. Lexington, MA: Heath, 1973.
"Miracle Caught on Camera—Part One." Online: http://www.youtube.com/user/BABYPEARS#p/search/2/rMUOr9po2gU [accessed 16.11.2010].
"Miracle Caught on Camera—Part Two." Online: http://www.youtube.com/watch?v=ho4HEqwEa7U [accessed 20.11.2010].
"Miracle Caught on Camera—Final Part." Online: http://www.youtube.com/watch?v=LnA4FlWP-Ho&feature=related [accessed 22.11.2010].
"Miracle of blind eye opening!" http://www.youtube.com/user/BABYPEARS#p/search/4/szcrnSXXTLY [accessed 16.11.2010].
Mooney, Annabelle. *The Rhetoric of Religious Cults: Terms of Use and Abuse*. Basingstoke, UK: Palgrave Macmillan, 2005.
Murphy, Nancey. *Beyond Liberalism and Fundamentalism*. Harrisburg, PA: Trinity, 1996.
Nelson, Geoffrey K. "Communal and Associational Churches." *Review of Religious Research* 12.2 (1971) 102–10.
Newman, Albert H. "Recent Changes in the Theology of Baptists." *The American Journal of Theology* 10 (1906) 600–609.
Niebuhr, H. Richard. *The Social Sources of Denominationalism*. 1929. Reprint. Cleveland, OH: Meridian, 1967.
Niles, John D. *Homo Narrans*. Philadelphia: University of Pennsylvania Press, 1999.
"No Miracles No Jesus—Part One." Online: http://www.youtube.com/watch?v=unoKG-2xrsw&NR=1 [accessed 4.11.2010].
"No Miracles No Jesus—Part Two." Online: http://www.youtube.com/watch?v=x9Jsgdc8qVA&feature=related [accessed 15.11.2010].
"No Miracles No Jesus—Part Four." Online: http://www.youtube.com/watch?v=T1gMEvozTHU [accessed 4.11.2010].
Noll, Mark A. *The Scandal of the Evangelical Mind*. Grand Rapids: Eerdmans, 1994.
"One of Savelle's Visits to London in 2012." Online: http://destinychristiancentre.org/whats-coming-up/jerry-savelle-18th-march-2012 [accessed 14.1.2012].
Osborn, Lawrence, and Andrew Walker. *Harmful Religion: An Exploration of Religious Abuse*. London: SPCK, 1997.
Osborn, T. L. *Healing the Sick and Casting Out Devils, Vol. 3, Faith's Testimony*. Tulsa, OK: Voice of Faith, 1953.
———. *The Message That Works*. Tulsa, OK: OSFO, 1997.

"Osteen Webpage." Online: http://joelosteen.lakewood.cc/site/PageServer?pagename =JOM_media_player&printer_friendly=1 [accesed 18/3/2007].

Owen, Huw Parri. *Concepts of Deity*. London: Macmillan, 1971.

Parsons, Talcott. "Introduction." In *The Sociology of Religion*, by Max Weber, xix–lxvii. Boston: Beacon, 1964.

Pattison, Stephen. *The Faith of the Managers*. London: Cassell 1997.

———. "Mystical Management: A Religious Critique of General Management in the Public Sector." *MC (Modern Believing)* 33.3 (1991) 17–27.

Peale, Norman Vincent. *Positive Thinking for a Time like This*. Englewood Cliffs, NJ: Prentice-Hall, 1975. (A revision and condensation of *The Tough-Minded Optimist* by the same author.)

Peel, Robert. *Mary Baker Eddy: The Years of Discovery*. New York: Holt, Richart and Winston, 1966.

"Peniel Belgium." Online: http://www.peniel.be/ [accessed 17.12.2010].

Percy, Martyn. "Confirming the Rumour of God: Why Every Church Needs a Sociologist." In *Restoring the Image: Essays on Religion and Society in Honour of David Martin*, edited by Andrew Walker and Martyn Percy, 185–86. Sheffield, UK: Sheffield Academic, 2001.

———. *Engaging with Contemporary Culture*. Aldershot, UK: Ashgate, 2005.

———. *Power and the Church: Ecclesiology in an Age of Transition*. London: Cassell, 1998.

———. *Words, Wonders and Power*. London: SPCK 1996.

Perriman, Andrew, ed. *Faith Health and Prosperity*. Milton Keynes, UK: Paternoster, 2003.

Peters, John. *Colin Urquhart: A Biography*. London: Hodder and Stoughton, 1994.

Peters, Shawn Francis. *When Prayer Fails: Faith Healing, Children, and the Law*. New York: Oxford University Press, 2008.

Phelan, J. W. *Philosophy Themes and Thinkers*. Cambridge: Cambridge University Press, 2005.

Pintar, Judith, and Steven Jay Lynn. *Hypnosis: A Brief History*. Chichester, UK: Willey-Blackwell, 2008.

Poling, Donald, and James E. Miller. *Foundations for a Practical Theology*. Nashville: Abingdon, 1985.

Poloma, Margaret. *Main Street Mystics: The Toronto Blessing and Reviving Pentecostalism*. Walnut Creek, CA: Altamira, 2003.

Ponsonby, Simon. *More: How You Can Have More of the Spirit When You Already Have Everything in Christ*. Colorado Springs: Victor, 2004.

Potter, Jonathan. *Representing Reality: Discourse, Rhetoric and Social Construction*. London: Sage, 2007.

"Premier Radio series." Five interviews with Colin Urquhart on the subject of faith, with Julia Fisher. Online: http://www.kingdomfaith.com/RSS.aspx?BlogID=12 [accessed 14.4.2008].

Pullum, Stephen J. *Foul Demons, Come Out: The Rhetoric of Twentieth Century American Faith Healing*. Westport, CT: Praeger, 1999.

Quimby, Phineas Parkhurst. *The Complete Collected Works of Dr. Phineas Parkhurst Quimby*. Edited by the Phineas Parkhurst Quimby. Philosophical Society, 2008. Online: http://www.seedoflifepublishing.com/Complete_Collected_Works_of_

Dr_Phineas_Parkhurst_Quimby_Look_Inside_Book_Free_PDF.pdf [accessed 13.5.2010].
———. "Imagination II." Online: http://www.phineasquimby.com/imagination_II.html [accessed 14.10.2011].
———. "Jesus—His Belief or Wisdom." Online: http://www.phineasquimby.com/jesus_belief_wisdom.html [accessed 14.6.10].
———. "Parables." Online: http://www.phineasquimby.com/parables.html [Accessed 11.10.2011].
———. *The Quimby Manuscripts*. Edited by H. W. Dresser. 1921. Reprint. London: Forgotten Books, 2008.
Ramzy, Rasha I. "Communicating Cosmopolitanism: The Analysis of the Rhetoric of Jimmy Carter, Vaclav Havel, and Edward Said." PhD thesis, Georgia State University, 2006.
Randi, James. *The Faith Healers*. Buffalo, NY: Prometheus, 1987.
"Reachout Trust, Bishop Michael Reid." Online: http://www.reachouttrust.org/phpbb3/viewtopic.php?f=12&t=2036&start=0 [accessed 14.7.2008].
"Reachout Trust, Peniel Church 2008." Online: http://www.reachouttrust.org/phpBB3/viewtopic.php?f=12&t=2072&start=0&st=0&sk=t&sd=a [accessed 14.7.2008].
Reichley, A. James. *Religion in American Public Life*. Washington, DC: Brookings, 1985.
Reid, Daniel G. *Dictionary of Christianity in America*. Downer's Grove, IL: IVP, 1990.
Reid, Michael S. B. "Attitudes that Destroy." Audio CD. Michael Reid, 2006.
———. "Bitter or Blessed." DVD. Michael Reid, 2007.
———. *Faith It's God Given*. Brentwood, UK: Alive UK, 2002.
———. "Faith or Fatalism." DVD. Brentwood, UK: Alive UK, 2005.
———. *It's So Easy*. Brentwood, UK: Alive UK, 2005.
———. *Strategic Level Spiritual Warfare: A Modern Mythology*. Brentwood, UK: Michael Reid Ministries, 2002.
———. *What God Can Do for You*. Brentwood, UK: Michael Reid, 2006.
———. *Whose Faith is it Anyway*. Brentwood, UK: Sharon, 1990.
Reid, Michael S. B., and Judson Cornwall. *Whose Mind Is It Anyway*. Brentwood, UK: Sharon, 1993.
Reid, W. Stanford, ed. *John Calvin: His Influence in the Western World*. Grand Rapids: Zondervan, 1982.
Reimer, Sam. *Evangelicals and the Continental Divide*. Montreal: McGill-Queen's University Press, 2003.
"Revival." Online: http://www.kingdomfaith.com/ and at internet, http://www.youtube.com/watch?v=XbZHocbhiDo&feature=player_embedded&list=PL5F3C38DE1DA0B822 [accessed 8.2.2012].
Richardson, Robert D. *William James: In the Maelstrom of American Modernism*. Boston: Houghton Mifflin, 2006.
Richter, Philip J. "God is Not a Gentleman." In *The Toronto Blessing—Or is it?*, edited by Stanley E. Porter and Philip J. Richter, 5–37. London: Darton Longman and Todd, 1995.
Romanowski, William D. *Pop Culture Wars: Religion and the Role of Entertainment in American Life*. Downers Grove, IL: IVP, 1996.
Rosenfeld, Lawrence, and Jean Civikly. *With Words Unspoken: The Nonverbal Experience*. New York: Holt, Reinhart & Winston, 1976.

Rubin, Julius H. *Religious Melancholy and Protestant Experience in America*. New York: Oxford University Press, 1994.

Saler, Michael. *As If: Modern Enchantment and the Literary Prehistory of Virtual Reality*. New York: Oxford University Press, 2012.

———. "Modernity and Enchantment: A Historiographic Review." *The American Historical Review* 111.3 (2006) 692–716.

Sargant, William. *Battle for the Mind: A Physiology of Conversion and Brain-Washing*. London: Heinemann, 1957.

Savage, Minot J. *Belief in God: An Examination of Some Fundamental Theistic Problems*. Boston: Ellis, 1881.

"Savelle a 'Regent' of Oral Roberts University and on Its Executive Committee." Online: http://selfstudy.oru.edu/vrr/Accreditation/HLC%20recorded%20in%20catalog06–07.pdf [accessed 16.1.2012].

Savelle, Jerry. *Biblical Partnership*. Crowley, TX: Jerry Savelle, 1999.

———. *Called to Battle Destined to Win*. Ventura, CA: Regal, 2009.

———. *Expect the Extraordinary*. Tulsa, OK: Harrison House, 2000.

———. *If Satan Can't Steal Your Dreams He Can't Control Your Destiny*. Tulsa, OK: Harrison House, 2004.

———. *If Satan Can't Steal Your Joy He Can't Keep Your Goods*. Tulsa, OK: Harrison House, 2002.

———. *In the Footsteps of a Prophet*. Crowley, TX: Jerry Savelle, 1999.

———. *Receive God's Best*. Crowley, TX: Jerry Savelle, 2006.

———. Tape of sermon at Kings Church, Medway, Bible week, 8th November 1999.

"Savelle's Visit to Hillsongs, London on 13th Sept 2009." Online: http://www.jerrysavelle.org/meetings/events.asp?id=4000 [accessed 12.1.2012].

Schiffer, Irvine. *Charisma: A Psychoanalytic Look at Mass Society*. Toronto: University of Toronto Press 1973.

Schmidt, Rosemarie, and Joseph F. Kess. *Television Advertising and Televangelism: Pragmatics and Beyond VII:5* Amsterdam: Benjemins, 1986.

Schweitzer, Arthur. "Theory and Political Charisma." *Comparative Studies in Society and History*, March 1974, 150–86.

Seldes, Gilbert. *The Stammering Century*. New York: Harper & Row, 1965.

Selznick, Philip. *Leadership in Administration: A Sociological Interpretation*. Los Angeles: University of California Press, 1984.

———. *The Moral Commonwealth*. Berkeley: University of California Press, 1994.

———. *The Organizational Weapon: A Study of Bolshevik Strategy and Tactics*. New York: McGraw-Hill, 1952.

———. *The Organizational Weapon: A Study of Bolshevik Strategy and Tactics*. Glencoe, IL: Free, 1960.

Shakarian, Demos, with John and Elizabeth Sherill. *The Happiest People on Earth*. London: Hodder and Stoughton, 2006.

Sheler, Jeffrey L. *Believers: A Journey into Evangelical America*. New York: Viking Adult, 2006.

Shelton, Sally Jo. Review of Andrew Perriman, *Faith, Health and Prosperity*. *PNUEMA: The Journal for the Society for Pentecostal Studies* 26.1 (2004) 164–66.

Sicherman, Barbara. "The Paradox of Prudence: Mental Health in the Gilded Age." *Journal of American History* 62 (1976) 880–912.

Simmons, Dale. H. *E. W. Kenyon and the Postbellum Pursuit of Peace, Power and Plenty.* Lanham, MD: Scarecrow, 1997.
Simmons, John K. "Christian Science and American Culture." In *America's Alternative Religions*, edited by Timothy Miller, 61–68. Albany, NY: State University of New York Press, 1995.
Simons, Herbert. W. "Introduction: The Rhetoric of Inquiry as an Intellectual Movement." In *The Rhetorical Turn: Invention and Persuasion in the Conduct of Inquiry*, edited by H. W. Simons, 1–31. Chicago: University of Chicago Press, 1990.
Smail, Tom, et al. *The Love of Power or the Power of Love: A Careful Assessment of the Problems within the Charismatic and Word-of-Faith Movements.* Minneapolis, MN: Bethany House, 1994.
Spencer, Martin. "What is Charisma?" *The British Journal of Sociology* 24 (1973) 341–54.
Strathern, Andrew. *The Rope of Moka.* Cambridge: Cambridge University Press, 1971.
"Supply." Out of print Article attributed to Mary Baker Eddy. Online: http://www.soularenergy.net/subpage1.html [accessed 6.11.2011].
Swales, John M. *Genre Analysis: English in Academic and Research Settings.* London: Cambridge University Press, 1990.
Swedenborg, Emmanuel. *Arcana Coelestia Vol. 1 of 8.* Translated by John F. Potts, 1905–10. Reprint. London: Forgotten Books, 2008.
———. *Arcana Coelestia Vol. 6 of 8.* Translated by John F. Potts, 1905–10. Reprint. London: Forgotten Books, 2008.
———. *Heaven and Hell.* Translated by John C. Ager, 1900. Reprint. London: Forgotten Books, 2010.
———. *The True Christian Religion.* Translated by John Whitehead. 1906. Reprint. London: Forgotten Books, 2008.
Sweeney, Douglas. *The American Evangelical Story.* Grand Rapids: Baker Academic, 2005.
Sweeney, John. "Sects, Power and Miracles in the Bible Belt of Essex." *The Guardian* 31 December 2000. Online: http://www.guardian.co.uk/uk/2000/dec/31/johnsweeney.theobserver.
Symonds, Melanie. *The Coming Revival: Colin Urquhart's Vision.* Guildford, UK: Highland, 1993.
Teahan, John F. "Warren Felt Evans and Mental Healing: Romantic Idealism and Practical Mysticism in Nineteenth Century America." *Church History* 48.1 (1979) 63–80.
"Terri." Online: http://www.terri.com/ [accessed 16.1.2012].
Thayer, H. S. *Meaning and Action: A Critical History of Pragmatism.* Indianapolis: Hacket, 1981.
The Church of England Board of Mission. *The Search for Faith and the Witness of the Church.* London: Church House, 1996.
Thomas, Alan Berkley. *Research Concepts for Management Studies.* Oxford: Routledge, 2006.
Thomas, George M. *Revivalism and Cultural Change: Christianity, Nation building, and the Market in the Nineteenth-Century United States.* Chicago: The University of Chicago Press, 1989.
Thoreau, Henry David. *Walden, or, Life in the Woods.* Mineola, NY: Dover, 1995.

Thouless, Robert H. *An Introduction to the Psychology of Religion*. London: Cambridge University Press, 1971.
Tillich, Paul. *Systematic Theology. Volume 1*. Chicago: University of Chicago Press, 1951.
Timko, Michael. "Ralph Waldo Emerson and American Identity." *The World and I* 23.12 (2008) 1.
Tönnies, Ferdinand. *Community and Society*. Translated by C. P. Loomis. East Lansing, MI: Michigan State University Press, 1957.
Trine, Ralph Waldo. *In Tune With The Infinite*. Radford, VA: Wilder, 2007.
Turner, Frederick. J. *The Frontier in American History*. 1920. Online: http://www.forgottenbooks.org [accessed 7.5.2011].
Tyner, Paul. "The Metaphysical Movement." *American Monthly Review of Reviews* 25.3 (1902) 312–20.
Urquhart, Colin. *Anything You Ask*. London: Hodder and Stoughton, 1978.
———. *Explaining Deception*. Tonbridge, UK: Sovereign Word, 2002.
———. *Faith for the Future*. London: Hodder and Stoughton, 1982.
———. *Having Confidence in God*. Audio tape set, undated.
———. *The Positive Kingdom*. London: Hodder and Stoughton, 1985.
———. *Receive Your Healing*. London: Hodder and Stoughton, 1986.
———. *True Faith*. Horsham, UK: Kingdom Faith, 2002.
———. *The Truth That Sets You Free*. London: Hodder and Stoughton, 2004.
———. *When the Spirit Comes*. London: Hodder and Stoughton, 1974.
"Urquhart's National Revival Centre." Online: http://www.kingdomfaith.com/AboutUs/WhereWeAre/NationalRevivalCentre.aspx [accessed 18.1.2012].
"Victims of Bishop Michael Reid." Online: http://victimsofbishopmichaelreid.blogspot.com/ [accessed 14.12.2010].
Wacquant, Loïc. "Habitus." In *International Encyclopedia of Economic Sociology*, edited by Jens Becket and Milan Zafirovski, 315–19. London: Routledge, 2005.
Wagner, C. Peter. *Apostles Today*. Ventura, CA: Regal, 2006.
———. *Your Church Can Grow*. Glendale, CA: Regal, 1976.
———. *Your Spiritual Gifts Can Help Your Church Grow*. Ventura, CA: Regal, 1994.
Wagstaff, Graham F. "Compliance, Belief, and Semantics in Hypnosis: A Nonstate, Sociocognitive Perspective." In *Theories of Hypnosis: Current Models and Perspectives*, edited by Graham F. Wagstaff et al., 362–96. New York: Guilford, 1991.
———. "The Semantics and Physiology of Hypnosis as an Altered State: Towards a Definition of Hypnosis." *Contemporary Hypnosis* 15 (1998) 149–65.
Währisch-Oblau, Claudia. "Material Salvation: Healing, Deliverance, and 'Breakthrough' in African Migrant Churches in Germany." In *Global Pentecostal and Charismatic Healing*, edited by Candy Gunther Brown, 62–80. New York: Oxford University Press, 2011.
Waller, George M., ed. *Puritanism in Early America*. Lexington, MA: Heath, 1973.
Wallis, Roy. *The Elementary Forms of the New Religious Life*. London: Routledge and Kegan Paul, 1984.
Walter, Otis M. "On the Varieties of Rhetorical Criticism." In *Essays on Rhetorical Criticism*, edited by Thomas R. Nilsen, 158–72. New York: Random House, 1968.
Ward, Pete. *Selling Worship: How What We Sing Has Changed The Church*. Milton Keynes, UK: Paternoster, 2005.

Ward, W. R. *Early Evangelicalism: A Global Intellectual History, 1670–1789.* Cambridge: Cambridge University Press, 2006.
Warfield, Benjamin B. *Counterfeit Miracles.* New York: Scribner's Sons, 1918.
Warner, Robert, E. "Fissured Resurgence: Developments in English Pan-Evangelicalism 1966–2001." PhD Thesis, Kings College, University of London, 2006.
———. *Reinventing English Evangelicalism, 1966–2001.* Milton Keynes, UK: Paternoster 2007.
———. *Secularization and Its Discontents.* London: Continuum, 2010.
Warren, Michael. *Seeing through the Media: A Religious View of Communications and Cultural Analysis.* Philadelphia: Trinity, 1997.
Warren, Rick. *The Purpose Driven Church.* Grand Rapids: Zondervan, 1995.
Weatherhead, Leslie D. *Psychology Religion and Healing.* Nashville: Abingdon, 1952.
Webber, George. *God's Colony in Man's World.* New York: Abingdon 1960.
Weber, Max. *Economy and Society: An Outline of Interpretive Sociology.* 2 vols. Edited by Guenther Roth and Claus Wittich. Berkeley: University of California Press, 1978.
———. *From Max Weber: Essays in Sociology.* Edited and translated by H. H. Gerth and C. W. Mills. London: Routledge and Kegan, 1948.
———. *On Charisma and Institution Building.* Edited by S. N. Eisenstadt. Chicago: University of Chicago Press, 1968.
———. *The Protestant Ethic and the Spirit of Capitalism.* Translated by Talcott Parsons. London: Allen & Unwin 1930.
———. *The Theory of Social and Economic Organization.* New York: Oxford University Press, 1947.
Whyte, William Foote. *Street Corner Society: The Social Structure of an Italian Slum.* 2nd ed. Chicago; London: University of Chicago Press, 1955.
Wigglesworth, Smith. *Ever Increasing Faith.* Radford, VA: Wilder, 2007.
———. "The Words of This Life." Sermon. Online: http://www.smithwigglesworth.com/sermons/eif9.htm [accessed 22.09.2010].
Williams, Gary. "Enlightenment Epistemology and Eighteenth-Century Evangelical Doctrines of Assurance." In *The Emergence of Evangelicalism: Exploring Historical Continuities*, edited by Michael A. G. Haykin and Kenneth J. Stewart, 372–74. Nottingham, UK: IVP, 2008.
Williams, J. Rodman. *Renewal Theology: Systematic Theology from a Charismatic Perspective.* Grand Rapids: Zondervan, 1996.
Williams, Peter W. *America's Religions: From Their Origins to the Twenty-first Century.* 3rd ed. Champaign, IL: University of Illinois Press, 2008.
Williams, Raymond. *Culture and Society 1780–1950.* Harmondsworth, UK: Penguin, 1966.
———. *Keywords: A Vocabulary of Culture and Society.* London: Fontana, 1983.
Williams, Rhys H. "Visions of the Good Society and the Religious Roots of American Political Culture." *Sociology of Religion* 60.1 (1999) 1–34.
Wilner, Ann R. *Charismatic Political Leadership: A Theory.* Center of International Studies. Princeton, NJ: Princeton University, 1968.
Wimber, John, with Kevin Springer. *Power Evangelism.* London: Hodder and Stoughton, 1985.
———. *Power Healing.* London: Hodder and Stoughton, 1986.
Wolffe, John. *Evangelical Faith and Public Zeal: Evangelicals and Society in Britain, 1780–1980.* London: SPCK, 1995.

Woods, Tim. "Giving and Receiving: Nuruddin Farah's *Gifts*, or, the Postcolonial Logic of Third World Aid." *The Journal of Commonwealth Literature* 38 (2003) 91–112.

World Council of Churches Department on Studies in Evangelism. *Planning for Mission: Working Papers on the New Quest for Missionary Communities*. Edited by Thomas Wieser. New York: United States Conference for the World Council of Churches, 1966.

World Council of Churches. *The Church for Others and the Church for the World*. Geneva: WCC, 1967.

Worley, Robert C. *A Gathering of Strangers: Understanding the Life of Your Church*. Philadelphia: Westminster, 1976.

Wright, C. *A Stream of Light: A Short History of American Unitarianism*. Boston: Unitarian Universalist Assoc., 1975.

Ziff, Larzer. *Puritanism in America*. New York: Viking, 1973.

Zweig, Stephen. *Mental Healers: Franz Anton Mesmer, Mary Baker Eddy, Sigmund Freud*. Garden City, NY: Viking, 1932.

Index

Abuse, vii–viii, 4, 16, 178, 251n68, 291
Activism, 51–52, 74
ACUTE (The Evangelical Alliance Commission on Unity and Truth among Evangelicals), 24
Adams, John, 62
Addiction (to new teaching and manifestations), 251
Addiction Model of Abuse, 237n5, 251n68
Adventures in Faith Magazine, 188, 190, 219, 250
Agent, Agency 29, 66, 113, 126, 235, 242, 253–55
Ahlstrom, Sydney, 66, 281
Albanese, A, 50n83, 81n15, 82n18, 112n199, 281
Allen, A. A., 37
Alpha Course, 55
Alternative Medicine, 18
America a land of opportunity, 78, 80
America a nation founded by God, 50, 54, 59, 76
America as a uniquely religious country with a God given mission, 59
American Declaration of Independence, 55
American Ethnicity, 50
American Exceptionalism, 8, 50–51, 55, 262
American Historical Cultural Theory, 8, 33

American New Thought, 14
American Protestants having special saving knowledge, 72
American Transcendentalism, 8, 56, 263, 268
Americanization, 1
Amplified Bible, 198, 202
Amputated Finger Tips Regeneration, 203–4
Anabaptism, 258
Anabaptists, 57–58, 259, 285
Anderson, C. Alan, 18n28, 89, 281
Andrews, James, 39, 126–27
Angley, Ernest, 37
Animal Magnetism, 85, 93–94
Animalists, 85
Anker, Roy M., 66n172, 97, 281
Annacondia, Carlos, 237n1
Anointed Men of God, 191, 194, 205, 257
Anthropology of Clothing and Ambiance, 219–220
Anthropology of Religion, 33
Anthropology, Anthropological 13, 28–29, 31–33, 211, 219–20, 228, 261, 267, 286
Anti-Intellectualism, 60, 75–76, 262, 288
Anti-rationalism, 70, 84
Anti-Trinitarian, 87
Appadurai, Arjun, 28
Apple, 1, 106, 238

Arcana Coelestia, 83–84, 295
Argyle, Michael, 46, 282
Aristotle, 14, 37, 41, 43, 61, 126, 281
Arminian Theology, Arminian Views, 63, 77, 87
Ascetic Protestantism, Protestant Asceticism, 68–69, 80, 156, 259
Assemblies of God, 15
Ataxic, 47
Assemblies of God, 15
Atonement, 25–26, 84, 100, 202
Ayer, A. J. 14n2, 281

Babypears, 171, 286, 288, 290–91
Baconian Inductive Philosophy, 60
Baker Eddy, Mary, 3n14, 18, 78, 93n81, 97n110, 104, 107, 109, 110n187, 111, 115n223, 122 281–82, 286, 291–92, 295, 298
Baker, Robert, 46, 282
Bakker, Jimmy, x, 247
Barbarin, Chevalier, 86
Barrington College, 119
Bates, Ernest S., 97n110, 282
Bebbington, David, 51–55, 74, 262, 282, 288
Becker, Judith, 159, 282
Beit-Hallahmi, Benjamin, 46, 282
Bercovitch, Sacvan, 59, 282
Berger, Peter, 28, 38, 133, 225, 282
Bethany Fellowship, 144
Bethel Bible Institute, 119
Bettinghaus, Erwin, 248, 282
Biblicism, 8, 51, 58, 74, 76
Big man, 234, 266
Billboards, 160
Billig, Michael, 38, 282
Black, Edwin, 36, 282
Body Language, 29, 152, 247, 252, 258
Bourdieu, Pierre, 29, 252–55, 282–283
Bourgeois psychology, 76
Braden, Charles, 3, 14, 82, 93n81, 95n99, 100, 107n171, 108n180, 112n197, 283
Braid, James, 46, 86, 283
Bramadat, Paul A., 133–34, 237, 283
Branham, William, x, 20, 37, 122, 175, 176 182, 238n10, 283

Bremer, Francis J., 58n125, 283, 285
Brock, Bernard L., 38, 283
Brown, Callum, 237n2, 283
Browning, Don, 32, 283
Budworth Hall, 155–156
Bultmann, Rudolf, 70, 283
Burke, Kenneth, 126, 283
Burton, Robert, 79n8, 114, 283

Cady, H. Emilie, 78, 110, 112, 113n201, 283
Calvin, 52, 58, 68–69, 288, 290, 293
Calvinism, 8, 57, 59, 63, 70, 74, 76, 78–81, 87, 97–98, 103, 114, 122
Calvinist Predestination, 115
Calvinist Puritanism, 50
Cameron, Helen, 31, 284
Campbell, James, 61–62, 284
Canons of Rhetoric, 36
Capital Accumulation, 229, 287
Capitalist Asceticism, 155
Capitalist Consumers of Religion, 29
Capitalist Mindset, 66
Capitalistic, 35, 68, 229, 266, 268
Capps, Charles, 187–88, 284
Caring Hands Hostel, 215
Carrier, James G., 229, 284
Caughey, James, 54
Cave, Dave, 25
Celsus, 257
Cerullo, Morris, viii, ix, x, 25, 170, 290
Cessationist Perspective, 13
CFS (Chronic Fatigue Syndrome), 172
Channing, William Henry, 77, 89
Chapman, Jonathan (Johnny Appleseed), 92
Chariots of Light, 181–182, 193, 207, 215, 219, 249, 255, 284
Charisma, vi, 7, 9, 47, 152, 189, 209, 235–41, 243, 245–47, 249–53, 255, 257, 259, 266, 285–86, 290, 294–95, 297
Charisma Magazine, 189
Charismatic authority, 94, 239
Charismatic Evangelicals, 17
Charismatic leaders, 8, 30, 72, 235, 239–41, 245, 247
Charismatic Movement, 4, 16, 154, 220

INDEX

Charismatic Renewal, vii–viii, 4, 17, 130, 238
Charles, George B., 112
Charm, 152, 238
Charms, 262
Chesebro, James W., 38, 283
Choate, Clara, 112
Christian Idealism, 14
Christian Perfectionism, 168
Christian Science, 3, 14, 18, 21, 77, 86, 92–94, 101, 104, 109–12, 122, 282, 287, 295
Christian Science Church, 18
Christian Science Journal, 110, 112
Christian Science Theological Seminary, 112
Church Growth Principles, 216
Church of Christ Scientist, 110
Church of England, 3–4, 58, 170, 222, 246, 258, 288, 295
Church of the New Jerusalem, 83
Churches run like businesses, 262
Civikly, Jean 249, 293
Clairvoyance, 78, 94, 96
Clairvoyant, 45, 94, 95, 96, 106
Classification of believers into classes, 70
Cleminson, Meidre, 247
Cognitive Dissonance, 9, 209, 255, 264–65, 286
Cognitive Therapy, 171
Coleman, Johnnie, 28
Coleman, Simon, 1n1, 28–29, 33n12, 227, 228n59, 229, 233–35, 252, 254–55, 261, 263n4, 284
Collective Amnesia, 237, 265
Collective Identity, 243
Collyer, Robert, 93
Come Together, 236
Commodification of Religion, 266
Commodification of Renewal, 238
Commonsense Philosophy, 1, 8, 60, 65, 75–76, 262
Competitiveness in giving, 231
Compliance, 46–48, 94, 227, 296
Confession of Sickness, 23
Congregational Church, 110

Congregational Studies, vi, 9, 31, 33, 209, 211, 261, 264, 267, 287
Congregationalist, 87, 116
Conkin, Paul K., 62n154, 284
Contextual, 211–12, 214–16, 220–23
Contextuality, 215
Conversionism, 51, 74
Copeland Gloria, 25, 182, 197, 284
Copeland viewed as a prophet, 192
Copeland, Kenneth, x, 6, 15–16, 24, 77, 122, 145, 179, 181–82, 185–87, 189–92, 194–95, 197, 201–3, 205–6, 215, 219, 246–47, 255n90, 257, 263, 284
Cornwall, Judson, 151, 157–58, 161, 284, 293
Coué, Émile, 46
Coueism, 86
Cranmer, Thomas, 58
Creative Speech, 22, 119
Creeping ascendency of secularization, 71
Critical Correlation, 32–33
Critical Correlative Approach, 31
Critical views of Scripture, 56
Crucicentrism, 51, 74
Cruz, Nicky, 153, 178, 284
Csordas, Thomas J., 255, 284
Cullis, Charles, 118
Cult, 3, 20, 110, 255, 289, 291
Cults, 3, 15, 17, 20, 37, 40–41, 44, 70, 87–88, 118, 122, 231, 261, 281, 291
Cultural, 1–3, 8, 32–33, 35, 40, 48, 50–51, 56–57, 61, 64, 76, 81, 133, 170, 229, 239, 245, 250, 252–53, 255, 261–63, 281, 284, 295, 297
Culture, x, xiii, 1–3, 8, 11, 20, 28–32, 34, 48–54, 56, 58, 60–62, 66, 76–78, 80, 82, 84, 86–88, 92–94, 96, 98, 114–15, 122–23, 133–34, 156, 182, 223, 228–29, 234, 252, 263, 268, 281, 285, 287, 290, 292–93, 295, 297
Cunnison, Ian 231, 290
Cursing Disease, 174–77, 269, 271–72, 274, 279

D'Andrade Hugh, 112n198, 285
Darwinism, 56
De Puysegur, Count Maxim, 85–86
De Tocqueville, Alexis, 51, 285
Dearing, Trevor, 154–55, 157
DeArteaga, William, 21n53, 157, 285
Deists, Deistic, 87–88
Delbanco, Andrew 63n156, 288
Delivery, 36, 44, 199, 242, 247, 250
Delsarte, 116
Demerath, N. J., 224–25, 285
Demystification and Secularization of the World, 251
Denial of Sensory Reality, 18, 84, 121, 164–65, 169
Denzin, Norman K., 33, 285
Depositing Money in Your Heavenly Account, 24
Depression, 79, 98, 132
Direct Influx, 91
Discourse Community, 37, 39, 44, 127, 233, 235, 261, 265–67
Disenchanted, 6–7, 34, 266
Disenchantment, 4, 9, 134, 209, 250–51, 288
Disposition, Dispositions, 242, 253–55
Dittemore, John V., 97, 282
Divine Influx, 84, 91–92
Divine Mind, 91, 101, 110–11, 122–23
Divine Science, 111, 281
Doctrine of Correspondence, 83–84, 89, 92, 107
Dollar, Creflo, 73
Double Atonement, 26
Double Predestination, 66, 69
Double, Don, 189
Douglas, Frederick, 62
Dow, Lorenzo, 54
Dow, Thomas, 240, 285
Dress/Clothing of preachers—significance, 36, 47, 219–20, 249, 250
Dresser, Annetta, 95, 107n172, 285
Dresser, Horatio W., 83, 84, 88n49, 93n81, 95, 100, 105–6, 107n172, 285, 293
Dresser, Julius, 95, 99, 107
Driggers, B. Carlisle, 214, 285

Dualism, 60, 70
Dualistic Epistemology, 117–19, 121
Duplantis, Jesse, 231, 255n90
DuPlessis, David, 163
Dyton, Simon, 58n121, 285

Ecclestone, Giles, 222, 225, 285, 290
Edwards, Jonathan, 54, 62–64, 76, 263, 290
Ehrenreich, Barbara, 80, 81n16, 109n183, 113n203, 113n205, 114n208, 114n210, 114n216, 114n219, 115, 285
Eistenstadt, S. N., 251
Ekman, Ulf, 227
El-Faizy, Monique, 53n102, 285
Elizabeth I, Queen of England, 57–58
Elizabethan Compromise/Settlement, 58
Electionism, 8, 50, 57, 59, 76, 87, 103
Emerson College, 15, 113, 115–18
Emerson College of Oratory, 113, 115
Emerson School of Oratory, 15
Emerson, Charles Wesley, 15, 116–17
Emerson, Ralph Waldo, 81–82, 88–92, 99, 263, 285, 296
Empiricism, 87
Empowering Presence of God, 237–38
Enchanted illusory world, 267
Enchanted Worldview, 251
Enchantment, 9, 209, 250–52, 255, 286, 288–89, 294
Enchantment, Disenchantment, 4, 9, 134, 251, 209, 250, 288
Enchants, 262
English Skepticism, 8
Enlightenment, 49, 51–52, 87, 297
Entrepreneur, Entrepreneurial, ix, 35, 134, 155–56, 208, 237
Entrepreneurship, 155
Epistemology, 17, 50, 52, 87–88, 91, 118–19, 121, 267–68, 297
Epistemology of the Faith Movement, 17
Established Church (of England), 60, 246
Ethnography, Ethnographic, 27–28, 133
Ethos or Reputation, 126
European Skepticism, 1, 267

INDEX 303

Evangelical Alliance, 24–25
Evangelical Alliance Commission on Unity and Truth among Evangelicals, 24
Evangelical counsels of Poverty, Chastity and Obedience, 70
Evangelical Faith Cure Movement, 20
Evangelical Revivalism, iii–iv, 3, 13, 15, 115
Evangelicalism, Definition, 52
Evans, Warren Felt, 3n14, 78, 82–83, 90, 95, 107–9, 112, 123, 286, 295
Evans-Pritchard, E. E., 228
Experience a priority over intellect, 63
Experience validation of God's activity, 63
Extreme Biblicism, 8, 58, 76

Faith Camp, 6, 220, 227, 244, 246, 255–56
Faith for Today, 139, 244
Faith in God's faith, 163–65, 168
Faith Movement, iv, xii, 15–18, 20–22, 25–29, 40, 50, 70, 74, 81, 120–21, 141, 151, 189, 201, 227, 230, 232, 290
Faith Principles, 29, 35, 186, 192, 227, 245
Faith Teachings, 84, 151, 261, 267
Faith-filled Words, 22, 119
Falling Back (Slain in the Spirit), 173
Farah, Nurudin, 230, 233, 286, 298
Fee, Gordon, 15–16, 203, 286
Festinger, Leon, 255–56, 286
Fideistic, 17
Fieldwork, 34
Fillmore, Charles and Myrtle, 112–13, 285
Financial Partners, 215
Finney, Charles G., 63, 151, 161, 174, 263–64, 286
First Great Awakening, 56, 63, 262
Fisher, Julia, 139–41, 145–46, 292
Fisher, Walter, 44, 134–35, 152, 251, 265n13, 286
Fisherfolk, 236
Flanagan, Kieran, 252, 286
Fluidists, 85

Formulaic approach, 26–27, 36
Formulaic Spirituality, 26
Francke (Lutheran Pietist), 52
Franklin, Benjamin, 61–62, 66, 67–68, 263–64, 284
Franciscan Movement, 258
Free Will Baptists, 118
Freeman, James Dillet, 112n198, 286
Freud, 46, 286, 298
Freudian psychoanalysis, 46
Freudism, 86
Friends University, 161
Frontier Spirit, 56, 76
Fundamental Practical Theology, 32, 283
Fundamentalists, 65, 237

Gademer, Hans-Georg, 32
Geertz, Clifford, 34, 39, 50, 127, 286
Gemeinschaft (Community), 223
Gesellschaft (Society), 223
Gifford, Paul, 25
Gill, Grant, 179–80, 182
Gill, Robin, xiii
Global Gospel Fellowship, 158
Globalization, 1, 25, 28–29, 50, 263, 268
Gnosticism, 9, 18, 50, 70–75, 83, 125, 168, 209, 256–57, 262–64, 267–68, 289
God a business God, 110
God as Supply, 110, 112, 295
God Himself having faith, 163–64
God TV, 2
God unable to override Spiritual laws, 23, 120, 196
God's Thinking, 98, 100
God's Words, 22, 119
God-chosen people, 262
Goodman, Ann, 214, 287
Gordon College, 119
Gordon, A. J. 117–19
Gossett, Don, 22, 122, 287
Gottschalk, Stephen, 110, 287
Graham, Billy, 55
Grammar of Assent, 38
Gregory, C.A. 229, 234, 287
Grubb Institute, 222
Guest, Matthew, 31, 287

Guinness, Os, 60, 65, 287
Gumbel, Nicky, 55

Habitus, 9, 29, 209, 250, 252–55, 296
Hagin, Kenneth, 15, 17–18, 20, 23–25, 27, 77, 119, 120–22, 140–41, 145, 168, 184n28, 189, 191, 194, 201, 207, 215, 263–64, 287
Half Way Covenant, 63–64, 263
Hall, W. D., 230, 290
Hamner, Gail, 1, 59, 61n147, 64, 287
Hand Gestures, 248
Hanegraff, Hank, 21, 167n113, 189n46, 287
Harrison, Milmon, 27–29, 287
Hatch, Nathan, 54, 287
Hau, 232–33, 266
Health, Wealth, and Prosperity Movement, vii, viii, 5, 8, 13, 16, 31, 263
Hegel, Georg, 82
Heimert, Alan, 63n156, 288
Hell-fire Theology, 114
Helm, Paul, 52, 288
Hermenuetics, Hermenuetical, xi,15, 26, 32, 92, 241
Heroic Medicine, 98, 114
Herskovitz, Melvin, 49, 288
Hervieu–Lèger, Daniele, 133
High Church movement, British, 60
Higher Christian Life Movement, 19, 21, 79
Higher Life, 21, 80, 118
Higher Life Teachers, 118
Hilborn, David, 25, 133, 288
Hilgard, Ernest R. 85
Hillsongs Church, London, 7, 179, 193n69, 294
Hindu Sacred Literature, 89
Hinn, Benny, 37, 73, 171n130, 173n140, 249
Hodder and Stoughton, 220
Hodge, A. A., 61
Hodge, Charles, 61
Hoffer, Eric, 247, 288
Hofstadter, Richard, 60, 288
Homo Donum (Gift Giving Man), 229

Homo Narrans, 134–35, 152, 229, 251, 291
Hopewell, James, 33, 211–12, 214–18, 264, 288
Hopkins, Emma Curtis, 78, 90, 112
Househunting, 211, 220, 264
   Four Approaches, 211
      Contextual, 211–12, 214–16, 220–23, 264
      Mechanistic, 31, 37, 75, 169, 211, 214–18, 220–21, 262, 264, 267
      Organic, 211, 215, 217–18, 220–21, 224–25, 264
      Symbolic, 211, 218–21, 224, 264
Houston, Brian, 237n1
Houston, J, 170, 288
Howell, Harris, 54
Hume, David, 61, 170, 288
Hunter, James D., 134, 288
Huskins, David, 162n89, 289
HWPM, vii–xi, 5–6, 35, 40, 113, 263–64
Hyde, Lewis, 232, 288
Hypnosis, 45–48, 85, 94, 171, 173, 282, 287, 292, 296

Idahosa World Outreach, 158
Idahosa, Benson, 35, 151, 158, 161–63, 174, 176, 238, 246, 264, 273–74, 289
Ideal Types, 222, 230
Idealism, Objective, 97
Idealism, Subjective, 8, 82, 88, 97, 107, 119, 122, 196, 263, 267–68
Ideas in the air of nineteenth-century America culture, 20, 62, 263
Ideas like seeds, 106, 116, 196, 198
If it works it must be good, 64
Illingworth, Cythia M., 204, 288
Illinois Christian Science College, 112
Illinois Metaphysical College, 112
Implicit Rhetorical Theories, 39–40
Industrial Revolution, 66
Infant Baptism, 58
Institute of Christian Science, 112
Instrumentalism, 65
International Charismatic Bible Ministries, 159

INDEX

International Communion of Charismatic Churches (ICCC), 162–63, 246, 288–89
Interpretive Principles, 180, 193
Invalidism, 109, 114–15
iPhones, 238

James Stuart, King of Scotland, 58
James, William, 61, 64–65, 114, 293, 288
Jamieson, Kathleen, 36, 284
Jefferson, Thomas, 62
Jenkins, David, 170, 288
Jenkins, Jerry B., 73
Jenkins, Richard, 251, 288
Jobs, Steve, 238n8
Johnson, Bill, 236n1
Jones, Sarah, (Caroline Green), 243, 289
Journard, Sidney, 249n56, 289
Judah, J. Stillson, 14, 289, 90n60, 91n68, 92n72, 107n171, 108n174, 108n180
Jung, Carl, 46
Jungian analytical psychology, 46

Kansas City Prophets, 236
Kant, Immanuel, 1, 61
Kenneth Copeland, x, 6, 15–16, 24, 77, 122, 179, 181, 185, 187, 189–90, 192, 194, 197, 201–2, 205–6, 247, 284
Kenyon, E. W., 8, 13–15, 17–24, 27, 70, 77–78, 79n5, 84, 91–92, 94n91, 113, 115–23, 142, 151, 158, 163–64, 168, 191, 194, 201, 207, 263–64, 287, 289–90, 295
Keswick, 21
Khulman, Kathryn, 238n10
King's Church, Medway, 180, 190, 192, 197, 203–204, 215, 218, 257
Kingdom Faith, 5–6, 42, 131, 139, 147, 188, 215, 218–19, 234, 243, 246, 282, 296
Kingdom Faith Teaching Course, 131
Kleeneze, 188, 202
Klyn, Mark S., 36, 289
Knapp, Mark, 248, 289
Kyle, Richard, 53, 55, 289

LaHaye, Tim, 73
Lake, John. G., 20
Lakeland Revival, 4, 236n1
Latimer, Hugh, 58
Law of Faith, 24–25, 201, 287
Law of Hundredfold Return, 194
Law of Reciprocity, 201
Law of Seedtime and Harvest, 194–95, 198, 233
Law of Sevenfold Return, 200
Lee, Philip J., 71–74, 257, 289
Lessnoff, Michael, 66, 289
Levi-Strauss, Claude, 49, 230, 290
Lewis, C. S., 55
Liberal Christians, 87
Liberalism, 1, 61, 291
Lindsay, James "Gordon", 176
Lindsey, Hal, 54n106, 290
Linnecar, Peter, 151, 155–56, 161, 218, 220
Livets Ord, 1, 28, 227, 233–34, 252, 263–64
Locke, John, 61
Lollardy, 57, 258
Longevity of Ministry, 130
Luckmann, Thomas, 28, 38, 282

MacArthur, John, 16–17, 290
MacIver, R. M., 223, 225, 290
Management Language, 2
Managerial Theories, 2
Maori, 232–33
Marsden, George, 54n108, 55–56, 59–60, 66, 262, 287, 290
Martin, David, 223–224, 290, 292
Massachusetts Bay Colony, a city upon a hill, 58–59
Massachusetts Metaphysical College, 110
Mather, Cotton, 52, 66
Mauss, Marcel, 49, 227–34, 252, 290
Maussian Analysis, 9, 209, 227–28, 265
May, Peter, 170, 265, 290
McAlister, Robert, 163
McLaren, Brian, 237n6
McConnell, Dan, xii, 14–15, 17–22, 27, 29, 70, 84, 92, 115, 118, 121, 189, 263, 290

McGrath, Alister, 52, 290
McIntyre, Joe, 14–15, 18n33, 19, 22, 115, 117–18, 290
ME (Myalgic Encepalomyelitis), 152, 170n122, 171–72, 175, 269, 270–71
Meaning the plain man gets out of the bible the correct one, 54n108, 61n143
Mechanistic, 31, 37, 75, 169, 211, 214–18, 220–21, 262, 264, 267
Mechanistic Language, 37
Mechanistic Pragmatism, 31
Media as Product, 35, 214, 238
Mental Suggestion, 45, 86, 94, 107, 262, 265
Mercy Seat, 63
Mesmer, Franz Anton, 46, 78, 85–86, 93, 298
Mesmerism, 8, 18, 45, 78, 85–86, 93–94, 113, 282, 286
Metaphysical cults, 17, 20, 70
Metaphysical healing, 82, 112
Metaphysical Sects, 90
Metaphysics, Metaphysical, 8, 13–15, 18, 20–22, 56, 65, 70, 74, 78, 81–84, 86, 88, 90–93, 97, 107, 108n174, 110–12, 118–119, 122, 233, 263, 281, 289, 298, 296
Meyer, F. B.
Mill, James, 61
Milbank, John, 234, 291
Miller, James E. 33, 292
Miller, Perry, 57, 79n7, 286, 291
Mind Cure, 8, 77, 80–84, 86–88, 97, 108, 111–12, 167, 263, 265, 286
Mind Techniques, 95
Mind-science cults, 3, 15
Missio Dei, 212
Models of Church, Associational, 222–226, 264, 267, 290–91
Models of Church, Communal, 222–226, 291
Models of Church, Contextual, 211–12, 214–216, 220–23, 264
Models of Church, Parish, 212, 216, 222–23, 225, 285, 290
Modern Commodity Societies, 229

Modern Western Capitalism, 66, 68
Modernism, 51, 293
Monism, 88–90
Montanism, 258
Moody, Dwight L., 54
Mooney, Annabelle, 37, 40–44, 261, 291
Motivational material, 193
Mottos, Motto, 193, 195, 198–99, 208
Muller, George, 118

Narrative, 22, 44, 125–26, 134–36, 148, 152, 207, 215, 219, 242, 251, 256, 262, 265, 267, 288
Narrative Fidelity, 135
Narrative Paradigm, 44, 251, 265
Narrative Probability, 135, 215
National Revival Centre, 6, 220, 240, 296
Nelson, Geoffrey K., 222–26, 291
Neo-Gnostic, 4, 8, 65, 165
Neo-Gnostic Tendencies, 8
Neo-Gnosticism, 9, 18, 50, 70, 125, 209, 256–57, 262–64, 267–68
Neurasthenia, 109, 113–14
Neurypnology, 86, 283
New Measures to bring in revival, 63, 174, 263
New Thought attitude to sickness, 18, 21, 94, 96–98, 107, 123
New Thought Metaphysics, New Thought, xi, 3n14, 8. 13–15, 18–21, 28, 50, 56, 65, 74, 77–83, 88–93, 95, 100n119, 101, 105, 108, 110, 112–19, 123, 125, 263, 281, 283, 285
New Wine Conference, 4n19, 6, 236, 237n6
Niebuhr, H. Richard, 76, 122, 257–59, 263, 266, 291
Niles, John, 134, 152, 229, 251, 291
Noll, Mark, 60, 282, 291
Non-State Theorists, 45
Norman, Larry, 236n1
North American Pragmatism, 1

Ongar Christian Fellowship, 155
Oral Roberts University, 5, 17, 159, 162, 190, 246, 255, 294

Ordinary person is as capable of interpreting scriptures as well as anyone else, 54, 61n143
Organization, x, 6, 29, 36, 44–45, 110, 130, 159, 225, 229, 239, 243, 297
Organizational Theory, vi, 9, 33, 209, 211, 222, 226, 261, 264, 267, 294
Organizations, 62, 134, 223–24
Origen, 257
Osborn, T. L., 35, 122, 151, 158, 161, 182, 252, 264, 291
Osteen, Joel, 77, 193n68, 292
Over-soul, 90–92, 285
Owen, Hugh, 89, 292
Owens, Jimmy and Carol, 236n1

Packer, J. I., 55
Page, Charles M., 223, 290
Paine, Thomas, 87
Paloma, Margaret, 159
Panentheism, 89
Pantheism, 89–90
Parsons, Talcott, 250, 292, 297
Participant Observer Study, Observer as participant, 27, 33
Pattison, Stephen, 2–3, 266, 292
Peale, Norman Vincent, x, 77, 193, 291–92
Peddlers of the Gospel, 213
Peirce, Charles S., 61, 64, 284
Peniel Academy, 156–57
Peniel Bible Assembly, 155
Peniel Church, 5, 150–51, 153–58, 160–62, 170, 227, 247, 252, 288, 293
Peniel College of Higher Education, 162
Peniel, Fee paying school, 218, 243
Pensacola Revival, 4, 236n1
People attracted by fresh move of God, 252
Percy, Martyn, iii, iv, v, xi, xiii, 38, 223, 228, 235, 238, 240, 245, 247, 292
Performative Rhetoric, 8, 32–36, 125, 152, 172, 180, 190, 207, 251, 261, 263, 267
Persuasion, 1, 31, 33, 37–38, 41–44, 46, 239, 242, 249–50, 284, 295
Peters, John, 129–132, 241, 243, 292
Phlogiston, 85

Pietism, 60
Placing of Billboard Posters, 160, 220
Plagiarizm, Plagiarize, 17–18, 27, 119
Planting an uncommon seed, 201
Plato, 116
Plymouth Colony, 59
Polarized Aggression, 243
Poling, Donald, 33, 292
Pope Paul VI, 163, 246, 288
Portraiture, 126
Positive Confession, x, 20, 22, 24–25, 27, 120, 123, 187, 189, 191
Positive formula prayers, 108
Positive Thinking, x, 8, 50, 65, 77–78, 80, 93, 108, 122, 166, 192–93, 285, 292
Positivist transcendentalist movement, 80
Possibility levels, 191, 257
Postbellum, 18–19, 295
Posthypnotic Amnesia, 85
Potlatch, 230–31, 266
Potter, Jonathan, 38, 292
Power of Spoken Words, 108
Poyen, Charles, 78, 86, 93
Practical Theological Framework, 31
Practical Theology, 32–33, 162, 283, 292
Pragmatic Instrumentality, 37
Pragmatism, ix, 1–2, 8, 31, 50, 53, 59–62, 64–65, 74–77, 88, 114, 125, 174, 208, 216, 237, 262–64, 266–68, 284, 287–88, 295
Pragmatism, Consecrated, 216
Prestations, 231
Price, Fred, 189
Prince, Derek, 236n1
Princeton, Princeton School, 55, 60, 61, 65
Principles that bind God, 120
Prosperity, iv, vii–xii, 5, 8, 13, 16, 18, 21, 24–29, 31, 35, 65, 73, 78, 101, 112–13, 116, 123, 180, 182, 185, 189, 191, 197, 202–4, 219, 227, 238, 259, 263–64, 266, 284–85, 292, 294
Prosperity Gospel, xii, 24, 264
Protestant Ascetic Lifestyle, 66

INDEX

Protestant Ethic, 66–68, 80, 156, 251, 289, 297
Protestant Work Ethic, 50
Providence Bible Institute, 119
Psychologists, 45–46, 48
Psychology, 9, 31–33, 46–47, 64, 76–77, 86, 261, 282, 289, 291, 296–97
Psychosomatic Illnesses, 47
Publicity, Publicity of Church, 35, 44, 160–61, 177, 190, 208, 214
Pulkingham, Betty, 236n1
Pullum, Stephen J., 37–40, 130, 238n10, 261, 292
Puritan, 8, 50, 52–53, 57–59, 62–64, 66–67, 70, 74–76, 78–79, 87, 156, 161, 262, 267, 282, 290–91
Puritan Ascetic Culture, 8
Puritan Heritage, 57, 75, 267
Puritan Imaginary, 64
Puritan Legacy, 50, 64
Puritan Principles, 59
Puritan settlers viewing themselves as the New Israel, 59
Puritanism, 50, 57, 59, 63–64, 74, 76, 283–285, 291, 296, 298
Puritans, 55, 57–59, 62–63, 76, 79–80, 114, 263, 283–85, 288, 291
Pyramid Selling, 188–89, 202
Pytches, David, 236n1

Qualitative Research, 32
Quimby and Jesus as the exemplary healer, 103
Quimby, George, 100
Quimby, Phineas, 3n14, 8, 15n10, 18, 45–46, 56, 65, 78, 81–83, 86, 92–107, 109–12, 114–15, 123, 263, 265, 285, 292–93
Quimby's talking cure, 94–95, 263
Quimby's Understanding of Death, 103
Quimby's Understanding of Jesus and The Christ, 99–105
Quimby's Understanding of Man, 105

Randi, James, 170, 293
Rationalist Skepticism (European), 1, 8, 40, 61, 75, 87, 267
Rationalization (Weber), 250–51

Reachout Trust, 150, 293
Reagan, Ronald, 80–81, 291
Reciprocity, xi, 201, 229, 232
Re-enchantment, 251–52, 288–89
Reflexivity, 252
Refugees, 4–5, 7, 34, 79, 222, 251, 266
Reichley, A. James, 63n158, 293
Reid, Ruth, 150, 152, 158, 161, 170n122, 220, 278
Reid, Thomas, 60–61
Reimer, Sam, 53n102, 293
Religious Interpretive Theory, 8, 33, 61
Religious Melancholy, 79–80, 114, 294
Reputation, 39, 126–127, 207, 218, 220, 232, 235, 261, 266–67
Rev. Ike, 28
Revelation Knowledge, 17, 25, 91, 118, 121, 123, 189–91, 194, 257
Revival Camp Fireside Meetings, 56
Revival Steps and Principles, 63, 65, 75
Revivalism, iii–iv, 3, 8, 13, 15, 48, 51, 54, 59–61, 63–65, 77–80, 87, 95, 115, 123, 170, 263–64, 266, 290, 295
Revolutionary Message, 240
Rhetoric, v, 4–5, 8, 29, 32–41, 43–44, 47–48, 125–27, 129–31, 150–53, 163, 172, 177, 180–81, 207–8, 211, 242, 245, 251, 261, 263, 267, 281, 289, 291–93, 295
Rhetorical Analysis, 7–8, 33, 37–38, 40, 261, 290
Rhetorical Constructs, 38
Rhetorical Devices, 1, 40, 193
Rhetorical Studies, 33, 261
Richardson, Robert D., 114n209, 293
Richter, Philip, 31, 133, 284, 293
Ridley, Nicholas, 58
Riecken, Henry W., 255
Roberts, Oral, ix, x, 5, 17, 20, 37, 158–162, 182, 190, 194, 195, 201, 206, 246, 255, 284, 294
Roberts, Richard, 158, 161, 162
Robertson, Roland, 28
Roffey Place, 6, 132, 215, 220, 241, 246, 252
Romanowski, William, 49, 293
Romanticism, 51

INDEX 309

Rosenfeld, Lawrence, 249, 293
Rossiter, Clinton, 62
Routinization of Charisma, 240, 245
Rowland, Daniel, 54
Rudd, Brian, 184–85
Ryle, James, 236n1, 237n6

Saler, Michael, 251, 289, 294
Salvation Army, Salvationists, 74n216, 227n57, 259, 284
Sargant, William, 159, 294
Satan, 60, 154, 192, 194, 200, 203, 205, 244–45, 294
Savelle, Carolyn, 181–86, 192, 195, 198–200, 247
Savelle-Foy, Terri, 182, 188, 203, 204, 295
Scanlon, Paul, 35n16
Schachter, Stanley, 255
Schenck, Ruthanna, 113
Schiffer, Irvine, 243, 294
Schleiermacher, Friedrich, 1, 61
Schuler, Robert, 77
Scott, Robert L., 38, 283
Scottish Commonsense Philosophy, 8, 60, 65, 76
Scottish Commonsense Realism, 50, 60, 75
Scripture treated as contractual or covenantal document, 26
Secret insights into Christian Truth, 237, 262, 267
Secularization, 4, 71, 133–34, 237, 251–52, 283, 286, 297
Seed Faith, ix, 151, 159, 194, 197
Seed faith gifts, 151, 159
Seldes, Gilbert, 73, 294
Self understood as embodied history, 253
Self-centered faith, 65, 72–74
Self-presentation, 29, 126, 129, 152, 160, 163, 180, 182, 207, 246, 262
Selznick, Philip, 223–25, 283–84, 294
Sense Knowledge, 118, 121–22, 194
Sense Knowledge Faith, 122
Sensory Evidence, 17
Sensory Knowledge, 17, 70

Shakarian, Demos, 153–54, 157, 176, 178, 294
Shaller, Lyle, 216
Sheler, Jeffrey L., 53n102, 294
Shelton, Sally Jo, 27, 294
Silvoso, Ed, 4n20, 237n1
Simmons, Dale H., 17, 18n29, 19, 21–22, 79, 115–18, 122, 158, 295
Simmons, John K., 92–93, 94n88, 101n24, 101n25, 295
Simpson, A. B., 20, 118
Smail, Tom, 17–18, 189, 295
Small Thinking, 191
Social and Theological Construction of Reality, 7, 239, 261, 266–67
Social Class, 9, 209, 224–25, 238, 285
Social Compliance, 46
Social Construction of Reality, 28, 38, 282
Social Constructionism, 33, 47
Societies (Gift), Societies (Commodity), 230
Socio-economic reasons that people are drawn to churches, 7, 8, 229, 266
Socrates, 61
Sola Fide, 68
Sola Scriptura, 52, 58, 76
Somnambulism, 85
Sowing Money, Sow Money, 188, 202, 232
Speaking in tongues, 129, 153, 183, 185
Speaking to your problems/ troubles, 143, 145
Speech delivery amongst charismatic leaders, 247
Speech Faith, 23
Spencer, Martin, 243, 295
Spinoza, 170
Spirit of Capitalism, traits
  Frugality, 67–68
  Honesty, 67–68
  Industry, 67–68
  Punctuality, 67–68
Spiritual Laws, 20, 23–24, 26, 35, 91–92, 120, 123, 165, 191, 194, 196, 201, 208, 264, 286
Spiritualism, 14
Spurling, Evva, 117–119, 289

St Hugh's Lewsey, 131, 138, 241n18
St. Andrew's Chorleywood, 236n1
St. Philip & St. James, Chatham, xiii, 4–7, 222, 226
Stanton, Elizabeth Cady, 62
State Theorists, 45
Steps and Principles to bring about revival, 63, 75
Stoddard, Solomon, 63–64
Storefront Churches, 212
Stories, Story, 38, 40, 42–44, 125–26, 134–38, 145–46, 148, 151–52, 180, 182–85, 188–89, 194, 198–200, 203–4, 207, 217, 219–20, 229, 231, 233, 238, 247, 251, 274, 280, 288
Story Telling Man, 134, 207
Stott, John, 55
Stranger quality, 245
Strathern, Andrew, 234, 295
Style, 6, 29, 36, 44–45, 95, 97, 217, 238, 241–42, 247, 249, 252, 256
Subjective Idealism, 8, 82, 88, 97, 107, 119, 122, 196, 263, 267–68
Subritsky, Bill, 237n1
Suggestibility, Suggestible people, 46–47, 159–60, 262, 267
Suggestion, 8, 23, 30, 45–48, 78, 86, 94, 107, 120, 134, 160, 169, 171, 173, 178, 185, 212, 227, 238, 247, 258, 262, 265–66, 268
Suggestive Persuasion Techniques, 46
Susceptibility, 94, 239
Suspension of sensory knowledge, 70
Swaggart, Jimmy, x, 247
Swales, John M., 37, 44, 261n1, 295
Swartz, A. J. 112
Swedenborgianism, 8, 78, 83, 92, 107
Sweedenborg, Emmanuel, 78, 83–84, 91–93, 99–100, 107, 116, 123, 167, 263, 295
Sweeney, Douglas, 53, 295
Syncretism, Syncretized, 13, 15, 78, 118, 263

Talking Cure, 94–95, 173, 263
Talking to Sickness, 174
Telepathy, 94

Tent Campaigns, 176, 238
Tertullian, 257
Thatcher, Margaret, 80
Thayer, H.S., 62, 65n67, 295
The Faith of God, 109, 141–42
The Scripture is Clear, 141
Theological Construction of Reality, xi, 7, 38, 40, 125, 239, 261, 266–67
Theory of Secularization, 133
Theosis, 168
Theosophy, 14
Thomas, Alan Berkley, 81, 295
Thomas, George M., 64, 295
Thoreau, Henry David, 62, 89, 295
Thouless, Robert H., 47, 296
Thunder Over Texas, 255
Tillich, Paul, 32, 296
Tithe, Tithing, viii, xi, 24, 201–2, 243, 289
Tönnies, Ferdinand, 223, 296
Toronto Blessing, viii, 4, 132–33, 236, 292–93
Torrey, R. A., 54n108, 61n143
Touch, 23, 85, 174, 176, 249, 272, 279
Tracy, David, 32
Trance State, 46
Transatlantic influence, 54
Transcendentalism, 8, 56, 77–81, 88–89, 91, 122, 263, 268
Tree, Geogina, 113
Trine, Ralph Waldo, 78, 113, 116–17, 296
Trinity, 4, 87, 104, 150, 159, 214, 291, 297
Trinity Church, Brentwood, 150, 159, 214
Troeltsch, Ernst, 71
Trumpet Call Newspaper, 218
Tudor, Mary, 58
Turner, Frederick J., 80–81, 296
Tusting, Karin, 31

Union Theological Seminary, 212
Unitarianism, 8, 77–78, 87–89, 107, 122–23, 284, 298
Unitarianism's emphasis on natural law, 107
Unitarians, 65, 87–88

INDEX 311

Unity Church, 112
Unity School of Christianity, 112, 283, 286
Universal fluid, 85
Universalist view of salvation, 87
Unreality of matter, 110
Urquhart, Clive, 146, 188, 240, 246
Use of magnets in healing, 85
Utilitarianism, 67, 88

Videos, 6–7, 29, 34, 48, 151–52, 156, 170–74, 177, 180, 182, 188, 214, 219, 238, 242, 246, 249, 251, 269–80
Videos as Quasi-Relics, 29
Vineyard, 236, 238
Vision Inflation, 237
Visualizing, 193
Vocal Cues, 248
Vocal force, 247–48

Wacquant, Loïc, 254, 283, 296
Wagner, C. Peter, 216, 245, 246n44, 296
Wagstaff, Graham, 46–48, 296
Währisch-Oblau, Claudia, 251, 296
Waldesianism, 258
Walker, Andrew, xiii, 17–18, 25, 189, 237n5, 251n68
Wallis, Roy, 37, 41, 42n50, 214, 261, 264, 296
Ward, Frances, 31
Ward, Pete, 156n39, 296
Ward, W.R., 51
Warfield, B. B., 61, 170, 297
Warner, Rob, 2, 4n20, 133n19, 134, 237, 252n69
Warren, Rick, 216, 297
Weatherhead, Leslie D., 46n66, 47, 297
Webber, George, 212–14, 266, 297
Weber, Max, 8, 39, 66–69, 74, 127, 134, 156n39, 239, 245, 250–51, 259, 285, 288, 292, 297
Weberian Ideal Type, 71, 222, 224, 226, 230

Wesley, John, 54, 63, 74n216, 161, 168n114
Wheelchairs provided for sick People, 171, 173, 270, 272
Whitefield, George, 54
Whitehouse, Deborah G., 18, 89, 90n59, 281
Whitman, Walt, 62
Whitney, Alice M., 118
Wigglesworth, Smith, 151, 161, 175–76, 297
Wilkerson, David, 153
Williams, Gary J., 52, 297
Williams, Rhys H., 62n155, 297
Williams, J. Rodman, 170
Willner, Ann R., 247
Willow Creek Community Church, 216, 236
Wimber, John, 55, 236n1, 237–38, 244, 297
Winthrop, Adam, 58
Winthrop, John, 58–59
Wisdom, Higher State of, 98
Witherspoon, John, 55, 60
Woodhead, Linda, 31
Woods, Tim, 230, 233, 298
Word of Faith Movement, 17, 25–28, 40, 50, 151
Word of Faith Theology, 8, 28, 119, 157, 169–70, 182
World Accommodating, 42
World Affirming, 42
World Council of Churches, 212, 298
World Rejecting, 42
Worley, Robert, 217, 298
Wright, Nigel G., 17–18, 189
Wrong Thinking, 96, 107, 109, 121, 123, 166, 169, 287
Wyclif, John, 57
Wycliffe, John, 258

Yongi Cho, Paul, 237n1

Ziff, Larzer, 63n157, 298
Zweig, Stephen, 85n37, 298

www.ingramcontent.com/pod-product-compliance
Lightning Source LLC
Chambersburg PA
CBHW050619300426
44112CB00012B/1577